Real-Time Systems

Systems

Modeling, Design, and Applications

T0322034

AMAST SERIES IN COMPUTING

Managing Editor: T. Rus
Advisory Board: A. Arnold, E. Astesiano, A. Fleck, W. Lawvere, P. Mosses,
M. Nivat, V. Pratt, C. Rattray, G. Scollo, R. Wachter, M. Wirsing

---

Published

AMAST Series in Computing: Vol. 8

Real-Time Systems

Modeling, Design, and Applications

Editors

Dan Ionescu
University of Ottawa, Canada

Aurel Cornell
Brigham Young University, USA

 **World Scientific**

NEW JERSEY • LONDON • SINGAPORE • BEIJING • SHANGHAI • HONG KONG • TAIPEI • CHENNAI

Published by

World Scientific Publishing Co. Pte. Ltd.

5 Toh Tuck Link, Singapore 596224

USA office: 27 Warren Street, Suite 401-402, Hackensack, NJ 07601

UK office: 57 Shelton Street, Covent Garden, London WC2H 9HE

British Library Cataloguing-in-Publication Data
A catalogue record for this book is available from the British Library.

AMAST Series in Computing — Vol. 8
REAL-TIME SYSTEMS
Modeling, Design and Applications

ISBN-13 978-981-02-4424-8
ISBN-10 981-02-4424-X

Printed in Singapore.

To all our beloved ones

Preface

This book collects the efforts developed by a series of researchers, presented at AMAST Workshops on Real-Time Systems. The authors whose papers were selected for this book are major players in this area, and they were given the opportunity to refine the text of their papers as a result of the lively discussions that took place during the workshops. The refining of the papers continued all through the editing process as well. The papers were carefully selected and revised by the editors and grouped into six parts debating subjects on the modeling and analysis, verification, synthesis, tools, and applications of real-time systems. The editors considered that these divisions made the book more coherent, and therefore, more readable.

It is almost futile to say that there is a large amount of research and literature on the subject of real-time systems. The subject is of great importance and it is resuscitating large interest in the research community. Great efforts have been made towards a clear understanding of the nature, features and particularities of real-time systems. As a result, a series of approaches of the field problems have been attempted. The variety of the latter spans over a vast spectrum of theoretical frameworks, from finite state machines to mathematical models expressed in various versions of the lambda calculus — and so are also the practical methodologies that have resulted by applying the above. As real-time systems are, as the name shows, systems, a systemic approach is needed, which unfortunately is very difficult to set. The difficulty stems from the combination of processes, some modeled by a set of differential/difference equations, and others by logic statements and their computer control algorithms, which usually involve first-order and/or temporal logic statements. The above facts have led to an arabesque of mathematical symbols and "theories" generated for the purpose of finding an appropriate model for the above combination of processes. It is needless to say that the field has attracted the attention of mathematicians, computer engineers, and computer and control theory scientists. It is also needless to say that the application of theoretical findings has had a large echo in the designers' and implementers' of real-time systems communities activating in the domains of telecommunications, power generation, metallurgy, aviation, and many other industries. Confronted with the difficulty of the field, the practitioners' community is in permanent expectation of new approaches and results, which should show them the light: a unified theory and practice capturing the essence of designing correct and at least sound real-time applications. As in other fields, designers and implementers of real-time applications expect to map in a coherent way the theoretical conquests to the reality of their projects. Thus, any book in this field should be in great demand. Related to the above, a fact must be mentioned: "*the book*" is not yet out. Here, the book we are trying to set is a reasonable combination of theory and practice, amalgamating a series of trends in the area of real-time systems in a readable sequence. However, it is clear to us that almost each chapter of this book can be easily developed into a book on its own. This reflects the diversity of problems and aspects that are currently under investigation in the area of real-time systems. We evaluate that this book is representative for the research efforts, which have been deployed in recent times in this area.

The first part of the book is a snapshot of the research done in the area of theory of real-time systems debating models of time, distributed, probabilistic, and process algebra models, and finally transition systems, at the time of the workshops.

The second part groups together the papers related to real-time system verification. This aspect is researched from different angles by using symbolic model checking, automated transition systems, process algebra methods, and for unpredictable real-time systems using suspension automata.

Part three contains subjects related to synthesis methods of real-time systems, while in part four the semantics expressed by urgent timed process algebras and the compositional semantics of real-time systems are studied.

Part five presents different programming paradigms and frameworks for real-time systems like the Llull system, the OSA model, and an algebraic implementation of the model checking methodology.

Part six is dedicated to the reality of real-time systems and contains industrial applications of some methodologies, considered appropriate by the authors, for providing a solution to the problem described.

As mentioned above, the combination of real world processes (continuous in their nature), man-made processes and devices (sometimes discrete) with one or many computers controlling the above processes, leads to a combination of continuous and/or discrete models which have to be dealt with by a computer. The difficulty of dealing with such a combination is aggravated by the fact that a computer does not yet have a unitary model as a process. It is also aggravated by the complexity of the computer system and by the sometimes severe safety conditions of the overall application. These are some of the challenges that have to be faced by a researcher or a practitioner when dealing with the design, implementation, and testing of a real-time system.

Obviously, there are plenty of models of time, execution models, logics, languages, theories, and applications that attempt to overcome these challenges. The literature of the domain already mentions a series of approaches to the modeling of real-time systems, including: automata theory, real-time process algebra, lambda calculus in real-time, and timed transition systems, to quote just a few.

Very often all of these may seem contradictory and practitioners may have difficulties in obtaining a clear picture of the direction they have to take in the design process of real-time systems. This might be explained by the lack of unified models and techniques. Although abstract and formal methods, provide very strong and versatile tools for a designer, they are only applied by academics. This state of the theoretical and practical developments in the area of real-time systems indicates that much work is needed before the field can mature with a unified and accessible theory available for practitioners.

No book will ever present a final solution to the multitude of problems mentioned above. The best we can hope for is that by presenting different aspects of real-time programming systems as they were researched by the authors, the book will help to enrich the general knowledge in this area, stimulating the creativity of other researchers.

Dan Ionescu
Aurel Cornell
Ottawa, April 2005

Contents

PART 2   Verification Methods for Real-Time Systems   135

PART 1

Theoretical Aspects of Real-Time Systems

Chapter 1

A Discrete Model for Real-Time Environments

Dan Ionescu and Cristian Lambiri

1.1 Introduction

The notion of real-time system, as it is currently accepted, describes a computational process that has to respond to internal or external stimuli in determined periods of time. Such processes have to consider time as the independent variable as in all theoretical system approaches. In real-time systems the time variable has discrete values and it is considered in a different manner than their non real-time counterparts, where time is implied but never stated. This chapter tries to establish an abstract model for real time systems, which blends the discrete nature of computational processes with the continuous nature of the time constraints.

Real-time systems have been studied in the realm of control systems and/or computer related processes for a very long time. The models and solutions for control systems, brought forward by various recent researchers which consider it a domain of differential equations, are based on the mathematical apparatus that has been a staple of control theory since its inception: functional analysis [Curtain 97]. The rise of discrete computational processes has given way to new methods of investigating this class of very important systems. Logic based (temporal logic [Ostroff 89b]), as well algebraic based (*I/O automata* [Gawlick 93; Sogaard-Anderson 93; Segala 95], real-time process algebra [Baeten 91]) have been proposed and studied in extensively.

What this chapter tries to achieve is to combine the control theory insight within a computationally viable model. An early attempt to bridge the gap between control theory and computer science has been done by Arbib [Arbib 75] who pointed out that the notion of finite automaton is just a particular case of his and Kalman's [Kalman 69] notion of dynamical system. Control theory based works provided tools for a powerful insight in the modeling, analysis, and synthesis of continuous or discrete systems using abstract mathematical models which can span from complex or functional analysis to category theory. This can be leveraged by combining it with the well-established computational models that have been in use in the computer science world which lately arrived also at the category theory abstractions.

1.2   Time and Events

A starting point for the study is represented by the general properties of real-time systems. It is a consensus in all research work that all models should respect the principle of causality, that the system should react to events or stimuli and that it should have a discrete representation. For this property to be well founded the time is of essence.

Time

The notion of time has been formalized in several ways, depending on the properties that we consider important. In the classical automata theory it is modeled as the set of natural numbers N and it is considered implicit in the definition of the automata. Using this mapping one can appreciate the running time complexity of programs by expressing it in number of transitions. Time can be made explicit by describing it as a special, infinitely recurring, event called *clock* [Ostroff 89b; Ostroff 90b; Brandin 94b], or by explicitly presenting it in the system definition as another component of the system [Kalman 69]. The former view is a natural extension of the classical automata theory. Its drawback stems from the special rules that have to be introduced in order to ensure the acceptance of the clock event. This chapter considers the second view and identifies time with the set of positive real numbers R^+, together with the usual binary relation $<=$, as a model for time. It is easy to see that R^+ has a cpo (complete partial order) structure.

Time is relative to the system of reference in which it is measured and so each system is considered to have its own *local time (LT)*. In order to be able to synchronize various parts of a distributed system a global entity called *global time (GT)* has also to be considered. Between any *LT* and *GT* a Newtonian time relation exists. If τ is the *GT* moment when system S started, a time moment in the two reference systems, t_g in *GT* and t_l in *LT* is in the following relation: $t_g = t_l + \tau$.

Let us consider two parts P_1 and P_2 of the same system S. Each part has its own local time T_1 and T_2 respectively. Considering that both parts started to function at the same *GT* moment τ, there is obviously an isomorphism between T_1 and T_2: $id : T_1 \longrightarrow T_2$. This isomorphism implies that both systems measure the time in the same manner.

Discrete event systems [Lin 93] have the property that events appear at discrete moments in time, but these moments can be anywhere on the time axis. R^+ is continuous from zero to ∞ and can, therefore, handle events that appear at any time moments.

Time moments are not the only kind of temporal structures. Of equal importance are the time intervals. We will denote a time interval $[t_1, t_2)$ by $\sigma_{t_1}^{t_2}$. Depending on the values of t_1 and t_2 several special cases that are more important will have separate denotations. A time interval that has only an upper limit $[0, t)$ will be denoted by σ^t. Similarly for a time interval that has only a lower limit, $[t, \infty)$, the following notation will be used σ_t. Single point intervals of the form $[t, t]$ will be denoted by $\bar{\sigma}_t$.

Let us consider now the set Σ of all time intervals over R. Over this set, let us define a partial operation, (denoted by $+$), called *interval concatenation*, in the following manner:

$$\sigma_{t_1}^{t_2} + \sigma_{t_2}^{t_3} = \sigma_{t_1}^{t_3},$$

$$\sigma_{t_1}^{t_2} + \sigma_{t_4}^{t_3} = \begin{cases} \sigma_{min(t_1,t_3)}^{max(t_4,t_2)} & \text{, if } [t_1, t_2) \cap [t_3, t_4) \neq \phi \\ \text{undefined} & \text{, if } [t_1, t_2) \cap [t_3, t_4) = \phi \end{cases}$$

Events

Based on their time existence, events can be classified in *discrete* and *duration* events. In our model we consider the *discrete* variety as the base event type, with the *duration* events modeled as strings of discrete events. We will denote *discrete events* with dt and with it the interval events.

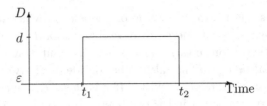

Fig. 1.1   Timed events

Events are defined by two time constants t_1 and t_2 that give a lower and an upper bound for the event's validity as shown in Fig. 1.1. An event is therefore a triple (e, t_1, t_2). The first component $e \in D$, where D is a set called the domain (Fig. 1.1), and $t_1, t_2 \in R^+$ specify the time value when the event starts to have an impact in the system while t_2 specifies the time value when the event ends to have an impact on the system. Events are described in their own reference system. To be more precise, if an event (e, t_1, t_2) appears at a moment t_d in a system's local time, it has to be executed in the interval $[t_d + t_1, t_d + t_2)$ in order to have an effect. The same interval in GT is given by $[\tau + t_d + t_1, \tau + t_d + t_2)$.

Definition 1.1 The set of timed events over the domain D is the set of triples (e, t_1, t_2), where $t_1, t_2 \in R^+$, with the property that $t_1 <= t_2$.
$E = \{(e, t_1, t_2) | e \in D, t_1 \in R^+, t_2 \in R^+, t_1 <= t_2\}$

The dynamics of the system is given by the interaction with the environment through its inputs and outputs. When an event is received, the time of entry in the system becomes part of the event. As an example, let us consider a set of events E as defined above. The set of possible event strings that can be generated by the environment is a subset of $(E \times T)^*$, with the obvious condition that if $i = \ldots (e_\alpha, t_\alpha)(e_\beta, t_\beta) \ldots$, then $t_a < t_b$. Let us denote by $\omega_{t_1}^{t_o}$ an input string that starts at t_1 and ends at t_2. If t_2 is finite then the length of such a string has to be finite.

The above condition ensures that the so-called Zeno executions, over a finite interval, do not appear.

Events are described in their own reference system. Thus, if an event $e_{t_1}^{t_2}$ appears at moment t_d in the local time of a system, it has to be executed in the interval $[t_d + t_1, t_d + t_2)$ in order to affect the system. The same interval in GT is given by $[\tau + t_d + t_1, \tau + t_d + t_2)$. Of course, an even more sophisticated interpretation can be brought up, where the event has a

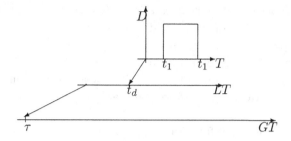

Fig. 1.2   Relation between time referentials

"good" behavior in the enabling interval and a "bad" one outside it. If the
time interval is $[0, \infty)$ then the events are untimed. The interval addition
can be used to simplify the event description. Let $e_{d_{t_1}^{t_2}}$ and $e_{d_{t_3}^{t_4}}$ be two
timed events for the same symbol d. If the operation $\sigma_{t_1}^{t_2} + \sigma_{t_2}^{t_3}$ is defined,
then $e_{d_{min(t_1,t_3)}^{max(t_4,t_2)}}$ (Figure 1.2) represents both events.

The set of admissible input functions is defined over subsets of T and
with the co-domain in E. Events on the other hand are formalized as
discussed above. The set of all events that appear on any *finite* time interval
has to have finite cardinality. This is true because a real-time system reacts
in a finite amount of time to any event. In the case when an *infinite* number
of events are allowed to appear over a finite interval, the system will not
finish processing those events over a finite interval. Such a behavior is
considered unacceptable and hence, the above condition is imposed. If $\omega_{t_1}^{t_0}$
is an acceptable input function defined over a time interval, with n the
number of time points where ω is defined, the system will process all the
inputs in a $n * \mu$ period of time. Ω is composed of functions ω defined in the
following manner: $\Omega = \{\omega : T \longrightarrow E \mid \omega = e_k(t_{e_k})\}$. Thus, any function
ω has to be defined in a *countable* set of time points. If $T_d \in T$ is the
set of time points where the function ω is defined there exists a morphism
$f : T_d \longrightarrow N$. If $Card(T_d) = \infty$ then f is an isomorphism.

The above condition ensures that the so-called Zeno executions
[Sogaard-Anderson 93], over a finite interval, do not appear. In such a
behavior, the processing time of a set of events that appear over a finite
interval takes an infinite amount of time. There is also another type of
Zeno behavior. This occurs when the number of events that appear over
any finite interval is greater that the number of entries in the input buffer

plus the number of events that can be processed in that interval. If K is the maximum number of events that can be buffered, the number of events that can appear over an interval $\sigma_{t_1}^{t_2}$ is given by: $N \leq K + | (t_2 - t_1)/\mu |$. If the number of events that appear over a period of time is greater than $K + [(t_2 - t_1)/\mu]$ then some of them will be lost. Over an infinite interval this means that the arrival rate of the events has to be less than or equal to $1/\mu$.

The acceptable input functions can be viewed as words in a language L_E. The language is defined over an *infinite* alphabet $E \times T$ where E is a set of events (timed and untimed) and T is the time set. A word in the language w is defined as follows: $\forall \omega \in \Omega, \forall t \in T$ where $w = \omega(t_0)\omega(t_1)\ldots\omega_{t_n}$. The language ($L_E$) is composed of the set of all words w such that $w = e_0(t_0)e_1(t_1)\ldots e_n(t_n)$ and $t_0 < t_1 < \ldots < t_n$, where $e_0, e_1, \ldots, e_n \in E$ and $t_0, t_1, \ldots, t_n \in T$. Hence, L_E is a subset of $(E \times T)^*$.

Another way of introducing timed events is by relating a *timer* with each event [Brandin 94b; Alur 90c]. There, the authors present similar approaches in the way they introduce the timed events, with the difference that in [Brandin 94b] timers for events are integrated in the notion of state of the system as in [Alur 90c] they are considered a separate entity.

1.3 Discrete Real-Time Systems

The system model that we consider is a discrete one, in the sense that the states set is countable. The duration of a state transition depends on the type of event that the system is processing. Thus the *transition interval* is given by the function $\mu : D \longrightarrow T$. This means that on any finite interval, the system will make a countable number of steps of different lengths.

Definition 1.2 A Discrete Real Time System **DRTS** is a tuple $A = (T, Q, E, Y, \phi, \beta, \mu)$ where:

- $T = \mathsf{R}^+$ is a set of **time values**
- E is a set of **events** and $I = E \times T$ is the input alphabet.
- Q is a set of symbols called **states**.
- $Y = (Y_j \mid j \in J)$ is an indexed set of **output values** with $Y_j \in D \times T \times T$.
- $\mu : prj_1(e) \longrightarrow T$ is the transition function.
- ϕ is a function $\phi : T \times Q \times I \longrightarrow Q$, called the **next state function**.

If the system is in the state q at t it will be in state q_1 at $t + \mu(prj(e))$, where $e_{t_1}^{t_2} \in E$ is the event, t_d is the moment when the event appears and $t \geq t_d$ is the moment when the event is processed.

- β is a set of total functions $\beta = \{\beta_j | \beta_j : Q \longrightarrow Y_j\}$, called **output functions**.

The definition above is missing the initial and final states. It is easy to particularize the DRTS definition to make it accommodate such states.

Definition 1.3 An ifDRTS is an DRTS together with $q_0 \in Q$, a special state called initial state, and $F \in Q$ a set of final states.

The class of *reactive systems* also fall into the above definition, by considering the set F to be empty. Such a system will be denoted by *iDRTS*.

An input-output run of a DRTS is a string of triples (e, t, y) where e is an event, t the moment when it appears, and y the output of the system. All the runs will be considered in LT and therefore will start at $t = 0$. For reactive systems runs have infinite length, while for other types of DRTS' might have finite runs. Considering a DRTS A, we will denote by Ω_q the set of all possible runs of A when it starts in state q. For $iDRTS$, where the initial state is known, the set will be simply denoted by Ω. Two states q_1 and q_2 are said to be equivalent if $\Omega_{q_1} = \Omega_{q_2}$. Since *iDRTS* always starts from the same state, q_0 we will call two iDRTS' A and B equivalent if $\Omega_A = \Omega_B$.

1.4 Composition and Decomposition of iDRTS Structures

The main point of interest, in this section, is the way we can combine simpler structures in order to obtain more complicated ones. Another way of obtaining new systems from known ones is by transforming them. The following definition gives the restrictions needed in order to build a morphism between two iDRTS.

Definition 1.4 Let $M_1 = (T, E_1, Q_1, Y_1, \delta_1, \beta_1, q_{01})$ and $M_2 = (T, E_2, Q_2, Y_2, \delta_2, \beta_2, q_{02})$ be two iDRTS. A **morphism** between M_1 and M_2 is a set of functions $\{tm : T \longrightarrow T, h : Q_1 \longrightarrow Q_2, ev : E_1 \longrightarrow E_2\} \cup \{g_j : Y_{1j} \longrightarrow Y_{2j} \mid \forall j \in J\}$ satisfying the following conditions: $f(\tau_1) = \tau_2$, $f(\mu_1) = \mu_2$, $h(q_{01}) = q_{02}$, $h(\delta_1(t, q_1, (e_1, t_d))) = \delta_2(tm(t), h(q_1), (ev(e_1), tm(t_d)))$ and $\forall j \in J, g_j(\beta_{1j}(q_1)) = \beta_{2j}(h(q_1))$.

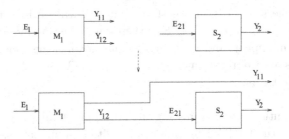

Fig. 1.3   Series composition of iDRTS

Using three types of compositions, *series*, *parallel* and *feedback*, we can obtain complex systems from simpler ones. Although used a lot by system theory, composition is weakly represented in the domain of formal models. Most of the authors seem concerned with the monolithic description of the system and except for parallel composition [Alur 90c; Sogaard-Anderson 93; Lin 93; Manna 92; Brandin 94b] none of the other is considered. Parallel composition provides an fairly accurate description of the behavior for *non interacting* systems functioning simultaneously. For systems that also interact with each other more sophisticated constructions are needed. Some define [Ostroff 89b] *parallel compositions* although the system is a series construction with feedback. Following classical work in system theory [Mesarovic 75] and automata theory [Arbib 69] the *series*, *parallel* and *feedback* composition will be defined.

In the *series* configuration (Figure 1.3) two automata are linked so that outputs from one automaton are connected to inputs of the other automaton. Of course the connection can be made if and only if the set $Y_{12} \subset E_{21}$. Without this connection compatibility the second system will not make any transitions. In the composed system both components start at the same time τ and thus, the set T is the same on both systems. Furthermore the output of the first system has to be event driven in order to have the same structure as the other events. Without this, the output would generate an uncountable number of events and this would be a Zeno behavior.

The sets of admissible inputs are, usually, different between iDRTS as a result of different transitions times and input queue lengths. To have a resulting system with non-Zeno behaviors, it is necessary to impose restrictions on the admissible input runs for the composed system. The admissible runs are determined by the transition time. To obtain them for the composed system let us compare the transition times for the parts. If $\mu_1 \geq \mu_2$ then the actions generated by the first system are at least μ_1 apart and this second system will synchronously process them as they appear. Hence, the set of acceptable inputs for M_1 is the set of acceptable inputs for the composed system. If $\mu_1 < \mu_2$ the set of admissible inputs for the composed system should be reduced such that the arrival rate is smaller than $1/\mu_2$. Therefore the arrival rate for the composed system should be: $1/max(\mu_1, \mu_2)$.

In the sequel only the case when $\mu_1 > \mu_2$ is considered. The transition time of the composed system is then $\mu = \mu_1 + \mu_2$. The above equation states that the outputs are considered to change only after the effect of an input event had propagated through the system.

Definition 1.5   Let $M_1 = (T, E_1, Q_1, Y_1, \delta_1, \beta_1, q_{01})$ and

$$M_2 = (T, E_2, Q_2, Y_2, \delta_2, \beta_2, q_{02})$$

be two iDRTS', where $Y_1 = (Y_{11}, Y_{12})$, $\beta = (\beta_{11}, \beta_{12})$. The series composition of M_1 and M_2 denoted by $(M_1 \odot M_2)$ is a system

$$M = M_1 \odot M_2 = (T, E, Q, Y, \delta, \beta, q_0)$$

where

- $Q = Q_1 \times Q_2$ is the state set.
- $E = E_1$ is the event set and $I = E_1 \times T$ is the input alphabet.
- $Y = (Y_{11}, Y_2)$ is the output set.
- $\delta : T \times Q \times I \longrightarrow Q$ is the next state function.

$$\delta(t, (q_1, q_2), (e_1, t_d)) = (\delta_1(t, q_1, (e_1, t_d)), \delta_2(t, q_2, (\beta_{11}(q_1), t_d))).$$

- $\beta = (\beta_{11}, \beta_2)$ is the set of output functions.
- $q_0 = (q_{01}, q_{02})$ is the *initial state*.

Let us consider the case when several inputs are applied to the same system. There are two possible points of views for these kinds of structured inputs. The first one considers the events to be synchronized [Ionescu 94].

To explain this, let us consider two iDRTS M_1 and M_2 working in parallel. Let E_1 is the set of admissible events for M_1, and E_2 for M_2. Then the set of events for the resulting system is $E' = \{(e_1, \varepsilon) \mid e_1 \in E_1\} \cup \{(\varepsilon, e_2) \mid e_2 \in E_2\} \cup \{(e_1, e_2) \mid e_1 \in E_1, e_2 \in E_2\}$. The set of

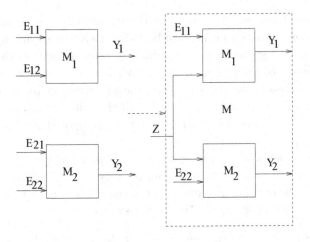

Fig. 1.4   Parallel composition of iDRTS

events for the parallel composition denotes that the events can appear at the same moment in time. Therefore they can be synchronized, or appear at different moments and be desynchronized. In each case the composed events are the doubles (e, ε) or (ε, e) where ε represents a "non-event". This point of view considers all the events queued in a single unit and processed synchronously. If $I_j = E_j \times T$ is the input alphabet for one input then because $T \times T \times \ldots T \cong T$ the alphabet of the composed inputs is $E_1 \times E_2 \ldots E_n \times T$.

A second point of view is to consider the inputs to be independently processed. Considering the inputs independent though, contradicts our intuition that systems behave like monoliths.

In the *parallel* configuration the set of events E of the resulting machine is a subset of the Cartesian product of the sets of events of the composing machines $E \subset E_1 \times E_2$. As with the *serial connection*, both machines have the same time reference, with the same initial moment. This ensures that the elements of the Cartesian product are valid events for the composed machine.

Definition 1.6   Let $M_1 = (T, E_1, Q_1, Y_1, \delta_1, \beta_1, q_{01})$ and

$$M_2 = (T, E_2, Q_2, Y_2, \delta_2, \beta_2, F_2, q_{02})$$

be two iDRTS' (Figure 1.4), with $E_1 = (E_{11})$ and $E_2 = (E_{21} \times E_{22})$. The parallel composition of M_1 and M_2 denoted by $(M_1 \oplus M_2)$ is a system

$$M = M_1 \oplus M_2 = (T, E, Q, Y, \delta, \beta, q_0)$$

where

- T is the set of time values.
- $Q = Q_1 \times Q_2$ is the set of states and $q_0 = (q_{01}, q_{02})$.
- $E = (E_{11} \times Z \times E_{22})$, with $Z \subseteq E_{12} \cap E_{21}$, is the set of events and $I = E_{11} \times Z \times E_{22} \times T$ is the input alphabet.
- $Y = (Y_1, Y_2)$ is the set of output values.
- $\delta : T \times \times Q \times I \longrightarrow Q$ is the next state function, defined by:

$$\delta(t, (q_1, q_2), (e_1, z, e_2, t_d)) = (\delta_1(t, q_1, (e_1, z, t_d)), \delta_2(tq_2, (e_2, z, t_d))),$$

- $\beta = \{\beta_1, \beta_2\}$ is the set of output functions.

The transition time of the composed system is equal to $max(\mu_1, \mu_2)$.

In the *feedback* connection some of the system's outputs are connected with its inputs thus forming another system. The feedback system can make more than one transition for certain inputs, because the output that is generated will be another event for the system. The iDRTS of the Definition 1.2 makes only one transition after it receives an event. In this case we define the transition of the feedback system to take place only when it reaches a state that will not change unless it receives an input event. Evidently the system can make several internal transitions in order to enter such a state. The set of admissible input functions for the feedback system is only a subset of that of the original system. This is due to the increased processing time.

Definition 1.7 Let $M_1 = (T, E_1, Q_1, Y_1, \delta_1, \beta_1, F_1, q_{01})$ be a iDRTS (Figure 1.5), with $E_1 = (E_{11} \times E_{12})$ and $Y_1 = (Y_{11}, Y_{12})$. The **feedback** connection of M_1 is a system

$$M = (T, E, Q, Y, \delta, \beta, q_0, F),$$

where:

- T is the set of time values.
- $Q = Q_1$ is the set of states, with $q_0 = q_{01}$.
- $E = E_{12}$ is the set of events and $I = E \times T$ is the input alphabet.

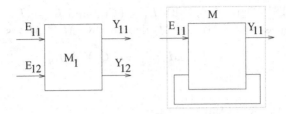

Fig. 1.5   Feedback composition of iDRTS

- $Y = Y_{12}$ is the set of outputs.
- $\beta = \{\beta_1\}$ is the set of output functions.
- $\delta : T \times Q \times I \longrightarrow Q$ is the next state function:

$$q_1(t + n * \mu) = \delta(t, q, (e_{11}, t_d)) = \delta_1(\ldots(\delta_1(t, q, (e_{11}, t_d)))).$$

Due to their nature, some feedback systems can have an infinite transition time. This is because the system will make internal transitions forever. This suggests that the class of all iDRTS' is not closed under the feedback operation. Thus, such an operation has to be applied with caution.

1.5   DRTS as Algebras

The relation between automata theory and algebra, an idea that seems almost natural now, has been first pointed out by Büchi [Buchi 89], who studied automata as *unary algebras*. By reducing the class of abstract automata to a unary algebra, only one set of the structure can be studied and therefore simplifications have to be made. Pointing out the problem Büchi [Buchi 89] also noted that means of a more general approach can study the same structures. He proposed *multi sorted algebra* which, presents the advantage of allowing an indexed carrier for the algebra. Therefore, the totality condition imposed for algebra operators can be satisfied over subsets of the carrier. Noticing the relation of universal algebra with another mathematical field of study, category theory, automata theorists and mathematicians tried to link the two fields together. Manes and Arbib [Arbib 75] have started a categorical approach by proving that the class of automata is a category and also, that the automaton itself can be viewed as a category. In this case automata properties are derived using categorical concepts. Adamek [Adamek 89] used an interesting variant to the categorical approach, by studying automata as *functors* between categories.

The algebraic methods of study are at help when one tries to make the transition from the automata as models of computations to logic theories that describe them. The relation of universal algebra with logic, by the means of model theory, means that a link between logical theories and the abstract models can be made. This is the reason of approaching the DRTS and therefore distributed systems through an algebraic theory.

Let us now consider the **DRTS** framework in the light of universal algebra. The multi set nature of the framework makes it a natural candidate for their study using *multi sorted* algebra.

Let $M = (T, Q, E, Y, \delta, \beta)$ be a **DDES**. The condition $t \leq t_d$ makes δ partial. To make a **DDES** suitable for study using the universal algebra framework, it is needed to make δ a total function. This can be done by considering an extension of δ such that, for all the doubles (t, t_d) where the function is undefined, $\delta(t, q, (e, t_d)) = q$. In the remainder of the section δ will be considered to be the extended *next state function* $\bar{\delta}$. As previously stated, for **DRTS** only the reactive case with $F = \phi$ is considered where $F = \{f | f : Td \rightarrow N\}$ Hence, the set F does not appear explicitly. As expected the *DRTS*, with the extended transition function, have the structure of universal algebras as proven by the following theorems.

Theorem 1.1 *A* **DDES** *is a multi-sorted algebra.*

Proof. Let $M = (T, Q, E, Y, \delta, \beta)$ be a **DDES**. Let us attach a sort to each of the sets. Hence, we'll consider T of having sort s_1 and Q of having sort s_2. The set of output values is made of several subsets: $Y = (Y_1, \ldots, Y_j)$. Each Y_j is considered to have sort j. Finally consider E of having sort i. Thus, the set S of sorts is composed of: $\{s_1, s_2, i\} \cup \{j | mid j \in J\}$. Over S consider the signature $\Sigma = (\delta, q_0, \beta_j \mid j \in J)$ with the following arities: $ar(\delta) = (s_1 s_1 s_2 i, s_2)$, $ar(\beta_j) = (s_2, j)$.

We consider the set $C = (T_{s_1}, Q_{s_2}, E_i, \{Y_j \mid j \in J\})$ to be the carrier and the functions δ and $\beta_j \in \beta$ from M to be realizations of the operation symbols from Σ. Then by the definition of multi sorted algebras, $A = (C, \delta, \{\beta_j \mid j \in J\})$ is a multi sorted algebra. Therefore, M is a *multi sorted algebra*. □

Theorem 1.2 *An* **iDRTS** *is a multi-sorted algebra.*

Proof. Let $M = (T, Q, E, Y, \delta, \beta, q_O)$ be a **DRTS**. As in the case of
DDES let us consider the set $C = \{T_{s_1}, Q_{s_2}, E_i, \{Y_j \mid j \in J\})$ with the
arities specified by the indexes.

If q_0 is considered to be an operation symbol, then we obtain the sig-
nature $\Sigma = (\delta, \{\beta_j \mid j \in J\}, q_0,)$. The signature has the following arities:
$ar(\delta) = (s_1 s_1 s_2 i, s_2)$, $ar(\beta_j) = (s_2, j)$, $ar(q_0) = s_2$. Hence, the set C with
the operation defined by σ form, is a multi sorted algebra. Therefore, M is
a *multi sorted algebra*. □

DRTS are therefore *multi-sorted* algebras. In this context, it is interesting to notice that morphisms between DRTS are homomorphisms in the
universe of multi sorted algebras.

Corollary 1.1   *A morphism between two DRTS is a homomorphism be-*
tween the underlying algebras.

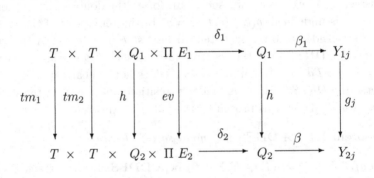

Proof.   Let $M_1 = (T, E_1, Q_1, Y_1, \delta_1, \beta_1, q_{01})$ and
$M_2 = (T, E_2, Q_2, Y_2, \delta_2, \beta_2, q_{02})$ be two DRTS' with Y_1 and Y_2 defined over
the same J. By Lemma 1.2 M_1 and M_2 are algebras over the same signature
$\Sigma = (\delta, \{\beta_j \mid j \in J\}, q_0)$.

The set of functions $\{tm_1 : T \longrightarrow T, tm_2 : T \longrightarrow T, h : Q_1 \longrightarrow Q_2, ev :$
$E_1 \longrightarrow E_2\} \cup \{g_j : Y_{1j} \longrightarrow Y_{2j} \mid \forall j \in J\}$ satisfying the morphism conditions
of Definition 1.4 also satisfy the conditions for multi sorted homomorphism.

Over the signature Σ, we have:

- $h(q_{01}) = q_{02}$ by hypothesis.
- $\forall f_1 \in F_1 \exists f_2 \in F_2$ such that $h(f_1) = f_2$ by hypothesis.
- $h(\delta_1(t_1, t_2, q_1, e_1)) = \delta_2(tm(t_1), tm(t_2), h(q_1), ev(e_1))$ and
- $\forall j \in J, g_j(\beta_{1j}(q_1)) = \beta_{2j}(h(q_1))$.

Therefore, by the definition of morphisms $[tm_1, tm_2, h, ev, (g_j \mid j \in J)]$ is a Σ-homomorphism. $\square$

The concept of **direct product** of algebras captures the behavior of parallel working automata. Let $A_1 = (T, E_1, Q_1, Y_1, \delta_1, \beta_1, q_{01})$ and $A_2 = (T, E_2, Q_2, Y_2, \delta_2, \beta_2, q_{02})$ be two iDRTS' and B their parallel composition with respect to Definition 1.6. The direct product $A = A_1 \times A_2$ is the algebra $A = (T \times T, E_1 \times E_2, Q_1 \times Q_2, Y_1 \times Y_2, \delta, \beta, (q_{01}, q_{02}))$, where the functions δ and $\beta \in \beta$ are defined point wise. Let us study the relation between the Cartesian product of two algebras and the *parallel* composition of the iDRTS.

More precisely, let us first consider the parallel connection of two iDRTS' as in Figure 1.4. Let $B = (T, E, Q, Y, \delta, \beta, q_0)$ be the multi sorted algebra obtained from the result of the parallel composition of the A_1 and A_2. For the parallel connection to have meaning, we have to impose the condition $E = E_{12} \cap E_{21}$. Considering the subset $E_s = \{(e, e) \mid e \in E\} \subset E_{12} \times E_{21}$ we can build a sub-algebra A' of A (the direct product of A_1 and A_2), formed with the same sets as A except for the event set, where we will take only a subset $E_v = E_{11} \times E_s \times E_{22} \subset E_{11} \times E_{12} \times E_{21} \times E_{22}$. Furthermore let us consider the following function $f : E_{11} \times E \times E_{22} \longrightarrow E_{11} \times E_s \times E_{22}$ defined as $f(e_{11}, e, e_{22}) = (e_{11}, e, e, e_{22})$. As previously discussed for the time set $T \times T \cong T$. Let us consider the function $id_{T \times T} : T \longrightarrow T \times T$, defined as: $id_{T \times T}(t) = (t, t)$. Hence, $h = [id_{T \times T}, id_{Q_1 \times Q_2}, f, id_{Y_j}]$ is a homomorphism between B, the algebra representing the parallel connection, and A'. Let us denote $E_1 = E_{11} \times E_{12}$, $E_2 = E_{21} \times E_{22}$ and $Q_{1 \times 2} = Q_1 \times Q_2$.

$$
\begin{array}{ccccccc}
T \times T \times Q_{1 \times 2} \times E_{11} \times E \times E_{22} & \xrightarrow{\delta} & Q_{1 \times 2} & \xrightarrow{\beta_j} & Y_{1j} \times Y_{2j} \\
\downarrow{\scriptstyle id_{T \times T}\ id_{T \times T}\ id_{Q_1 \times Q_2}\ f} \quad \downarrow{\scriptstyle id_{Q_1 \times Q_2}} & & \downarrow{\scriptstyle id_{Y_{1j} \times Y_{2j}}} & & \downarrow \\
T \times T \times T \times T \times Q_{1 \times 2} \times E_1 \times E_s \times E_2 & \xrightarrow{\delta} & Q_{1 \times 2} & \xrightarrow{\beta_j} & Y_{1j} \times Y_{2j}
\end{array}
$$

However, A' is a sub algebra of A. Therefore, there exists a homomorphism $in_A : A' \longrightarrow A$. By applying the Universal Property of Algebra we obtain a homomorphism from B to A. Hence, there exits a homomorphism from the underlying algebra of the parallel connection and the Cartesian product of A_1 and A_2.

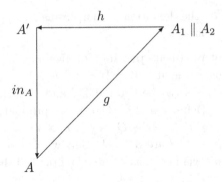

A characterization from $A_1 \times A_2$ to B is also possible. In this case we need a function $tm : T \times T \longrightarrow T$ and a function $g : E_{11} \times E_{12} \times E_{21} \times E_{22} \longrightarrow E_{11} \times E \times E_{22}$. The function tm can be defined as

$$tm(t_1, t_2) = \begin{cases} t & \text{if } t_1 = t_2 \\ 0 & \text{otherwise} \end{cases}$$

and the function g by the following description:

$$g(e_{11}, e_{12}, e_{21}, e_{22}) = \begin{cases} (e_{11}, e, e_{22}) & \text{if } e_{12} = e_{21} \\ (e_{11}, \varepsilon, e_{22}) & \text{otherwise} \end{cases}.$$

Thus, $k = [tm, tm, g, id_{Q_1 \times Q_2}, id_{Y_j}]$ is a homomorphism from $A_1 \times A_2$ to B.

1.6 A Model for Sequential Processes

This section examines the structure of computer processes, using the formal model that was built in the previous paragraphs. The abstraction process uses a "reversed engineering" method by trying to formalize a concept derived from a human made tool to produce other tools. Our technological perception of the "computational process" biases this type of abstraction.

Multitasking systems appeared after the sequential ones and tried to mimic their behavior, by creating the illusion of multiple parallel processes executed on a single physical unit. Thus the notion of "sequential process" is crucial to the formalization process.

In this chapter sequential processes are considered to be collections composed of two entities that interact with each other. One entity ensures the dynamics of the process and therefore, acts as a *controller*, while the other

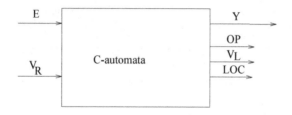

Fig. 1.6   C-automata

one acts as a *memory* that stores variables for the controller. Let us examine both parts from the perspective of the **iDRTS** model developed in the previous sections.

The *control* part of the process will be considered to be a **iDRTS**. The abstraction can be made because the controller has discrete states and accepts discrete events.

Let us consider a particular kind of **iDRTS** with the structure of inputs and outputs depicted in Figure 1.6. Let us call this type of system a *C-automaton*. The set of inputs for the system is structured, as visible in Figure 1.6. This is because some inputs (V_R) are needed to interact with the *memory* part of the process, as the others are needed for external interaction E. The set of outputs is also composed of several subsets. Part of the outputs are inputs in the memory subsystem (OP, V_l, LOC) and the rest are the outputs of the process. Thus, a C-automaton is an iDRTS with the following structure:

$$A_c = (T, \{E, V_R\}, Q, \{LOC, OP, V_L\}, Y, F, \delta, \{\beta_1, \beta_2\}, q_0)$$

where

- $E_c = V_R \times E$ is a set of events.
- Q is a set of states. $q_0 \in Q$ is the initial state.
- $\beta = V_L \times OP \times LOC \times Y$ is the a set of output events.
- $\delta : T \times T \times Q \times E_c \longrightarrow Q$ is the next state function, $\delta(q, e_c) = q_{next}$
- $\beta = (\beta_1, \beta_2), \beta_1 : Q \longrightarrow Y, \beta_2 : Q \longrightarrow OP \times V_L \times LOC$ is the output function.

The system, as shown in Fig. 1.7 has two output functions, β_1 and β_2, to make the distinction between the process output and the commands for the memory.

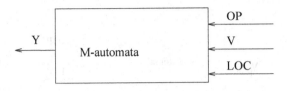

Fig. 1.7   M-automata

To be able to make a suitable abstraction for the memory we must analyze how a real memory behaves. The term can mean many things, but here we refer to a device that can store and access information by direct addressing. In the technology used for most of today's computers a memory system is just a conglomerate of units called *memory cells*. A *memory cell* is a place where a quantity of information can be stored at times and retrieved afterwards. The number of different symbols that can be stored depends on the memory and is always finite. All the events that a memory receives are un-timed. Furthermore the memory system is time invariant and thus the time set can be omitted from the definition of the system. By considering the stored symbols as the *states* of the memory we can abstract it as an iDRTS with the following structure: $(Q, Q, Q, \delta, \{\beta\}, F, q_0)$. The notion of final state does not make sense for a storage facility. We will consider $F = \phi$ and omit it from subsequent references.

We can expand the model by considering several memory units running in parallel. If we use parallel composition we can obtain a memory with n cells: $(Q^n, Q^n, Q^n, \delta, \beta, q_0^n) = (Q^n, \delta, \beta, q_0^n)$ where $\delta : Q^n \times Q^n \longrightarrow Q^n$ and $\beta : Q^n \longrightarrow Q^n$. Let $\beta_m : Q^n \times E \longrightarrow Q^n$.

Let $E_m = \{(-, -, \ldots, q_i, \ldots, -) \mid q_i \in Q\} \subset Q^n$ such that only one memory cell receives an event at a certain time moment. And let OP, V_L, LOC be three sets of symbols such that $OP = \{R, WR\}, V_L \subset Q, LOC \subset \mathsf{N}$. Let $f : OP \times V_L \times LOC \longrightarrow E_m$ be a function such that

$$f(x, y, z) = \begin{cases} \lambda & \text{if } x = R \\ (\underbrace{-, -, \ldots}_{z}, y, \ldots) & \text{if } x = WR \end{cases}$$

and $\delta_M : OP \times V_L \times LOC, \delta_M = \delta \circ f$. We can now define a model for the memory that we'll call *M-automaton*.

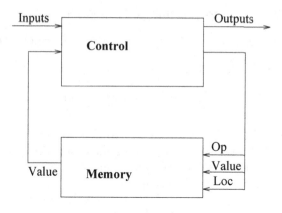

Fig. 1.8   Process abstraction

Definition 1.8   An M-automaton is iDRTS,
$A_M = (\{OP, V_L, LOC\}, Q^n, Q, \delta, \beta, q_0^n)$ where

- E is the set of events $E = OP \times V_L \times LOC$, where:

  - $OP = \{R, W\}$ is a set of symbols called operations;
  - V_L, LOC are finite sets of symbols called values and locations.

- δ is the next state function $\delta : Q^n \times E \longrightarrow Q^n$
- β is the output function $\beta : Q^n \times LOC \longrightarrow Q$
- q_0^n is the initial state: $q_0^n \in Q^n$

We can now present a formal definition of the notion of a computational process. As previously said a computational process is considered to be composed of two parts that interact with each other: a control part that is described by a *C-automaton* and a memory part that is formalized by an *M-automaton*. Let us consider the two automata to be connected as depicted in Figure 1.8. This type of connection can be expressed as a combination of serial and feedback connections: $P = \mathcal{F}(M \odot C)$. Let us call the resulting system a *P-automaton*.

Definition 1.9   Let

$$A_c = (T, \{E_c, V_R\}, Q_c, \{LOC, OP, V_L\}, Y_c, F_c, \delta_c, \{\beta_{1c}, \beta_{2c}\}, q_{0c})$$

be a C-automaton and

$$A_M = (\{OP, V_L, LOC\}, Q_M^n, Q_M, \delta_M, \beta_M, q_{0M}^n)$$

be a M-automaton. A **P-automaton** is a septuple

$$A_p = \mathcal{F}(A_C \odot A_M) = (T, E_p, Q_p, Y_p, \delta_p, \beta_p, q_{0p}, F_p, \{LOC, OP, V_L, V_R\})$$

resulting by the composition of the A_C and A_M where

- $Q_p = Q_C \times Q_M^n$ is the set of states, and $q_{0p} = (q_{0C}, q_{0M}^n)$ is the initial state.
- β_p is the output function. $\beta_p((q_1, q_2)) = (\beta_{1C}(q))$
- $F_p = \{(f_C, q) | f_c \in F, q \in Q_M\} \subseteq Q_p$ is the set of final states.
- $E_p = E_c$ is the set of (external) events.
- δ_p is the next state function,

$$\delta : T \times T \times q_p \times E_p \longrightarrow Q_p,$$

$$\delta(t, t, (q_1, q_2), e) = (\delta_C(t, q, ((e, v_R), t_e)), \delta_M(q_2, (op, v_L, loc)))$$
$$= (\delta_C(t, q_1, ((e, \beta_M(q_2), t))), \delta_M(q_2, \beta_{2C}(q)))$$

For a sequential process, its state is determined state by the values of its variables plus the state of the processor. For a *P-automaton* the state is the state of the control part plus the state of all the memory locations (values found in the memory cells). Therefore, using the above definition, the state of the process corresponds with the state of the *P-automaton*. This model is related with the *fair transition systems (FTS)* [Manna 89]. Let us consider the state set of *P-automata* $Q_p = Q_c \times Q_M^n$. A variable $v \in Q_p$ is a tuple $v = (v_c, v_M^1, \ldots, v_M^n)$. The composing elements of this variable are *state variables* of *FTS*. The transition τ is the same as our function δ and the *initial condition* from *FST* is our q_0. In [Manna 89], the authors add two more classes of restrictions to their models called *justice* and *fairness* in order to insure proper operation of the system.

From Definition 1.9 we can derive the definition of a reactive process.

Definition 1.10 A **reactive process** is a sequential process that has an empty set of final states.

A typical concurrent system has a variable number of processes during its life-time that are created and killed at the request of other processes. The program that does this work is called *operating system (OS)*. After a process is created the relation between the processes that asked for the service and the new process is determined by the specifics of the system.

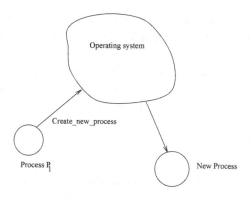

Fig. 1.9   Creation of new processes

From the point of view of process creation, the *operating system* can be abstracted by considering an entity that contains a set of *P-automaton*. This is the set of processes that the system can create. Furthermore, an automaton that has a special type of next state function is needed to start a new process when needed. When the *OS* automata receives an event requesting a new process it will make not only an internal transition, but will also start another *P-automata*. Let us call the abstraction of the *OS* an *S-automaton*.

Definition 1.11   An S-automata is septuple

$$A_{s_i} = (T, E, Q, \delta, Y, \mathcal{A}_P, \beta, q_0)$$

where:

- T is a set of time values,
- E is a set of events,
- Q is a set of states with $q_0 \in Q$ the initial state,
- $\mathcal{A}_P$ is a set of P-automata and Y a set of output values,
- $\delta : T \times T \times Q \times E \longrightarrow Q$ is the next state function,
- β is the output function, $\beta : Q \longrightarrow Y \times \mathcal{A}_P$,

An *S-automaton* is thus, a DES whose set of output values is a set of *P-automata*. The *S-automaton* can output two types of actions: one is the same as in the case of iDRTS, a simple output, while the other is a new process. The set T is considered to be the set of real numbers as in all the other formalization discussed before. The new process will start its work in its initial state. One major difference between this abstraction and a real system is that once it starts a new process the operating system loses control over it and cannot stop it. Although this might seem like a major drawback, in the authors' opinion it is not. To be more precise, once the process is started, if the process has a reactive behavior it should not stop.

1.7   Conclusions

In this chapter we describe a discrete model for real-time systems and prove that it can be casted in the universal algebra framework. Furthermore the parallel composition operator can be described in the algebraic framework using direct product morphisms and sub-algebras.

Chapter 2

Distributed Synchronous Processes

Frédéric Boniol

2.1 Introduction: Real-Time and Reactive Systems

Real-time systems are often considered as composed of three layers. The first one is an interface with the environment that is in charge of input receptions and output productions. It transforms external physical events into internal logical signals and conversely. The second layer is a reactive subsystem that contains the logical and temporal control of the system. It handles the logical inputs and decides, with respect to the current time, what outputs and what actions must be generated in reacting to the environment. The last layer is a set of transformational tasks that perform classical computations requested by the reactive subsystem. From this point of view, the reactive part is one of the most critical, and needs particular attention.

Temporal and Logical Safety — By construction, the reactive part of a real time system contains the temporal and logical control of the whole application, and then requires (a) *logical* properties, i.e. respect of the input/output specification, and (b) *temporal properties*, i.e. respect of the timing constraints. In this sense, the development of techniques and methods that could help to design such reactive systems, to give readable, concise and meaningful descriptions of them, and finally to prove their logical and temporal correctness, is one of the most relevant aims of real time programming.

Concurrency — From an architectural point of view, the reactive part of a real time system is generally composed of concurrent communicating subunits, either for geographical requirements, or for safety and fault tolerance criteria. For instance the global avionics system of modern aircrafts (such as Airbus A340, Boeing B777...) is composed of more than 100 computers communicating through numerical buses; each computer implementing specific avionics processes or functions defined and developed by different partners. Such an architecture requires concurrency expression means within specification and programming languages, and distributed implementation capabilities.

Determinism — Finally, determinism is an important requirement of critical embedded systems. From an observational point of view, a process is considered as deterministic if it produces identical output sequences when fed with identical (timed) input sequences. Deterministic systems are generally an order of magnitude simpler to specify, debug, and analyze than non-deterministic ones. Consequently, the behavior of critical real time applications, such as embedded systems, must be as predictable as possible. It means that the behavior of its reactive part must be reproducible, and then deterministic. Purely sequential systems are obviously deterministic. However, as noted above, reactivity often means concurrency. This requires then specification and programming languages defined by deterministic semantics of communication and concurrency.

The literature on real time systems is unanimous in recognizing the difficulty in specifying complex and critical reactive systems. Several *asynchronous* solutions have been proposed to this problem: Petri Nets, CSP, Occam, CCS ... But, due to the asynchronous concurrency semantics generally based on interleaving principles, most of these solutions are non-deterministic.

Another approach involving *strong synchronous* languages such as LUS-TRE [Caspi 91], ESTEREL [Berry 92; Boussinot 91], SIGNAL [Le Guernic 91], STATECHARTS [Harel 87]... have been proposed as a deterministic solution to the problem of concurrent reactive system design. These languages consider ideal reactive systems that produce outputs synchronously with inputs, their reactions taking no observable time. Such an approach is interesting in that it tackles real time and reactive programming in a formal and deterministic way, and provides a powerful way to produce centralized reactive processes. But it is rather more unrealistic in the area of distributed applications, where by definition, communication time cannot be neglected.

In this sense, both strong synchronism and asynchronism are not adequate answers (separately) to the problem of designing critical and distributed real-time systems.

In this chapter we explore another approach to reactivity called *weak synchronism*. The aim of this paradigm is to make a compromise between asynchronism and strong synchronism, avoiding the non-determinism difficulties met within the asynchronous approach, and permitting distributed implementations. The idea we explore is twofold: (a) as well as the strong synchronism, to guarantee determinism by controlling reaction time, i.e. assuming that reactions take exactly a constant duration δ, and (b) to allow physical distribution by assuming that δ is strictly positive. We consider then reactive systems, that react synchronously with an implicit global clock, and that produce outputs exactly one time unit after inputs, their reactions taking one time unit of this clock. The aim of the first part of this chapter is to introduced formally the weak synchronism by defining a weak synchronous calculus of communicating reactive automata, called CoREA (COmmunicating REactive Automata).

We build afterwards in a second part a weak synchronous extension of strong synchronous languages. This extension is based on the idea that it could be more convenient sometimes to describe a complex concurrent application by a set of communicating agents developed separately, than by a single global program which would be afterwards distributed. Following that idea, we formally introduce in section 2.5 a model of concurrent ESTEREL modules communicating in a weak synchronous way, and we show that such a mixed strong-weak synchronous approach could be a simple and adequate model for specifying distributed deterministic reactive applications, such as avionics systems of modern aircrafts.

This chapter is organized as follows. Section 2.2 presents a very short state of the art of reactive programming techniques. We discuss the advantages and drawbacks (a) of the asynchronous solution, (b) of the class of strong synchronous languages, and (c) of the approach proposed by G. Berry coupling ESTEREL and CSP [Berry 93]. Section 2.3 is then devoted to an informal introduction of the weak synchronous paradigm, which shall be formally instantiated in section 2.4 by defining a weak synchronous process algebra named CoREA. We introduce then in section 2.5 a programming model of concurrent reactive systems, mixing both ESTEREL and CoREA, and we investigate in the next section a distributed execution model of such concurrent reactive systems.

2.2   Reactive Programming: Asynchronism versus Strong Synchronism

Asynchronous Approaches

Several "asynchronous" solutions, such as Ada or Occam, have been proposed to the problem of reactive programming. They are interesting in that they permit hierarchical, modular and concurrent program developments. However, because of the asynchronous nature of tasks units, the semantics of asynchronous languages is intrinsically non-deterministic. Concurrent tasks are viewed as being loosely coupled independent execution units, each task evolving at its own pace. Inter-task communication is done by mechanisms such as message passing or rendezvous. Communication as a whole is asynchronous in the sense that an arbitrary amount of time can pass between the desire of communication and its actual completion. Furthermore when several communication can take place, their actual order is also arbitrary. Consequently, the semantics of time-handling primitives of these languages is intrinsically non-deterministic.

More generally, asynchronous techniques force the user to choose between determinism and concurrency, for they base concurrency on asynchronous implementation models where processes non-deterministically compete for computing resources. This leads to the problem of temporal interpretation of programs. Temporal primitives such as watchdogs (e.g. "do a task in less than 3 seconds") have only tentative meanings, for nothing forces them to be accurately executed. Consequently, execution times may be sometimes unpredictable, implying difficulties in proving correctness properties and in preserving reactivity.

In that sense, asynchronous calculi such as CSP provide a convenient approach for designing distributed applications composed of asynchronous communicating processes. Implementing them on networks of processors is natural, since the linguistic asynchronous communication mechanisms are close to actual communication mechanisms in networks. However, the lack of determinism of most of those approaches can actually become an impediment for critical systems, such as embedded systems which requires strong determinism.

The Strong Synchronous Approach

In order to avoid the previously mentioned problem, a more recent approach called "strong synchronism", has been proposed by D. Harel et G. Berry in Statecharts [Harel 87], and Esterel [Berry 92; Boussinot 91] respectively. This approach is based on the strong synchronous hypothesis [Benveniste 91]: each reaction of a reactive system is assumed to be instantaneous. Such ideal reactive systems produce outputs synchronously with their inputs, their reactions being assumed to take no observable time. To "take no time" has actually to be understood in two ways. First, a strong synchronous reaction is considered as "taking no time" with respect to its external environment if this environment remains invariant during the reaction; that supposes that the system reacts faster than its environment. Second, each subprocess of a global strong synchronous system is also assumed to "take no time" with respect to other subprocesses. That means that all subprocesses of the same strong synchronous application are supposed to react instantaneously at the same time, and to share the same (unchanged) environment; concurrent subprocesses evolve in a tightly coupled input-driven way and communication is performed by instantaneously broadcasting, the receiver receiving a message exactly at the same time it is sent. It provides a deterministic semantics of concurrency, and a formal straightforward interpretation of temporal statement. For instance, the watchdog "await 10 SECOND" lasts exactly 10 seconds. In the same way, a sequence of two processes "$P_1; P_2$" means that P_2 begins exactly when P_1 ends. Hence, the statement "await 10 METER ; P_1" (written in the ESTEREL style) means that the subprocess P_1 starts exactly when the 10th occurrence of signal "METER" arrives.

However, in order to guarantee as much as possible the strong synchronous hypothesis, synchronous programs are compiled into deterministic sequential implementations, yielding excellent run-time efficiency and predictability. Distribution of LUSTRE, ESTEREL or SIGNAL programs is then based on automated tool producing distributed code from those sequential implementations and from user-provided distribution commands [Ghezal 90; Girault 94]. This allows a whole application to be programmed in LUSTRE or ESTEREL without taking care of distribution problems, and then to be easily debugged and validated using standard LUSTRE or ESTEREL methods. However, distributed code generation onto multiprocessor architectures may be sometimes difficult while preserving accurate temporal predictability. Accurate bounds on reaction time (and then accurate temporal predictability) could be difficult to get, and their evaluation constitutes a real problem to be studied [Halbwachs 93].

In that sense, strong synchronous languages are adequate answers for programming centralized or strongly coupled systems. However, those languages may be more inadequate for designing large distributed systems, potentially loosely coupled, such as avionics systems.

Asynchronous-Synchronous Coupling: CRP

G. Berry has proposed an interesting attempt to combine ESTEREL and CSP for proposing a formal model of distributed reactive programming, called CRP [Berry 93]. The general idea is to describe a distributed reactive system as a network of communicating reactive kernels. Each kernel is a strong synchronous process (ESTEREL), while communication rules between kernels follow the CSP style, i.e. are based on the "*one to one*" rendezvous paradigm.

This approach is interesting in that it considers complex reactive systems as composed of a network of deterministic reactive kernels, and in that it bases concurrency and communication between kernels on a convenient and well known asynchronous implementation model (such as transputers network for instance ...). However in such an implementation model, processes non-deterministically compete for communication resources. Then as in CSP, the time taken between the possibility of communication and its actual achievement can be arbitrary. This problem is partially avoided in each ESTEREL kernel by controlling communication requests by temporal primitive as watchdogs. Nevertheless, this leads to possible non-deterministic behaviors at the global level, depending on the activity of communication resources.

Such a drawback is not really an impediment for a large class of reactive systems. It could be even a convenient way to introduce again non-determinism into strong synchronous systems. However, as mentioned in introduction, critical real time systems such as large embedded applications require both distribution and predictability, and need then another paradigm. We present in the next sections the weak synchronous paradigm as a possible response to this problem.

2.3 The Weak Synchronous Paradigm

The idea of weak synchronism has been initially proposed by R. Milner in his synchronous calculus SCCS [Milner 83], and by E. M. Clarke *et al.* in the area of hardware controllers and digital circuits [Browne 86]. The Milner's idea for introducing determinism into process algebra was twice: first to build the semantics of concurrency on *simultaneity* (and not interleaving as in CCS), and second to force processes which can perform an action to do it. For instance, contrary to the CCS process "$a.p$" which either may perform "a" immediately if it so wishes or wait for another tick (according to the asynchronous paradigm described briefly above), the SCCS process "$a : p$" performs "a" immediately and becomes "p" at the next tick. Consequently, the SCCS concurrent process "$(a : p) \parallel (b : q)$" reacts in a deterministic way by performing the double action "$a \times b$" and becomes "$p \parallel q$" at the next tick.

The aim of this chapter is to extend the SCCS paradigm to reactive distributed programming. The main idea developed in the following sections is, as well as in SCCS, to guarantee determinism by controlling reaction and communication time. But, contrary to strong synchronous languages, we assume that reactions and communications take a constant strictly positive duration. In other words, inputs and outputs of weak synchronous systems shall be separated by exactly one constant time unit. For instance, execution at time t of the broadcast statement "emit α" performs exactly at time $t + 1$ an occurrence of signal α. As in SCCS, weak synchronous systems behaves then synchronously with an implicit global clock, called *reference clock*. They react exactly at each "tick" of this clock to input signals emitted by the environment since the last tick, and to output signals emitted by the system itself during the last reaction, and they produce outputs for the next tick; their reactions taking one time unit exactly.

Weak synchronous systems are then *weakly reactive*: they interact with their environment only at each tick of their reference clock, and not continuously as *ideal* reactive systems. In this sense the reference clock defines the *reactivity granularity* of such systems. However, note that from an implementation point of view, strong synchronous programs lead also to weakly reactive systems whose granularity is determined by the maximal reaction time of their concrete implementation. The point of view we adopt here is then to take into account the concept of *reactivity granularity* directly at the modeling level (and not only at the implementation one).

The aim of the next sections is now to propose, in a formal way, an operational characterization of the weak synchronism. We proceed in two stages. First, we define in the next section a small calculus of weak synchronous communicating automata called CoReA (COmmunicating REactive Automata). Second we build in section 2.5 a weak synchronous extension of a strong synchronous language (ESTEREL) as a candidate model for designing distributed embedded systems; the semantics of this extension being based on both ESTEREL and CoReA.

2.4   CoReA: A Weak Synchronous Process Algebra

We follow the algebraic point of view of R. Milner. From this point of view, a process algebra may be defined by

- an abstract syntax (a free algebra $\mathcal{L}$)
- an operational semantics defined in a Plotkin style [Plotkin 81]
- and finally a congruence $\sim \subset \mathcal{L} \times \mathcal{L}$.

The next subsections are devoted to the definition of CoReA according to the three points above.

2.4.1   *Abstract Syntax*

A reactive automaton may be considered as an agent which reacts to input signals by broadcasting output and local signals, and becomes a new agent. Let S_{in}, S_{out}, and S_{loc} be disjoined countable sets of inputs signals, output signals and local signals.

We define first a signal calculus as a propositional logic where propositions are input and local signals. Formulae g of this calculus are defined by the following grammar:

$$g ::= \textbf{true} \mid \pi \mid g \wedge g \mid \neg g \qquad \text{with } \pi \in S_{in} \cup S_{loc}$$

Let $\mathcal{G}$ be the free algebra of formulae g. For conciseness, we define "**false**" and "∨" as abbreviations:

$$\textbf{false} \stackrel{\text{def}}{=} \neg\textbf{true} \quad \text{and} \quad g_1 \vee g_2 \stackrel{\text{def}}{=} \neg(\neg g_1 \wedge \neg g_2)$$

Let $Var = \{x, y, \ldots\}$ be a countable set of variables. Reactive automata of our calculus are terms a of the free algebra $\mathcal{L}$ defined by the following grammar:

$$
\begin{aligned}
a ::= \ &\textbf{nil} && \text{with } \textbf{nil} \notin Var \cup S_{in} \cup S_{loc} \cup S_{out} \\
| \ &g/O \cdot x && \text{with } x \in Var, \ g \in \mathcal{G}, \ O \subset S_{loc} \cup S_{out} \\
| \ &g/O \cdot a && \text{with } g \in \mathcal{G}, \ O \subset S_{loc} \cup S_{out} \\
| \ &a + a \\
| \ &a \parallel a \\
| \ &fix(x = a) \text{ with } x \in Var \text{ and } x \text{ sequential in } a
\end{aligned}
$$

where as usual "**nil**" stands for the process which does nothing. The construction "$g/O \cdot a$" stands for a transition guarded by a formula g and an action O and leading to an automaton a. Whenever g is true, the automaton $g/O \cdot a$ becomes a by broadcasting signals in O. Such a construction may be graphically represented by the following automaton:

"$\parallel$" and "$+$" are respectively the parallel composition and a deterministic choice operator between two branches. For instance the term "$g_1/O_1 \cdot a_1 + g_2/O_2 \cdot a_2$" may be graphically represented by the following automaton:

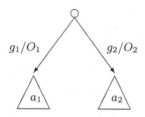

Finally, "$fix(x = a)$" stands for the recursive definition. For instance, the term "$fix(x = g/O \cdot x)$" may be graphically represented by the following automaton:

$$g/O$$

As usual, we denote by "$free(a)$" the set of variables free in a. Note then that fix is the only binding operator of our calculus. If x is free in a, then it is bound in $fix(x = a)$.

Furthermore, we denote as usual by "$a\{a'/x\}$" the result of simultaneously replacing a' for free occurrences of x in a, with change of bound variables as necessary to avoid clashes. Finally we define as usual "$a \equiv a'$" to mean that a and a' are identical up to change of bound variables.

The set $\mathcal{A}$ of well formed automata is then the greatest subset of $\mathcal{L}$ containing only closed terms:

$$\mathcal{A} \stackrel{\text{def}}{=} \{a \in \mathcal{L} \mid free(a) = \emptyset\}$$

Finally, let $\mathcal{A}_{seq} \subset \mathcal{A}$ be the set of sequential closed automata (obtained by removing the expression "$a \parallel a$" in the previous grammar).

2.4.2 *Weak Synchronous Operational Semantics*

A guard $g \in \mathcal{G}$ is a logical composition of signals. Its truth depends on the set I of signals present in the current environment. Let $I \subset S_{in} \cup S_{loc}$, and let $g \in \mathcal{G}$, we write "$I \models g$" to mean that g is valid over I, and we define such a relation inductively by:

$$
\begin{aligned}
&I \models \textbf{true} \\
&I \models \pi && \textbf{iff } \pi \in I \\
&I \models g_1 \wedge g_2 && \textbf{iff } I \models g_1 \text{ and } I \models g_2 \\
&I \models \neg g && \textbf{iff } \text{it is not the case that } I \models g
\end{aligned}
$$

By extension, "$g_1 \equiv g_2$" means that g_1 and g_2 have the same models:

$$g_1 \equiv g_2 \quad \textbf{iff} \quad (\forall I \subset S_{in} \cup S_{loc}, \ I \models g_1 \ \textbf{iff} \ I \models g_2)$$

Definition 2.1 Let $a \in \mathcal{L}$, we denote by "$guard(a)$" the formula characterizing the evolution condition of a:

$$guard(\mathbf{nil}) \stackrel{\text{def}}{=} \mathbf{false}$$
$$guard(g/O \cdot x) \stackrel{\text{def}}{=} g$$
$$guard(g/O \cdot a) \stackrel{\text{def}}{=} g$$
$$guard(a_1 + a_2) \stackrel{\text{def}}{=} guard(a_1) \vee guard(a_2)$$
$$guard(a_1 \parallel a_2) \stackrel{\text{def}}{=} guard(a_1) \vee guard(a_2)$$
$$guard(fix(x = a)) \stackrel{\text{def}}{=} guard(a)$$

Let $a \in \mathcal{L}$ and $I \subset S_{in} \cup S_{loc}$, then "$I \models guard(a)$" means that a is reactive to I, i.e. there is at least one transition leaving the initial state of a and which is labelled by a guard valid over I. For instance the evolution condition of automaton **nil** is always false. In other terms, **nil** cannot evolve. Conversely, the evolution condition of automaton "$g_1/O_1 \cdot a_1 + g_2/O_2 \cdot a_2$" is $g_1 \vee g_2$. Such an automaton can evolve to a_1 when g_1 becomes true, or to a_2 when g_2 becomes true.

We can now define the weak synchronous operational semantics of terms $a \in \mathcal{L}$ by a step relation $\longrightarrow \subset (S_{loc} \times \mathcal{L}) \times S_{in} \times S_{out} \times (S_{loc} \times (\mathcal{L} \cup Var))$. We write:

$$L_t \times a_t \xrightarrow[I_t]{O_t} L_{t+1} \times a_{t+1} \quad \text{with} \quad \begin{array}{l} L_t, L_{t+1} \subset S_{loc}, \ I_t \subset S_{in}, \ O_t \subset S_{out} \\ a_t \in \mathcal{L}, \ a_{t+1} \in \mathcal{L} \cup Var \end{array}$$

to mean that:

(1) at tick t the automaton a_t reacts (or does not react) to local signals L_t and to input signals I_t, by broadcasting output signals O_t and local signals L_{t+1}, and becomes a new automaton a_{t+1} at $t+1$;

(2) I_t is the set of input signals emitted by the environment during $[t-1, t[$;

(3) L_t is the set of the local signals broadcast by the system at $t-1$ (during the last reaction), and present as input at t (i.e. one time unit after);

(4) L_{t+1} is the set of local signals broadcast by the system at t and which will be exploited at $t+1$ for the next reaction (i.e. one tick later).

In that sense, broadcasting takes one time unit. The relation $\longrightarrow$ characterizes the dynamic evolution of a reactive system when the time is running, each step taking exactly one time unit of the reference clock.

Formally, the operational semantics of automata $a \in \mathcal{L}$ is given by the least relation $\longrightarrow \subset (S_{loc} \times \mathcal{L}) \times S_{in} \times S_{out} \times (S_{loc} \times (\mathcal{L} \cup \mathcal{V}ar))$ satisfying the structural definition below given. We follow a SOS style [Plotkin 81] by defining the semantics of our calculus by means of inference rules. We write in the following

$$\frac{P_1 \ldots P_n}{\underset{C}{\longrightarrow}} \qquad H_1 \ldots H_m$$

to mean that the conclusion C is true if premises $P_1 \ldots P_n$ are true provided that hypotheses $H_1 \ldots H_m$ are satisfied.

(a)   Transition

Whenever $I \cup L \models g$, then $g/O \cdot a$ reacts by emitting signals in O and becomes a:

$$L \times (g/O \cdot a) \quad \frac{\mathbf{true}}{\overset{O \cap S_{out}}{\underset{I}{\longrightarrow}}} \quad (O \cap S_{loc}) \times a \qquad I \cup L \models g \qquad \textbf{(Op1)}$$

(b)   Inaction

Whenever a is not reactive to its environment, then it remains invariant, no output is emitted, and the local context is lost (signals are not persistent):

$$L \times a \quad \frac{\mathbf{true}}{\overset{\emptyset}{\underset{I}{\longrightarrow}}} \quad \emptyset \times a \qquad I \cup L \not\models guard(a) \qquad \textbf{(Op2)}$$

(c)   Case

$+$ is the choice operator, choosing deterministically (like in ESTEREL and unlike in SCCS) between two branches. An automaton $a_1 + a_2$ is seen as a list of branches sorted in decreasing order of priority. If two branches are reactive simultaneously, only the first one in the ordered list is selected:

$$\frac{L \times a_1 \xrightarrow[I]{O} L' \times a_1'}{L \times (a_1 + a_2) \xrightarrow[I]{O} L' \times a_1'} \qquad I \cup L \models guard(a_1) \qquad \textbf{(Op3)}$$

$$\frac{L \times a_2 \xrightarrow[I]{O} L' \times a_2'}{L \times (a_1 + a_2) \xrightarrow[I]{O} L' \times a_2'} \qquad \begin{cases} I \cup L \not\models guard(a_1) \\ I \cup L \models guard(a_2) \end{cases} \qquad \textbf{(Op4)}$$

Note that $+$ is then associative but not commutative.

(d)   Concurrency
According to the weak synchronous paradigm, concurrent automata react synchronously at each tick of the global clock by adding their outputs to form a global output event and a global local event which will be seen everywhere at the next tick:

$$\frac{L \times a_1 \xrightarrow[I]{O_1} L_1' \times a_1' \qquad L \times a_2 \xrightarrow[I]{L_2} L_2' \times a_2'}{L \times (a_1 \parallel a_2) \xrightarrow[I]{O_1 \cup O_2} (L_1' \cup L_2') \times (a_1' \parallel a_2')} \qquad \textbf{(Op5)}$$

Note that this rule provides a deterministic semantics of concurrency and broadcasting. Furthermore, $\parallel$ is associative and commutative.

(e)   Recursion
$fix(x = a)$ reacts as a in which all free occurrences of x are substituted by $fix(x = a)$:

$$\frac{L \times a \xrightarrow[I]{O} L' \times a'}{L \times fix(x = a) \xrightarrow[I]{O} L' \times (a'\{fix(x = a)/x\})} \qquad I \cup L \models guard(a)$$

$$\textbf{(Op6)}$$

Rules **Op1**...**Op6** define then a causal and deterministic semantics of CoREA; that is, every automaton $a \in \mathcal{L}$ is executable and deterministic whatever its environment (Theorem 2.1).

Definition 2.2   Let $a \in \mathcal{L}$, a is causal and deterministic if and only if for all $I \subset S_{in}$, and $L \subset S_{loc}$ there exists unique $O \subset S_{out}$, $L' \subset S_{loc}$ and $a' \in \mathcal{L} \cup \mathcal{V}ar$ such that:

$$(L \times a) \xrightarrow[I]{O} (L' \times a')$$

Theorem 2.1   *For all a in $\mathcal{L}$, a is causal and deterministic.*

Proof.   By induction on rules **Op1**...**Op6**.   □

Furthermore, let $a \in \mathcal{A}$, i.e. a closed term of $\mathcal{L}$. Then, a is causal and deterministic and evolves to another closed automaton also in $\mathcal{A}$.

Theorem 2.2   *Let $a \in \mathcal{A}$, let $I \subset S_{in}$, let $L \subset S_{loc}$, let $a' \in \mathcal{L}$ such that:*

$$(L \times a) \xrightarrow[I]{O} (L' \times a')$$

then $a' \in \mathcal{A}$.

Proof.   By induction on rules **Op1**...**Op6**.   □

This last result is interesting in that, for all automaton $a \in \mathcal{A}$, it allows to tell about infinite behaviors as sequences of reactions

$$(L \times a) \xrightarrow[I_1]{O_1} (L_2 \times a_2) \xrightarrow[I_2]{O_2} (L_3 \times a_3) \ldots (L_n \times a_n) \xrightarrow[I_n]{O_n} (L_{n+1} \times a_{n+1}) \ldots$$

and then to characterize the semantics of a term $a \in \mathcal{A}$ as a *function* $[\![a]\!]$ associating a unique infinite sequence of output events to a (possibly infinite) sequence of input signals (Definition 2.5).

Definition 2.3   We denote by "input real-time history" a finite or infinite sequence "$\hat{I}$" of pairs (π, t) consisting of an input signal $\pi \in S_{in}$ and occurrence date $t \in \mathsf{R}^+$:

$$\hat{I} = ((\pi_i, t_i))_{i \geq 0}$$

such that for each $i \geq 0$, $\pi_i \in S_{in}$, $t_i \in \mathsf{R}^+$, and $t_i \leq t_{i+1}$.

$(\pi, t) \in \hat{I}$ means that the signal π occurs in history $\hat{I}$ at time t. An input real-time history can be considered as a temporal trace of an asynchronous environment, by taking R^+ (positive real numbers) as the temporal domain.

Definition 2.4   Let $\hat{I}$ be an input real-time history, we denote by "$obs(\hat{I})$" the result of synchronizing $\hat{I}$ on the discrete clock:

$$obs(\hat{I}) \stackrel{\text{def}}{=} (I_i)_{i>0}$$

such that

$$I_i \stackrel{\text{def}}{=} \{\pi_k \mid (\pi_k, t_k) \in \hat{I} \text{ and } i - 1 \le t_k < i\} \qquad \text{for each } i > 0$$

In other terms, $obs(\hat{I})$ denotes the behavior of the environment observed by the system by taking N (positive natural numbers) as discrete clock. Signals broadcast by the environment during $[n, n+1[$ are exploited simultaneously by the system at $n + 1$.

The relation "$\rightarrow$" being causal and deterministic, we can now define formally the weak synchronous semantics of an agent $a \in \mathcal{A}$ by a function $[\![a]\!]$ which associates an output history to each input real-time history:

Definition 2.5   Let $\hat{I}$ be an input real-time history, let $(I_1, \ldots, I_n, \ldots) = obs(\hat{I})$, let $a \in \mathcal{A}$, then:

$$[\![a]\!](\hat{I}) \stackrel{\text{def}}{=} (O_1, O_2, O_3, \ldots, O_n, \ldots)$$

such that

$$(\emptyset \times a) \xrightarrow[I_1]{O_1} (L_2 \times a_2) \xrightarrow[I_2]{O_2} (L_3 \times a_3) \ldots (L_n \times a_n) \xrightarrow[I_n]{O_n} (L_{n+1} \times a_{n+1}) \ldots$$

For each $a \in \mathcal{A}$, $[\![a]\!]$ defines the observable behavior of a in reacting to an asynchronous environment. In that sense, the function $[\![.]\!]$ defines the weak synchronous semantics of automata in $\mathcal{A}$.

2.4.3   *Congruence*

We do not wish to distinguish automata which have the same behavior. We define then the notion of bisimulation between automata, and we show that it is a congruence relation.

Definition 2.6 A binary relation $R \subset \mathcal{A} \times \mathcal{A}$ is a strong bisimulation over $\mathcal{A}$ if, whenever $a_1 \; R \; a_2$ then for all $I \subset S_{in}$, $L \subset S_{loc}$:

> (i) if $(L \times a_1) \xrightarrow[I]{O} (L' \times a_1')$,
>
> > then for some a_2', $(L \times a_2) \xrightarrow[I]{O} (L' \times a_2')$ and $\; a_1' \; R \; a_2'$
>
> (ii) if $(L \times a_2) \xrightarrow[I]{O} (L' \times a_2')$,
>
> > then for some a_1', $(L \times a_1) \xrightarrow[I]{O} (L' \times a_1')$ and $\; a_1' \; R \; a_2'$
>
> (iii) $I \cup L \models guard(a_1)$ **iff** $I \cup L \models guard(a_2)$

Definition 2.7 Let $a_1, a_2 \in \mathcal{A}$, a_1 and a_2 are strongly equivalent, denoted by $a_1 \sim a_2$, if and only if there exists a strong bisimulation $R \subset \mathcal{A} \times \mathcal{A}$ such that $a_1 \; R \; a_2$.

Proposition 2.1 $\sim$ *is the greatest strong bisimulation over agents in* $\mathcal{A}$.

Hitherto, we have only defined strong equivalence over agents in $\mathcal{A}$, i.e. terms with no free variable. To remedy this, we naturally extend the definition of $\sim$ over $\mathcal{L}$ as follows:

Definition 2.8 Let $a_1, a_2 \in \mathcal{L}$, let $\vec{x} = (x_1, \ldots, x_n) \in \mathcal{V}ar$ such that $free(a_i) \subset \vec{x}$ $(i = 1, 2)$. a_1 and a_2 are strongly equivalent, denoted by $a_1 \sim a_2$, if and only if for all $\vec{b} = (b_1, \ldots, b_n) \in \mathcal{A}$, $a_1\{\vec{b}/\vec{x}\} \sim a_2\{\vec{b}/\vec{x}\}$.

That defines then a strong congruence over $\mathcal{L}$; i.e. $\sim$ is substitutive under all the combinators of our calculus, and also under recursive definition.

Proposition 2.2 $\sim$ *is a congruence, i.e. for all* $a_1, a_2, a_3, a_4 \in \mathcal{L}$ *such that* $a_1 \sim a_2$ *and* $a_3 \sim a_4$, *then:*

(1) $(g/O \cdot a_1) \sim (g/O \cdot a_2)$
(2) $(a_1 + a_3) \sim (a_2 + a_4)$
(3) $(a_1 \parallel a_3) \sim (a_2 \parallel a_4)$
(4) $fix(x = a_1) \sim fix(x = a_2)$

The three first items can be directly obtained by induction on the structure of $\mathcal{L}$. In return, the last item is more difficult, and its proof is rather long and can not be given here. The way to demonstrate it is very similar to the idea followed by R. Milner for proving that CCS strong bisimulation is a congruence [Milner 89]. The reader interested by the proof of the third item is invited to refer to the full version of the present article [Boniol 97].

Finally, processes of our calculus are elements of the quotient algebra

$$\mathcal{P} \overset{\text{def}}{=} \mathcal{A}/\sim$$

$\mathcal{P}$ is then an algebra of deterministic synchronous reactive processes (cf. Theorem 2.1).

2.4.4 *Equational Laws*

Having established our congruence $\sim$, we may now consider the quotient algebra $\mathcal{P}$, and determine in this section a complete and sound set of equational laws in $\mathcal{P}$.

Let Σ be the theory defined by axioms **A1-A12** below and by the classical inference rules of equality (stating that "=" is a congruence). We denote by "$\Sigma \vdash a = a'$" to mean that a and a' are provably equal in Σ:

$$\text{if} \quad a \equiv a' \quad \text{then} \quad a = a' \tag{A1}$$

$$\textbf{false}/O \cdot a = \textbf{nil} \tag{A2}$$

$$\text{if} \quad g \equiv g' \quad \text{then} \quad g/O \cdot a = g'/O \cdot a \tag{A3}$$

$$(g/O \cdot a) + (g'/O \cdot a) = (g \vee g')/O \cdot a \tag{A4}$$

$$(g/O \cdot a) + (g'/O' \cdot a') = (g/O \cdot a) + ((g' \wedge \neg g)/O' \cdot a') \tag{A5}$$

$$\text{if} \quad (guard(a) \vee \neg guard(b)) \equiv \textbf{true} \quad \text{then} \quad a + b = a \tag{A6}$$

$$\text{if} \quad (guard(a) \wedge guard(b)) \equiv \textbf{false} \quad \text{then} \quad a + b = b + a \tag{A7}$$

$$a + (b + c) = (a + b) + c \tag{A8}$$

$$a \parallel \textbf{nil} = \textbf{nil} \parallel a = a \tag{A9}$$

$$\left(\sum_{i=1...n} g_i^1/O_i^1 \cdot a_i^1 \right) \parallel \left(\sum_{j=1...m} g_j^2/O_j^2 \cdot a_j^2 \right)$$

$$= \sum_i \sum_j ((g_i^1 \wedge g_j^2)/(O_i^1 \cup O_j^2) \cdot (a_i^1 \parallel a_j^2))$$

$$+ \sum_i ((g_i^1 \wedge \bigwedge_j \neg g_j^2)/O_i^1 \cdot \left(a_i^1 \parallel \left(\sum_j g_j^2/O_j^2 \cdot a_j^2 \right) \right))$$

$$+ \sum_j ((g_j^2 \wedge \bigwedge_i \neg g_i^1)/O_j^2 \cdot \left(\left(\sum_i g_i^1/O_i^1 \cdot a_i^1 \right) \parallel a_j^2 \right))$$

$$\text{(A10)}$$

$$fix(x = a) = a\{fix(x = a)/x\} \qquad \text{(A11)}$$

$$\text{if} \quad b = a\{b/x\} \quad \text{then} \quad b = fix(x = a) \qquad \text{(A12)}$$

These axioms describe the basic identities in $\mathcal{P}$. Automata which are identical up to change of bound variables are equal (**A1**). Transitions labelled by **false** can never be taken, and then are equal to **nil** (**A2**). Transitions, which are identical up to change of guards having same models, are equal (**A3**). The operator $+$ is distributive (**A8**), and commutative whenever guards are exclusive (**A7**). **nil** is the unit element for parallelism (**A9**). Axiom **A10** defines parallelism in terms of summation (expansion axiom). Finally, the two last axioms define the recursion construction. Firstly, $fix(x = a)$ is a solution of the fixed-point equation $b = a\{b/x\}$ (**A11**), and secondly this fixed-point is unique (**A12**).

This defines a sound and complete axiom system with respect to the congruence $\sim$.

Theorem 2.3   *For each $a, a' \in \mathcal{L}$, $\Sigma \vdash a = a'$ * **iff**   *$a \sim a'$*

A sound result ($\Rightarrow$) can be directly obtained by induction on axioms **A1**...**A12**. In return, the completeness result ($\Leftarrow$) is more difficult to obtain, and its proof is also rather long and detailed and cannot be given here. The way to demonstrate it is very similar to the idea followed by R. Milner for proving completeness of CCS equational laws [Milner 84; Milner 89]. The reader who is interested by the proof of this theorem is invited to refer again to the full version of the present chapter [Boniol 97].

This concludes the definition of our process algebra.

2.4.5 Brief Comparison with CCS

As briefly mentioned in introduction, concurrency in CCS is based on the "interleaving" paradigm, where processes non-deterministically compete for computing resources. In other terms, concurrent actions are executed sequentially in a non-deterministic order. Hence, CCS processes can behave non-deterministically and are not temporally predictable. On the contrary, concurrency in CoREA is based on the weak synchronous paradigm, where concurrent processes react simultaneously at each tick of the reference clock. It defines then a global deterministic semantics (cf. Theorem 2.1).

Furthermore, according to the interleaving paradigm, CCS concurrent processes are asynchronous; they evolve independently, and the only way to synchronize them is to achieve a communication action. In that sense, CCS communication mainly means synchronization between two processes (note besides that emission and reception actions are tackled in a symmetrical way), also called "rendezvous" in CSP. It only allows one process to communicate with another one, at a time.

The communication mechanism in CoREA is quite different. First of all, by definition CoREA concurrent processes are synchronous. Then it is not necessary to synchronize them by explicit "hand shaking" actions. Secondly, broadcasting is the unique communication mechanism in CoREA. Broadcasting, in opposition to "hand shaking", can be seen as "hand raising": when one wants to communicate, one raises its hand, so everybody can see it. It is analogous to radio communication where there are many receptors that all receive the same information at the same time, whatever the number of receptors (eventually zero). Then from this point of view, emission and reception actions are not tackled in a symmetrical way: (a) reception is necessarily synchronous with emissions, however (b) unlike in CCS, an emission action is not delayed until a receptor is ready; i.e. emission actions in CoREA can be performed without receptions. In other terms, communication does not force synchronization.

2.5   Application to Distributed Reactive Programming

Sections 2.4 has defined formally a minimal calculus of synchronous deterministic reactive processes, named CoREA. However, that calculus does not provide a user-friendly language for designing complex and distributed systems. The next step is then to build a more high level programming approach, formally based on COREA, preserving its deterministic semantics, and providing distributed implementation capabilities.

We propose then in this section a model of concurrent reactive systems mixing both ESTEREL and COREA.

2.5.1 ESTEREL: *Brief Overview*

ESTEREL [Boussinot 91; Berry 92] is a high level programming language introduced by G. Berry for designing tightly coupled reactive systems. The basic object of ESTEREL is the *signal*. Signals are used for communication with the environment as well as for internal communication.

The ESTEREL programming unit is the module. A module has an interface that defines its input and output signals, and a body that is an executable statement.

```
module M:
    input I₁, I₂;
    output O₁, O₂;

    body
end module
```

For instance the previous module describes a reactive system M reacting to each occurrence of the input signals I_1 and I_2 by eventually producing occurrences of output signals O_1 and O_2.

At execution time, a module is activated by repeatedly giving it an input event consisting of a possibly empty set of input signals assumed to be present. The module reacts by executing its body and outputs the emitted output signals. This reaction is assumed to be instantaneous or strongly synchronous in the sense that the outputs are produced in no time. Hence, all necessary computations are also done in no time. The only statements that consume time are the ones explicitly requested to do so.

The main statements of the ESTEREL language are statements emitting and waiting for input and/or output signals; those statements being put in sequence or in parallel. Some of the major statements of ESTEREL are then:

```
emit S
await S
present S then stat₁ else stat₂ end
loop stat end
stat₁ ; stat₂
stat₁ || stat₂
```

At each instant, each signal is consistently seen as present or absent by all statements, ensuring determinism. By default, signals are absent; a signal is present if and only if it is an input signal emitted by the environment or a signal internally broadcast by executing an `emit` statement.

An "`emit` S" statement is assumed to take no time. It broadcasts the signal S and terminates right away, making the emission of S transient. Signals broadcast by such a statement are instantaneously observed by the environment and by all the parallel components of the program.

Moreover, control transmission by the sequencing operator ";" takes no time by itself. In the same way, the "||" operator takes also no time by itself.

The only statement assumed to take time is "`await` S". When it starts executing, this statement simply retains the control up to the first future instant where S is present. If such an instant exists, the `await` statement terminates immediately; that is, the control is released instantaneously. If no such instant exists, then the `await` statement waits forever, and never terminates.

More generally, ESTEREL statements are imperative in nature. Then ESTEREL modules can be easily transformed into sequential state-transition systems where concurrency and communication are compiled away. In that sense, ESTEREL modules can be compiled into sequential CoREA automata reacting to input signals by emitting output signals and changing state. The idea we explore now in the next subsection is mainly based on this result.

2.5.2 $\mathcal{E}C$ = ESTEREL + CoREA

As proposed by G. Berry in CRP [Berry 93], we consider reactive systems as composed of ESTEREL kernels communicating via an interconnection network. However, contrary to CRP, concurrency and communication in our model are based on the weak synchronous semantics of CoREA. Formally, we consider reactive processes composed of n $(n > 0)$ ESTEREL modules broadcasting by broadcasting through a weak synchronous communicating medium. Let $\mathcal{E}C$ be the free algebra defined by the following grammar:

$$ p \quad ::= \quad K_E \quad | \quad p \parallel\!\parallel p $$

where K_E stands for causal and deterministic ESTEREL modules which do not contain any variable and which communicate with their environment only through pure signals (belonging to S_{in}, S_{loc} et S_{out}).

As mentioned at the end of subsection 2.5.1, ESTEREL modules can be transformed into finite deterministic and sequential automata, and then into sequential COREA processes. Let $\mathcal{S}_{Est}$ be this transformation function:

$$ \mathcal{S}_{Est} \; : \; K_E \to a \in \mathcal{A}_{seq} $$

We extend then this function to concurrent terms by:

$$ \mathcal{S}(K_E) \stackrel{\text{def}}{=} \mathcal{S}_{Est}(K_E) $$
$$ \mathcal{S}(p_1 \parallel\!\parallel p_2) \stackrel{\text{def}}{=} \mathcal{S}(p_2) \parallel \mathcal{S}(p_1) $$

where "$\parallel$" is the COREA parallel operator. We define then the operational semantics of terms $p \in \mathcal{E}C$ by the least relation $\Longrightarrow \subset (S_{loc} \times \mathcal{E}C) \times S_{in} \times S_{out} \times (S_{loc} \times \mathcal{E}C)$ satisfying the structural definition below:

$$ \frac{L \times \mathcal{S}(p) \; \xrightarrow[I]{O} \; L' \times \mathcal{S}(p')}{L \times p \; \xrightarrow[I]{O} \; L' \times p'} \qquad \textbf{(Op7)} $$

Globally speaking, this definition confers a weak synchronous semantics to the parallel composition " $\parallel\!\parallel$ " of $\mathcal{E}C$. Let $(K_1 \parallel\!\parallel \ldots \parallel\!\parallel K_n)$ be a concurrent term of $\mathcal{E}C$, then according to the previous definition:

(1) kernels $K_1 \ldots K_n$ are assumed to share a same global clock, called the reference clock;

(2) kernels $K_1 \ldots K_n$ react instantaneously at each "tick" of the reference clock;

(3) kernels $K_1 \ldots K_n$ communicate by broadcasting;

(4) broadcasting takes exactly one time unit of the reference clock.

At each "tick", each kernel reads its input signals coming from other kernels or from the environment, and computes its new internal state and output signals that will be received by other kernels and by the environment at the next tick. In that sense, the system operates exactly the same as a parallel composition of abstract machines in which the next state is computed instantaneously and in which changing state and broadcasting outputs require waiting for the next clock tick.

Definition 2.9 Let $p \in \mathcal{E}C$, p is causal and deterministic if and only if for all $I \subset S_{in}$, and $L \subset S_{loc}$, there exists unique $O \subset S_{out}$, $L' \subset S_{loc}$ and $p' \in \mathcal{E}C$ such that:

$$L \times p \xrightarrow[I]{O} L' \times p'$$

Theorem 2.4 *Let $p \in \mathcal{E}C$, p is causal and deterministic.*

Proof. Direct, from rule **Op7** and from Theorem 2.1. □

Then we may define a relation $\sim_E \subset \mathcal{E}C \times \mathcal{E}C$ by:

$$p_1 \sim_E p_2 \quad \text{iff} \quad \mathcal{S}(p_1) \sim \mathcal{S}(p_2)$$

Proposition 2.3 $\sim_E$ *is a congruence.*

Proof. Direct, from proposition 2.2. □

In that sense, the quotient algebra $\mathcal{E}C/ \sim_E$ is a weak synchronous extension of ESTEREL*. The main advantage of this extension is to provide a high level formal model, based on ESTEREL, for programming reactive applications which can be explicitly described as a set of communicating components.

2.6 Towards Weak Synchronous Distributed Implementations

By construction, after applying the ESTEREL compiler on each module K_i, a concurrent system $p \equiv (K_1 \;|||\; \ldots \;|||\; K_n) \in \mathcal{E}C$ may be considered as composed of n sequential sub-automata loosely coupled, communications between sub-automata taking one time unit of the reference clock. Such

---

*From an expressive point of view, terms of $\mathcal{E}C$ can be described in pure strong synchronous languages by modeling the weak synchronous communicating medium by ES-TEREL or LUSTRE modules which implement the delay of one time unit between broadcasting and reception. In that sense, the extension of ESTEREL proposed in this section is only a *conceptual* extension.

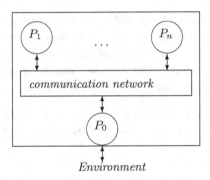

Fig. 2.1   A distributed execution machine

a system may be naturally implemented onto multiprocessor architectures provided that maximal physical communication time between processors is bounded by a constant which can be evaluated statically. In that case the maximal cycle duration (real reaction time of all kernels plus real communication time), and then the step of the reference clock of the system, may be evaluated at compile time from characteristics of the application and of the multiprocessor architecture.

Let us consider a distributed architecture Figure 2.1 composed of n communicating processors $P_1 \ldots P_n$ and of an *interface* processor P_0 broadcasting signals from the environment to processors $P_1 \ldots P_n$ and conversely. Let us suppose that such an architecture satisfies hypotheses 2.1 and 2.2.

Hypothesis 2.1   The drift rates of the hardware clocks $H_0 \ldots H_n$ associated to each processor $P_0 \ldots P_n$ are bounded.

■

Hypothesis 2.2   Communication time between two processors (through the communication network) is bounded.

■

Let $(K_1 \; ||| \; \ldots \; ||| \; K_n)$ be a concurrent system of $\mathcal{EC}$ composed of n communicating ESTEREL modules. The aim of this subsection is to build an execution model of this program over architecture Figure 2.1, and then to show that the coupling ESTEREL+CoReA admits distributed implementations.

For conciseness, we consider in the following that processors $P_0 \ldots P_n$ communicate via a single multiplex bus and store input signals in a mailbox (one mailbox per processor). Other execution models for other networks (multiple buses, Omega networks. . .) are studied in the full version of this chapter [Adelantado 93].

Mapping Rules:

Using the ESTEREL compilers, each module K_i is transformed into a sequential process that is mapped onto the processor P_i:

$$\forall i = 1 \ldots n, \quad K_i \mapsto P_i$$

Under hypothesis 2.1, the reaction time of each kernel K_i is then bounded by a constant L_i that can be evaluated at compile time. Let us suppose that:

$$L_1 \geq \ldots \geq L_{n-1} \geq L_n$$

Execution Model:

A run of a weak synchronous system is a sequence of cycles. Cycles begin at each tick of the reference clock by activating each kernels with its new input signals (received during the previous cycle), and terminate by broadcasting related output signals as input for the next cycle. Let us consider the following protocol:

(f) Protocol SB (Single Bus)

At the beginning of the cycle, let I be the input event received by P_0 from the environment, O_i the input event of P_i, and a_i the sequential automaton implementing the current state of the ESTEREL module on P_i $(i = 1 \ldots n)$:

Step 1: *P_0 broadcasts I to $P_1 \ldots P_n$, and then waits for new input signals from the environment;*

Step 2: *after receiving I from P_0, each P_i $(i = 1 \ldots n)$ reacts to its new input event $I \cup O_i$ by computing the transition:*

$$O_i \times a_i \xrightarrow[I]{O_i'} O_i' \times a_i'$$

Step 3: *when P_n ends its reaction, it broadcasts output signals O_n' to $P_0 \ldots P_n$;*

Step 4: *when P_i ($i = 1 \ldots n - 1$) has finished its reaction and has received O'_{i+1} from P_{i+1}, it broadcasts output signals O'_i to $P_0 \ldots P_n$;*

Step 5: *when P_0 has received O'_1 from P_1, it broadcasts output signals received from $P_1 \ldots P_n$ to the external environment;*

The cycle ends when step 5 ends.

Let us note **SB** the function implementing this protocol:

$$\mathbf{SB} : I, (O_i, p_i)_{i=1 \ldots n} \to (O'_i, p'_i)_{i=1 \ldots n}$$

SB implements the relation $\Longrightarrow$.

Proposition 2.4 *For any events $I, O \subset S$, the two following statements are equivalent:*

(i) $\mathbf{SB}(I, (O,)_{i=1 \ldots n}) = (O'_i, \llbracket K'_i \rrbracket)_{i=1 \ldots n}$

(ii) $O \times (K_1 \;\vert\vert\vert\; \ldots \;\vert\vert\vert\; K_n) \xrightarrow[I]{O'} O' \times (K'_1 \;\vert\vert\vert\; \ldots \;\vert\vert\vert\; K'_n)$

where $O' = O'_1 \cup \ldots \cup O'_n$, $a_i = \mathcal{S}_{Est}(K_i)$ and $a'_i = \mathcal{S}_{Est}(K'_i)$.

Proof. By induction on n. $\qquad\qquad\qquad\qquad\qquad\qquad\qquad\qquad$ $\square$

Furthermore, cycles **SB** involve parallel reactions, and sequential communications. This avoids collisions on the bus. Then under hypothesis 2.2, the broadcasting time from P_i to $P_0 \ldots P_n$ is bounded by a constant D_i that can be evaluated at compile time. Consequently, the cycle duration can also be bounded:

Proposition 2.5 *Under hypotheses 2.1 and 2.2, the duration T of cycles* **SB** *is bounded by:*

$$T \le \max_{k=1 \ldots n} \left(L_k + \sum_{j=0}^{k} D_j \right) + d_0$$

where L_i, D_i and d_0 are respectively the maximal reaction time of the reactive process mapped onto processor P_i, the maximal broadcasting time from P_i to $P_0 \ldots P_n$, and the maximal broadcasting time from P_0 to the environment.

Proof. By induction on n. $\qquad\qquad\qquad\qquad\qquad\qquad\qquad\qquad$ □

Finally, cycles are executed synchronously with the reference clock of the system. They begin at each tick of this clock and must end before the next tick. The weak synchronous paradigm imposes then

$$cycle\ duration \leq \Delta t$$

where Δt is the period of the reference clock (w.r.t to the absolute time). We can then deduce the minimal value of Δt such that sequences of cycles **SB** implement the weak synchronous semantics.

Corollary 2.1 *The execution model based on the function* **SB** *implements the weak synchronous semantics of $\mathcal{EC}$ if:*

$$\Delta t \geq \max_{k=1...n} \left(L_k + \sum_{j=0}^{k} D_j \right) + d_0 \qquad\qquad \textbf{(Ex8)}$$

where Δt is the period of the reference clock.

This defines the minimal granularity of reactivity of such an implementation.

Sequentiality of broadcasting permits to bound communication time and then cycle duration. However, this leads to a minimal value of Δt proportional to n (number of strong synchronous kernels). This is a serious drawback when increasing the size of the system (for instance the avionics system of a modern aircraft such as Airbus A340 is composed of more than 100 computers). More efficient synchronization protocols, supported by other interconnection networks allowing parallel communication, are studied by M. Cubéro-Castan [Adelantado 93]. Particularly, he has proved that, in the case of Omega networks interconnecting processors $P_0 \ldots P_n$, broadcasting of signals can be done in parallel. The lower bound of the reference clock step Δt becomes then:

$$\Delta t_{min} \geq \max_{k=1...n} (L_k) + \max_{k=1...n} (D_k)$$

and does not depend directly on the size of the system.

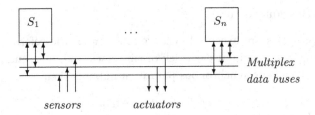

Fig. 2.2   General avionics system architecture

That shows the distributed implementation capabilities of the weak synchronous model $\mathcal{E}C$.

2.7   Application to Embedded Systems

Avionics systems of modern aircrafts (such as Airbus A340/A330, Boeing B777, EuroFighter Aircraft, or DASSAULT-AVIATION Rafale...) are mainly composed of functions and/or processes running in parallel and communicating through multiplex data buses. Such an avionics architecture may be represented by Figure 2.2 where each S_i is a tightly coupled subsystem (such as engine control processes, global positioning subsystems, a central air data computers, a digital flight control subsystem...); all those subsystems communicating through MIL-STD-1553 or ARINC 629 multiplex buses. Such an architecture is then very close to the abstract distributed machine Figure 2.1.

Moreover, subsystems S_i are generally specified and realized by a different partners. From this point of view, an avionics system can be seen as a term

$$S \equiv (S_1 \mid \ldots \mid S_n)$$

composed of communicating and concurrent subunits which cannot be compiled into a global automaton. Such a construction is then very close (from a syntactical point of view) to $\mathcal{E}C$ terms.

Last, avionics systems are often critical and require then determinism. Each subsystem S_i is then assumed to behave in a deterministic way; in the same manner, the global system S is also assumed to define a deterministic behavior. Hence, communication and concurrency between subsystems S_i must be deterministic.

In that sense, the $\mathcal{E}C$ model previously defined (extended eventually with other languages such as LUSTRE and STATECHARTS) provides a formal and simple framework for specifying such avionics systems.

We have experimented the $\mathcal{E}C$ model (extended to full ESTEREL involving statements operating on data and valued signals) on an military assistant system, named "Pilot's Associate" [Champigneux 95] (DASSAULT-AVIATION). The global objective of this application is to help a human pilot, by recognizing eventually unexpected threats, by planning his mission, by proposing several counter-attacks, and by planning their executions if human pilot agrees. By definition, this application is an actual reactive system facing strong timing constraints, and involving communicating subsystems.

The $\mathcal{E}C$ specification we have realized of such an embedded system involves 5 ESTEREL modules:

(1) a "sensor fusion" module, named Fusion, recognizing threats by merging information from sensors (radar...) with already known threats;

(2) a "tactical assessment" module, named Tact_Ass, evaluating consequences of a given threat onto the mission, according to the nature of the threat, relief, and flight plan;

(3) a "mission assessment" module, named Mission, managing and eventually replanning the flight plan according to outside situation and aircraft parameters;

(4) a "tactical management" module, named Tact_Man, computing a set of counter-attacks for a given threat;

(5) and a last module, named Visu which synthesizes all information from previous modules to be presented to human pilot according to outside situation and to pilot workload.

The $\mathcal{E}C$ modelization of that system may then be defined by:

$$\text{PA} \stackrel{\text{def}}{=} (\text{Fusion} \,|||\, \text{Tact\_Ass} \,|||\, \text{Mission} \,|||\, \text{Tact\_Man} \,|||\, \text{Visu})$$

A prototype of PA has been implemented [Adelantado 94]. That prototype has allowed the evaluation of an actual implementation of the "Pilot's Associate" system on a distributed architecture composed of 5 processors communicating through a simple multiplex data bus:

- Let us note L the maximal reaction time of the ESTEREL modules evaluated on a SUN4C/30 processor:

$$L \approx 8 \; ms$$

- Let us note C the maximal number of bits broadcast at each tick by all kernels:

$$\sum_{i=1...5} C_i = 16000 \; bits$$

Then, the maximal broadcasting time required by each kernel is:

$$\sum_{i=1...5} D_i = \frac{16000}{5 \; 10^6} \; s = 3.2 \; ms$$

when considering that the multiplex bus operates at 5 Mbit/s for effective data (other bits being used for control words).

Finally, by applying equation **Ex8**, the minimal tick duration on such an architecture is:

$$\Delta T \geq L + \sum_{i=1...5} D_i \approx 11.2 \; ms$$

(when considering that d_0 is already contains in L, i.e. in the kernel reactions). This defines the level of responsiveness of this application on such a distributed architecture.

2.8 Conclusion

This chapter presents a process algebra of deterministic concurrent reactive automata, named CoREA, based on a weak synchronous semantics. We have then define a formal model based on ESTEREL+CoREA, for programming reactive application which are conceptually distributed, i.e. explicitly composed of communicating reactive components, such as avionics systems. The main advantage of this model is to allow distributed implementation which are logically and temporally predictable.

Furthermore, avionics systems are often heterogeneous in the sense that they often are composed of functions or processes specified by different partners with different languages. For instance, languages LUSTRE, STATECHARTS, SDL... are intensively used for specifying different concurrent and communicating parts of the Airbus A340 avionics system. The next objective of the work presented above is then to define a more general model, multi-languages in nature, and mixing synchronous approaches such as ESTEREL, LUSTRE and STATECHARTS in a weak synchronous way, with asynchronous languages such as SDL. That leads to the problem of synchronous/asynchronous conjunction.

Chapter 3

A Model of Probabilistic Processes

Fernando Cuartero, Valentín Valero and David de Frutos

Abstract: We present a model of probabilistic processes, which is an extension of CSP, on the basis of replacing internal non-determinism by generative probabilistic choices, and external non-determinism by reactive probabilistic choices. Our purpose when defining the model has been to maintain, as far as possible, the meaning of all the operators in classical CSP, generalizing them in a probabilistic way. Thus we try to keep valid (once probabilistically generalized), as far as possible, the laws of CSP. It is the combination of both internal and external choice that makes strongly difficult the definition of a probabilistic version of CSP. We can find in the literature quite a number of papers on probabilistic processes, but only in a few of them internal and external choices are combined trying to preserve their original meaning. The denotational semantics here presented is based on a domain of probabilistic trees with two kinds of nodes, representing the internal and external choices, the root being an internal one, which generalizes in a very natural way the corresponding trees for nonprobabilistic process algebras. We present also a testing semantics fully abstract with respect to our denotational semantics.

This work has been partially supported by CICYT under grant number TIC-97-0669-c03-02

3.1 Introduction

There are mainly two trends when trying to define the semantics of probabilistic processes. The first is the so called *generative*, which distributes the probabilities among all the possible computations. This clearly corresponds to the natural probabilistic generalization of the internal choice of CSP. On the other hand, the *reactive* approach distributes the probabilities among all the computations beginning with the same action; this is, in our opinion, the reasonable way to cope with the external choice of CSP. These models are separately studied [Glabbeek 90].

Papers studying the semantics of probabilistic processes have appeared in the literature. First of them just studied probabilistic transition systems [Christoff 90]; others [Giacalone 90; Glabbeek 90] focus on probabilistic versions of the SCCS calculus [Milner 83], a synchronous version of the more popular CCS [Milner 89]. Hansson [Hansson 90] presents an asynchronous CCS, but maintaining the non-determinism mixed with a random behavior of the environment. Wang Yi [Yi 92] presents a proposal for a testing semantics of a probabilistic extension of CCS, also including both non-deterministic and probabilistic choices.

A group of researchers from Oxford University have spent a considerable effort on the subject, and two Ph.D. Thesis have been produced. Karen Seidel [Seidel 92] has developed two different probabilistic models of CSP. In the first one, she gives a semantics in terms of probability measures on the space of infinite traces, but as this first model raises some problems when defining the semantics for the external choice operator, she develops a second semantics, using conditional probability measures. On the other hand, Gavin Lowe [Lowe 91] has also defined a denotational model covering both internal and external probabilistic behavior in Timed CSP, but there are several important differences with our approach, both at the intuitive and at the technical level. The most important difference is that he maintains a pure (without any probabilistic information) non-deterministic choice operator.

Another contribution is [Yuen 94], which presents a fully abstract characterization of the testing semantics defined in [Cleveland 92]. That characterization is based on finding a complete subset of tests, with the same strength that the full set of tests. Finally, in [Núñez 95] is studied a *generative* interpretation of probabilities for a language with two choice operators. This model is very close to ours. A testing semantics is presented for that model, and also a fully abstract denotational semantics, based on *acceptance trees* following similar ideas to that presented here.

In Section 2 we present the syntax of the language. In Section 3 we introduce the mathematical objects representing semantics processes. Semantics of the operators is defined in Section 4. Afterwards, a simple protocol is presented as example in Section 5. In Section 6 the testing semantics is presented, and we show that it is fully abstract with respect to the denotational semantics. Finally, in Section 7 some conclusions and the future work are presented.

3.2 Syntax of PCSP

Definition 3.1 Given a finite alphabet of actions Σ, and a set of identifiers Id, the set of PCSP processes is defined by the following BNF-expression:

$$P ::= STOP \mid DIV \mid X \mid a \to P \mid P \lceil \rceil_p P \mid P \square_p P \mid P \parallel_A^p P \mid \mu X.P$$

where $p \in [0, 1]$, $a \in \Sigma$, $A \subseteq \Sigma$ and $X \in Id$.

$\square$

We have omitted the study of the hiding operator, due to its special difficulties, although a discussion on the subject can be found in the final section.

The intuitive meaning of each operator is as follows:

- *STOP*, $a \to P$ and $\mu X.P$: They are similar to the corresponding CSP operators.
- *DIV* is a *divergent* process, unable to execute any action, but also unable to stop.
- INTERNAL CHOICE: $P \lceil \rceil_p Q$ is a process that behaves as P with probability p and as Q with probability $1 - p$.
- EXTERNAL CHOICE: $P \square_p Q$ is a process whose behavior is mainly deterministic. If the environment offers an action which can be executed either by P or by Q, but not for both of them, then it will be executed for the corresponding process with the probability with which this process can execute it. If both processes can execute the

offered action, then the choice is made randomly according to the parameter p (as in the internal choice). With this intuition behind, there is a reactive interpretation of the external choice.

- PARALLEL COMPOSITION: $P \parallel_A^p Q$ is a process which represents the parallel execution of P and Q synchronizing on the actions in A, and the meaning of the parameter p is similar to that in the external choice when an action not belonging to A is offered by the environment.

3.3 Domain of Probabilistic Processes

In order to obtain a denotational model of PCSP, we have to define the kind of mathematical objects representing semantics processes. For that, let us have a look at the behavior of a process in our model. Along the execution of a process we find two different stages at each step of its evolution. Firstly, the process reaches a *stable state* after the execution of several internal choices. After that, the environment selects, among all the actions of that state, which is the concrete action to be executed.

Thus, the main idea to define the behavior of a process will be the description of the reached states along its execution. Naturally, due to the probabilistic characteristics of our model, we need to add, in the appropriate way, the adequate probabilistic information.

We define a probabilistic process by means of a tree with two kinds of alternating nodes, which we call internal and external nodes, the root being an internal one. Arcs leaving internal nodes are labeled with a pair (A, p), where A is a state (i.e. a set of actions) and p is a probability. These arcs reach external nodes, from which as many arcs as actions of A leave, labeled each one with a different action of that state; and reaching again another internal node. Graphically, a partial representation can be seen in Fig. 3.1.

Definition 3.2 (Probabilistic Processes)

We define *semantical probabilistic processes* by the following regular expression:

$$P := \bigcap_{A \in \mathcal{A}} [p_A] \bigsqcup_{a \in A} a.P$$

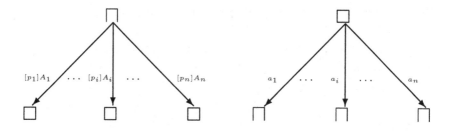

Fig. 3.1   Internal and External nodes of probabilistic processes

where $\mathcal{A} \subseteq \mathcal{P}(\Sigma)$, $\mathcal{A} \neq \emptyset$ and $\forall A \in \mathcal{A} : p_A \neq 0 \wedge \sum_{A \subseteq \mathcal{A}} p_A \leq 1$.

We will denote by $\mathcal{P}$ the set of semantical probabilistic processes.

$\square$

Definition 3.3   (Probability to reach a state)

Let $P = \bigsqcap_{A \in \mathcal{A}} [p_A] \bigsqcup_{a \in A} a.P_{a,A}$ a semantical probabilistic process and $A \subseteq \Sigma$.
We define the probability with which P reaches the state A, which we
denote by $p(P, A)$, by

$$p(P, A) = \begin{cases} p_A \text{ if } A \in \mathcal{A} \\ 0 \quad \text{otherwise} \end{cases}$$

We will also denote by $P/(a, A)$ the process obtained after executing
the action a at the state A, i.e. $P_{a,A}$.

$\square$

External nodes of a semantical probabilistic process can be characterized by means of a unique sequence of alternating states and actions. We
will denote by SEQ the set of these sequences characterizing all possible
external nodes:

$$SEQ = \{ \langle A_1 \cdot a_1 \dots A_n \rangle \mid a_i \in A_i, A_i \in \mathcal{P}(\Sigma), n \geq 1 \}$$

We can associate to each such a sequence the probability with which a
corresponding computation will be executed, as follows:

Definition 3.4   (Probability to reach an external node)

Let $P \in \mathcal{P}$, $s = \langle A_1 \cdot a_1 \dots A_n \rangle \in SEQ$. We define the probability with

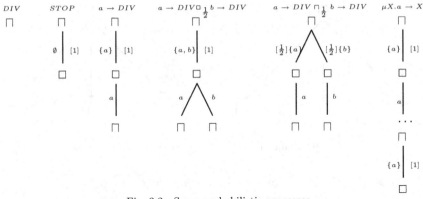

Fig. 3.2   Some probabilistic processes

which P reaches the external node represented by the sequence s, denoted by $p(P, s)$, as follows:

$$p(P, \langle A_1 \rangle) = p(P, A_1)$$
$$p(P, \langle A_1 \cdot a_1 \rangle \cdot s) = p(P, A_1) \cdot p(P/(a_1, A_1), s)$$
□

Once we have the objects of our domain of processes, we introduce the partial order between them.

Definition 3.5   (Order between semantical probabilistic processes)
Let $P, Q \in \mathcal{P}$. We say that $P \sqsubseteq Q$ if and only if for any sequence $s \in SEQ$, we have $p(P, s) \le p(Q, s)$.
□

The following result (whose proof is immediate) allows us to state that with this ordering we can define a denotational semantics using the *fixed point* approach.

Theorem 3.1 $(\mathcal{P}, \sqsubseteq)$ is a complete partial order (cpo).
□

3.4   Operator Semantics

The semantics of the considered operators is defined in a denotational style, by associating a function between semantical probabilistic processes to each operator. As usual, in the sequel $[\![P]\!]$ will denote the semantics of P.

3.4.1 *Simple Operators*

— $[\![DIV]\!]$ is defined by a tree with a single node (the root), and no arcs at all. Thus

$$p([\![DIV]\!], s) = 0 \quad \forall s \in SEQ$$

— $[\![STOP]\!]$ is defined by a tree with two nodes: one internal and one external. The arc connecting them is labeled by $(\emptyset, 1)$.

$$p([\![STOP]\!], s) = \begin{cases} 1 & \text{if } s = \langle \emptyset \rangle \\ 0 & \text{otherwise} \end{cases}$$

— $[\![a \to P]\!]$ is defined from $[\![P]\!]$, adding two new nodes to it: one internal (new root) and one external. The arc connecting them is labeled by $(\{a\}, 1)$, and the arc connecting this new external node and the root of $[\![P]\!]$ is labeled by a. Thus, we have:

$$p([\![a \to P]\!], s) = \begin{cases} p([\![P]\!], s') & \text{if } s = \langle \{a\} \cdot a \rangle s' \\ 0 & \text{otherwise} \end{cases}$$

— Branches of $[\![P \sqcap_p Q]\!]$ are obtained from the branches of $[\![P]\!]$ and $[\![Q]\!]$, weighted by p and $1-p$ respectively. When $[\![P]\!]$ and $[\![Q]\!]$ have two branches with identical sequences, only one of them appears in $[\![P \sqcap_p Q]\!]$, taking as probability the weighted addition of the probabilities associated to them. Thus, we have:

$$p([\![P \sqcap_p Q]\!], s) = p \cdot p([\![P]\!], s) + (1-p) \cdot p([\![Q]\!], s)$$

3.4.2 *External Choice*

To obtain the tree $[\![P \square_p Q]\!]$ firstly we must consider all the possible states of $[\![P]\!]$ and $[\![Q]\!]$ at the first level. Then, the arcs of $[\![P \square_p Q]\!]$ leaving the root are obtained considering all the union sets of them. For each state C so obtained, its associated probability is calculated adding up the products of the probabilities corresponding to all the pairs A, B such that $C = A \cup B$.

Thus, at the first level we have:

$$p([\![P \square_p Q]\!], \langle C \rangle) = \sum_{\substack{A,B \\ A \cup B = C}} p([\![P]\!], \langle A \rangle) \cdot p([\![Q]\!], \langle B \rangle)$$

This way, we have solved the internal choices at the first level of P and Q, and then we have to face with the external ones under those. For that, let us consider a pair A, B,such that $C = A \cup B$, and let $a \in C$. Then, either this action just belongs to one of these sets, or it does to both of them. In the first case, the corresponding process executes the action and continues its execution. Thus, in this case the corresponding branches of $[\![P\Box_pQ]\!]$ are obtained from the branches of the process executing the action. On the other hand, when the action belongs to both sets, branches of $[\![P\Box_pQ]\!]$ are obtained by combining those of both processes in a very similar way to that used for the internal choice.

$$p([\![P\Box_pQ]\!], \langle C \cdot a \rangle s) = \sum_{\substack{a \in A-B \\ C=A \cup B}} p([\![P]\!], \langle A \cdot a \rangle s) \cdot p([\![Q]\!], \langle B \rangle)$$

$$+ \sum_{\substack{a \in B-A \\ C=A \cup B}} p([\![Q]\!], \langle B \cdot a \rangle s) \cdot p([\![P]\!], \langle A \rangle)$$

$$+ \sum_{\substack{a \in A \cap B \\ C=A \cup B}} [p \cdot p([\![P]\!], \langle A \cdot a \rangle s) \cdot p([\![Q]\!], \langle B \rangle)$$

$$+ (1-p) \cdot p([\![Q]\!], \langle B \cdot a \rangle s) \cdot p([\![P]\!], \langle A \rangle)]$$

3.4.3 *Parallel Composition*

The semantical probabilistic process $[\![P\|_A^pQ]\!]$ is defined in a similar way as the external choice, considering all the possible states of $[\![P]\!], [\![Q]\!]$. However, now we cannot only consider simple unions of states, due to the presence of the synchronization set A, and we must remove from each union set $B \cup C$ the actions in A belonging just to one of the sets B or C, because these actions should be executed by both processes P and Q simultaneously. Thus, the reached state will be $D = ((B \cup C) - A) \cup (B \cap C)$.

To simplify our notation we will split the states reached by the process P into two components, B and X_1 (resp. for Q, C and X_2), where sets B and C do not hold any actions belonging to both sets A and $B \cap C$. However, all these kind of actions will be taken into account in two sets, X_1, X_2, where X_1 holds the actions belonging to the synchronization set which can be executed only by process P, and respectively X_2.

Then, at the first level we have to consider all the possible states $B \cup X_1$

of $[\![P]\!]$ and $C \cup X_2$ of $[\![Q]\!]$, for $X_1 \cap X_2 = \emptyset$, $X_1, X_2 \subseteq A$, and $B \cap C \subseteq A$.

$$p([\![P\|_A^p Q]\!], \langle D \rangle) = \sum_{B \cup C = D} \sum_{\substack{X_1, X_2 \subseteq A \\ X_1 \cap X_2 = \emptyset}} p([\![P]\!], \langle B \cup X_1 \rangle) \cdot p([\![Q]\!], \langle C \cup X_2 \rangle)$$

Let $\langle D \cdot a \rangle s \in SEQ$, and B, C, X_1, X_2 as previously. We have to distinguish four cases to define $p([\![P\|_A^p Q]\!], \langle D \cdot a \rangle s)$:

— If $a \in B - C$, then P executes the action a, and the parallel process $P/(a, B \cup X_1)\|_A^p Q$ must execute the sequence s.
— If $a \in C - B$, then Q executes the action a, and the parallel process $P\|_A^p Q/(a, C \cup X_2)$ must execute the sequence s.
— When $a \in (B \cap C) - A$, this action is executed randomly either by P or Q with the associated probability. Then, the process $P/(a, B \cup X_1)\|_A^p Q$ must execute the sequence s with probability p, and $P\|_A^p Q/(a, C \cup X_2)$ with probability $1 - p$.
— When $a \in A \cap B \cap C$, both processes must cooperate to execute the action, and the process $P/(a, B \cup X_1)\|_A^p Q/(a, C \cup X_2)$ must execute the sequence s.

$$p([\![P\|_A^p Q]\!], \langle D \cdot a \rangle s)$$

$$= \sum_{\substack{B \cup C = D \\ A \cap B = A \cap C}} \sum_{\substack{X_1, X_2 \subseteq A \\ X_1 \cap X_2 = \emptyset}} p([\![P]\!], \langle B \cup X_1 \rangle) \cdot p([\![Q]\!], \langle C \cup X_2 \rangle)$$

$$\cdot \begin{cases} p([\![P/(a, B \cup X_1)\|_A^p Q]\!], s) & \text{If } a \in B - C \\ p([\![P\|_A^p Q/(a, C \cup X_2)]\!], s) & \text{If } a \in C - B \\ p \cdot p([\![P/(a, B \cup X_1)\|_A^p Q]\!], s) \\ \quad + (1 - p) \cdot p([\![P\|_A^p Q/(a, C \cup X_2)]\!], s) & \text{If } a \in B \cap C - A \\ p([\![P/(a, B \cup X_1)\|_A^p Q/(a, C \cup X_2)]\!], s) & \text{If } a \in B \cap C \cap A \end{cases}$$

3.4.4 Recursion

To define the semantics of $\mu X.P(X)$, where $P(X)$ is a process where X appears as free variable X, we use the fix point technique, because we know [Cuartero 97] that semantical definitions of the previous operators are monotonous and continuous.

$$[\![\mu X.P(X)]\!] = \sqcup [\![P^n]\!]$$

where $P^0 = DIV, \ldots, P^n = P(P^{n-1}), \ldots$.

3.5   Example

We present a modeling of the AUY-protocol for data transmission. This protocol ensures a reliable transmission in a system in which the channels can fail.

The system consists of two agents, a transmitter and a receiver, which communicate messages. The transmitter sends a message to the receiver using an unreliable channel, which can lose it with some known probability p. We suppose that if the original message is lost, the channel will transmit a null message λ to the receiver. The receiver takes a message from its input channel, and if it is not λ, it sends the message to the outside world, and an acknowledgement message to the transmitter using a second channel. Again, this channel can lose the message (we suppose that with the same probability p although this is not necessary at all), in which case it sends a null message λ' to the transmitter. If the transmitter receives through this second channel a λ', it will repeat the emission, sending again the original message. Finally, when it receives the acknowledgement it accepts a new incoming message, and a new cycle begins.

The PCSP process modeling this protocol is just the P process defined as follows:

Transmitter:
$$T = in \rightarrow T_1$$
$$T_1 = msg \rightarrow (ack \rightarrow T \Box \lambda' \rightarrow T_1)$$
First channel:
$$C_1 = msg \rightarrow ([p]\lambda \rightarrow C_1 \sqcap [1-p]msg' \rightarrow C_1)$$
Second channel:
$$C_2 = (ack' \rightarrow ([p]\lambda' \rightarrow C_2 \sqcap [1-p]ack \rightarrow C_2))\Box(\lambda'' \rightarrow \lambda' \rightarrow C_2)$$
Receiver:
$$R = (msg' \rightarrow out \rightarrow ack' \rightarrow R)\Box(\lambda \rightarrow \lambda'' \rightarrow R)$$
AUY-protocol:
$$P = T\|_{\{msg,ack,\lambda'\}}((C_1\|_\emptyset C_2)\|_{\{msg',ack',\lambda,\lambda''\}}R)$$

We have omitted the probabilities in the appearances of the external choice and parallel operators all along the example, since in fact they are not necessary in this particular case, because the first actions of the components are different.

The application of the semantic definitions allows us to observe that this system is essentially deterministic. There are only two internal nodes representing real random choices, and in all the external nodes there is only one action to choice among. Both internal nodes represent the possibility of losing information (messages or acknowledgements).

3.6 Testing Semantics

In this section, we will present a testing semantics based on the idea of offering tests to processes, being a test a probabilistic tree, where each level represents a set of different actions offered by the observer at that step, from which one will be selected to be executed. The arcs of these probabilistic trees are labeled both by an action and a probability, thus the accepted subset of actions at each step of the process evolution will have associated a certain probability distribution, so that the action to be executed is selected from this set according to it. We only study the finite case; the study of infinite processes being very similar to the denotational semantics.

3.6.1 *Probabilistic Tests*

A first idea to define the semantics of PCSP, is to analyze the behavior of each process when we offer to it any trace of actions to be executed. For each trace of actions we would have the probability with which it is accepted. However, we have found several problems when trying to apply this idea. Concretely, with this sole information it is not possible to differentiate some processes, which intuitively should be distinguished.

As a consequence, in order to define the semantics of PCSP, instead of offering to processes just traces, we will offer to them (probabilistic) trees of actions. Each level of such a tree represents a set of different actions offered by the observer at that step, from which one will be selected to be executed. The arcs of these probabilistic trees are labeled both by an action and a probability, thus the accepted subset of actions at each step of the process evolution will have associated a certain probability distribution, so that the action to be executed is selected from this set according to it. In this way, the semantics of each process is defined by the probabilities to pass each possible test.

Definition 3.6   (Probabilistic Tests)

We define the set of Probabilistic Tests (*PTEST* for short) as follows:

$$ t ::= \omega \mid 0 \mid a.t \mid \sum_{i=1}^{n} [p_i] a_i.t_i $$

where $a_i \in \Sigma$, $a_i \neq a_j$ if $i \neq j$, $p_i \in [0,1]$ and $\sum_{i=1}^{n} p_i = 1$.

$\square$

The ω test stands for *success;* thus it will always be accepted. The 0 test stands for *failure;* that is, it is a test impossible to accept. The $a.t$ test stands for a sequential test, which first offers the action a and, if it is accepted, afterwards behaves like the test t. Finally, the test $\sum_{i=1}^{n} [p_i] a_i.t_i$ stands for a test which offers the actions a_i. If all of them are accepted, one of them will be selected, according to the probabilities p_i's, and after the execution of that action we apply the corresponding continuation t_i. On the other hand, if only a subset of actions is accepted, the probabilities of the remaining actions will be distributed among the accepted ones, according to their own probabilities.

If the probability of any branch is 0, our aim is that it has the least priority to be selected, i.e., we select it only if no other branch having positive probability can be selected. If several branches with null probability can be accepted and no one with positive probability can be, then we choose between the first ones with uniform probabilities. In fact, null probabilities could have been avoided, since the information given by the tests including them can be inferred from corresponding tests that are obtained from them, taking small probabilities converging to 0 instead of those null probabilities. But we have preferred to maintain them, because we think that its explicit use is more intuitive.

Definition 3.7   (Some operations over Probabilistic Tests)

- **First Level**: If t is a test, t_0 represents the first level of t, which is a test in which each action offered by t is followed by ω.

- **After:** If t is a test and a an action, t/a is the test after the action a in t.
- **Initial Set:** We denote by $Ft(t)$ the set of actions of the first level of a test t.

□

For every process P, and every observation tree t, we are going to define the probability with which P passes t, denoted by $P \mid t$. As usual, it is defined in a recursive way, by the syntactical structure of processes.

3.6.2 *Simple Operators*

The $STOP$ process, due to its definition, cannot perform any action, and thus, it refuses any test but ω.

$$STOP \mid t = \begin{cases} 1 & \text{if } t = \omega \\ 0 & \text{if } t \neq \omega \end{cases}$$

The prefixed process $a \to P$ is only able to accept the execution of the action a, and afterwards it becomes P. Thus it will pass any test containing in its first level an action a, with a probability equal to that of process P accepting t/a. If a is not offered at the first level of the test, then it will fail.

$$(a \to P) \mid t = \begin{cases} 1 & \text{if } t = \omega \\ P \mid (t/a) & \text{if } a \in Ft(t) \\ 0 & \text{if } a \notin Ft(t) \text{ and } t \neq \omega \end{cases}$$

If P and Q are processes, the process $P \sqcap_p Q$ will make an internal choice between them, in a generative way according to the indicated probabilities, without any influence from the environment. Thus, this process will accept any test that either P or Q can accept, but with a probability that is obtained by adding those corresponding to both processes, weighed by the respective probabilities.

$$(P \sqcap_p Q) \mid t = p \cdot (P \mid t) + (1 - p) \cdot (Q \mid t)$$

3.6.3 *External Choice*

The process $P \square_p Q$ will also behave either like P or like Q, but now the observer will have the main role in the selection. Thus, an action will only be refused if it is simultaneously refused by both processes. Besides, when not a single action, but a set of them, is offered to the process, we expect that its behavior will be at worst the same that in the previous case. This means that a set of actions will be refused if and only if all the actions in the set are simultaneously refused by both processes. The main difficulty appears when some of the offered actions are accepted by one of the processes, and the remaining by the other, as in the following example:

$$(a \to c \to STOP) \square_{\frac{1}{2}} b \to STOP)$$

If we consider the test $[\frac{1}{2}]a.c.\omega + [\frac{1}{2}]b.c.\omega$, and we apply the corresponding first level test to the given process, then $\{a, b\}$ will be the set of actions offered to the process. Thus, this first level test should be accepted surely. But if a is the selected action to pass it, then the rest of the test will be accepted, while for action b, the rest of the test will not be accepted.

Moreover, as we have previously commented, in this case the probabilities associated to the arguments of the choice are useless since the sets of actions accepted by both arguments are disjoint. Therefore, the only way to decide which will be the action to be executed, and thus to choose between both processes, consists on relying on the probabilities associated to the branches of the test.

We will follow the same procedure to select the action to be executed in the general case, in which the sets of actions accepted by both processes are not disjoint. In such a case, if the selected action can be executed by both processes, we will still have to decide which will be the process that will do it, and for that we will use the probabilities associated to the arguments of the external choice. Besides, we must note that the probabilities of the non accepted actions offered by the test must be distributed between the accepted ones in order to get that the sum of the probabilities of all the accepted actions will be 1.

Therefore, in order to define the semantics of the external choice operator we must be able to talk about the different *states* at which the process can be once the internal choices on its top have been solved. Here we mean by *state* the set of actions which can be accepted after the resolution of those internal choices.

More exactly, in order to define the probability with which a test t is passed by a process $P \square_p Q$, we will calculate all the contributions of the different actions offered on the first level of the test. For each action a in that set, the probability of accepting t through a depends on the current states of both processes P and Q. For each state of a process we have a probability of reaching it which we must formally define. To do it, we offer to the process some simple tests with depth one. With each of them we can calculate the sum of the probabilities of reaching any of the possible states containing some actions offered by the test. Once we know those probabilities, we can combine them to obtain the probability to reach each possible state. The probability of passing this kind of tests is rather easy to calculate.

Definition 3.8 Let P, Q be two processes, and t_0 a test of depth one. The probability with which the process $P\square_p Q$ accepts t_0 is given by

$$(P\square_p Q) \mid t_0 = (P \mid t_0)(1 - (Q \mid t_0)) + (Q \mid t_0)(1 - (P \mid t_0)) + (P \mid t_0)(Q \mid t_0)$$

$\square$

Definition 3.9 (Process state probabilities)

Let P be a process and A a possible state of it, i.e. a set of actions. We denote by $p(P, A)$ the probability with which process P reaches state A, defined as follows:

(1) $p(P, \emptyset) = 1 - P \mid t_\Sigma$

(2) $p(P, A) = 1 - (P \mid t_{\Sigma - A}) - \sum_{B \subset A} p(P, B)$

where for each set of actions $A = \{a_1, \ldots, a_n\}$, t_A is defined by

$$t_A = \sum_{i=1}^{n} [1/n]\, a_i \,.\, \omega$$

$\square$

As we have previously commented, when a state is reached, the probabilities of the actions offered by the test, which are not in the reached state, must be distributed between the accepted actions. The probability thus obtained will be called *normalized probability*.

Definition 3.10 (Normalized probabilities)

Let t be a test, $A \subseteq \Sigma$ and $a \in Ft(t) \cap A$. The probability of selecting a as the action to be executed by a process P being in the state A, when the test t is offered to it, denoted by $s(a, A, t)$, is given by

$$
s(a, A, t) = \begin{cases}
\dfrac{p_a}{1 - \sum_{b \in Ft(t) - A} p_b} & \text{If } p_a \neq 0 \\[4mm]
\dfrac{1}{|Ft(t) \cap A|} & \text{If } \forall b \in Ft(t) \cap A, \ p_b = 0 \\[4mm]
0 & \text{Otherwise}
\end{cases}
$$
□

If $p_a \neq 0$, the probability to execute a will be p_a when all the actions in $Ft(t)$ are accepted. In opposition, if some of the actions offered by the test are not executable in the current state, then the probability to execute them will be 0, and the probabilities associated to them in the test should be proportionally distributed between the remaining actions. If all the actions that can be executed have null probability (which means low priority), the choice between them will be made uniformly; but if there are still some executable actions with positive probability, the normalized probability of those actions with null probability remains 0.

Now, we just need to define the probability of accepting the rest of the test, once some action a has been selected, to complete the definition of the probability of accepting the test.

But in order to calculate the probability of accepting the rest of the test, first we need to know the process which will execute the selected action a.

Definition 3.11 Let P, Q be two processes, $A, B \subseteq \Sigma$, $a \in A \cup B$, t a test, and $p \in [0, 1]$. The probability of accepting the rest of the test t by the process $P \square_p Q$, once the action a has been executed and assuming that before the execution of a, P was at state A and Q at state B, is defined by

$Cont(P \square_p Q, t, A, B, a)$
$$
= \begin{cases}
P/(a, A) \,|\, t/a & \text{If } a \in A - B \\
Q/(a, B) \,|\, t/a & \text{If } a \in B - A \\
p \cdot (P/(a, A) \,|\, t/a) + (1 - p) \cdot (Q/(a, B) \,|\, t/a) & \text{If } a \in A \cap B
\end{cases}
$$

where $P/(a, A)$ denotes the rest of the process P after the execution of a, when this process is at the state A. This new operator will be defined in the next subsection.

For short, to denote the probability $Cont(P \square_p Q, t, A, B, a)$, we will write $Cont(\square, t, A, B, a)$. □

Finally, we can define the probability with which an external choice accepts a test. If A is the state reached by the first argument, and B is the state reached by the second one, then $A \cup B$ will be the set of actions the external choice may perform, i. e., the state of it. But after the execution of one action, the rest of the acceptation will depend on both, the action executed, and the process argument executing it, i.e. the function *Cont*. Thus, we have

Definition 3.12 (Probability of accepting a test by an external choice) Let P, Q be two processes, $t \notin \{\omega, 0\}$ a test, $p \in [0, 1]$. The probability with which the test t is accepted by the process $[p]P\square[1-p]Q$, is defined by

$$(P\square_p Q) \,|\, t = \sum_{a \in Ft(t)} \sum_{\substack{A, B \subseteq \Sigma \\ a \in A \cup B}} s(a, A \cup B, t) \cdot p(P, A) \cdot p(Q, B) \cdot Cont(\square, t, A, B, a)$$
□

3.6.4 *Continuation of a Process after an Action in a State*

In this subsection we define the behavior of the process $P/(a, A)$, introduced above. Contrary to what happens in ordinary CSP, we need to distinguish the state of the process P to define its behavior after the execution of the action a. For example, let us consider the following process:

$$Q_1 = (a \to b \to STOP\square_{\frac{1}{2}} b \to STOP) \sqcap_{\frac{1}{2}} a \to STOP)$$

It can be at two different states: one in which the actions in the set $\{a, b\}$ can be executed, and another in which only the action a can be executed. Then, depending on the state at which P will be, the behavior of P after the execution of a will be different, because $Q_1/(a, \{a, b\})$ can execute the action b, while $Q_1/(a, \{a\})$ cannot.

In general, to define the behavior of $P/(a, A)$ we consider a family of tests $t^{(a,B)}$, derived from any test $t \in PTEST$, such that $P/(a, A) \,|\, t$ can be calculated from the probabilities $P \,|\, t^{(a,B)}$.

If A is not a state of P, or equivalently $p(P, A) = 0$, we will take $P/(a, A) \,|\, t = 0$; otherwise, to define $P/(a, A) \,|\, t$ when A is a state of P, and $t \neq \omega$, we will proceed recursively, beginning from $A = \{a\}$.

To this state, we can calculate the probability with which P reaches it, and afterwards accepts t from it, by offering the test:

$$t^{(a,\emptyset)} = [0]a.t + \sum_{b \in \Sigma - \{a\}} \left[\frac{1}{|\Sigma| - 1}\right] b.0$$

then, the probability $P/(a, \{a\}) \,|\, t$ is obtained as follows:

$$P/(a, \{a\}) \,|\, t = \frac{P \,|\, t^{(a, \emptyset)}}{p(P, \{a\})}$$

now, let us consider a state with just two actions a and b. Let us consider:

$$t^{(a, \{b\})} = [0]a.t + [0]b.0 + \sum_{c \in \Sigma - \{a, b\}} \left[\frac{1}{|\Sigma| - 2} \right] c.0$$

then, $P \,|\, t^{(a, \{b\})}$ gives us the sum of the probability with which P reaches the state $\{a\}$, accepting the test $a.t$ from it, plus a half of the probability of reaching the state $\{a, b\}$, accepting the test from it. As a consequence, $P/(a, \{a, b\}) \,|\, t$ can be calculated as follows:

$$P/(a, \{a, b\}) \,|\, t = \frac{2 \cdot (P \,|\, t^{(a, \{b\})} - P \,|\, t^{(a, \emptyset)})}{p(P, \{a, b\})}$$

finally, for a general state A, the test to be considered depends on whether this set is the full alphabet Σ or not. It is defined as follows:

$$t^{(a, A - \{a\})} = \begin{cases} [0]a.t + \displaystyle\sum_{b \in A - \{a\}} [0]b.0 + \displaystyle\sum_{c \in \Sigma - A} \left[\frac{1}{|\Sigma - A|} \right] c.0 & \text{If } A \neq \Sigma - \{a\} \\[4ex] \left[\dfrac{1}{|\Sigma|} \right] a.t + \displaystyle\sum_{c \in \Sigma - \{a\}} \left[\frac{1}{|\Sigma|} \right] c.0 & \text{If } A = \Sigma - \{a\} \end{cases}$$

then, we have

$$P \,|\, t^{(a, A - \{a\})} = \sum_{B \subseteq A - \{a\}} \frac{p(P, B \cup \{a\}) \cdot (P/(a, B \cup \{a\}) \,|\, t)}{|B \cup \{a\}|}$$

hence, if $p(P, A) \neq 0$, we obtain

$$P/(a, A) \,|\, t = \frac{|A| \cdot (P \,|\, t^{(a, A - \{a\})} - \displaystyle\sum_{C \subset A - \{a\}} \frac{(P/(a, C \cup \{a\}) \,|\, t) \cdot p(P, C \cup \{a\})}{|C| + 1})}{p(P, A)}$$

and unfolding this recursive definition, we obtain

$$P/(a, A) \,|\, t = \frac{|A| \cdot (P \,|\, t^{(a, A - \{a\})} - \displaystyle\sum_{C \subset A - \{a\}} (-1)^{|A - C|} \cdot P \,|\, t^{(a, C)})}{p(P, A)}$$

Theorem 3.2 (Equivalence)

Let $P, Q \in PCSP$ be two processes, then $[\![P]\!] \equiv [\![Q]\!]$ if and only if for all test t we have $P \mid t = Q \mid t$.

$\square$

3.7 Conclusion

In this chapter we have presented a denotational and a testing semantics for a probabilistic version of CSP, whose mathematical objects are semantical trees with two kinds of nodes, representing internal and external choices, the root being an internal one. Arcs of these trees are differently labeled, depending on the kind of the starting node: if this is an internal one, the label is a set and a probability; while for the external nodes arcs are only labeled with an action. Thus, only the arcs leaving internal nodes have associated a probabilistic information, which are points where the system makes probabilistic (internal) decisions. Then, the external nodes represent the deterministic participation of the environment.

On the other hand, the testing semantics is based on the idea of offering tests to processes, being a test a probabilistic tree, where each level represents a set of different actions offered by the observer at that step, from which one will be selected to be executed. The arcs of these probabilistic trees are labeled both by an action and a probability, thus the accepted subset of actions at each step of the process evolution will have associated a certain probability distribution, so that the action to be executed is selected from this set according to it. In this way, the semantics of each process is defined by the probabilities to pass each possible test.

We have also defined a system proof [Cuartero 97], consisting of a set of axioms and inference rules for algebraically reasoning about the behavior of processes. We have proved that this proof system is sound and complete with respect to the denotational semantics. The main interesting points here are that our normal forms are quite similar to those of the classical CSP, but we have no need to introduce convexity requirements and processes after the execution of the same action do not need to be equal. Furthermore, our normal forms are very similar of Hanssons's probabilistic processes [Hansson 90].

A natural extension of our language would consist on the introduction of a hiding operator. We have also studied this concrete extension concluding that for defining this hiding operator we must add some probabilistic information to it if we want to maintain the classical interpretation of this operator. A sketch of the meaning of our hiding operator is showed by means of the following equation valid in CSP:

$$\Box_{a \in A} a \to P_a \backslash c \equiv \begin{cases} \Box_{a \in A} a \to (P_a \backslash c) & \text{if } c \notin A \\ P_c \backslash c \sqcap (P_c \backslash c \,\Box\, \Box_{a \in A} a \to (P_a \backslash c)) & \text{if } c \in A \end{cases}$$

In our model, we were looking for a probabilistic interpretation of this behavior, but we faced the problem of associating a probability to the new internal appearing in the right hand side. A first idea could be to consider the same probability associated to the external choice, but this is not possible, because we have that probabilities are meaningless in the context of an external choice among processes prefixed (axioms A8 and A10). Then, it is necessary to introduce a new probability for this new internal choice, taking it from the syntax of our hiding operator. With respect to the external choice of the right hand side, we cannot use the probability associated to the external choice of the left hand side because the generalized external choice is not probabilistic; thus, we have chosen 0 as value for the probability of this external choice, on the base of the classical interpretation. Thus, with our model we have the following equation:

$$\Box_{a \in A} a \to P_a \backslash (c, q)$$

$$\equiv \begin{cases} \Box_{a \in A} a \to (P_a \backslash (c, q)) & \text{if } c \notin A \\ P_c \backslash (c, q) \sqcap_q (P_c \backslash (c, q) \,\Box_0\, \Box_{a \in A} a \to (P_a \backslash (c, q))) & \text{if } c \in A \end{cases}$$

Chapter 4

Modeling and Proving Grafcets with Transition Systems

D. L'her, P. Le Parc and L. Marcé

4.1 Introduction

Grafcet is a graphical programming language used mainly in the field of automatisms. Its powerful control structures can express particularly parallelism. This last notion is often awkward to handle. So it is necessary to be able to prove some properties on systems programmed in Grafcet.

The Grafcet semantics has been defined, in a previous work[Le Parc 94a] [Le Parc 93], with the SIGNAL language. In this paper, we present a different approach using transition systems.

After an overview of the Grafcet language [Bouteille 92], two methods are given to build a transition system equivalent to a particular grafcet. The first one is based on the synchronized product, while the second one is more algorithmic. Then the properties we want to verify on Grafcet are presented and the way of validating them is given.

4.2 Grafcet

Grafcet is a graphical model to describe the behavior of the control part of an automated system. This formalism has become a very popular programming language in industrial world and has been integrated in the international standard IEC1131.

4.2.1   Graphical Elements

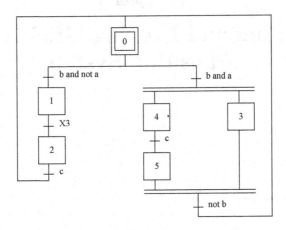

Fig. 4.1   A small Grafcet program

The basic graphical elements of the Grafcet language are (see Figure 4.1):

- the steps: they represent the different states of a system. A step is either active or inactive. The set of active steps of a grafcet at a given time represents the grafcet's situation.
- the transitions: they control the evolutions between steps. The control is taken by the boolean expression called receptivity associated to the transition.
- the links: they are used to connect steps and transitions and must respect the following rule: two steps (resp. transitions) must no be linked together. With the links, classical control structures may be express such as sequentiality, choice, parallelism, synchronization, iteration.

4.2.2   Temporal Aspect

In the receptivities, a particular function enabling to count time can be found: the temporization.

The temporization $t_1/X_i/t_2$ indicates a boolean condition which is true if the step X_i stays active at least t_1 time units and becomes false t_2 time units after the step X_i deactivation. No structural relation is fixed between the use of temporization and the reference's step X_i. The notation t_1/X_i is an abbreviation for $t_1/X_i/0$.

The temporizations can be synchronized on logical time, that is to say they change at the rate of acquisition of streams of events.

4.2.3 *Evolution Rules and Interpretation*

Five rules have been defined to explicit the way a grafcet works.

Rule 1: At the beginning, the initial steps are active.
Rule 2: A transition can be fired if its condition is true and if all the preceding steps are active.
Rule 3: When a transition is fired, all the preceding steps are simultaneously deactivated and all the following steps are simultaneously activated.
Rule 4: If several transitions can be fired, they are all fired simultaneously.
Rule 5: If a step is simultaneously activated and deactivated, it remains active.

The behavior of a grafcet is described by those five evolution rules. Interpretation algorithms complete them. The main ones are the interpretation WithOut Stability Research (WOSR) and the interpretation With Stability Research (WSR).

WOSR interpretation

In the case of the WOSR interpretation, an evolution step fits with a simple evolution step that is to say with a simultaneous firing of all fired transitions. At time t, the achievement of a simple evolution step, fits with an acquisition of inputs stream, with a computation of the new situation and with an emission to the external world.

WSR interpretation

In the case of the WSR interpretation, an evolution step fits with an acquisition of an inputs stream, with obtaining a stable situation by a repeated firing of transitions which can be fired and with an emission to the external world. A stable situation is obtained when no more transition may be fired without any acquisition of new inputs.

On the example of Figure 4.1, with the WSR interpretation, if we suppose that the step 0 is active and that the input c is true, then the program evolves from the situation {0} to the situation {3,5} when the inputs a and b become true. With the WOSR interpretation, the program evolves from the situation {0} to the situation {3,4}. Then new inputs are acquired and if the input c remains true then the situation will become {3,5} else it will remain {3,4}.

In the following, only the WOSR interpretation is presented. However for the second method, the WSR interpretation has been treated. Other limits are imposed on the language: the grafcets are without action, or macro-step or forcing order. Only the first modeling takes the receptivities of temporized types into account.

For the modeling seen here, the Grafcet is presented as a synchronous language. Several input signals can start in simultaneously a Grafcet evolution. In other works [Roussel 94], the asynchronous approach is chosen for the building of an equivalent automaton.

4.3   First Modeling

In this part, to avoid ambiguities between a grafcet transition and a transition of transition systems [Arnold 92], Grafcet transitions are called Gtransitions.

4.3.1   *Transition System*

To model the Grafcet, three transition systems are used:

- The first one is useful to describe the feasible evolutions of a step not initial. The initial state of this system is the state "*inactive*".
- The second one is distinguishable from the first one by its initial state. Indeed, this is the state "*active*" because it represents an initial step.
- The third one describes the evolution of a receptivity linked to a Gtransition.

As shown on Figure 4.2, a step can be active or inactive. It can remain inactive (eI transition), become active (A transition), become inactive (I transition), remain active without being activated or deactivated (eA transition), remain active being activated (eA− transition) or be activated and

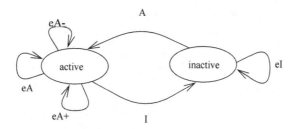

Fig. 4.2   The transition system for a step

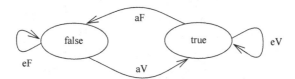

Fig. 4.3   The transition system for a Gtransition

deactivated simultaneously (eA+ transition).

The receptivity linked to a Gtransition may be false or true. Four evolutions are feasible: the receptivity remains false (eF transition), it remains true (eV transition), it becomes false (aF transition) or it becomes true (aV transition) (Figure 4.3).

Then the transition systems for steps and Gtransitions must be synchronized.

4.3.2   *Synchronization Constraints*

To obtain the synchronization constraint, we proceed in two stages: first we locally build vectors of synchronization linked to each Gtransition (partial constraint) then we merge these sets (global constraint).

Partial constraint

In the following, we will note: ens1 = {eI, eA, A(*), I(*), eA+(*), eA−(*)}, ens2 = {eI, A(*)}, ens3 = {I, eA+(*)}, ens4 = {A, eA−, eA+(*)}.

For a Gtransition t, preceded by a step X_i and followed by a step X_j, the set of synchronization vectors is written in the following table, where (*) means that the vector depends on the grafcet structure and might not be encountered. For example, the vector [eF .eI .A(*)] is accepted only if the X_j step is preceded by another Gtransition.

Table 4.1   Table of synchronization constraints

t	X_i	X_j
eF aF	eI eA A(*) I(*) eA+(*) eA−(*)	eI eA A(*) I(*) eA+(*) eA−(*)
eV aV	eI A(*)	eI eA A(*) I(*) eA+(*) eA−(*)
eV aV	I eA+(*)	A eA− eA+(*)

Table 4.1 is read as follows: if the receptivity linked to the Gtransition is false (transitions eF, aF), then the steps X_i and X_j can evolve according to an element of ens1. If the receptivity is true (transitions eV, aV), two cases may happen:

- the step X_i is inactive, then it can be activated or remain inactive. So it evolves according to an element of ens2. In this case, X_j evolves according to an element of ens1.
- the step X_i is active, then it is deactivated (unless it is activated again by a preceding step) and X_j is activated. So ens3 brings together the feasible evolutions for the step X_i and ens4 for the step X_j.

The transition eA+ is always followed by (*). Indeed, we may not conclude from the constraints of evolution linked to a single transition whether if a step can be simultaneously activated and deactivated or not. This transition is fired when a step is deactivated (I transition) and simultaneously activated (eA− transition).

For a transition followed and/or preceded by several steps, local synchronization vectors are built in a similar way with the same sets.

Global constraint

Then we want to build the whole synchronization vectors. If the grafcet has n steps and k Gtransitions, each vector has n+k components. We proceed step by step. First we merge two Gtransitions. Then as long as there is a remaining Gtransition, we merge it with the result.

What does merging mean? For two local vectors which do not share steps, the merging is simply a Cartesian product. For two vectors sharing steps, the product is done with a pseudo-intersection on shared steps.

The pseudo-intersection is defined as follows: for each element of $\{eI, eA, A, I, eA+, eA-, A(*), I(*), eA+(*), eA-(*)\}$, the following rules apply : $el \bigcap el = el$; $el \bigcap el(*) = el$; $I \bigcap eA- = eA+$.

Once synchronization vectors are obtained, we keep elements without *. In fact, as all the Gtransitions have been treated, elements with * are evolutions that we do not encounter because of the grafcet structure.

Remark. Transitions eA+ and eA− must be distinguished from a transition eA when the constraints are built. They may express the following facts:

- a step remains active being deactivated only if it is activated (transition eA+).
- a step remains active being activated (transition eA−).

Then, as in the transition system, the transitions eA, eA+ and eA− have the same source and the same target, we can replace all eA+ and eA− by an transition eA in the synchronization system and suppress the transitions eA+ and eA− in the transition system. This reduces the number of the synchronization vectors.

With the tool MEC [Crubillé 89], the transition system equivalent to the complete grafcet is obtained by synchronizing the transition systems describing steps and Gtransitions with the set of synchronization vectors which are defined earlier.

4.3.3 *Temporization*

For a temporization k_1/X_i, the equivalent automaton is shown on Figure 4.4. The automaton has k_1 states where the temporization is false $(F_1, \ldots, F_{k1})$ and a state where the temporization is true.

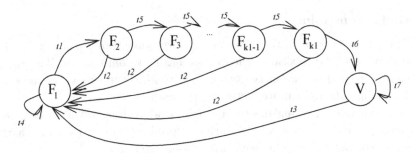

Fig. 4.4   Equivalent automaton at k_1/X_i

Table 4.2   Table of synchronization constraints

tempo	X_i	t	tempo	X_i	t
$t1$	A	eF	$t4$	eI	eF
$t1$	eA	eF	$t5$	eA	eF
$t2$	I	eF	$t6$	eA	aV
$t3$	I	aF	$t7$	eA	eV

The transition $t1$ is fired only if step X_i is activated (or remains active for an initial step). The $t5$ and $t6$ transitions are fired when the step X_i remains active. The $t6$ transition is different from the $t5$ transitions because the temporization becomes true. And last, the $t4$ transition is fired when the step X_i remains inactive.

The synchronization system is defined in Table 4.2 where t points out the Gtransition which is associated with the temporization tempo.

For a temporization $k_1/X_i/k_2$, the equivalent automaton is shown on Figure 4.5.

The automaton has now k_2 states where the temporization is true. Three new kinds of transitions are added. The $t8$ transition is fired when the step X_i is deactivated. In this case the temporization remains true. The $t9$ transition is fired when the step remains inactive and the temporization remains true. The $t10$ transition is fired when the step X_i is activated whereas the temporization is true.

For the synchronized system, the constraints for a temporization linked to the receptivity t are described in Table 4.3.

These partial synchronization constraints are introduced in the synchronized system describing the evolution, in the same way that the merging.

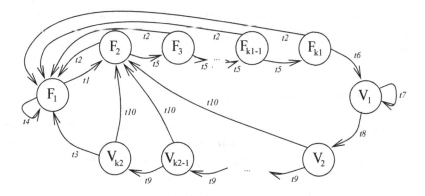

Fig. 4.5   Equivalent automaton for $k_1/X_i/k_2$

Table 4.3   Table of synchronization constraints

tempo	X_i	t	tempo	X_i	t
t1	A	eF	*t6*	eA	aV
t1	eA	eF	*t7*	eA	eV
t2	I	eF	*t8*	I	eV
t3	eI	aF	*t9*	eI	eV
t4	eI	eF	*t10*	A	aF
t5	eA	eF			

4.3.4   *Limits*

This method makes possible to model the different elements of Grafcet by transition systems and to synchronize them to obtain the transition system equivalent to the complete grafcet. Moreover, we introduce a discrete time in modeling.

But this building is very expensive. Indeed for a Gtransition preceded by a step and followed by a step, 16 synchronization vectors may be used. So for a grafcet having n Gtransitions of this kind, the global synchronization system includes in the order of 16^n synchronization vectors. The number of synchronization vectors grows up in an exponential way and so this method can not be used for large grafcets. Moreover with this method, even if no temporization is used, a single situation of grafcet is described by several states of the transition system according to the values of Gtransitions.

The method presented below, associates to each grafcet situation a single state of the transition system to decrease the size of the associated model.

4.4   Second Modeling

This modeling [Le Parc 94b] of a grafcet with a transition system is based on the association of a situation to each state of the system. The transitions between states represent the evolution condition from one situation to another.

Given a situation Si, we should be able to know all the transitions and then all the immediately following situations. As a situation consists of a finite number of steps which may be seen as parallel processes, the evolutions from Si fit with the evolutions from the steps of Si.

To construct the Global Transition System (GTS) equivalent to a grafcet program, a two stages iterative method has been developed:

(1) Building of basic transition systems (BTS) associated to each step. They model the possible evolution from a step by firing only its directly connected transitions.

(2) Iterative construction of GTS from the initial situation with the BTS.

4.4.1   *Construction of Basic Transition Systems*

The BTS building is realized from the Atomic Transition Systems (ATS) which for each step E_i define the reached situation after firing a single downstream transition T_j. The obtained transition system consists of two states and two transitions (see Figure 4.7 on the left).

The system is labeled to take into account that it represents a part of a grafcet. The state 1 is labeled by the ($<E_i>$) step it represents. The label associated to the state 2 corresponds to the list of the activated states when firing the transition T_j. The transitions t_1 and t_2 are respectively labeled by $<R(T_j)>$ and $<$not $R(T_j)>$; so the determinism of the interpretation is guaranteed.

Figure 4.6 shows the ATS generated when the transition T_j is followed by one or several steps. It can be shown easily that the two transition systems are equivalent to the two grafcets.

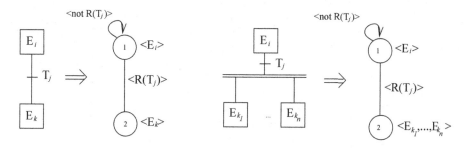

Fig. 4.6   Atomic Transition System

Once all the ATS are computed, the building of BTS is straightforward in the case of steps followed by a single transition. In fact, the BTS is equivalent to the ATS.

On the other hand, for the steps having n downstream transitions, n ATS are built and represent the different possibilities to fire simultaneously these transitions: so they may be seen as parallel processes. To compute the BTS equivalent to the considered step, we must compute the product of the n transition systems. It corresponds to a "synchronized product" * where the synchronization constraint depends on the label of each transition. All the n-uples of the constraint must check this property: the logical "and" of labels must not be always false. If this property is not checked, then we may define transitions which are never fired for the grafcet because always false.

For example on Figure 4.7, if instead of <b> there is <not a>, then the transition between the (1,1) and (2,2) states does not exist.

In addition to compute on states and transitions , a computation on labels takes place during the product of ATS. The label which is associated to a transition fits with the logical "and" of all the labels of transitions which take part in its building. We can prove by recurrence on transitions systems that such a labeling guarantees the interpretation determinism of transition systems : from the initial state and for a given inputs vector, one single label is true.

---

*Inspired by synchronized product defined in [Arnold 89] and used previously.

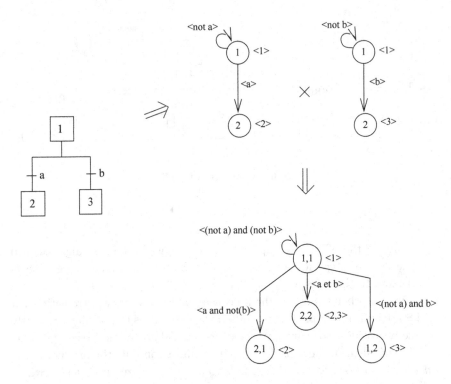

Fig. 4.7   Basic Transition System

4.4.2   *Building of the Global Transition System*

The building of the Global Transition System is done in an iterative way. The initial state matches the initial situation of grafcet. If it includes a single step, then the BTS built for this step is used.

If the initial situation consists of several steps, there is a set of simultaneously active steps which represent parallel processes. The GTS computation is the result of synchronization of the BTS associated to the steps of initial situation. We use again the "synchronized product" with a constraint checking the same property (logical "AND" of labels not always false).

At this stage of computation, a transition system with an initial state and its following states is built. It represents the feasible evolutions from the initial situation of the grafcet.

Then for each of the p following states, the equivalent transition system is computed and integrated in the system already built.

Using the same method as for the initial step, the global transition system is built step by step. If we avoid computing again the transition system for a situation, the construction ends. In fact, each state represents a situation and the number of situations of a grafcet having p steps is at most 2^p.

Once the GTS is built, we add to each step E_i, a set e_i which defines the states where this step is active. These sets are computed from the labels associated to each state. It allows us to check more easily properties with the tool MEC.

This modeling has the advantage of associating a single state to a grafcet situation. On the other hand, it does not take into account of the temporal aspect which was treated by the first method.

Afterwards, some properties are checked on this model.

4.5 Proof

The previous modelings take only the evolution system of Grafcet into account. The verifications are limited to proofs at the level of steps or more generally of situations. Some properties we want to check are:

- Does it exist steps which are always active? Does it exist never activated steps? The first one, like the second one may point out a conception mistake.
- Does it exist situations where the steps E_{i_1}, E_{i_2} ,..., E_{i_n} are simultaneously active or activated? The answer may detect conflicts at the time of actions valuation.
- From a situation S0, is the situation S1 accessible? Moreover we may check that from S0, S1 is accessible (possibly unavoidably) through situation S2. That may also show that from a given situation it's possible to come back.
- Does it exist situations which are accessible from the initial state and which don't allow evolution (deadlock)? More generally, does it exist a set of situations from where we can't leave?

4.5.1 *Second Modeling*

We show how these properties can be expressed in MEC for the transition system built in the Section 4.4.

- To know if a step E_i is always active, we compute the number of states of the set e_i and we compare it to the total number of states of the automaton. In the case of equality, the step is active in each state of the transition system.

  On the other hand, the steps which are never activated have an empty set e_i.

- To check if n steps $E_{i_1}, \ldots, E_{i_n}$ may simultaneously be active, we compute the intersection of sets $e_{i_1}, \ldots, e_{i_n}$ and we check whether it is empty. In MEC, the instruction is `ei1 /\ \dots /\ ein` where `/\` defines intersection of sets.

  To show that n steps may simultaneously be activated, we compute the set of states where no one of these steps is active and the set of states where they are simultaneously active. That is to say in MEC:

  ```
  et_inactives:= * - (ei1 \/ \dots \/ein);
  et_actives  := ei1 /\ \dots /\ ein;
  ```

  where `*` means all the states. If there exists at least one transition from `et_inactives` to a state of `et_actives`, then the property is true. So we compute the intersection between the set of transitions which have their source in `et_inactives` and the set of transitions having their target in `et_actives`.

  ```
  tr_origine := rsrc(et_inactives);
  tr_but     := rtgt(et_actives);
  tr_resultat:= tr_origine /\ tr_but;
  ```

- To verify the reachability of a situation S1 from a situation S0, we must find the states q1 and q0 associated to these situations: to do this we study the labels associated to each state of the transition system. We use the operator `reach(S,T)` which defines the set of reachable states from the set of states S only through the transitions of set T:

  ```
  et_accessibles:= reach(!state='q0', *);
  ```

  Then we must only see if the state q1 is a member of `et_accessibles`.

A second method based on the temporal logic function potential (X1, X2) defined in [Arnold 89] may be used. This function defines the set of states from which we may reach at least a state of X2 through only states of X1. We use it with all the states for X1, with the state associated to the situation q1 for X2. The property is true only if q0 must belongs to the result. The function potential is defined as follows:

```
function potential(X1:state; X2:state)
return Z:state;
begin
  Z = X2 \/ (X1 /\ src(rtgt(Z)) )
end.
```

To prove the reachability of situation S1 from the situation S0 through the situation S2, we use twice the previous methods (with S0 and S2, then with S2 and S1). If we want to check that S2 must be on the way, we compute the set of reachable states from q0 through transitions having target in q2.

```
tr_arrivant_q2:= rtgt(!state='q2');
et_accessibles:= reach(!state='q0',
                 *-tr_arrivant_q2);
```

If the set et_accessibles is empty, we have then proved that S1 is reachable from S0 only by a way through S2.

- To detect deadlocks, situations that the system can not evolve from, we may use the least fixed points function unavoidable defined in [Arnold 89]. This one computes all states having no successor.

```
function unavoidable(Zt:trans ; Zs:state)
return X:state;
var Y:_trans
begin
  X = Zs \/ (* - src(Y));
  Y = Zt /\ rtgt(* - X)
end.
```

We use this function with the following parameters : the set of all transitions without transitions having the same source and target, the empty set for the states. If the result is the empty set, the grafcet has no deadlock.

4.5.2 *First Modeling*

The properties checked on the transition system built by the second method may be proved too on the transition system built by the first method. However, the first method is limited by the exponential growth of the number of states. The benefit of this one consists in implementing temporal proofs.

- To check that step X_i remains active at most d time units:
  - First we compute the set act$\_X_i$ of states where the step X_i is active
  - Then we compute the set succ$\_1$ of successors of this set taking only those which are members of act$\_X_i$. If succ$\_1$ is empty then we have checked that X_i remains active at most d time units, else:
  - We compute the set succ$\_2$ of the successors of this set taking only the members of act$\_X_i$.
    If succ$\_2$ is empty then the property is verified else the method is repeated to succ$\_$d-1.
  - Then we compute the set of successors of succ$\_$d-1: succ$\_$d
    If succ$\_$d $/\backslash$ act$\_X_i$ is empty then the property is checked else it is not.

- To verify that the step X_i remains active exactly d time units:
  - We define the set FM$\_X_i$ of states where X_i is active at the beginning and states where X_i is activated.
    The states where X_i is active at the beginning consist of the intersection between the initial states and the states where X_i is active (act$\_X_i$).
    The states where X_i is activated are obtained by:
    succ(**pred**(act$\_X_i$)-act$\_X_i$).
    So FM$\_X_i$:=(**succ**(**pred**(act$\_X_i$)-act$\_X_i$) $\backslash/$ initial) $/\backslash$ act$\_X_i$
  - Then we compute the set succFM1 of the successors of FM$\_X_i$. We verify that all the states of this set belong to act$\_X_i$. If it's not the case, the property is not true, else we apply the same method on succFMd-1.

Without the following checking, we have proved that X_i remains active at least d time units.

— To show that X_i remains active exactly d time units, we check that no successor of succFMd-1 belong to act_X_i. If so, the property is true else it's not.

4.6 Example and Results

4.6.1 *Example*

For the grafcet presented on Figure 4.1, the transition system built by the second method is the one of Figure 4.8 in MEC.

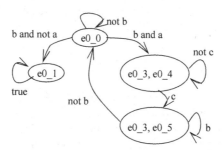

Fig. 4.8   Transition system associated to grafcet

This system is made of four states numbered 1, 2, 4 and 9 which are associated to the situation {step 0}, {step 1}, {step 3, step 4} and {step 3, step 5}. The definition of sets e0_i indicates the states of the system where step i is active.

```
transition_system grafcet
  < width = 0 >;
1   <e0_0>
    |- T_1_1 -> 4,
       T_1_2 -> 2,
       e -> 1;
2   <e0_1>
    |- e -> 2;
4   <e0_3; e0_4>
    |- T_4_1 -> 9,
```

```
            e -> 4;
     9    <e0_5; e0_3>
          |- T_9_1 -> 1,
            e -> 9;

   < initial = {1}; e0_0 = {1}; e0_1 = {2};
     e0_3 = {9, 4}; e0_4 = {4}; e0_5 = {9}>.
```

On this example, different properties may be verified :

- Steps 1 and 3 may never be active simultaneously, because of $e0\_1 \wedge e0\_3 = \emptyset$.
- The step 2 is never activated because the set $e0\_2$ doesn't exist.
- We may find deadlocks. The call of unavoidable(*-!label='e',{}) gives $e0\_1$. So the step 1 is a dead situation.

4.6.2 Results

With the first method, the results obtained on a SPARC ELC (memory space: 42 Mo) are summed up in Table 4.4. The grafcets are distinguished by the number of steps (**et**) and by the number of transitions (**t**). To complete this description, we specify if the grafcet includes parallelism (**par**). The parameter (**nbv**) is the number of synchronized vectors built for the considered grafcet and (**tf**) the time used for the building. The parameter (**tf**) is measured using the UNIX command time. The parameters (**tc**) and (**ts**) point out the time needed to load the constraint and the time needed to build the complete transition system. They are obtained by the MEC command timer. For resulting transition systems, we specify the number of states (**ne**) and the number of transitions (**nt**).

Table 4.4   Results for the first method

grafcet			nbv	tf	tc	ts	transition system	
et	t	par					ne	nt
2	2	no	64	0s	0s	0s	6	24
3	3	no	512	0.2s	0s	0s	18	144
3	5	yes	2048	1.1s	1s	0s	62	992
4	4	no	4096	2.3s	1s	1s	48	768
4	5	yes	16386	10.4s	13s	2s	232	7424

The results in Table 4.4 show that the number of synchronized vectors grows very fast according to the number of steps and of transitions, and to the parallelism. For a grafcet having 6 steps, 7 transitions and parallelism, the building fails because of lack of memory space.

Also, we notice that the number of states (respectively the number of transitions) is larger than the number of steps (respectively transitions) of the associated grafcet.

For the second method, performances are described in Table 4.5. To describe the grafcets and the transition systems, the same notations are used. The parameter (**time**), obtained by the command time, is the time needed to build the transition system and (**espm**) the memory space used.

Table 4.5   Results of the second method

grafcet			time	espm	transition system	
et	t	par			ne	nt
2	2	no	0s	—	2	4
3	3	no	0.1s	—	3	6
3	5	yes	0.2s	1608 ko	7	37
4	4	no	0.1s	1104 ko	4	8
4	5	yes	1.2s	1740 ko	15	123
6	7	yes	15.8s	3252 ko	63	1191
15	20	yes	100s	6064 ko	229	1082

In the sequential case, the number of states of the transition system is equal to the number of steps of the grafcet. When parallelism is introduced, the number of states is larger but remains significantly smaller than the number obtained by the first method.

The needed time and memory space increase according to the size of the grafcet and to the parallelism. The form of the grafcet has an important effect on results, so a grafcet with 15 steps, 20 transitions and parallelism cannot be treated because of lack of memory space. But these limits may be pushed forward on a machine more powerful having more memory. Moreover, this software is only a prototype and it can be improved (factor 5 at least).

4.7   Conclusion

Two methods to model grafcet on transition systems have been presented. The first one allows time introduction in the model but leads to an exponential number of states. The second one gives the smallest transition system when the transitions do not contain any temporization. Nevertheless the problem is still the quick growth of number of states. In fact for a grafcet with n steps, there is at most $2^n - 1$ states.

On the transition system equivalent to the grafcet, the use of the tool MEC allows to check some properties. For the verification of temporal properties, we must introduce in the second model the notion of time. We could use the timed graphs [Olivero 94] which limit the number of states while dealing with time.

Chapter 5

Focus Points and Convergent Process Operators

Jan Friso Groote and Jan Springintveld

5.1 Introduction

One of the main aims of process theory is to be able to formally specify distributed systems and to verify their correctness w.r.t. some specification. Process algebra and assertional methods both have proven to be fruitful in this area. In this chapter we propose a verification method that incorporates elements of the assertional approach into an algebraic framework.

The incorporation of assertional methods into the algebraic framework is based on a particular format for the notation of processes, the so-called *linear process operators*. This format, similar to the UNITY format of Chandy and Misra (1988) and to the precondition/effect notation of Jonsson (1987), and Lynch and Tuttle (1987), enriches the process algebraic language with a symbolic representation of the (possibly infinite) state space of a process by means of state variables and formulas concerning these variables. Thus it combines the advantages of a compact and easy to manipulate algebraic notation with the advantages of the precondition/effect style. In this chapter, the linear process format is used to apply assertional techniques such as invariants and simulations for the algebraic verification of parallel systems.

In our algebraic framework, proving that an implementation satisfies a specification means proving that they are equal w.r.t. some given equality relation. Exploiting the symbolic representation of state spaces, we reduce the task of proving equality of implementation and specification to proving the existence of a *state mapping*, satisfying certain constraints, which we call the *matching criteria*. A state mapping maps states of the implementation to matching states of the specification. Here, matching means that the same set of external actions can be executed directly. The matching criteria are comparable to the defining clauses of weak refinements as used by Lynch and Vaandrager (1995). The criteria are formulated as simple formulas over the data parameters and conditions occurring in implementation and specification. Thus we reduce a large part of the correctness of the implementation w.r.t. the specification to the checking of a number of elementary facts concerning data parameters and conditions occurring in implementation and specification. This greatly simplifies protocol verifications.

The method described in this chapter has been used (explicitly or implicitly) in a number of non-trivial case studies. Bezem and Groote (1994) verified a sliding window protocol and Fredlund *et al.* (1997) proved an efficient, but complex leader election protocol in a ring topology correct. In Shankland and van der Zwaag (1998), part of the IEEE P1394 high-speed bus protocol (see IEEE, 1995) is proven correct and in Groote *et al.*, (1997) a distributed summation algorithm is verified. The latter verification has been checked mechanically with the theorem prover PVS (see Shankar *et al.*, 1993). In our view these case studies clearly show that our method is practically useful and is well-suited for mechanization.

Organization

In Section 5.2, we present the preliminaries of the theory. In Section 5.3, we present a general result that formulates sufficient conditions for two processes to be equal in the case where there are no infinite chains of internal action in the implementation. This result is applied in Section 5.4 to the verification of communication protocols that do have unbounded internal activity. In Section 5.5, we illustrate the proof strategy with some positive and negative examples. One of the positive examples is the Concurrent Alternating Bit Protocol. Appendix A contains technical lemmas that are used in the chapter. Finally, Appendix B contains the μCRL axioms plus some additional axioms that are used in the verification.

5.2   Preliminaries

In this section, we present some basic definitions, properties and results that we use in this chapter. We apply the proof theory of μCRL as presented by Groote and Ponse (1993) which can be viewed as ACP (see Baeten and Weijland, 1990, and Bergstra and Klop, 1984) extended with a formal treatment of the interaction between data and processes.

5.2.1   *A Short Description of μCRL*

The language μCRL is a process algebra comprising data developed by Groote and Ponse (1994). We do not describe the treatment of data types in μCRL in detail, as we make little use of it in this chapter. For our purpose it is sufficient that processes can be parameterized with data. We assume the data sort of booleans $\mathcal{B}$ with constants true T and false F, and the usual operators. Furthermore, we assume for all data types the existence of an equality function eq that faithfully reflects equality, and an *if_then_else*-function such that $if(b, t_1, t_2)$ equals t_1 if b equals T and equals t_2 otherwise.

Starting from a set Act of actions that can be parameterized with data, processes are defined by means of guarded recursive equations and the following operators. (In Subsection 5.2.2, we will discuss a useful variant of guarded recursive equations.)

First, there is a constant δ ($\delta \notin \mathsf{Act}$) that cannot perform any action and is henceforth called deadlock or inaction.

Next, there are the sequential composition operator $\cdot$ and the alternative composition operator $+$. The process $x \cdot y$ first behaves as x and if x successfully terminates continues to behave as y. The process $x + y$ can either do an action of x and continue to behave as the rest of x or do an action of y and continue to behave as the rest of y.

Interleaving parallelism is modeled by the operator $\parallel$. The process $x \parallel y$ is the result of interleaving actions of x and y, except that actions from x and y may also synchronize to a communication action, when this is explicitly allowed by a communication function. This is a partial, commutative and associative function $\gamma : \mathsf{Act} \times \mathsf{Act} \to \mathsf{Act}$ that describes how actions can synchronize; parameterized actions $a(d)$ and $b(d')$ synchronize to $\gamma(a, b)(d)$, provided $d = d'$. A specification of a process typically contains a specification of a communication function.

In order to axiomatize the parallel operator there are two auxiliary parallel operators. First, the left merge $\lfloor\!\lfloor$, which behaves as the parallel operator, except that the first step must come from the process at the left. Secondly, the communication merge $\mid$ which also behaves as the parallel operator, except that the first step is a communication between both arguments.

To enforce that actions in processes x and y synchronize, we can prevent actions from happening on their own, using the encapsulation operator ∂_H. The process $\partial_H(x)$ can perform all actions of x except that actions in the set H are blocked. So, assuming $\gamma(a, b) = c$, in $\partial_{\{a,b\}}(x \parallel y)$ the actions a and b are forced to synchronize to c.

We assume the existence of a special action τ ($\tau \notin \mathsf{Act}$) that is internal and cannot be directly observed. A useful feature is offered by the hiding operator τ_I that renames the actions in the set I to τ. By hiding all internal communications of a process only the external actions remain. In this way we can obtain compact descriptions of the external functionality of a set of cooperating processes. A nice example is provided in Theorem 5.5.1 where the external behavior of a set of parallel processes modeling the Concurrent Alternating Bit Protocol appears to be the same as that of a simple one place buffer.

Another useful operator is the general renaming ρ_f, where $f : \mathsf{Act} \to \mathsf{Act}$ is a renaming function on actions. If process x can perform an action a, then $\rho_f(x)$ can perform the action $f(a)$.

The following two operators combine data with processes. The sum operator $\Sigma_{d:D}p(d)$ describes the process that can execute the process $p(d)$ for some value d selected from the sort D. The conditional operator $\_\triangleleft\_\triangleright\_$ describes the *then-if-else*. The process $x \triangleleft b \triangleright y$ (where b is a boolean) has the behavior of x if b is true and the behavior of y if b is false.

We apply the convention that $\cdot$ binds stronger than Σ, followed by $\_\triangleleft\triangleright\_$, and $+$ binds weakest. Moreover, $\cdot$ is usually suppressed. Axioms that characterize the operators are given in Appendix B.

5.2.2 *Linear Process Operators*

We recapitulate some terminology that has been introduced in both referenced articles by Bezem and Groote (1994). Especially the notion of a linear process forms the cornerstone for the developments in this chapter.

Intuitively, a linear process is a process of the form $X(d:D) = RHS$, where d is a parameter of type D and RHS consists of a number of summands of the form

$$\sum_{e:E} a(f(d,e)) \, X(g(d,e)) \triangleleft b(d,e) \triangleright \delta$$

Such a summand means that if for some e of type E the guard $b(d,e)$ is satisfied, the action a can be performed with parameter $f(d,e)$, followed by a recursive call of X with new value $g(d,e)$.

The main feature of linear processes is that for each action there is a most one alternative. This makes it possible to describe them by means of a finite set Act of actions as indices, giving for each action a the set E_a over which summation takes place, the guard b_a that enables the action, the function f_a that determines the data parameter of the action and the function g_a that determines the value of the recursive call.

In the next definition the symbol Σ, used for summation over data types, is also used to describe an alternative composition over a finite set of actions. If $Act = \{a_1, \ldots, a_n\}$, then $\Sigma_{a \in Act} \, p_a$ denotes $p_{a_1} + p_{a_2} + \cdots + p_{a_n}$. The p_a's are called *summands* of $\Sigma_{a \in Act} \, p_a$. Note that for summation over actions the symbol $\in$ is used (instead of the symbol :).

Formally, we define linear processes by means of linear process operators.

Definition 5.1 Let $Act \subset \mathsf{Act}$ be a finite set of actions, possibly extended with τ. A *linear process operator* (*LPO*) over Act is an expression of the form

$$\Phi = \lambda p.\lambda d{:}D. \sum_{a \in Act} \sum_{e_a:E_a} a(f_a(d, e_a)) \, p(g_a(d, e_a)) \triangleleft b_a(d, e_a) \triangleright \delta.$$

We will give an example below. Note that the bound variable p ranges over processes parameterized with a datum of sort D.

LPOs are defined having a single data parameter. The LPOs that we will consider generally have more than one parameter, but using cartesian products and projection functions, it is easily seen that this is an inessential extension. Often, parameter lists get rather long. Therefore, we use the following notation for updating elements in the list. Let $\vec{d}$ abbreviate the vector $d_1, \ldots, d_n$. A summand of the form

$$\Sigma_{e_a:E_a} a(f_a(\vec{d}, e_a)) \, p(d'_j/d_j) \triangleleft b_a(\vec{d}, e_a) \triangleright \delta$$

in the definition of a process $p(\vec{d}\,)$ abbreviates

$$\Sigma_{e_a:E_a} a(f_a(\vec{d}, e_a))\, p(d_1, \ldots, d_{j-1}, d'_j, d_{j+1}, \ldots d_n) \triangleleft b_a(\vec{d}, e_a) \triangleright \delta.$$

Here, the parameter d_i is in the recursive call updated to d'_i. This notation is extended in the natural way to multiple updates. If no parameter is updated, we write the summand as $\Sigma_{e_a:E_a} a(f_a(\vec{d}, e_a))\, p \triangleleft b_a(\vec{d}, e_a) \triangleright \delta.$

LPOs are often defined equationally. We give an example of an LPO K which is a channel that reads frames consisting of a datum from some data type D and an alternating bit. It either delivers the frame correctly, or loses or garbles it. In the last case a checksum error ce is sent. The non-deterministic choice between the three options is modeled by the actions j and j'. If j is chosen the frame is delivered correctly and if j' happens it is garbled or lost. The state of the channel is modeled by the parameter i_k.

proc $K(d{:}D, b{:}Bit, i_k{:}\mathsf{N}) =$

$$\sum_{d':D} \sum_{b':Bit} r(\langle d', b' \rangle)\, K(d'/d, b'/b, 2/i_k) \triangleleft eq(i_k, 1) \triangleright \delta +$$
$$(j'\, K(1/i_k) + j\, K(3/i_k) + j'\, K(4/i_k)) \triangleleft eq(i_k, 2) \triangleright \delta +$$
$$s(\langle d, b \rangle)\, K(1/i_k) \triangleleft eq(i_k, 3) \triangleright \delta, +$$
$$s(ce)\, K(1/i_k) \triangleleft eq(i_k, 4) \triangleright \delta$$

Note that we have deviated from the pure LPO format: in the last three summands there is no summation over a data type E_i, in the second summand j and j' do not carry a parameter (like the τ-action) and the $+$ operator occurs. But, using axiom SUM1 from Appendix B, we can always add a dummy summation over some data type. Also, it is possible to give j and j' some dummy argument. Finally, using axiom SUM4, the $\sum$-operator can be distributed over the $+$. In the sequel we will allow ourselves these deviations.

Processes can be defined as solutions for convergent LPOs.

Definition 5.2   A *solution* or *fixed point* of an LPO Φ is a process p, parameterized with a datum of sort D, such that, for all $d : D$, $p(d) = \Phi p d$.

Definition 5.3   An LPO Φ written as in Definition 5.1 is called *convergent* if there is a well-founded ordering $<$ on D such that for for all $e_\tau : E_\tau$, $d : D$ we have that $b_\tau(d, e_\tau)$ implies $g_\tau(d, e_\tau) < d$.

For each LPO Φ, we assume an axiom which postulates that Φ has a canonical solution, which we denote by $\langle \Phi \rangle$. Then, we postulate that every *convergent* LPO has at most one solution. In this way, convergent LPOs define processes. The two principles reflect that we only consider process algebras where every LPO has at least one solution and converging LPOs have precisely one solution.

Thus we assume the following two principles:

- Recursive Definition Principle (L-RDP) : For all d of sort D and LPOs Φ over D we have $\langle\Phi\rangle(d) = \Phi\langle\Phi\rangle d$
- Recursive Specification Principle (CL-RSP): Every convergent linear process operator has at most one fixed point (solution): for all d of sort D and convergent LPOs Φ over D we have $p(d) = \Phi p d \rightarrow p = \langle\Phi\rangle$.

Usually, we do not mention $\langle\Phi\rangle$ explicitly and just speak about solutions for Φ.

The following general theorem, taken from the article of Bezem and Groote (1994) on invariants is the basis for our proofs. Roughly, it says that if an LPO is convergent in the part of its state space that satisfies an invariant I, then it has at most one solution in that part of the state space.

Definition 5.4 An *invariant* of an LPO Φ written as in Definition 5.1 is a function $I : D \rightarrow \mathcal{B}$ such that for for all $a \in Act$, $e_a : E_a$, and $d : D$ we have:

$$b_a(d, e_a) \wedge I(d) \rightarrow I(g_a(d, e_a)).$$

Theorem 5.2.1 (Concrete Invariant Corollary) *Let Φ be an LPO. If, for some invariant I of Φ, the LPO $\lambda p.\lambda d.\Phi p d \triangleleft I(d) \triangleright \delta$ is convergent and for some processes q, q', parameterized by a datum of type D, we have*

$$I(d) \rightarrow q(d) = \Phi q d,$$
$$I(d) \rightarrow q'(d) = \Phi q' d,$$

then

$$I(d) \rightarrow q(d) = q'(d).$$

Remark 5.2.2 In this chapter we will restrict ourselves to processes defined by LPOs. This is not as restrictive as it may seem. First, general μCRL processes can be effectively rewritten to equivalent processes in LPO format. Secondly, the linearization of the parallel composition of linear processes can be done symbolically and efficiently. These insights are currently being implemented in a μCRL tool set (Dams and Groote, 1995). Thus, general (parallel) μCRL processes can be easily made to fit in the framework of the present chapter.

5.2.3   *Internal Actions*

We work in the setting of branching bisimulation (Glabbeek and Weijland, 1989), but provide results for weak bisimulation too in those cases where they differ. So, we generally use the following two laws.

B1: $x\tau = x$
B2: $z(\tau(x+y)+x) = z(x+y)$

We write $x \subseteq y$ if there exists a z such that $x + z = y$. It is easily verified that if $x \subseteq y$ and $y \subseteq x$ then $x = y$. Using this notation, we have the following easy fact.

Lemma 5.2.3

$$y \subseteq x \rightarrow \tau x = \tau(\tau x + y)$$

Proof. $\tau x = \tau(x+y) \overset{\text{B2}}{=} \tau(\tau(x+y)+y) = \tau(\tau x + y).$ $\square$

We also assume a principle of fair abstraction, in the form of Koomen's Fair Abstraction Rule (KFAR). The formulation below is the one valid in branching bisimulation:

$$\frac{p(d) = i\,p(d) + y}{\tau\,\tau_{\{i\}}(p(d)) = \tau\,\tau_{\{i\}}(y)}$$

Here p represents a process that can be parameterized, y represents a process and i represents an action.

5.3   Sufficient Conditions for the Equality of LPOs

In this section, we are concerned with proving equality of solutions of LPOs Φ and Ψ. The LPO Φ defines an implementation and the LPO Ψ defines the specification of a system. We assume that τ-steps do not occur in the specification Ψ. Example 5.3 in Section 5.5 shows that this restriction is necessary. On the other hand, Theorem 5.3.2 will show that the restriction is less severe than it seems. We want to show that after abstraction of internal actions in a set Z the solution of Φ is equal to the solution of

Ψ. In this section we assume that Φ cannot perform an infinite sequence of internal actions, but in the next section we relax this restriction. It turns out to be convenient to consider Φ where the actions in Z are already renamed to τ. Hence, we speak about an LPO Ξ which is Φ where actions in Z have been hidden. Note that Ξ is convergent, and hence defines a process. We fix the LPOs Ξ and Ψ as follows (where the actions are taken from a set *Act*):

$$\Xi = \lambda p \cdot \lambda d{:}D_\Xi \cdot \sum_{a \in Act} \sum_{e_a:E_a} a(f_a(d, e_a)) \, p(g_a(d, e_a)) \lhd b_a(d, e_a) \rhd \delta$$

$$\Psi = \lambda q \cdot \lambda d{:}D_\Psi \cdot \sum_{a \in Act \setminus \{\tau\}} \sum_{e_a:E_a} a(f'_a(d, e_a)) \, q(g'_a(d, e_a)) \lhd b'_a(d, e_a) \rhd \delta$$

The issue that we consider is how to prove the solutions of Ξ and Ψ equal. This is done by means of a *state mapping* $h{:}D_\Xi \to D_\Psi$. The mapping h maps states of the implementation to states of the specification. It explains how the data parameter that encodes states of the specification is constructed out of the data parameter that encodes states of the implementation. In order to prove implementation and specification branching bisimilar, the state mapping should satisfy certain properties, which we call *matching criteria* because they serve to match states and transitions of implementation and specification.

We first describe what a perfect match is for h. This means that in states of the implementation and specification that are h-related, the same set of external actions can be executed directly, with the same data parameter and leading to h-related states. In general, it may be the case that the implementation, say in state d, has to do some internal computation before it can perform the external actions that are possible from $h(d)$ in the specification. In this case, h accomplishes only an "indirect" match: whatever the implementation can do, the specification can do, but not necessarily vice versa. Since the implementation is convergent, it is guaranteed that after finitely many internal steps the internal computation stops and we reach a so-called *focus point*. A focus point is a state in the implementation without outgoing τ-steps. We demand that the focus point that is reached by the implementation should be h-related to $h(d)$ in the specification, and the match should be perfect. The set of states from which a focus point can be reached via internal actions is called the *cone* belonging to this focus point. Now the matching criteria below express that focus points in the

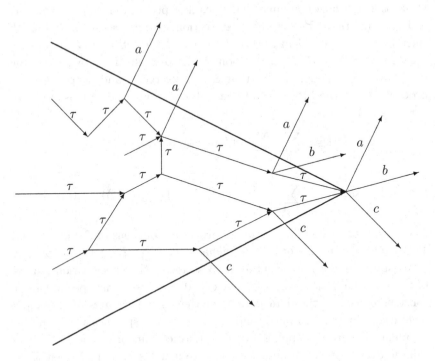

Fig. 5.1   A cone with its focus point

state space of the implementation must match perfectly with their h-image in the specification, whereas points in a cone only have to match indirectly.

States without outgoing τ-steps are in the literature also known as *stable states*. We use the terminology *focus points* to stress that in a focus point there is a perfect match between implementation and specification, and in this sense, a focus point is a *goal* of the implementation, and the internal actions in the cone (which are directed to the focus point) are *progressing* towards this goal. The situation is depicted very schematically in Fig. 5.1. Here the dashed arrows are internal actions (τ-steps) that are all directed towards the focus point.

Note that as we have assumed that Ξ is convergent, each internal step in a cone is indeed directed towards the focus point. In general there may be loops of internal actions, for instance if data must be retransmitted over unreliable channels. Actions that give rise to such loops may be considered *non-progressing* (w.r.t. the focus point). We will deal with them in Section 5.4.

Before presenting the matching criteria, we give a formal characterization of focus points of Ξ by means of the *focus condition* $FC_\Xi(d)$, which is true if d is a focus point, and false if not. It simply states that in state d there is no element e of E_τ such that the enabling condition $b_\tau(d, e)$ of the τ-action is satisfied.

Definition 5.5 The *focus condition*, $FC_\Xi(d)$, of Ξ is the formula

$$\neg\exists e{:}E_\tau\,(b_\tau(d, e))\quad(\text{``in state } d, \tau \text{ is not enabled''})$$

Now we formulate the criteria. We discuss each criterion directly after the definition. Here, $=$ binds stronger than $\neg$, which binds stronger than $\wedge$ and $\vee$, which in turn bind stronger than $\rightarrow$.

Definition 5.6 Let $h{:}D_\Xi \rightarrow D_\Psi$ be a state mapping. The following criteria referring to Ξ, Ψ and h are called the *matching criteria*. We refer to their conjunction by $C_{\Xi,\Psi,h}(d)$.

$$\Xi \text{ is convergent} \tag{Ex1}$$

$$\forall e_\tau{:}E_\tau(b_\tau(d, e_\tau) \rightarrow h(d) = h(g_\tau(d, e_\tau))) \tag{Ex2}$$

$$\forall a \in Act \setminus \{\tau\}\forall e_a{:}E_a\,(b_a(d, e_a) \rightarrow b'_a(h(d), e_a)) \tag{Ex3}$$

$$\forall a \in Act \setminus \{\tau\}\forall e_a{:}E_a\,(FC_\Xi(d) \wedge b'_a(h(d), e_a) \rightarrow b_a(d, e_a)) \tag{Ex4}$$

$$\forall a \in Act \setminus \{\tau\}\,\forall e_a{:}E_a\,(b_a(d, e_a) \rightarrow f_a(d, e_a) = f'_a(h(d), e_a)) \tag{Ex5}$$

$$\forall a \in Act \setminus \{\tau\}\,\forall e_a{:}E_a\,(b_a(d, e_a) \rightarrow h(g_a(d, e_a)) = g'_a(h(d), e_a)) \tag{Ex6}$$

To recapitulate: if in a (non-focus) point d of the implementation a visible action can be done, then this action must also be possible in $h(d)$ in the specification (criterion (**Ex3**)). But, conversely, if $h(d)$ in the specification can perform an action, the non-focus point d need not match it directly. As the implementation is convergent (criterion (**Ex1**)) a focus point will be reached after a finite number of internal steps. Due to criterion (**Ex2**) this focus point will have the same h-image as d. By criterion (**Ex4**) the focus point can perform the same actions as $h(d)$. These actions carry the same data parameter (**Ex5**) and lead to h-related states (**Ex6**).

Now we come to the main result of this section. Its formulation and proof reflect the discussion above except for two points. First, the theorem is formulated under the condition of an invariant of Ξ. The reason for this is that a specification and an implementation are in general only equivalent for the reachable states in the implementation. A common tool to exclude non-reachable states is an invariant, which is therefore added.

As to the second point. Assume that r and q are solutions of Ξ and Ψ, respectively. Let $d : D_\Xi$ be given and assume that $I(d)$ and $I(d) \to C_{\Xi,\Psi,h}(d)$ hold. We distinguish two cases. If $FC_\Xi(d)$ holds, so $r(d)$ is in a focus point and cannot perform a τ-action, we prove that $r(d) = q(h(d))$. If $FC_\Xi(d)$ does not hold then $r(d)$ can perform a τ-action, while $q(h(d))$ can't (Ψ does not contain τ). So $r(d)$ and $q(h(d))$ can't be equal. In the setting of branching bisimulation we can in this case only prove $\tau\, r(d) = \tau\, q(h(d))$. (In the setting of weak bisimulation this simplifies to $r(d) = \tau\, q(h(d))$).

Theorem 5.3.1 (General Equality Theorem) *Let Ξ, Ψ and h be as above (recall that Ψ does not contain τ-steps). Assume that r and q are solutions of Ξ and Ψ, respectively. If I is an invariant of Ξ and $\forall d{:}D_\Xi\,(I(d) \to C_{\Xi,\Psi,h}(d))$, then*

$$\forall d{:}D_\Xi\ I(d) \to r(d) \triangleleft FC_\Xi(d) \triangleright \tau\, r(d) = q(h(d)) \triangleleft FC_\Xi(d) \triangleright \tau\, q(h(d)).$$

Proof.   Define the LPO Ω by:

$$\Omega = \lambda r \cdot \lambda d{:}D_\Xi \cdot \Xi rd \triangleleft FC(d) \triangleright \tau\, \Xi rd.$$

We prove the theorem as an application of the Concrete Invariant Corollary (Theorem 5.2.1) with Ω as LPO. We verify the conditions of that result.

As the invariant implies that Ξ is convergent, it is straightforward to see that the LPO $\lambda r \cdot \lambda d{:}D_\Xi = \Omega rd \triangleleft I(d) \triangleright \delta$ is convergent too.

Using Lemma 5.5.10 and the fact that r is a solution of Ξ, it is also easy to see that $\lambda d{:}D_\Xi \cdot r(d) \triangleleft FC(d) \triangleright \tau r(d)$ is a solution of Ω.

It is slightly more involved to check that $\lambda d{:}D_\Phi \cdot q(h(d)) \triangleleft FC(d) \triangleright \tau q(h(d))$ is a solution of Ω. After applying Lemma 5.5.10, this boils down to proving the following equation.

$$q(h(d)) \triangleleft FC(d) \triangleright \tau\, q(h(d))$$
$$= \Xi[\lambda d{:}D_\Xi \cdot q(h(d))]d \triangleleft FC(d) \triangleright \tau\, \Xi[\lambda d{:}D_\Xi \cdot q(h(d))]d.$$

We distinguish two cases. The first case is where $FC(d)$ holds. We must show that

$$q(h(d)) = \sum_{a \in Act} \sum_{e_a : E_a} a(f_a(d, e_a)) \, q(h(g_a(d, e_a))) \lhd b_a(d, e_a) \rhd \delta \, .$$

We proceed as follows:

$q(h(d)) =$

$\sum_{a \in Act} \sum_{e_a : E_a} a(f'_a(h(d), e_a)) \, q(g'_a(h(d), e_a)) \lhd b'_a(h(d), e_a) \rhd \delta \overset{\text{(Ex3),(Ex4)}}{=}$

$\sum_{a \in Act} \sum_{e_a : E_a} a(f'_a(h(d), e_a)) \, q(g'_a(h(d), e_a)) \lhd b_a(d, e_a) \rhd \delta \overset{\text{(Ex5),(Ex6)}}{=}$

$\sum_{a \in Act} \sum_{e_a : E_a} a(f_a(d, e_a)) \, q(h(g_a(d, e_a))) \lhd b_a(d, e_a) \rhd \delta \, .$

The second case is where $FC(d)$ does not hold. Now we must show that

$$\tau \, q(h(d)) = \tau \sum_{a \in Act} \sum_{e_a : E_a} a(f_a(d, e_a)) \, q(h(g_a(d, e_a))) \lhd b_a(d, e_a) \rhd \delta \, .$$

First note the following Fact:

$q(h(d)) =$

$\sum_{a \in Act} \sum_{e_a : E_a} a(f'_a(h(d), e_a)) \, q(g'_a(h(d), e_a)) \lhd b'_a(h(d), e_a) \rhd \delta \supseteq$

$\sum_{a \in Act \setminus \{\tau\}} \sum_{e_a : E_a} a(f'_a(h(d), e_a)) \, q(g'_a(h(d), e_a))$

$\qquad\qquad \lhd b'_a(h(d), e_a) \wedge b_a(d, e_a) \rhd \delta \overset{\text{(Ex5),(Ex6)}}{=}$

$\sum_{a \in Act \setminus \{\tau\}} \sum_{e_a : E_a} a(f_a(d, e_a)) \, q(h(g_a(d, e_a)))$

$\qquad\qquad \lhd b'_a(h(d), e_a) \wedge b_a(d, e_a) \rhd \delta \overset{\text{(Ex3)}}{=}$

$\sum_{a \in Act \setminus \{\tau\}} \sum_{e_a : E_a} a(f_a(d, e_a)) \, q(h(g_a(d, e_a))) \lhd b_a(d, e_a) \rhd \delta \, .$

The theorem now follows by:

$\tau \, q(h(d)) \overset{\ddagger}{=}$

$\tau \, (\tau \, q(h(d)) +$

$+ \sum_{a \in Act \setminus \{\tau\}} \sum_{e_a : E_a} a(f_a(d, e_a)) \, q(h(g_a(d, e_a))) \lhd b_a(d, e_a) \rhd \delta) \overset{\star}{=}$

$\tau \, (\sum_{e_\tau : E_\tau} \tau \, q(h(g_\tau(d, e_\tau))) \lhd b_\tau(d, e_\tau) \rhd \delta +$

$\qquad \sum_{a \in Act \setminus \{\tau\}} \sum_{e_a : E_a} a(f_a(d, e_a)) \, q(h(g_a(d, e_a))) \lhd b_a(d, e_a) \rhd \delta) =$

$\tau \, (\sum_{a \in Act} \sum_{e_a : E_a} a(f_a(d, e_a)) \, q(h(g_a(d, e_a))) \lhd b_a(d, e_a) \rhd \delta)$

At $\ddagger$, we have used Lemma 5.2.3 and the Fact stated above. At $\star$, we have used Lemma 5.5.9 and matching criterion (**Ex2**). Recall that, since $\neg FC_\Xi(d)$ holds, there exists an e_τ such that $b_\tau(d, e_\tau)$. For the same reason, $\tau \in Act$; this justifies the last step. $\qquad\square$

The following result, whose proof we omit, states that in the setting of branching bisimulation, the restriction to specifications without τ-steps is not a genuine restriction.

Theorem 5.3.2 *Let Ξ and Ψ be convergent LPOs over Act. Let p and q be solutions of Ξ and Ψ, respectively. Suppose there exists a μCRL-expressible functional, rooted branching bisimulation h between $\tau\, p(d)$ and $\tau\, q(h(d))$. Using a fresh action j, we can effectively construct LPOs Ξ_2 and Ψ_2, with solutions p_2 and q_2 respectively, such that*

(1) Ψ_2 *does not contain τ-steps*
(2) h *is a functional, rooted branching bisimulation between $\tau\, p_2(d)$ and $\tau\, q_2(h(d))$.*
(3) $\tau_{\{j\}}(p_2(d)) = p(d)$ *and* $\tau_{\{j\}}(q_2(h(d))) = q(h(d))$

We can formulate a result similar to Theorem 5.3.4 in the setting of weak bisimulation semantics, which is axiomatized by the following laws (where $a \neq \tau$).

$$\text{T1: } x\tau = x$$
$$\text{T2: } \tau x = \tau x + x$$
$$\text{T3: } a(\tau x + y) = a(\tau x + y) + ax$$

First, we prove the following variant of Lemma 5.2.3.

Lemma 5.3.3 (Lemma 5.2.3 for weak bisimulation)

$$y \subseteq x \rightarrow \tau x = \tau x + y$$

Proof. $\tau x \overset{\text{T2}}{=} \tau x + x = \tau x + x + y \overset{\text{T2}}{=} \tau x + y.$ $\qquad\square$

Using Lemma 5.3.3 rather than Lemma 5.2.3, we can prove the following adaptation of Theorem 5.3.1.

Theorem 5.3.4 (General Equality Theorem for Weak Bisimulation) *Let Ξ, Ψ and h be as above (recall that Ψ does not contain τ-steps). Assume that r and q are solutions of Ξ and Ψ, respectively. If I is an invariant of Ξ and $\forall d{:}D_\Xi\, (I(d) \rightarrow C_{\Xi,\Psi,h}(d))$, then*

$$\forall d{:}D_\Xi\; I(d) \rightarrow r(d) = q(h(d)) \triangleleft FC_\Xi(d) \triangleright \tau\, q(h(d)).$$

5.4 Abstraction and Idle Loops

The main result of this section, Theorem 5.4.4, is an adaptation of Theorem 5.3.1 to the setting where implementations can perform unbounded sequences of internal activity.

Recall that we are concerned with the following situation. We have an implementation, defined by the LPO Φ, and a specification, defined by the LPO Ψ. We want to prove that Φ is equal to Ψ, after abstraction of internal actions in Φ. In the previous section, we have shown how to prove equality of Ψ and Ξ, which is an abstract version of Φ, where internal actions, i.e. actions not in Ψ, are hidden.

Thus our next task is to rename internal actions in Φ in such a way that the resulting LPO Ξ is convergent, i.e. does not contain τ-loops, and such that a state mapping h from Ξ to Ψ, satisfying the matching criteria, can be defined.

In the previous section, we identified τ-steps with internal actions that make progress towards a focus point, and so make progress in the protocol. Following this intuition, we only rename those occurrences of actions that constitute progress in the protocol. Consider for instance the Concurrent Alternating Bit Protocol of Section 5.5, where a sender S repeatedly sends a datum with an alternating bit b attached to receiver R through the channel K of Section 5.2, until an acknowledgement arrives via channel L. Obviously, losing or garbling the datum in the channel K does not constitute progress in any sense; indeed, these events give rise to an internal loop, since the sender S retransmits the datum. So these transitions are not renamed to τ. Also, the transmission of the datum by the sender is useful only when the receiver has not yet received it, i.e. is still willing to accept data with alternating bit b. Suppose that we have a formula φ that expresses that R will accept data with alternating bit b. Then we split this transmission into two transitions: one where the transmission is renamed to τ and the enabling condition is strengthened by the conjunct φ, and one where the transition is unchanged but the enabling condition is strengthened by the conjunct $\neg\varphi$.

It requires experience to identify progressing internal actions for particular applications; we hope that the examples in Subsection 5.5.1 provide enough intuition.

We have seen that, when the implementation has unbounded internal behavior, not all occurrences of all internal actions can be renamed to τ, since this would give rise to a non-convergent LPO Ξ. Hence some occurrences of some internal actions in the implementation remain unchanged. However, in order to apply Theorem 5.3.1, the specification Ψ and abstracted implementation Ξ should run over the same set of actions, except that Ξ can perform τ-steps. To arrive at this situation, we augment Ψ with "idle" loops: for each internal action j that still occurs in Ξ, we augment Ψ with a j-loop of the form $j\,p(d) \triangleleft \mathsf{T} \triangleright \delta$. As a consequence, the augmented specification is in every state able to do a j-step. In general, the abstracted implementation Ξ is not in every state able to perform a j-step. To remedy this we also add a j-loop to Ξ.

After these preparations, Theorem 5.3.1 yields that Ξ plus idle loops is equal to Ψ plus idle loops. Now by KFAR, we can abstract from these idle loops to obtain equality of implementation Φ (after abstraction of *all* internal actions) and specification Ψ.

Since the internal actions are eventually all renamed to τ, we may as well rename them first to a single internal action i, and add just a single idle loop (an i-loop) to Ξ and Ψ. This considerably smoothens the presentation.

As opposed to the previous section, the main result of this section, Theorem 5.4.4, is the same for weak bisimulation and branching bisimulation. In the sequel, we assume that *Ext* (the set of external actions of Φ), Z (the set of internal actions of Φ), and $\{\tau\}$ are mutually disjoint and finite sets of actions.

First, we introduce a number of operator transformations that are instrumental in the proof. The operator $i(\Phi)$ is Φ extended with an i-loop; $\rho_{\mathsf{Z}}(\Phi)$ is Φ with all actions in Z renamed to i; $i_{\mathsf{Z}}(\Phi)$ is a combination of the two.

Definition 5.7 Let Φ be a convergent LPO over $Ext \cup \mathsf{Z} \cup \{\tau\}$. Let $i \in \mathsf{Act}$ be an action such that $i \notin Ext \cup \mathsf{Z} \cup \{\tau\}$. Let ρ_{Z} be a renaming operator renaming the actions in Z to i. We define the following operators on LPOs.

$$i(\Phi) \overset{\text{def}}{=} \lambda p.\lambda d{:}D_{\Phi}.\Phi p d + i\,p(d),$$
$$\rho_{\mathsf{Z}}(\Phi) \overset{\text{def}}{=} \lambda p.\lambda d{:}D_{\Phi}.\rho_{\mathsf{Z}}(\Phi p d),$$
$$i_{\mathsf{Z}}(\Phi) \overset{\text{def}}{=} i(\rho_{\mathsf{Z}}(\Phi)).$$

The following theorem gives the relevant properties of these operators. It is proved in Appendix A as Theorem 5.5.11; the proof uses KFAR and CL-RSP.

Theorem 5.4.1 *Let Φ be a convergent LPO over $Ext \cup \mathsf{Z} \cup \{\tau\}$ such that $i \notin Ext \cup \mathsf{Z} \cup \{\tau\}$. Assume that p_1 is a solution of Φ, p_2 is a solution of $i(\Phi)$, and p_3 is a solution of $i_{\mathsf{Z}}(\Phi)$. Then we have, for all $d : D$:*

(1) $\tau\, p_1(d) = \tau\, \tau_{\{i\}}(p_2(d))$,
(2) $\rho_{\mathsf{Z}}(p_2(d)) = p_3(d)$ *and*
(3) $\tau\, \tau_{\mathsf{Z}}(p_1(d)) = \tau\, \tau_{\{i\}}(p_3(d))$.

The essential technical concept in this section is a *pre-abstraction* or *partial abstraction* function ξ. The function ξ divides occurrences of internal actions in the implementation into two categories, namely the *progressing* and *non-progressing* internal actions. In this setting, a focus point is not defined in terms of τ-steps, as in the previous section, but in terms of progressing internal actions.

In order to apply Theorem 5.4.4 below, one must provide not only an invariant and a state mapping h, but also a pre-abstraction.

Definition 5.8 Let Φ be an LPO and let Z be a finite set of actions. A *pre-abstraction function* ξ is a mapping that yields for every action $a \in \mathsf{Z}$ an expression of sort $\mathcal{B}$. The *pre-abstraction* Φ_ξ is defined by replacing every summand in Φ of the form

$$\sum_{e_a : E_a} a(f_a(d, e_a))\, p(g_a(d, e_a)) \triangleleft b_a(d, e_a) \triangleright \delta$$

with $a \in \mathsf{Z}$ by

$$\sum_{e_a : E_a} (\tau\, p(g_a(d, e_a))) \triangleleft \xi(a)(d, e_a) \triangleright a(f_a(d, e_a))\, p(g_a(d, e_a))) \triangleleft b_a(d, e_a) \triangleright \delta$$

We extend ξ to all actions by assuming that $\xi(\tau)(d, e_\tau) = \mathsf{T}$ and $\xi(a)(d, e_a) = \mathsf{F}$ for all remaining actions.

Note that if $\xi(a)(d, e_a) = \mathsf{T}$, the action a in the summand is replaced by τ, while if $\xi(a)(d, e_a) = \mathsf{F}$, the summand remains unchanged. In the remaining case, a-transitions are divided into progressing ones (renamed to τ) and non-progressing ones. Observe that $D_\Phi = D_{\Phi_\xi}$ and that convergence of Φ_ξ implies convergence of Φ.

We redefine the notions *convergent* and *focus point* in a setting where there is a pre-abstraction.

Definition 5.9 Let Φ be an LPO with internal actions Z and let ξ be a pre-abstraction function. The LPO Φ is called *convergent w.r.t.* ξ iff there is a well founded ordering $<$ on D such that for all $a \in Z \cup \{\tau\}$, $d : D$ and all $e_a : E_a$ we have that $b_a(d, e_a)$ and $\xi(a)(d, e_a)$ imply $g_a(d, e_a) < d$. Note that this is equivalent to convergence of Φ_ξ, defined in terms of Φ and ξ.

The difference between Φ and Φ_ξ disappears when the internal actions in Z are hidden. This is stated in the next lemma, which is proven as Lemma 5.5.12 in Appendix A.

Lemma 5.4.2 *Let* Φ *be an LPO that is convergent w.r.t. a pre-abstraction function* ξ. *Let* p *be a solution of* Φ *and* p' *be a solution of* Φ_ξ. *Then*

$$\tau_Z(p) = \tau_Z(p').$$

Definition 5.10   Let ξ be a pre-abstraction function. The *focus condition* of Φ relative to ξ is defined by:

$$FC_{\Phi,Z,\xi}(d) \stackrel{\text{def}}{=} \forall a \in Z \cup \{\tau\} \ \forall e_a : E_a \ \neg(b_a(d, e_a) \wedge \xi(a)(d, e_a)).$$

Note that this is exactly the focus condition of Φ_ξ, defined in terms of Φ and ξ.

In the next definition we define the matching criteria for the case where the implementation can perform unbounded internal activity. After an instrumental technical lemma we formulate the main theorem.

Definition 5.11   Let Φ, Ψ be LPOs, where Φ runs over $Ext \cup Z \cup \{\tau\}$ (Ext, Z and $\{\tau\}$ mutually disjoint) and Ψ runs over Ext. Let $h : D_\Phi \to D_\Psi$ and let ξ be a pre-abstraction function. The following 6 conditions are called the *matching criteria for idle loops* and their conjunction is denoted by $CI_{\Phi,\Psi,\xi,h}(d)$.

$$\Phi \text{ is convergent w.r.t. } \xi \tag{Ex1}$$

$$\forall a \in Z \cup \{\tau\} \ \forall e_a : E_a \ (b_a(d, e_a) \to h(d) = h(g_a(d, e_a))) \tag{Ex2}$$

$$\forall a \in Ext \ \forall e_a : E_a (b_a(d, e_a) \to b_a'(h(d), e_a)) \tag{Ex3}$$

$$\forall a \in Ext \ \forall e_a : E_a \ (FC_{\Phi,Z,\xi}(d) \wedge b_a'(h(d), e_a) \to b_a(d, e_a)) \tag{Ex4}$$

$$\forall a \in Ext \ \forall e_a : E_a \ (b_a(d, e_a) \to f_a(d, e_a) = f_a'(h(d), e_a)) \tag{Ex5}$$

$$\forall a \in Ext \; \forall e_a{:}E_a \; (b_a(d, e_a) \rightarrow h(g_a(d, e_a)) = g'_a(h(d), e_a)) \qquad \textbf{(Ex6)}$$

Lemma 5.4.3 *Let Φ, Ψ, h and ξ as in Definition 5.11. We find:*

$$CI_{\Phi,\Psi,\xi,h}(d) \rightarrow C_{i_Z(\Phi_\xi),i(\Psi),h}(d).$$

Proof. Below we show that the conditions in $C_{i_Z(\Phi_\xi),i(\Psi),h}(d)$ follow from the conditions in $CI_{\Phi,\Psi,\xi,h}(d)$. In order to see this, we formulate the conditions of $C_{i_Z(\Phi_\xi),i(\Psi),h}(d)$ in terms of Φ, Ψ and ξ directly and show how they follow.

(1) We must show that $i_Z(\Phi_\xi)$ is convergent. This is an immediate consequence of the fact that Φ is convergent w.r.t. ξ.

(2) We must prove

$$\forall a \in Z \cup \{\tau\} \; \forall e_a{:}E_a$$
$$(\xi(a)(d, e_a) \wedge b_a(d, e_a) \rightarrow h(d) = h(g_a(d, e_a))).$$

(We must consider $a \in Z$ as these are renamed to τ if $\xi(a)(d, e_a)$ holds.) Note that this condition is a direct consequence of condition 2 of $CI_{\Phi,\Psi,\xi,h}(d)$.

(3) We get

$$\forall a \in Z \cup Ext \cup \{i\} \; \forall e_a{:}E_a$$
$$(b_a(d, e_a) \wedge \neg\xi(a)(d, e_a) \rightarrow b'_a(h(d), e_a)).$$

In case $a \in Z$ or a is the new action i, the action a appears as i in $i_Z(\Phi_\xi)$. In this case $b'_i(h(d), e_b)$ equals T and the condition trivially holds.

In case $a \in Ext$, this is exactly condition 3 of $CI_{\Phi,\Psi,\xi,h}(d)$.

(4) This condition yields

$$\forall a \in Z \cup Ext \cup \{i\} \; \forall e_a{:}E_a$$
$$(FC_{\Phi,Z,\xi}(d) \wedge b'_a(h(d), e_a) \rightarrow b_a(d, e_a) \wedge \neg\xi(a)(d, e_a)).$$

In case $a \in Z \cup \{i\}$, a occurs as i in $i_Z(\Phi_\xi)$ and $i_Z(\Psi)$. So the conditions $b_i(d, e_i)$ and $b'_i(h(d), e_i)$ are both equal to T. If $\xi(i)(d, e_i) = \mathsf{F}$, we are done; if $\xi(i)(d, e_i) = \mathsf{T}$, the focus condition is false and the theorem follows trivially.

In case $a \in Ext$ we have that $\xi(a)(d, e_a) = \mathsf{F}$ and the theorem follows from condition 4 of $CI_{\Phi,\Psi,\xi,h}(d)$.

(5) In this case we get

$$\forall a \in \mathsf{Z} \cup Ext \cup \{i\} \, \forall e_a{:}E_a$$
$$(\neg \xi(a)(d, e_a) \wedge b_a(d, e_a) \rightarrow f_a(d, e_a) = f'_a(h(d), e_a)) \, .$$

In case $a \in \mathsf{Z} \cup \{i\}$, a occurs as i in $i_\mathsf{Z}(\Phi)$ and $i_\mathsf{Z}(\Psi)$. As i has no parameter, this condition holds trivially.

In case $a \in Ext$ this is exactly condition 5 of $CI_{\Phi, \Psi, \xi, h}(d)$.

(6) The last condition is

$$\forall a \in \mathsf{Z} \cup Ext \cup \{i\} \, \forall e_a{:}E_a$$
$$(\neg \xi(a)(d, e_a) \wedge b_a(d, e_a) \rightarrow h(g_a(d, e_a)) = g'_a(h(d), e_a)) \, .$$

In case $a \in \mathsf{Z} \cup \{i\}$ the action a appears as i in $i_\mathsf{Z}(\Phi_\xi)$ and $i_\mathsf{Z}(\Psi)$. So, g'_i is the identity and we must prove that $h(g_a(d, e_a)) = h(d)$. This follows from condition 2 of $CI_{\Phi, \Psi, \xi, h}(d)$.

In case $a \in Ext$ this is an immediate consequence of condition 6 of $CI_{\Phi, \Psi, \xi, h}(d)$. $\qquad\square$

Theorem 5.4.4 (Equality theorem for idle loops) *Let Φ, Ψ be LPOs, where Φ runs over $Ext \cup \mathsf{Z} \cup \{\tau\}$ (Ext, Z and $\{\tau\}$ mutually disjoint) and Ψ runs over Ext. Let $h : D_\Phi \rightarrow D_\Psi$ and let ξ be a pre-abstraction function. Let p and q be solutions of Φ and Ψ, respectively.*

If I is an invariant of Φ and $\forall d : D_\Phi \, (I(d) \rightarrow CI_{\Phi, \Psi, \xi, h}(d))$, then

$$\forall d{:}D_\Phi \; I(d) \rightarrow \tau \, \tau_\mathsf{Z}(p(d)) = \tau \, q(h(d)).$$

Proof. Let p, q, p' and q' be solutions of Φ, Ψ, $i_\mathsf{Z}(\Phi_\xi)$ and $i_\mathsf{Z}(\Psi)$, respectively. The following three facts follow straightforwardly from the work done up to now.

(1) $\tau \, \tau_\mathsf{Z}(p(d)) = \tau \, \tau_{\{i\}}(p'(d))$ (Theorem 5.4.1.3),

(2) $\tau \, q(h(d)) = \tau \, \tau_{\{i\}}(q'(h(d)))$ (Theorem 5.4.1.1) and

(3) $I(d) \rightarrow \tau \, p'(d) = \tau \, q'(h(d))$ (Theorem 5.3.1 and Lemma 5.4.3).

The theorem follows straightforwardly by

$$\tau \, \tau_\mathsf{Z}(p(d)) \overset{(1)}{=} \tau \, \tau_{\{i\}}(p'(d))$$
$$\overset{(3)}{=} \tau \, \tau_{\{i\}}(q'(h(d)))$$
$$\overset{(2)}{=} \tau \, q(h(d))$$

$\qquad\square$

5.5   Examples

In this section we give some examples. We begin with three simple ones, where invariants, progressiveness of internal actions, and convergence hardly play a role. The first example is an easy application of Theorem 5.4.4. The next example shows that in some cases a state mapping as required by Theorem 5.3.1 or Theorem 5.4.4 does not exist, even though the processes in question are evidently branching bisimilar. The third example motivates our restriction to specifications without τ-steps. In Subsection 5.5.1, we present a larger example, the Concurrent Alternating Bit Protocol. As an application of Theorem 5.4.4, we prove the correctness of this protocol. Here, invariants, progressiveness of internal actions and convergence make their appearance.

Example 5.1   The following LPO describes a person who tosses a coin (this event is modeled by the internal action j). When *head* turns up the person performs an external action *out(head)*, when *tail* turns up the person tosses again. We write *Sides* for the sort consisting of *head* and *tail*.

proc $X(s{:}Sides) =$
$$\sum_{s':Sides} j\, X(s') \vartriangleleft eq(s, tail) \vartriangleright \delta +$$
$$out(s)\, X(tail) \vartriangleleft eq(s, head) \vartriangleright \delta$$

After hiding the internal action j, this process implements the process which does nothing but *out(head)*-steps, given by

proc $Y(s{:}Sides) = out(head)\, Y(s)$

Here we leave the condition T of the summand implicit. The parameter s is added to Y for convenience. We use Theorem 5.4.4 to prove that solutions for X and Y are branching bisimilar. More precisely, let p and q be solutions for X and Y, respectively: we prove that for all $s \in Sides$, $\tau\, \tau_{\{j\}}(p(s)) = \tau\, q(s)$. Here we take X for Φ, Y for Ψ, $\{j\}$ for Z and $\{out\}$ for *Ext*. First we define the ξ-function, which determines when the internal action j is renamed to τ. The coin is tossed when s equals *tail*. When the side that turns up, s', is again *tail*, we have a j-loop (which after renaming would lead to a τ-loop). To exclude this situation, we put $\xi(j) = eq(s', head)$. The focus condition $FC_{X,\{j\},\xi}(s)$ is now defined as $\forall s'{:}Sides\ \neg(eq(s, tail) \wedge eq(s', head))$, which is equivalent to $eq(s, head)$. As invariant we simply take the always true formula T and we define $h : Sides \to Sides$ by $h(s) = head$.

Spelling out the matching criteria of Definition 5.11, we get the following proof obligations:

(1) X is convergent w.r.t. ξ. This is easy: we let the required well-founded ordering on *Sides* be given by: *head* < *tail*.

(2) $eq(s, tail) \rightarrow head = head$. This formula is trivially proved.

(3) $eq(s, head) \rightarrow \mathsf{T}$. Equally trivial.

(4) $(FC_{X,\{j\},\xi}(s) \wedge \mathsf{T}) \rightarrow eq(s, head)$. Easy, since $FC_{X,\{j\},\xi}(s)$ is equivalent to $eq(s, head)$.

(5) $eq(s, head) \rightarrow s = head$. Trivial. Remember that we assume that eq faithfully reflects equality.

(6) $eq(s, head) \rightarrow head = head$. Trivial.

Example 5.2 Let Y be defined as in Example 5.1. Define a function $flip : Sides \rightarrow Sides$ with $flip(head) = tail$ and $flip(tail) = head$ (no other equations hold). Let Z be defined by

proc $Z(st{:}Sides) = out(head)\, Z(flip(st))$

Processes defined by Y and Z are evidently strongly bisimilar. However, we cannot give a state mapping $h : Sides \rightarrow Sides$ that satisfies the matching criteria. Towards a contradiction, suppose that h exists. By criterion (6), we have $h(s) = flip(h(s))$, which is clearly impossible.

We conjecture that in cases like this, one can always rewrite the implementation and specification in a simple way to (branching) equivalent ones, which can be dealt with by our strategy. (In the present case, just delete the parameter st in Z.) It remains to make this more precise.

Now we show that the restriction to specifications without τ-steps cannot be dropped. We present a counter example to this generalization of Theorem 5.3.1, which also serves to refute the same generalization of Theorem 5.4.4.

Example 5.3 Let U be defined by

proc $U(st{:}\mathsf{N}) =$
$$\tau\, U(2) \triangleleft eq(st, 1) \triangleright \delta +$$
$$b\, U(3) \triangleleft eq(st, 2) \triangleright \delta +$$
$$c\, U(st) \triangleleft eq(st, 3) \triangleright \delta$$

Solutions for this LPO can be written as $\tau\, b\, c^{\omega}$. Next, consider

proc $V(st{:}\mathsf{N}) =$
$$\tau\, V(2) \lhd eq(st,1) \rhd \delta +$$
$$b\, V(3) \lhd eq(st,2) \rhd \delta +$$
$$\tau\, V(3) \lhd eq(st,2) \rhd \delta +$$
$$c\, V(st) \lhd eq(st,3) \rhd \delta$$

We have that solutions to U and V are not in general branching (or weakly) bisimilar: the infinite trace c^ω is an (infinite) trace of a solution for V, but not of a solution for U. However, it is easy to show that the conditions of Theorem 5.3.1 are satisfied, contradicting this result.

We define a state mapping h from U to V, of type $\mathsf{N} \to \mathsf{N}$, by

$$h(st) = \begin{cases} 2 & \text{if } eq(st,1) \\ st & \text{otherwise} \end{cases}$$

The focus condition $FC_U(st)$ is equivalent to $\neg eq(st,1)$. It is easily seen that the matching criteria $C_{U,V,h}$ are satisfied. (For convergence, take the $>$ ordering on N (restricted to $\{1,2,3\}$) as the required well-founded ordering.)

The question arises whether our strategy can deal with τ-steps in the specification at all. Intuitively, these steps model that the specification internally and invisibly makes choices. In case the implementation is (after abstraction of internal actions) equal to the specification, these choices must also occur in the implementation. Usually, they will be modeled by internal but visible actions. An adaptation of our strategy could be to make the choices in the specification visible by replacing the τ-steps by the corresponding internal actions. Then one might prove this version of the specification equal to the (partially abstracted) implementation. Thereafter, hiding the internal actions in the specification yields the desired result.

5.5.1   *The Concurrent Alternating Bit Protocol*

In this subsection we prove the correctness of the Concurrent Alternating Bit Protocol ($CABP$), as an application of Theorem 5.4.4.

5.5.1.1   *Specification*

In this section we give the standard description of the Concurrent Alternating Bit Protocol and its specification. The system is built from six components. The overall structure of the $CABP$ is depicted in Fig. 5.2.

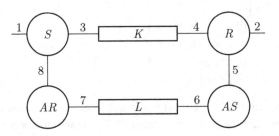

Fig. 5.2   The structure of the *CABP*

Information flows clockwise through this picture. The components can perform read $(r_n(\ldots))$ and send actions $(s_n(\ldots))$ to transport data over port n. A read and a send action over port n can synchronize to a communication action $(c_n(\ldots))$ over port n when they are executed simultaneously. In such a case the parameters of the send and read action must match.

We use the sort *Bit* with bits e_0 and e_1 with an inversion function *inv* and the sort N of natural numbers. We assume an unspecified sort D that contains the data elements to be transferred by the protocol. The sort *Frame* consists of pairs $\langle d, b \rangle$ with $d : D$ and $b : Bit$ (b models the alternating bit). This sort also contains two error messages, *ce* (for *checksum error*) and *ae* (for *acknowledgement error*).

The channels K and L read data at port 3, resp. port 6. They either deliver the data correctly (via port 4, resp. 7), or lose or garble the data (in the last case a checksum error *ce* (resp., acknowledgement error *ae*)) is sent. The non-deterministic choice between the three options is modeled by the actions j and j'. If j is chosen the data are delivered correctly and if j' happens they are garbled or lost. The state of the channels is modeled by parameters i_k and i_l.

proc $K(d_k{:}D, b_k{:}Bit, i_k{:}\mathsf{N}) =$
$$\sum_{d:D} \sum_{b:Bit} r_3(\langle d, b \rangle)\, K(d/d_k, b/b_k, 2/i_k) \lhd eq(i_k, 1) \rhd \delta +$$
$$(j'\, K(1/i_k) + j\, K(3/i_k) + j'\, K(4/i_k)) \lhd eq(i_k, 2) \rhd \delta +$$
$$s_4(\langle d_k, b_k \rangle)\, K(1/i_k) \lhd eq(i_k, 3) \rhd \delta +$$
$$s_4(ce)\, K(1/i_k) \lhd eq(i_k, 4) \rhd \delta$$

$$L(b_l{:}Bit, i_l{:}\mathsf{N}) =$$
$$\sum_{b:Bit} r_6(b)\, L(b/b_l, 2/i_l) \triangleleft eq(i_l, 1) \triangleright \delta +$$
$$(j'\, L(1/i_l) + j\, L(3/i_l) + j'\, L(4/i_l)) \triangleleft eq(i_l, 2) \triangleright \delta +$$
$$s_7(b_l)\, L(1/i_l) \triangleleft eq(i_l, 3) \triangleright \delta +$$
$$s_7(ae)\, L(1/i_l) \triangleleft eq(i_l, 4) \triangleright \delta$$

The sender S reads a datum of sort D at port 1 and repeatedly offers the datum (with a bit attached) at port 3 until it receives an acknowledgement ac at port 8 after which the bit-to-be-attached is inverted.

proc $S(d_s{:}D, b_s{:}Bit, i_s{:}\mathsf{N}) =$
$$\sum_{d:D} r_1(d)\, S(d/d_s, 2/i_s) \triangleleft eq(i_s, 1) \triangleright \delta$$
$$(s_3(\langle d_s, b_s \rangle))\, S + r_8(ac)\, S(inv(b_s)/b_s, 1/i_s)) \triangleleft eq(i_s, 2) \triangleright \delta$$

The receiver R reads a datum at port 4 and if the datum is not a checksum error ce and if the bit attached is the expected bit, it sends the datum via port 2 and sends (via port 5) an acknowledgement ac to the acknowledgement sender AS, after which the bit-to-be-expected is inverted. If the datum is a checksum error or the bit attached is not the expected bit, the datum is ignored.

proc $R(d_r{:}D, b_r{:}Bit, i_r{:}\mathsf{N}) =$
$$\sum_{d:D} r_4(\langle d, b_r \rangle)\, R(d/d_r, 2/i_r) \triangleleft eq(i_r, 1) \triangleright \delta +$$
$$(r_4(ce) + \sum_{d:D} r_4(\langle d, inv(b_r) \rangle))\, R \triangleleft eq(i_r, 1) \triangleright \delta +$$
$$s_2(d_r)\, R(3/i_r) \triangleleft eq(i_r, 2) \triangleright \delta +$$
$$s_5(ac)\, R(inv(b_r)/b_r, 1/i_r) \triangleleft eq(i_r, 3) \triangleright \delta$$

The acknowledgement sender AS repeatedly sends its acknowledgement bit via port 6, until it reads an acknowledgement ac at port 5, after which the acknowledgement bit is inverted.

proc $AS(b_r'{:}Bit) =$
$$r_5(ac)\, AS(inv(b_r')) + s_6(b_r')\, AS(b_r')$$

The acknowledgement receiver AR reads bits at port 7 and when the bit is the expected acknowledgement bit, it sends via port 8 an acknowledgement ac to the sender S, after which the bit-to-be-expected is inverted. Acknowledgements errors ae or unexpected bits are ignored.

proc $AR(b'_s : Bit, i'_s : N) =$
$$r_7(b'_s)\, AR(2/i'_s) \triangleleft eq(i'_s, 1) \triangleright \delta +$$
$$(r_7(ae) + r_7(inv(b'_s)))\, AR \triangleleft eq(i'_s, 1) \triangleright \delta +$$
$$s_8(ac)\, AR(inv(b'_s)/b'_s, 1/i'_s) \triangleleft eq(i'_s, 2) \triangleright \delta$$

The $CABP$ is obtained by putting the components in parallel and encapsulating the internal send and read actions at ports $n \in \{3, 4, 5, 6, 7, 8\}$. Synchronization between the components is modeled by communication actions at connecting ports.
We put $H = \{s_3, r_3, s_4, r_4, s_5, r_5, s_6, r_6, s_7, r_7, s_8, r_8\}$.

proc $CABP(d{:}D) =$
$$\partial_H(S(d, e_0, 1) \parallel AR(e_0, 1) \parallel K(d, e_1, 1) \parallel$$
$$L(e_1, 1) \parallel R(d, e_0, 1) \parallel AS(e_1))$$

The specification of the external behavior of $CABP$ uses the one-datum buffer B, which can read via port 1 if b is true, and deliver via port 2 if b is false.

proc $B(d{:}D, b{:}\mathcal{B}) =$
$$\sum_{e:D} r_1(e)\, B(e, \mathsf{F}) \triangleleft b \triangleright \delta +$$
$$s_2(d)\, B(d, \mathsf{T}) \triangleleft \neg b \triangleright \delta$$

After abstraction of internal actions, the $CABP$ should behave as a one-datum buffer, up to initial silent steps. We let $I = \{c_3, c_4, c_5, c_6, c_7, c_8, j, j'\}$. Our goal is to prove the following result.

Theorem 5.5.1 *For all d:D we have*

$$\tau\, \tau_I(CABP(d)) = \tau\, B(d, \mathsf{T}).$$

This result will be proved as Theorem 5.5.7, as an easy consequence of Theorem 5.4.4, taking a certain expansion Sys of $CABP$ for Φ, B for Ψ, the set I for Z, and $\{r_1, s_2\}$ for Ext. In the next section, we determine Sys.

5.5.1.2   *Expansion*

In this section we expand $CABP$ to a linear process term Sys. As a preparation, we first group S and AR, respectively R and AS, together. This has the advantage that we can dispose of the parameters b'_s and b'_r. For d_s, d_r, $d_k : D$, b_s, b_r, b_k, $b_l : Bit$ and i_s, i'_s, i_r, i_k, $i_l : N$, we define:

proc $SAR(d_s, b_s, i_s, i'_s) = S(d_s, b_s, i_s) \parallel AR(b_s, i'_s)$

$RAS(d_r, b_r, i_r) = R(d_r, b_r, i_r) \parallel AS(inv(b_r))$

$Sys(d_s, b_s, i_s, i'_s, d_r, b_r, i_r, d_k, b_k, i_k, b_l, i_l) =$
$\partial_H(SAR(d_s, b_s, i_s, i'_s) \parallel K(d_k, b_k, i_k) \parallel L(b_l, i_l) \parallel RAS(d_r, b_r, i_r))$

Lemma 5.5.2 *For all d:D we have*

$$CABP(d) = Sys(d, e_0, 1, 1, d, e_0, 1, d, e_1, 1, e_1, 1).$$

Proof.   Direct using the definitions.   □

Lemma 5.5.3 *For all d_s, d_r, d_k : D, b_s, b_r, b_k, b_l : Bit and i_s, i'_s, i_r, i_k, i_l : N, it holds that*

$Sys(d_s, b_s, i_s, i'_s, d_r, b_r, i_r, d_k, b_k, i_k, b_l, i_l) =$
$\sum_{d:D} r_1(d)\, Sys(d/d_s, 2/i_s) \triangleleft eq(i_s, 1) \triangleright \delta +$
$c_3(\langle d_s, b_s \rangle)\, Sys(d_s/d_k, b_s/b_k, 2/i_k) \triangleleft eq(i_s, 2) \wedge eq(i_k, 1) \triangleright \delta +$
$c_4(\langle d_k, b_r \rangle)\, Sys(d_k/d_r, 2/i_r, 1/i_k)$
$\qquad \triangleleft eq(i_r, 1) \wedge eq(b_r, b_k) \wedge eq(i_k, 3) \triangleright \delta +$
$c_4(\langle d_k, b_r \rangle)\, Sys(1/i_k) \triangleleft eq(i_r, 1) \wedge eq(b_r, inv(b_k)) \wedge eq(i_k, 3) \triangleright \delta +$
$c_4(ce)\, Sys(1/i_k) \triangleleft eq(i_r, 1) \wedge eq(i_k, 4) \triangleright \delta +$
$s_2(d_r)\, Sys(3/i_r) \triangleleft eq(i_r, 2) \triangleright \delta +$
$c_5(ac)\, Sys(inv(b_r)/b_r, 1/i_r) \triangleleft eq(i_r, 3) \triangleright \delta +$
$c_6(inv(b_r))\, Sys(inv(b_r)/b_l, 2/i_l) \triangleleft eq(i_l, 1) \triangleright \delta +$
$c_7(b_l)\, Sys(1/i_l, 2/i'_s) \triangleleft eq(i'_s, 1) \wedge eq(b_l, b_s) \wedge eq(i_l, 3) \triangleright \delta +$
$c_7(b_l)\, Sys(1/i_l) \triangleleft eq(i'_s, 1) \wedge eq(b_l, inv(b_s)) \wedge eq(i_l, 3) \triangleright \delta +$
$c_7(ae)\, Sys(1/i_l) \triangleleft eq(i'_s, 1) \wedge eq(i_l, 4) \triangleright \delta +$
$c_8(ac)\, Sys(inv(b_s)/b_s, 1/i_s, 1/i'_s) \triangleleft eq(i_s, 2) \wedge eq(i'_s, 2) \triangleright \delta +$
$(j'\, Sys(1/i_k) + j\, Sys(3/i_k) + j'\, Sys(4/i_k)) \triangleleft eq(i_k, 2) \triangleright \delta +$
$(j'\, Sys(1/i_l) + j\, Sys(3/i_l) + j'\, Sys(4/i_l)) \triangleleft eq(i_l, 2) \triangleright \delta$

Proof.   By straightforward process algebraic calculations.   □

Now this expanded version of *Sys* will play the role of Φ as introduced in section 4. As it would decrease readability, we have chosen not to transform *Sys* to an LPO. We have taken care that all theorems are correctly applied to *Sys*.

5.5.1.3 Invariant

The process Sys does not behave as the buffer for all its data states. Actually, there are cases where it can perform an r_1 in succession without an intermediate s_2, or two successive s_2 actions without an intermediate r_1. However, such states cannot be reached from the initial state. We formalize this observation by formulating six invariant properties of Sys. The first five invariants $I_1, \ldots, I_5$ state what values i_s, i'_s, i_r, i_k, and i_l may have. The last invariant I_6 is less trivial. We first provide the formal definition of the invariant, thereafter we give an informal explanation of I_6.

$$I_1 \equiv eq(i_s, 1) \vee eq(i_s, 2);$$
$$I_2 \equiv eq(i'_s, 1) \vee eq(i'_s, 2);$$
$$I_3 \equiv eq(i_k, 1) \vee eq(i_k, 2) \vee eq(i_k, 3) \vee eq(i_k, 4);$$
$$I_4 \equiv eq(i_r, 1) \vee eq(i_r, 2) \vee eq(i_r, 3);$$
$$I_5 \equiv eq(i_l, 1) \vee eq(i_l, 2) \vee eq(i_l, 3) \vee eq(i_l, 4);$$
$$I_6 \equiv (eq(i_s, 1) \rightarrow eq(b_s, inv(b_k)) \wedge eq(b_s, b_r) \wedge eq(d_s, d_k) \wedge$$
$$eq(d_s, d_r) \wedge eq(i'_s, 1) \wedge eq(i_r, 1)) \wedge$$
$$(eq(b_s, b_k) \rightarrow eq(d_s, d_k)) \wedge$$
$$(eq(i_r, 2) \vee eq(i_r, 3) \rightarrow eq(d_s, d_r) \wedge eq(b_s, b_r) \wedge eq(b_s, b_k)) \wedge$$
$$(eq(b_s, inv(b_r)) \rightarrow eq(d_s, d_r) \wedge eq(b_s, b_k)) \wedge$$
$$(eq(b_s, b_l) \rightarrow eq(b_s, inv(b_r))) \wedge$$
$$(eq(i'_s, 2) \rightarrow eq(b_s, b_l)).$$

The invariant I_6 can be understood in the following way. Every component can be in exactly two modes, which we call *involved* and *unaware*.

If a component is *involved*, it has received correct information about the datum to be transmitted and has the duty to forward this information in the clockwise direction. If a component is *unaware*, it is not (yet) involved in transmitting the datum. In particular the sender S is unaware if there is nothing to transmit. The idea behind the protocol is that initially all components are in the unaware mode. When the sender S reads a datum to be transmitted it gets involved. By transmitting data the components K, R, L and AR become subsequently involved. When AR signals the acknowledgement to S by $s_8(ac)$, it is clear that the datum has correctly been delivered, and all components fall back to the unaware mode. The invariant simply expresses that if a component is in the involved mode all components in the anti-clockwise direction up to and including the sender S must also be involved. With regard to the components K and R the invariant also expresses the property that if these components are involved, then the data that these contain must be equal to the datum of the sender.

Below we present a table indicating in which case a component is involved, and in case it is involved, what property should hold. It is left to the reader to check that the invariant indeed encodes the intuition explained above. Note that AS has been omitted as its parameters do not play a role in Sys.

Component	Condition for involvement	Property
S	$eq(i_s, 2)$	
K	$eq(b_s, b_k)$	$eq(d_s, d_k)$
R	$eq(i_r, 2) \vee eq(i_r, 3) \vee eq(b_s, inv(b_r))$	$eq(d_s, d_r)$
L	$eq(b_s, b_l)$	
AR	$eq(i_s', 2)$	

We write $\vec{d}$ for the vector $d_s, b_s, i_s, i_s', d_r, b_r, i_r, d_k, b_k, i_k, b_l, i_l$.

Lemma 5.5.4

$$I(\vec{d}) = \bigwedge_{j=1}^{6} I_j(\vec{d})$$

is an invariant of Sys.

5.5.1.4 *Abstraction and focus points*

The Concurrent Alternating Bit Protocol has unbounded internal behavior that occurs when the channels repeatedly lose data, when acknowledgements are repeatedly being sent by the receiver without being processed by the sender or when the sender repeatedly sends data to the receiver that it has already received. We define a pre-abstraction function to rename all actions in Z into τ except those that give rise to loops. So:

$$\xi(a)(\vec{d}) = \begin{cases} \mathsf{F} & \text{if } a = j', \\ eq(b_s, b_r) & \text{if } a = c_3, \\ \neg eq(b_s, b_r) & \text{if } a = c_6, \\ \mathsf{T} & \text{for all other } a \in \mathsf{Z}. \end{cases}$$

In case $a = j'$ either channel K or L distorts or loses data. In case $a = c_3$ and $\neg eq(b_s, b_r)$ data is being sent by the sender to the receiver that is subsequently ignored by the receiver. And in case $a = c_6$ and $eq(b_s, b_r)$, an acknowledgement sent by the receiver to the sender is ignored by the sender.

We can now derive the focus condition FC with respect to ξ. FC is the negation of the conditions that enable τ-steps in Sys. This results in a rather long formula, which is equivalent to the following formula (assuming that the invariant holds).

Lemma 5.5.5 *The invariant $I(\vec{d})$ implies that*

$$
\begin{aligned}
FC_{Sys,Z,\xi}(\vec{d}) = \\
eq(i'_s, 1) \wedge eq(i_l, 1) \wedge ((eq(i_s, 1) \wedge eq(i_k, 1)) \vee \\
(eq(i_r, 2) \wedge (eq(i_k, 3) \vee eq(i_k, 4)))).
\end{aligned}
$$

Lemma 5.5.6 $Sys(\vec{d})$ *is convergent w.r.t. ξ.*

Proof. We define a well-founded ordering $\sqsubset$ by means of the function f given below as follows: $\vec{a} \sqsubset \vec{b} \Leftrightarrow f(\vec{a}) < f(\vec{b})$, where $<$ is the usual "less than" ordering on the natural numbers. Since $<$ is well-founded on the natural numbers and — as can easily be checked — f decreases with every internal step of Sys_ξ as above, we see that $\sqsubset$ does the job.

Now we give the function f. For $\alpha \in \{k, l\}$, we let $(x_1, x_2, x_3, x_4)^\alpha$ abbreviate

$$
if(eq(i_\alpha, 1), x_1, if(eq(i_\alpha, 2), x_2, if(eq(i_\alpha, 3), x_3, x_4))).
$$

Define $f(d_s, b_s, i_s, i'_s, d_r, b_r, i_r, d_k, b_k, i_k, b_l, i_l)$ by

$$
if(eq(i_s, 2), 9, 0) + if(eq(i'_s, 2), 0, 3) + if(eq(i_r, 2), 0, 3) + if(eq(i_r, 3), 5, 0) +
$$
$$
if(eq(b_r, b_k), (2, 1, 0, 3)^k, (3, 5, 4, 4)^k) +
$$
$$
if(eq(b_s, b_l), (2, 1, 0, 3)^l, (3, 5, 4, 4)^l).
$$
$\hfill\square$

Theorem 5.5.7 *For all $d : D$ we have*

$$
\tau \tau_I(CABP(d)) = \tau B(d, \mathsf{T}).
$$

Proof. By Lemma 5.5.2 it suffices to prove, for all $d{:}D$:

$$
\tau \tau_I(Sys(d, e_0, 1, 1, d, e_0, 1, d, e_1, 1, e_1, 1)) = \tau B(d, \mathsf{T}).
$$

Note that the invariant I holds for the parameters of Sys such as displayed. So we can apply Theorem 5.4.4, taking Sys for Φ, B for Ψ, Sys' for Ξ, the set I for Z, $\{r_1, s_2\}$ for Ext, and I as invariant. It remains to pick an appropriate function h; this function will yield a pair consisting of a datum of type D and a boolean. We choose h to be:

$$h(\vec{d}) = \langle d_s, eq(i_s, 1) \vee eq(i_r, 3) \vee \neg eq(b_s, b_r) \rangle.$$

The first component is the datum that is read by the buffer when $eq(i_s, 1)$ and exported when $eq(i_r, 2)$. We can take d_s, because we can show that when action $s_2(d_r)$ happens, $d_s = d_r$.

The second component of the triple is the boolean formula that controls, in terms of the parameters $\vec{d}$ of Sys, whether the buffer is enabled to read (the formula is true) or enabled to write (the formula is false). Typically, Sys is able to read when $eq(i_s, 1)$ as the read action in the sender is enabled. The sender is also enabled to read (after some internal activity) when it is still waiting for an acknowledgement, but the proper acknowledgement is on its way. This case is characterized by $\neg eq(b_s, b_r)$. The same holds when the receiver has delivered a datum, but has not yet informed the acknowledgement handler AS. In this case $eq(i_r, 3)$ holds.

Next, we verify the conditions of Theorem 5.4.4. We get the following conditions (omitting trivial conditions):

(1) Sys is convergent w.r.t. ξ.
(2) (a) $eq(i_r, 3) \rightarrow \mathsf{T} = eq(i_s, 1) \vee \neg eq(b_s, inv(b_r))$
    (b) $eq(i_s, 2) \wedge eq(i'_s, 2) \rightarrow eq(i_r, 3) \vee \neg eq(b_s, b_r) = \mathsf{T}$.
(3) $eq(i_r, 2) \rightarrow \neg(eq(i_s, 1) \vee eq(i_r, 3) \vee \neg eq(b_s, b_r))$.
(4) (a) $FC_{Sys, \mathsf{Z}, \xi}(\vec{d}) \wedge (eq(i_s, 1) \vee eq(i_r, 3) \vee \neg eq(b_s, b_r)) \rightarrow eq(i_s, 1)$.
    (b) $FC_{Sys, \mathsf{Z}, \xi}(\vec{d}) \wedge \neg(eq(i_s, 1) \vee eq(i_r, 3) \vee \neg eq(b_s, b_r)) \rightarrow eq(i_r, 2)$.
(5) $eq(i_r, 2) \rightarrow d_r = d_s$.
(6) $eq(i_s, 1) \rightarrow eq(i_r, 3) \vee \neg eq(b_s, b_r) = \mathsf{F}$.

Lemma 5.5.6 takes care of condition 1. The remaining conditions are easily verified, under the invariant I. □

Acknowledgments

A preliminary version of this chapter was read by Doeko Bosscher, Dennis Dams, Wan Fokkink, David Griffioen, Henri Korver, Jaco van de Pol, Judi Romijn, Alex Sellink, and Frits Vaandrager. Their comments and subsequent discussions lead to many improvements. Example 5.3 is due to Frits Vaandrager.

Appendix A: Elementary Results

This appendix contains some technical lemmas, which are used in previous sections. We begin with simple properties of the $\_ \triangleleft \_ \triangleright \_$ operator and the $\sum$-operator.

Lemma 5.5.8 *For all processes x, y and (open) terms of sort $\mathcal{B}$ b, b_1, b_2 we have:*

(1) $x \triangleleft b \triangleright x = x$

(2) $x \triangleleft b \triangleright y = y \triangleleft \neg b \triangleright x$

(3) $x \triangleleft b \triangleright y = x \triangleleft b \triangleright \delta + y \triangleleft \neg b \triangleright \delta$

(4) $x \triangleleft b_1 \wedge b_2 \triangleright \delta = (x \triangleleft b_1 \triangleright \delta) \triangleleft b_2 \triangleright \delta$

(5) $x \triangleleft b_1 \vee b_2 \triangleright \delta = x \triangleleft b_1 \triangleright \delta + x \triangleleft b_2 \triangleright \delta$

Proof. (1), (2), (3): by induction on b, i.e. by distinguishing the cases where b equals T and where b equals F. (4), (5): by induction on b_1 and b_2. $\square$

Lemma 5.5.9 *If there is some $e{:}D$ such that $b(e)$ holds, then*

$$x = \sum_{d:D} x \triangleleft b(d) \triangleright \delta.$$

Proof.   Assume $b(e)$ holds.

$$\left(\sum_{d:D} x \triangleleft b(d) \triangleright \delta\right) \supseteq (x \triangleleft b(e) \triangleright \delta) = x = \left(\sum_{d:D} x\right) \supseteq \left(\sum_{d:D} x \triangleleft b(d) \triangleright \delta\right).$$

Note that in the first $\supseteq$-step we use axiom SUM3. In the second $=$-step, we use SUM1. The last step can be seen as follows.

$$
\begin{aligned}
\sum_{d:D} x &= \\
\sum_{d:D} (x \triangleleft b(d) \triangleright x) &= \\
\sum_{d:D} (x \triangleleft b(d) \triangleright \delta + x \triangleleft \neg b(d) \triangleright \delta) &= \\
\sum_{d:D} (x \triangleleft b(d) \triangleright \delta) + \sum_{d:D} (x \triangleleft \neg b(d) \triangleright \delta)
\end{aligned}
$$

We use Lemma 5.5.8.5.5.8 at the first step, and Lemma 5.5.8.5.5.8 at the second. At the last step SUM4 is used. Note that at the first two steps we also use SUM11. $\square$

The following result is a trivial corollary of τ-law B1.

Lemma 5.5.10 *Let Φ be an LPO. For all processes p and data $d : D$ we have*

$$\Phi p d = \Phi[\lambda d. p(d) \lhd b(d) \rhd \tau\, p(d)] d$$

The last two results concern LPOs extended with idle loops. They are used in Section 5.4. Remember that we assume that Ext, Z and $\{\tau\}$ are mutually disjoint and that $i \notin Ext \cup Z \cup \{\tau\}$.

Theorem 5.5.11 *Let Φ be a convergent LPO over $Ext \cup Z \cup \{\tau\}$ such that $i \notin Ext \cup Z \cup \{\tau\}$. Assume that p_1 is a solution of Φ, p_2 is a solution of $i(\Phi)$, and p_3 is a solution of $i_Z(\Phi)$. Then we have, for all $d : D$:*

(1) $\tau\, p_1(d) = \tau\, \tau_{\{i\}}(p_2(d))$,
(2) $\rho_Z(p_2(d)) = p_3(d)$ *and*
(3) $\tau\, \tau_Z(p_1(d)) = \tau\, \tau_{\{i\}}(p_3(d))$.

Proof.

(1) First we show $\lambda d. \tau\, p_1(d)$ and $\lambda d. \tau\, \tau_{\{i\}}(p_2(d))$ to be solutions of

$$\Psi \stackrel{\text{def}}{=} \lambda p. \lambda d{:}D_\Phi. \tau\, \Phi p d.$$

It is straightforward to see that $\lambda d. \tau\, p_1(d)$ is a solution of Ψ. We only prove that $\lambda d. \tau\, \tau_{\{i\}}(p_2(d))$ is a solution of Ψ.
As p_2 is a solution of $i(\Phi)$ it holds that

$$p_2(d) = \Phi p_2 d + i\, p_2(d).$$

By an application of KFAR we find:

$$\tau\, \tau_{\{i\}}(p_2(d)) = \tau\, \tau_{\{i\}}(\Phi p_2 d).$$

As i does not appear in Φ, we can distribute $\tau_{\{i\}}$ and we find:

$$\tau\, \tau_{\{i\}}(p_2(d)) = \tau(\Phi[\lambda d.(\tau_{\{i\}}(p_2(d)))]d).$$

So, $\lambda d. \tau\, \tau_{\{i\}}(p_2(d))$ is a solution of Ψ.
As Φ is convergent, Ψ is convergent. Hence, using the principle CL-RSP we find for all $d : D$

$$\tau\, p_1(d) = \tau\, \tau_{\{i\}}(p_2(d)).$$

(2) First observe that $i(\rho_Z(\Phi))$ and $\rho_Z(i(\Phi))$ are syntactically identical operators. So we may assume that p_3 is a solution of $\rho_Z(i(\Phi))$. Since p_2 is a solution of $i(\Phi)$, we also have that $\rho_Z(p_2(d))$ is a solution of $\rho_Z(i(\Phi))$. Since $\rho_Z(i(\Phi))$ is convergent, the desired equality follows from CL-RSP.

(3) By case 1 and 2 of this theorem we find:

$$\begin{aligned} \tau\, p_1(d) &= \tau\, \tau_{\{i\}}(p_2(d)) \\ \rho_Z(p_2(d)) &= p_3(d) \end{aligned} \qquad \textbf{(Ex7)}$$

Using the congruence properties we transform the second equation of (**Ex7**) above into:

$$\tau\, \tau_{\{i\}}(\rho_Z(p_2(d))) = \tau\, \tau_{\{i\}}(p_3(d)).$$

By axioms $R+$ and $T+$ this simplifies to:

$$\tau\, \tau_Z(\tau_{\{i\}}(p_2(d))) = \tau\, \tau_{\{i\}}(p_3(d)).$$

Using the first equation of (**Ex7**) and the Hiding laws TI, this is reduced to:

$$\tau\, \tau_Z(p_1(d)) = \tau\, \tau_{\{i\}}(p_3(d)),$$

which we had to prove. $\qquad\qquad\qquad\qquad\qquad\qquad\qquad\qquad\square$

Lemma 5.5.12 *Let Φ be an LPO that is convergent w.r.t. a pre-abstraction function ξ. Let p be a solution of Φ and p' be a solution of Φ_ξ. Then*

$$\tau_Z(p) = \tau_Z(p').$$

Proof. Consider the LPO Φ^ξ where every summand of the form

$$\sum_{e_a:E_a} a(f_a(d, e_a))\, p(g_a(d, e_a)) \lhd b_a(d, e_a) \rhd \delta$$

with $a \in Z$ is replaced by

$$\sum_{e_a:E_a} (i\, p(g_a(d, e_a)) \lhd \xi(a)(d, e_a) \rhd a(f_a(d, e_a))\, p(g_a(d, e_a))) \lhd b_a(d, e_a) \rhd \delta$$

where i is a fresh action. Assume Φ^ξ has solution p^ξ. Clearly, $\tau_{\{i\}}(p^\xi) = p'$ as both terms are a solution of Φ_ξ (use Lemma 5.5.8.5.5.8). Also $\rho_Z(p^\xi) =$

$\rho_Z(p)$ as both terms are solutions of $\rho_Z(\Phi)$. Furthermore, $\tau_{\{i\}}(p) = p$ as i does not occur in Φ (so both terms are solutions of Φ).

Using these observations and (at the second and fourth step) axioms R+ and T+, we derive:

$$\begin{aligned}
\tau_Z(p) &= \tau_Z(\tau_{\{i\}}(p)) \\
&= \tau_{\{i\}}(\rho_Z(p)) \\
&= \tau_{\{i\}}(\rho_Z(p^\xi)) \\
&= \tau_Z(\tau_{\{i\}}(p^\xi)) \\
&= \tau_Z(p')
\end{aligned}$$

$\square$

Appendix B: Axioms and Rules for μCRL

In this section, we present tables containing the axioms for the ACP operators, some axioms for the Sum and the conditional operator, plus some additional axioms that were necessary. In the tables, D is an arbitrary data type, d represents an element of D, x, y, z range over processes, a, b, i are actions, c, d represent either τ, δ or an action $a(d)$, and p, p_1, p_2 are process terms in which the variable d may occur. (Although some names are overloaded, the context makes clear what is meant. In Table 5.2, b also ranges over boolean terms.) Furthermore, R ranges over renaming functions, and I, I' and H range over sets of actions. If $R = \{a_1 \rightarrow b_1, \ldots, a_n \rightarrow b_n\}$, then $dom(R) = \{a_1, \ldots, a_n\}$ and $ran(R) = \{b_1, \ldots, b_n\}$. Finally, $\mathcal{D}$ in Table 5.2 ranges over derivations.

Beside these axioms, μCRL features two important principles: RSP, stating that guarded recursive specification have at most one solution, and an induction rule, for inductive reasoning over data types. For more information on μCRL, the reader is referred to Groote and Ponse (1994).

Table 5.1   Axioms for the ACP operators

A1 $x + y = y + x$	CM1 $x \parallel y = x \parallel\!\!\!\!\llcorner y + y \parallel\!\!\!\!\llcorner x + x \mid y$
A2 $x + (y + z) = (x + y) + z$	CM2 $c \parallel\!\!\!\!\llcorner x = c \cdot x$
A3 $x + x = x$	CM3 $c \cdot x \parallel\!\!\!\!\llcorner y = c \cdot (x \parallel y)$
A4 $(x + y) \cdot z = x \cdot z + y \cdot z$	CM4 $(x + y) \parallel\!\!\!\!\llcorner z = x \parallel\!\!\!\!\llcorner z + y \parallel\!\!\!\!\llcorner z$
A5 $(x \cdot y) \cdot z = x \cdot (y \cdot z)$	CM5 $c \cdot x \mid d = (c \mid d) \cdot x$
A6 $x + \delta = x$	CM6 $c \mid d \cdot x = (c \mid d) \cdot x$
A7 $\delta \cdot x = \delta$	CM7 $c \cdot x \mid d \cdot y = (c \mid d) \cdot (x \parallel y)$
B1 $x \cdot \tau = x$	CM8 $(x + y) \mid z = x \mid z + y \mid z$
B2 $z(\tau \cdot (x + y) + x) = z(x + y)$	CM9 $x \mid (y + z) = x \mid y + x \mid z$

CD1 $\delta \mid x = \delta$	DD $\partial_H(\delta) = \delta$
CD2 $x \mid \delta = \delta$	DT $\partial_H(\tau) = \tau$
CT1 $\tau \mid x = \delta$	D1 $\partial_H(a(d)) = a$ if $a \notin H$
CT2 $x \mid \tau = \delta$	D2 $\partial_H(a(d)) = \delta$ if $a \in H$
	D3 $\partial_H(x + y) = \partial_H(x) + \partial_H(y)$
	D4 $\partial_H(x \cdot y) = \partial_H(x) \cdot \partial_H(y)$
CF $a(d) \mid b(e) =$ $\begin{cases} \gamma(a,b)(d) & \text{if } d = e \text{ and} \\ & \gamma(a,b) \text{ defined} \\ \delta & \text{otherwise} \end{cases}$	

TID $\tau_I(\delta) = \delta$	RD $\rho_R(\delta) = \delta$
TIT $\tau_I(\tau) = \tau$	RT $\rho_R(\tau) = \tau$
TI1 $\tau_I(a(d)) = a(d)$ if $a \notin I$	R1 $\rho_R(a(d)) = R(a)(d)$
TI2 $\tau_I(a(d)) = \tau$ if $a \in I$	
TI3 $\tau_I(x + y) = \tau_I(x) + \tau_I(y)$	R3 $\rho_R(x + y) = \rho_R(x) + \rho_R(y)$
TI4 $\tau_I(x \cdot y) = \tau_I(x) \cdot \tau_I(y)$	R4 $\rho_R(x \cdot y) = \rho_R(x) \cdot \rho_R(y)$

Table 5.2 Axioms for Sum and Conditional

SUM1	$\Sigma_{d:D}p = p$	d not free in p
SUM2	$\Sigma_{d:D}p = \Sigma_{e:D}(p[e/d])$	e not free in p
SUM3	$\Sigma_{d:D}p = \Sigma_{d:D}p + p(d)$	
SUM4	$\Sigma_{d:D}(p_1 + p_2) = \Sigma_{d:D}p_1 + \Sigma_{d:D}p_2$	
SUM5	$\Sigma_{d:D}(p_1 \cdot p_2) = (\Sigma_{d:D}p_1) \cdot p_2$	d not free in p_2
SUM6	$\Sigma_{d:D}(p_1 \parallel p_2) = (\Sigma_{d:D}p_1) \parallel p_2$	d not free in p_2
SUM7	$\Sigma_{d:D}(p_1 \vert p_2) = (\Sigma_{d:D}p_1) \vert p_2$	d not free in p_2
SUM8	$\Sigma_{d:D}(\partial_H(p)) = \partial_H(\Sigma_{d:D}p)$	
SUM9	$\Sigma_{d:D}(\tau_I(p)) = \tau_I(\Sigma_{d:D}p)$	
SUM10	$\Sigma_{d:D}(\rho_R(p)) = \rho_R(\Sigma_{d:D}p)$	
SUM11	$\dfrac{\begin{array}{c}\mathcal{D}\\ p_1 = p_2\end{array}}{\Sigma_{d:D}(p_1) = \Sigma_{d:D}(p_2)}$	d not free in the assumptions of $\mathcal{D}$

BOOL1	$\neg(\mathsf{T} = \mathsf{F})$
BOOL2	$\neg(b = \mathsf{T}) \to b = \mathsf{F}$
COND1	$x \triangleleft \mathsf{T} \triangleright y = x$
COND2	$x \triangleleft \mathsf{F} \triangleright y = y$

Table 5.3 Some extra axioms needed in the verification

KFAR	$p(d) = i\,p(d) + y \to \tau\,\tau_{\{i\}}(p(d)) = \tau\,\tau_{\{i\}}(y)$	
T+	$\tau_I(\tau_{I'}(x)) = \tau_{I \cup I'}(x)$	
R+	$\tau_I(\rho_R(x)) = \tau_{I'}(x)$	if $ran(R) \subseteq I$ and $I' = I \cup dom(R)$
SC1	$(x \parallel y) \parallel z = x \parallel (y \parallel z)$	
SC3	$x\vert y = y\vert x$	
SC4	$(x\vert y)\vert z = x\vert(y\vert z)$	
SC5	$x\vert(y \parallel z) = (x\vert y) \parallel z$	

PART 2

Verification Methods for Real-Time Systems

Chapter 6

The Automatic Verification Using Symbolic Model-Checking

Satoshi Yamane

Abstract: It is important to verify timing conditions in real-time systems. The verification methods such as model checking and language inclusion algorithm, bisimulation method have been researched. Especially symbolic model checking is promising for verifying a large system. Time models are classified into discrete time model and dense time model. In discrete time model, symbolic model checker based on BDDs (Binary Decision Diagrams) has been developed. But in dense time model, symbolic model checking based on BDDs causes the state-explosion problem because of generating region graph from specification. In this chapter, we propose symbolic model checking based on BDDs in dense time model, which do not use region graph. In our proposed symbolic model checker, we represent state spaces by both BDDs and DBMs (Difference Bound Matrices). We have realized effective symbolic model checker based on BDDs in dense time model by proposed method.

Keywords: Real-time systems, verification, BDDs, symbolic model checking.

6.1 Introduction

It is important to formally verify whether specification satisfies verification properties or not in real-time systems, such as operating systems and communication protocols, logical circuits [Kavi 92]. In dense time model, formal verification methods are classified into language inclusion algorithm and model checking as follows [Alur 92c].

(1) If both specification and verification specification are described by timed automaton, verification problem reduces to language inclusion problem in formal language theory [Yamane 95a]. Language inclusion problem is decided if verification specification language is closed under complementation. Timed automaton is based on the ideas on coupling ω-automaton with timing constraints in dense time domain.

(2) If specification is described by timed Kripke structure and verification specification is described by real-time temporal logic, verification problem reduces to real-time model checking [Yamane 95b].

In this chapter, we focus on model checking, because many interesting verification properties are expressive. Especially, we focus on symbolic model checking [McMillan 93] based on BDDs (Binary Decision Diagrams) [Bryant 86], because we can avoid the state-explosion problem.

On the other hand, there are discrete time model and fictitious clock time model, dense time model [Alur 92c]. In discrete time model and fictitious clock time model, symbolic model checking systems such as [Campos 94] and [Yang 93] have been developed. But in discrete time model and fictitious clock time model, asynchronous real-time systems can not be specified and verified [Alur 91]. In this chapter, we try to specify real-time systems by dense time model and formally verify specification using model checking, especially symbolic model checking. In dense time model, symbolic model checkers such as the verifier of multi-clock automaton [Wang 93] and HYTECH [Alur 93b], KRONOS [Henzinger 92] have been developed. But there are some problems in these symbolic model checkers as follows.

(1) The verifier of multi-clock automaton requires large verification cost because of generating region graph [Alur 90a].

(2) HYTECH is implemented by both symbolic representation and semi-decision procedure using the Mathematica software package. But HYTECH is not implemented by BDDs.

(3) KRONOS is implemented by both symbolic representation and DBMs. But KRONOS is not implemented by BDDs.

From 1 and 2, 3, the dense time symbolic model checking based on BDDs without region graph have not yet been developed. For this reason, 1 and 2, 3 cause the state-explosion problem.

In this chapter, we develop symbolic model checking based on BDDs. In general, symbolic model checking is more effective than model checking because of image computation and BDDs. But in dense time model, it is difficult to verify systems because of timing constraints. We try to store state transitions and timing constraints by the form (s, x) where s is a set of states represented by BDDs and x is a set of timing constraints represented by DBMs. This form allows us to verify systems using dense time symbolic model checking. This form have been proposed for language inclusion algorithm by Dill D. and Wong-Toi H [Dill 95]. They have realized the real-time symbolic verification system based on BDDs and DBMs. We develop our real-time symbolic model checking based on their ideas. Our approach for verification of real-time systems is as follows.

(1) System specification, which is described by parallel composition of timed automata, is automatically transformed into timed Kripke structure.

(2) Dense time symbolic model checking is based on both BDDs and DBMs. For DBMs, we can avoid the state- explosion problem.

In Section 2 real-time specification is introduced. In Section 3 real-time temporal logic is introduced. In Section 4 real-time symbolic model checking is introduced. In Section 5 examples of formal specification and timing verification are introduced. In Section 6 conclusion is introduced.

6.2 Specification Method for Real-Time Systems

6.2.1 *Specification by Timed Buchi Automaton*

Each process is specified by timed Buchi automaton [Alur 92b] and system specification is the product automaton of timed Buchi automata. Because timed Buchi automaton is closed under union and intersection. Timed Kripke structure is automatically transformed from system specification.

Definition 6.1 Timed Buchi automaton is a $A = (\Sigma, S, S_0, C, E, F)$ where

(1) Σ: a finite set of events
(2) S: a finite set of states
(3) $S_0 \subseteq S$: a finite set of start states
(4) C: a finite set of clocks
(5) $E \subseteq S \times S \times \Sigma \times 2^C \times \Phi(C)$: a set of transitions

(6) $F \subseteq S$: accepting states
(7) $\Phi(C)$ represents timing constraints δ of clock C, and is recursively defined by a set X ($x \in X$) of clock variables and a time constant D as follows.

$$\delta ::= x \le D \,|\, D \le x \,|\, \neg\delta \,|\, \delta_1 \wedge \delta_2$$

An edge $(s, s', a, \lambda, \delta)$ represents a transition from state s to state s' on input symbol a. We represent this transition as follows.

$$s \xrightarrow{a, \lambda, \delta} s'$$

The set $\lambda \subseteq$ C gives the clocks to be reset with this transition. A run r of timed automaton over a word $\sigma \in \Sigma^\omega$ is an accepting run iff $inf(r) \cap F \ne 0$.

Definition 6.2   Consider timed Buchi automaton $A_i = (\Sigma, S_i, s_{0i}, C_i, E_i, F_i)$ ($i = 1, 2, \ldots, n$). Intersection can be implemented by a trivial modification of the standard product construction for Buchi automata as follows.

(1) The set of clocks for the product automaton A is $\cup C_i$.
(2) The states of A are of the form $(s_{j1} \times s_{j2} \times \ldots \times s_{jn})$, where each $s_{ji} \in S_i$, and $i = 1, 2, \ldots, n, j = 1, \ldots, m$.
(3) The initial state is of the form $(s_{01} \times s_{02} \times \ldots \times s_{0n})$, where each $s_{0i} \in S_i$, and $i = 1, 2, \ldots, n$.
(4) The set of transitions consists of $E_1 \times E_2 \times \ldots \times E_n$. The transition of A is obtained by coupling the transitions of the individual automaton having the same label. Let $\{\langle s_{ji}, s_{ki}, a, \lambda i, \delta i \rangle \in E_i | i = 1, 2, \ldots, n\}$ be a set of transitions with the same label a. Corresponding to this set, there is a joint transition of A out of each state of the form $(s_{j1} \times s_{j2} \times \ldots \times s_{jn})$ labeled with a. The new state is $(s_{k1} \times s_{k2} \times \ldots \times s_{kn})$ with j=k+1 mod n if $s_k \in F_k$ and $j = k$ otherwise.
(5) The set of clocks to be reset with the transition is $\cap \lambda i$, and the associated clock constraint is $\wedge \delta i$.
(6) The accepting set of A consists of $F_1 \times F_2 \times \ldots \times F_n$.

Theorem 6.1   *Timed Buchi automaton is closed under intersection.*
(Outline of proof)
According to [Definition 2], the class of timed language $L(A_1) \cap L(A_2)$ accepted by timed Buchi automaton $A_1 \times A_2$ is generated, where $L(A_i)$ is the class of timed language accepted by timed Buchi automaton A_i.

6.2.2 Generation of Timed Kripke Structure

It is necessary to generate timed Kripke structure from timed automaton in order to realize model checking. The generation method is the same as the reference [Hiraishi 90]. A timed Kripke structure T corresponding to a timed automaton A is defined to be a timed Kripke structure such that there exists one to one correspondence between the state-input sequences of A and the paths from one of an initial state. Next, we formally define the generation method of timed Kripke structure as follows.

Definition 6.3 $T = (S', \mu', R', \pi')$ be a timed Kripke structure. where

> (1) S': a finite set of states
> (2) μ': $S' \rightarrow 2^P$ assigns to each state the set of atomic propositions true in that state.
> (3) R': a binary relation on $S'(R' \subseteq S' \times S')$ which gives the possible transitions between states.
> (4) π': $S' \rightarrow 2^C \times \Phi(C)$ assigns to each state the set of clocks.

Next, we define operational semantics for a timed Kripke structure T in terms of a transition system. A timed-state of the system is a pair $q = (si', xi)$, $i = 0, \ldots, n$, where $s'_i \in S'$ is a state and x_i is a vector of clock values.

Definition 6.4   We define operational semantics for a timed Kripke structure T as follows.

> (1) The set q_0 of initial states is the set of all timed-states whose state component is an initial state in T, and whose clocks values are all equal to 0, as given by $q_0 = \{(s'_0, 0) | s'_0$ is the set of initial states$\}$.
> (2) For each transition $s'_i \rightarrow s'_{i+1}$, let
> $R' = \{(s'_i, x_i), (s'_{i+1}, x_{i+1}) | x_i \in \pi'(s'_i)$ and $x_{i+1} \in \pi'(s'_{i+1})$, $s'_i \times s'_{i+1} \in R'\}$.

Next, we define the generation of timed Kripke structure from a timed automaton.

Definition 6.5   Let $A = (\Sigma, S, S_0, C, E, F)$ be a timed automaton, and $T = (S', \mu', R', \pi')$ be a timed Kripke structure. The generation method is as follows.

> (1) $S' = E$

(2) $R' \subseteq E \times E$

(3) $\mu' = E \rightarrow 2^{\Sigma} = S' \rightarrow 2^{P}$

(4) $\pi' = E \rightarrow 2^{C} \times \Phi(C) = S' \rightarrow 2^{C} \times \Phi(C)$

Next, we explain that this transformation is compatible with the definition of truth of temporal logic.

Theorem 6.2 *For all timed automaton A and temporal logic ϕ, timed Kripke structures T, it holds that $\models_A \phi$ iff $\models_T \phi$*

(Proof)

From the definition of A, it follows that for each infinite sequence

$$s_0 \xrightarrow{a_0, \lambda_0, \delta_0} s_1 \xrightarrow{a_1, \lambda_1, \delta_1} s_2 \xrightarrow{a_2, \lambda_2, \delta_2} \cdots$$

of transitions of A there is a path $(s'_0, s'_1, s'_2, \ldots)$ of T,

such that

$$s_i \xrightarrow{a_i, \lambda_i, \delta_i} s_{i+1} \sim s'_i$$

for all

$$s_i \xrightarrow{a_i, \lambda_i, \delta_i} s_{i+1}$$

Conversely, for each infinite sequence $(s'_0, s'_1, s'_2, \ldots)$ of T, there is a path

$$s_0 \xrightarrow{a_0, \lambda_0, \delta_0} s_1 \xrightarrow{a_1, \lambda_1, \delta_1} s_2 \xrightarrow{a_2, \lambda_2, \delta_2} \cdots$$

of A such

$$s_i \xrightarrow{a_i, \lambda_i, \delta_i} s_{i+1} \sim s'_i$$

for all s'_i in the first sequence.

Next observe that if

$$s_i \xrightarrow{a_i, \lambda_i, \delta_i} s_{i+1} \sim s'_i$$

then $s_{i+1} \models_A \phi$ iff $si' \models_T \phi$. Using this observation and the above correspondence between sequences of transitions of A and sequences of states of T, we can induction over ϕ prove that for all transitions of A and states of T.

6.3 Real-Time Temporal Logic

Verification property specification is described in RTCTL (Real-Timed CTL), which expands TCTL (Timed CTL) [Alur 90a] with next state operator as follows.

Definition 6.6 The formulas ϕ of RTCTL are inductively defined as follows.

$\phi ::= p|\neg\phi|\phi_1 \to \phi_2|EX_{\sim}c\ \phi_1|\ E\ (\phi_1\ U_{\sim c}\ \phi_2)\ |EG_{\sim c}\ \phi_1$

(1) E: for some sequence of states a formula holds
(2) X: next states operator
(3) U: until operator
(4) G: always operator
(5) p $\in$ (atomic proposition)
(6) c $\in$ N (natural number)
(7) $\sim$ is binary relation $<, \leq, =, \geq, >$

Informally, E $(\phi_1\ U_{<c}\ \phi_2)$ means that for some sequence of states $s_0', s_1', s_2', \ldots$ there exits a sequence of states of time length less than C such that ϕ_2 holds at the last state and ϕ_1 holds at all its intermediate states.

Definition 6.7 We can specify all the temporal formulas using following syntactic abbreviations.

(1) EF $_{\sim c}\ \phi_1$ = E $(trueU_{\sim c}\ \phi_1)$
(2) AX $_{\sim c}\ \phi_1 = \neg E\neg X_{\sim c}\ \phi_1$
(3) AG $_{\sim c}\ \phi_1 = \neg EF_{\sim c}\ \neg\phi_1$
(4) A $\phi_1\ U_{\sim c}\ \phi_2 = E[\neg\phi_2\ U_{\sim c}\ \neg\phi_1 \wedge \neg\phi_2] \wedge \neg EG_{\sim c}\ \neg\phi_2$

Here we define RTCTL-semantics in order to interpret RTCTL-formula based on timed Kripke structure as follows.

Definition 6.8 For a timed Kripke structure $T = (S', \mu', R', \pi')$, a state $s_0' \in S_0'$, a sequence of states $s_0', s_1', \ldots, s_n'$ and a RTCTL-formula ϕ, the satisfaction relation $(T, s_0') \models \phi$ is defined inductively as follows.

(1) $(T, s_0') \models$ p iff p $\in \mu'\ (s_0')$.
(2) $(T, s_0') \models \neg\phi_1$ iff $(T, s_0') \models \phi_1$ is unsatisfiable.
(3) $(T, s_0') \models \phi_1 \to \phi_2$ iff $(T, s_0') \models \phi_1$ is unsatisfiable or $(T, s_0') \models \phi_2$.

(4) $(T, s'_0) \models EX_{\sim c} \phi_1$ iff for some state s'_1 such that (s'_0, s'_1) $\in R'$, $s'_1 \models \phi_1$ and $\sim c$ is satisfiable with $\mu'(s'_1)$.

(5) $(T, s'_0) \models E(\phi_1 U_{\sim c} \phi_2)$ iff for some sequence of states $(s'_0, \ldots, s'_n)$, $\exists i[i \geq \land (T, s'_i) \models \phi_2 \land \sim c$ is satisfiable with $\mu'(s'_i) \land \forall j[0 \leq j < i \rightarrow (T, s'_j) \models \phi_1 \land \sim c$ is satisfiable with $\mu'(s'_j)]]$

(6) $(T, s'_0) \models EG_{\sim c} \phi_1$ iff for some sequence of states $(s'_0, s'_1, \ldots, s'_n)$, $\forall i[0 \leq i \rightarrow (T, s'_i) \models \phi_1 \land \sim c$ is satisfiable with $\pi'(s'_i)]$

6.4 Verification Algorithm for Real-Time Symbolic Model Checking

In real-time symbolic model checking, for a timed Kripke structure T, we represent state transitions relation R' as BDDs and a set of states as the form (s'_i, x_i) $(i = 0, 1, \ldots, n)$, where $s'_i \in S'$ is a state represented by BDDs and x_i is a vector of clock values represented by DBMs(differences bounds matrices). In order to realize real-time symbolic model checking, we compute a set of states that satisfy the formulas by inverse image computation and test whether a set of states satisfy timing constraints using DBMs.

We define real-time symbolic model checking algorithm after defining inverse image computation and DBMs.

6.4.1 *Inverse Image Computation*

Many of the idea used in symbolic model checking can be explained by considering the problem of computing reachable state sets, since reachable state computations are at the heart of model checking [Burch 94]. Let s'_i be a set of states represented by the BDDs s'_i (V). We wish to compute a BDDs s'_j (V') that represents the states reachable from s'_i by the transitions in the transition relation R':

$$s'_j(V') = \exists V \cdot [s'_i(V) \land R'(V, V')].$$

This is called image computation. But in real-time symbolic model checking, we use inverse image computation. In inverse image computation, we compute a BDDs s'_i (V) that represents the states backward reachable from s'_j by the transitions in the transition relation R':

$$s'_i(V) = \exists V' \cdot [s'_j(V') \land R'(V, V')].$$

6.4.2 DBMs (*Differences Bounds Matrices*)

6.4.2.1 *Reachability Analysis (Test Timing Constraints)*

We can compute a set of states that satisfy the formulas using inverse image computation. But we must test whether a set of states satisfy timing constraints. We will test timing constraints (reachability analysis) using DBMs [Dill 89] [Alur 92a] as follows.

Definition 6.9 DBMs consists of the matrix of timer valuations. Timer valuations are defined as follows.

$\forall i, j \in C : t_i - t_j \leq d_{ij}$
where

(1) t_i: clock variable
(2) t_j: clock variable
(3) d_{ij}: clock constant

The (i, j)-element of DBMs is equal to d_{ij}. A fictitious clock t0 that is always exactly zero is introduced.

$d_{ij} \subseteq \{\ldots, -2, -1, 0, 1, 2, \ldots\} \cup \{\ldots, -2^-, -1^-, 0^-, 1^-, 2^-, \ldots\} \cup \{-\infty\} \cup \{\infty\}$.

The ordering $<$ over the integers is extended to d_{ij} by the following law: for any integer a, $-\infty < a^- < a < (a+1)^- < \infty$.

Next, we define reachability analysis using DBMs.

Definition 6.10 Generate the intersection of canonical DBMs, check reachability between two states. Here we check whether state $D \to D'$ is possible or not.

(1) **Canonical DBMs by Floyd-Warshall' algorithm.** Each inequality of DBMs is of the form $t_i - t_j \leq d_{i,j}$. An alternative formulation of it allows the construction of a constraint graph for a given set of inequalities. Each variable is represented as a node in the graph, and an inequality $t_i - t_j \leq d_{i,j}$ is represented by a directed edge with weight $d_{i,j}$ connecting t_i to t_j. For this reason, we can get canonical DBMs by Floyd-Warshall' algorithm [Cormen 90].

(2) **Intersect canonical DBMs.** Intersection DBMs = min $\{d_{ij}, d'_{ij}\}$ where

(a) $[d_{ij}]$: canonical DBMs of state D

(b) $[d'_{ij}]$: canonical DBMs of state D'

In dense time model, in order to reach D' from D, there is intersection DBMs between D and D'[19].

(3) **Test intersection DBMs.** If there is a negative-cost cycle in intersection DBMs, it is impossible to reach D' from D. If there is no negative-cost cycle in intersection DBMs, it is possible to do so.

Next, we explain the validity of reachability analysis as follows.

Theorem 6.3 *If there is a negative-cost cycle in intersection DBMs of D and D', it is impossible to reach D' from D.*
(*Proof*)
We call a sequence of clock variables $t_1, t_2, \ldots, t_n$. The cost of the path in intersection DBMs is $d_{t1,t2} + \ldots + d_{tn,t1}$. We can define $d_{t1,t2}, d_{t2,t3}, \ldots, d_{tn,t1}$ as follows.

$t_1 - t_2 \leq d_{t1,t2}$
$t_2 - t_3 \leq d_{t2,t3}$
$\ldots$

$t_n - t_1 \leq d_{tn,t1}$
The cost$=(t_1 - t_2) + (t_2 - t_3) + \ldots + (t_n - t_1) = t_1 - t_1$
If there is a negative-cost cycle $(t_1 - t_1 < 0)$, it is impossible to reach D' from D.

We must test whether a set of states satisfy $\sim cin \; \phi_1 \; U_{\sim c} \; \phi_2$. In other words, we test whether the time elapsed in traversing a sequence between ϕ_1 and ϕ_2 satisfies $\sim c$. We test it using a clock variable in DBMs as follows.

Definition 6.11 We define the computation of the time elapsed in traversing a sequence between s'_j and s'_k ($j < k$). We focus on some clock variable x in DBMs.

(1) **When x is not reset between s'_j and s'_k.** The timing constraint is $x \leq d$ or $x \geq d$ at s'_j and $x \leq h$ or $x \geq h$ at s'_k, where $d \leq h$. We compute the time elapsed in traversing a sequence between s'_j and s'_k.

(a) case $x \leq d$ and $x \leq h$: The elapsed time t is $t \leq h - d$.
(b) case $x \geq d$ and $x \geq h$: The elapsed time t is $t \geq h - d$.
(c) case $x \leq d$ and $x \geq h$: The elapsed time t is $t \geq h$.
(d) case $x \geq d$ and $x \leq h$: The elapsed time t is $t \leq h - d$.

(2) **When x is reset between s'_j and s'_k.** Assuming that x is reset at a state s'_l ($j < l < k$). We compute the time elapsed in traversing a sequence between s'_j and s'_l and the time elapsed in traversing a sequence between s'_l and s'_k. We compute the elapsed times using the same way as (1). Finally, we add the time elapsed in traversing a sequence between s'_j and s'_l and the time elapsed in traversing a sequence between s'_l and s'_k.

From (1) and (2), we can compute the time elapsed in traversing a sequence between s'_j and s'_k.

6.4.3 *Real-Time Symbolic Model Checking*

Finally, we define real-time symbolic model checking as follows.

Definition 6.12   The real-time symbolic model checking consists of following procedures.

(1) Firstly, we convert system specification into timed Kripke structure.

(2) Secondly, we represent state transitions relation R' as BDDs and a set of states as the form (s'_i, x_i) $(i = 0, 1, \ldots, n)$, where $s'_i \in S'$ is a state represented by BDDs and x_i is a vector of clock values represented by DBMs(differences bounds matrices).

(3) Next, we compute the set of states that satisfy every subformula using inverse image computation and we test whether the set of states satisfy timing constraints or not using DBMs. We test whether the time elapsed in traversing a sequence satisfy timing constraints in a formula(for example, $\sim c$ *in* E $(\phi 1 \ U_{\sim c} \ \phi 2)$.

(4) Finally, after determining the set S of states that satisfy the formula f, we test whether s'_0 is a subset of S(that is, whether $\neg s'_0$ (V) $\lor$ S(V) is the BDDs representing true.) If it is, then the timed Kripke structure satisfies f.

Next, we define real-time symbolic model checking algorithm as follows.

Definition 6.13   For given a structure $T = (S', \mu', R', \pi')$ and a temporal logic formula f, we determine whether $\models_T$ f. The algorithm is based on inverse image computation. Firstly, we compute the set of states that satisfy all subformulas of f of length 1, the second stage compute the set of states that satisfy all subformulas of f of length 2, and so on. At the end of ith stage, the set of states that satisfy the set of all subformula of length $\leq i$ will be computed. To perform computing the set of states at stage i, the set of states gathered in earlier stages is used. One can conclude that $\models_T f$ if the initial state (s_0') is a subset of the set of states. Let ϕ be a subformula of f. We compute the set of states that satisfy all subformulas ϕ of f of length 1 as follows.

(1) $\phi \in p$(atomic proposition)
   nothing to do

(2) $\phi = \neg\phi_1$
   return $\neg s\phi_1(V)$
   where $s\phi_1(V)$ means the set of states that satisfy ϕ_1 represented by BDDs

(3) $\phi = \phi_1 \rightarrow \phi_2$
   return $\neg s\phi_1(V) \vee s\phi_2(V)$

(4) $\phi = EX_{\sim c}\phi_1$
   return $functionEX\phi_1\ (EX\phi_1(V), \sim c)$
   functionEX $\phi_1\ (EX\phi_1(V)\ ,\sim c\ )$
   $EX\phi_1(V) = \exists V' \cdot [R'(V, V') \wedge \phi1(V)]$;
   If $\sim c$ is not satisfiable with $\phi'(EX\phi_1(V)')$, we compute $EX\phi_1(V)$ as follows.
   $EX\phi_1(V) := EX\phi_1(V) - EX\phi_1(V)'$;
   We test whether $EX\phi_1(V)$ is reachable from $\phi_1(V)$ satisfying timing constraints;
   If there is the set of states $EX\phi_1(V)'$ that does not satisfy timing constraints,
   we compute $EX\phi_1(V)$ as follows.
   $EX\phi_1(V) := EX\phi_1(V) - EX\phi_1(V)'$;
   return $EX\phi_1(V)$;
   end $functionEX\phi_1$;

(5) $\phi = E\phi_1\ U_{\sim c}\ \phi_2$
   $T(V) := \phi_2(V)$;
   repeat {
   $U(V) := \phi_1(V) \wedge \exists V' \cdot [R'(V, V') \wedge T(V')]$;
   If there is the set of states $\pi'(U(V)')$ that does not satisfy $\sim c$,
   we compute $U(V)$ as follows.
   $U(V) := U(V) - U(V)'$;

If there is the set of states $U(V)'$ that does not satisfy timing constraints, we compute $U(V)$ as follows.

$U(V) := U(V) - U(V)'$;

If $U(V)$ is included in $\phi_1(V)$, return $\phi_1(V)$;

If $U(V)$ is not included in $\phi_1(V)$, $T(V) := U(V) + T(V)$;

}

(6) $\phi = EG_{\sim c}\phi_1$

$T(V) := \phi_1(V)$;

repeat {

$U(V) := \phi_1(V) \wedge functionEX\phi_1(T(V), \sim c)$;

If $U(V)$ is equal to $\phi_1(V)$, $\phi_1(V) := T(V)$ and return $\phi_1(V)$;

$T(V) := U(V)$;

}

6.5 The Verification System

6.5.1 *Configuration of the Verification System*

We have developed the verification system based on this method using SBDD library [Minato 90]. It runs on SUN4/IP (12MB). The verification system consists of compiler (1kstep) and real-time symbolic model checker (3kstep), which are implemented in C language.

6.5.2 *Verification Example*

6.5.2.1 *Specification*

We present here the timed automata for the senders and the receivers of the CSMA/CD protocol [Ins 85] [Nicollin 92]. The specification consists of sender and receiver. The sender stays in initial state s_0 until it receives a message. Then, it tests the bus to see if it is ready or busy, collision detection. In receiver, at initial state R_0, it is ready to be in the transmission of a message. If one of the senders starts sending, the receiver sets to zero the timer y. When y is less than or equal to 5,the bus is sensed idle for the other sender.

Table 6.1　Verification cost

Verification property				Cost	
$EF_{\geq 0} send$				T	
		symbolic model checking		model checking	
states	trans.	memory(Kb)	time(s)	memory(Kb)	time(s)
124	355	1004	1.86	218	1.10
948	3984	1384	32.73	886	11.88
3484	19082	1517	270.29	2011	150.93
5665	32445	1470	646.88	not enough	not enough
11091	66057	1683	1829.96	not enough	not enough
14356	86102	1694	1998.86	not enough	not enough

6.5.2.2　*Verification*

We have verified using real-time symbolic model-checker whether verification properties by RTCTL are satisfiable in specification. We input timed automata into compiler by the programming language format.

The verification properties are (1) EF send and (2) EF(send $\vee$ E (ready U $_{\leq 5}$ end)), (3) EF(send $\vee$ E(ready U $_{\leq 10}$ end)), (4) EG($send \vee ready \wedge begin$) as shown in Fig. 6.1. In order to compare real-time symbolic model-checker and real-time model-checker, we have verified using real-time model-checker whether verification properties by RTCTL are satisfiable in specification in Tables 6.1, 6.2, 6.3 and 6.4. We have already reported real-time model-checker [Yamane 95b]. When we have verified it using real-time model-checker, we cannot verify 5665 states because of being not enough memory. But we can verify more than 14588 states using real-time symbolic model-checker in Table 6.2. For this, we can avoid the state-explosion problem. We can show symbolic model-checking fro dense time real-time systems is effective.

(a) $EF_{\geq 0} send$
(b) $EF_{\geq 0}(send \vee E[ready U_{\leq 5} end])$
(c) $EG_{\geq 0}(send \vee E[begin U_{\leq 5} end])$
(d) $AF_{\geq 0}(send \vee E[begin U_{\leq 20} end])$

Fig. 6.1　Verification property specification

Table 6.2   Verification cost

Verification property				Cost	
$EF_{\geq 0}(send \vee E[readyU_{\leq 5}end])$				T	
		symbolic model checking		model checking	
states	trans.	memory(Kb)	time(s)	memory(Kb)	time(s)
124	355	1046	2.33	239	1.03
948	3984	1076	41.31	905	12.06
3484	19082	1550	323.44	2104	151.64
5665	32445	1648	833.71	not enough	not enough
11091	66057	1481	3029.27	not enough	not enough
14356	86102	1743	4434.68	not enough	not enough

Table 6.3   Verification cost

Verification property				Cost	
$EG_{\geq 0}(send \vee E[beginU_{\geq 5}end])$				F	
		symbolic model checking		model checking	
states	trans.	memory(Kb)	time(s)	memory(Kb)	time(s)
124	355	1044	2.27	207	1.08
948	3984	1405	41.06	895	11.91
3484	19082	1531	307.71	2104	151.23
5665	32445	1372	813.03	not enough	not enough
11091	66057	1252	2839.80	not enough	not enough
14356	86102	1709	3346.28	not enough	not enough

Table 6.4   Verification cost

Verification property				Cost	
$AF_{\geq 0}(send \vee E[beginU_{le20}end])$				T	
		symbolic model checking		model checking	
states	trans.	memory(Kb)	time(s)	memory(Kb)	time(s)
124	355	1050	2.41	207	1.08
948	3984	1109	38.23	876	11.98
3484	19082	1371	256.49	2104	151.22
5665	32445	1508	618.21	not enough	not enough
11091	66057	1506	1960.00	not enough	not enough
14356	86102	1751	3419.47	not enough	not enough

6.6   Conclusion

In this chapter, we have proposed a real-time symbolic model checking method based on both BDDs and DBMs. We have developed the verification system and shown it effective by the CSMA/CD protocol. We can avoid the state-explosion problem. But we cannot verify 10^{20} states such as [McMillan 93]. This shows the verification system for dense time systems is high cost. But the dense time has a desirable feature for representing two causally independent events in asynchronous real-time systems. In order to verify very large systems, we are developing the compositional verification system.

Chapter 7

Property Verification within a Process Algebra Framework

A. Cerone and G. J. Milne

7.1 Introduction

Since the 1980s, process algebras have been successfully used to model concurrent systems and to verify equivalence between the specification and the implementation of a system. The combination of process algebra and temporal logic through the technique of *model checking* [Clarke 86] has allowed the development of tools for the automatic verification of properties of systems. The most recent tools are based on a symbolic representation of the state space (*symbolic model checking*) [McMillan 93] and allow the verification of systems with a large number of states.

Since such tools involve two different formalisms, the process algebra and the logic, their use is often very hard for non expert users. The critical step is the specification within the logic of the properties of a system that is modeled within the process algebra. Properties based on events performed by processes have to be thought again in terms of logical formulas and this procedure can easily generate errors.

In this chapter we present a methodology for the automatic verification of concurrent systems, which is based on the characterization of temporal properties within *Circal* [Milne 94; Moller 89], a process algebra in which processes can be guarded by sets of simultaneous actions and such actions can be shared over an arbitrary number of processes.

We introduce *SAUB* [Cerone 00], a branching time temporal logic whose temporal operators are based on actions rather than on states. Several modal and temporal logics based on actions [De Nicola 90; Hennessy 85; Stirling 96] have been developed to describe properties of processes. With respect to the previous logics, SAUB has the additional feature of expressing also simultaneity between actions and this makes it suitable to describe properties of Circal processes.

The distinctive features of Circal support a *constraint-based* modeling [Vissers 91; Milne 94]: the behavior of a process may be constrained simply by composing it with another process, which represents the constraints. This modeling technique is the basis for verifying properties within the process algebra. A property of a process can be characterized in terms of another process so that one of the two processes constrains the other only when the property does not hold. This approach can be applied when the property to be tested is characterized in terms of a well-known model that satisfies it (*model-based* characterization) and is very useful in the verification of safety properties.

A more sophisticated approach leads to a characterization of general SAUB formulas in terms of Circal processes (*formula-based* characterization). A property can be characterized within Circal through a translation of the SAUB formula that describes it into a set of processes and into the rules to compose these processes with one another. The two processes obtained by the application of the rules are then tested for equivalence.

In both approaches the property verification is reduced to an equivalence between processes that can be automatically verified within the *Circal System*, the mechanization of the Circal process algebra. This methodology has been successfully applied to the specification and automatic verification of an audio control protocol developed by Philips [Cerone 96; Cerone 97a] and to handshaking control circuits of asynchronous micropipelined processors [Cerone 97b; Cerone 99].

7.2   The Circal Process Algebra

In this section we give a brief description of the Circal operators and their semantics and refer the reader to the book by Milne [Milne 94] and the paper by Moller [Moller 89] for further explanations. To describe and analyze a system, the user works with the language XCircal, the extention of the Circal process algebra that is automated by the Circal System [Milne 94].

The syntax of Circal processes is summarized by the following BNF expressions, where P is a process, D a process definition, $\mathcal{A}$ is the set of possible actions, $m \subseteq \mathcal{A}$, $a, b \in \mathcal{A}$ and I is a process variable:

$$P ::= /\backslash \mid mP \mid P + P \mid P \,\&\, P \mid I \mid P * P \mid P - m \mid P\,[a/b]$$
$$D ::= I < - P$$

7.2.1 Informal Semantics

Each Circal process has associated with it a *sort*, which specifies the set of actions (ports) through which it may interact with other processes. Every sort will be a non empty subset of $\mathcal{A}$, the collection of all available actions. The set of processes of sort L is denoted by $\mathcal{P}_L$. The set of all processes is $\mathcal{P} \stackrel{\text{def}}{=} \bigcup_{L \subseteq \mathcal{A}} \mathcal{P}_L$. If some action $a \in \mathcal{A}$ is in the sort of some interacting process, then a communication (synchronization) cannot occur via the port a unless the process in question allows it. A synchronization event involving any port $a \in \mathcal{A}$ not in the sort of an interacting process may occur without regard to the process in question. Set of actions occur simultaneously in the communication and may be shared over arbitrary numbers of processes. The role of each Circal operator can be described as follows:

Termination. $/\backslash$ is a constant representing a process which can participate in no communication. This is a process that has terminated or deadlocked. There is actually a whole family $\{/\backslash_L\}_{L \subseteq \mathcal{A}}$ of such constants.

Guarding. Single or simultaneous guards are permitted. For example

$$P < - (a\ b)\ P'$$

represents the process P which will perform a and b simultaneously, and then evolve into P'. The fact that processes may be guarded by sets of simultaneously occurring actions is a key feature of Circal which greatly enriches the modeling potential of the algebra in contrast to process algebras such as CCS [Milner 89] and CSP [Hoare 85] which only permit a single action to occur at one computation instant. An example of a single guard is

$$P < - a\ P'$$

in which process P performs the single action a and evolves to P'. In this case a is a shorthand for (a).

Definition. A name can be given to a Circal process with the definition operator. Recursive process definitions are permitted; for example

$$P < - (a\ b)\ P$$

is interpreted as a process that continuously repeats the simultaneous actions $(a\ b)$.

Choice. The term $P + Q$ represents the process which can perform either the actions of the subterm P or the actions of the subterm Q. The choice is decided by the environment in which the process is executed. For example, the following process can perform a or b or c

$$P < - a\ P + b\ P + c\ P'$$

The choice is made depending on the action available from the environment.

Non-determinism. The term $P\&Q$ represents the process which can perform either the actions of the subterm P or the actions of the subterm Q. The computation path is decided autonomously by the process itself without any influence from its environment. For example, the following process can perform a or b or c

$$P < - a\ P\ \&\ b\ P\ \&\ c\ P'$$

independently of which actions are supplied by the environment. If P chooses to perform a, and a is not supplied by the environment, then P terminates.

Concurrent Composition. Given processes P and Q, the term $P * Q$ represents the process which can perform the actions of the subterms P and Q together (*composition*). Any synchronization which can be made between two terms, due to some atomic action being common to the sorts of both subterms, must be made, otherwise the actions of the subterms may occur asynchronously.

Abstraction. The term $P - a$ represents the process that is identical to P except that the port a is invisible to the environment. We will use $P - a\,b\,c$ as a shorthand for $((P - a) - b) - c$.

Relabeling. The term $P[b/a]$ is the new version of P in which the action b replaces a wherever a occurs in P.

7.2.2 Formal Semantics

The formal semantics of Circal [Moller 89] is given in terms of transition systems labeled with set of actions.

Definition 7.1 A *Labeled Transition System* (LTS) is a structure. $\mathcal{T} = \langle \mathcal{S}, \mathcal{A}, \rightarrow, s_0 \rangle$ where

- $\mathcal{S}$ is a finite set of *states*;
- $\mathcal{A}$ is a finite, non empty set of *actions*;
- $\rightarrow \subseteq \mathcal{S} \times 2^{\mathcal{A}} \times \mathcal{S}$ is a *transition relation*, whose generic element (s_1, μ, s_2) is usually written as $s_1 \xrightarrow{\mu} s_2$.

State s_0 is called the *initial state*.

A *generalized transition* $p \xRightarrow{\mu}_{\mathcal{T}} q$ is defined by

$$p \xRightarrow{\mu}_{\mathcal{T}} q \quad \text{iff} \quad p \xrightarrow{\emptyset}_* p' \xrightarrow{\mu} p'' \xrightarrow{\emptyset}_* q \quad \text{for some } p', p''$$

where $\xrightarrow{\emptyset}_*$ is the reflexive and transitive closure of $\xrightarrow{\emptyset}$. A path on $\mathcal{T}$ is an infinite sequence of states $s_1 s_2 s_3...$ such that for each $i \geq 1$ there exists $\mu \in 2^{\mathcal{A}}$ such that $s_i \xrightarrow{\mu} s_{i+1}$. The set of paths on $\mathcal{T}$ starting from $s \in \mathcal{S}$ is denoted by $\Pi_{\mathcal{T}}(s)$.

For each $s \in \mathcal{S}$ the *successor set* of s is

$$\Theta_{\mathcal{T}}(s) \overset{\text{def}}{=} \{ \mu \in 2^{\mathcal{A}} \mid \mu \neq \emptyset \ \text{ and } \ s \xRightarrow{\mu}_{\mathcal{T}} s' \ \text{ for some } s' \in \mathcal{S} \}.$$

Definition 7.2 Let $\mathcal{T}_1 = \langle \mathcal{S}_1, \mathcal{A}_1, \rightarrow_1, s_1 \rangle$ and $\mathcal{T}_2 = \langle \mathcal{S}_2, \mathcal{A}_2, \rightarrow_2, s_2 \rangle$ two LTS. Then

- $\mathcal{T}_1 \sqsubseteq_{\text{may}} \mathcal{T}_2$ if and only if for each $\mu \in 2^{\mathcal{A}}$ for each $p_1 \in \mathcal{S}_1$, $s_1 \xRightarrow{\mu}_{\mathcal{T}_1} p_1$ implies $s_2 \xRightarrow{\mu}_{\mathcal{T}_2} p_2$ for some $p_2 \in \mathcal{S}_2$;
- $\mathcal{T}_1 \sqsubseteq_{\text{must}} \mathcal{T}_2$ if and only if for each $\mu \in 2^{\mathcal{A}}$ for each $p_2 \in \mathcal{S}_2$, $s_2 \xRightarrow{\mu}_{\mathcal{T}_2} p_2$ implies $s_1 \xRightarrow{\mu}_{\mathcal{T}_1} p_1$ for some $p_1 \in \mathcal{S}_1$ such that $\Theta_{\mathcal{T}_1}(p_1) \subseteq \Theta_{\mathcal{T}_2}(p_2)$;
- $\mathcal{T}_1 \sqsubseteq \mathcal{T}_2$ if and only if $\mathcal{T}_1 \sqsubseteq_{\text{may}} \mathcal{T}_2$ and $\mathcal{T}_1 \sqsubseteq_{\text{must}} \mathcal{T}_2$.

Definition 7.3 Let $\mathcal{A}$ the set of all available actions. The semantics of a Circal program $R \in \mathcal{P}_L$ is the labeled transition system

$$\mathcal{B}(R) = \langle \mathcal{S}, \mathcal{A}, \rightarrow, R \rangle$$

such that $\rightarrow$ is the least relation that satisfies the following conditions:

- $P \rightarrow P$ and $\mu P \xrightarrow{\mu} P$;
- if $P \rightarrow P'$, then $P + Q \rightarrow P' + Q$ and $Q + P \rightarrow Q + P'$;
- if $P \xrightarrow{\mu} P'$ for $\mu \neq \emptyset$, then $P + Q \xrightarrow{\mu} P'$ and $Q + P \xrightarrow{\mu} P'$;
- $P\&Q \rightarrow P$ and $P\&Q \rightarrow Q$;
- if $P \in \mathcal{P}_{L_1}$, $Q \in \mathcal{P}_{L_2}$, $P \xrightarrow{\mu} P'$, $Q \xrightarrow{\nu} Q'$ and $\mu \cap L_2 = \nu \cap L_1$, then $P * Q \xrightarrow{\mu \cup \nu} P' * Q'$;
- for any $L \subseteq \mathcal{A}$ if $P \xrightarrow{\mu} P'$, then $P - L \xrightarrow{\mu \setminus L} P'$.

Definition 7.4 The *behavioral inclusion:* of $P \in \mathcal{P}_L$ in $Q \in \mathcal{P}_M$ is defined as follows.

$$P \sqsubseteq Q \quad \text{iff} \quad \mathcal{B}(P) \sqsubseteq \mathcal{B}(Q).$$

Definition 7.5 The *equivalence:* of $P \in \mathcal{P}_L$ and $Q \in \mathcal{P}_M$ is defined as follows.

$$P \cong Q \quad \text{iff} \quad P \sqsubseteq Q \quad \text{and} \quad Q \sqsubseteq P.$$

The equivalence between two processes is implemented by the Circal System giving to the expression

$$P == Q$$

the result `true`, if $P \cong Q$ and `false`, otherwise.

7.3   The Methodology

As with any process algebra, the Circal process algebra is a low level language containing the primitive constructs to model concurrency. For this reason it is a very flexible language and it is possible to develop modeling styles that allow the description of high level aspects of concurrent systems, as well as application-oriented modeling styles.

One modeling style that is very useful in several application domains, and in particular in the description of communication protocols [Cerone 96; Cerone 97a] is the *constraint-based* modeling style [Vissers 91; Milne 94].

7.4 Constraint-Based Modeling

The constraint-based modeling style is supported by the following distinctive features of the Circal process algebra:

- guarding of processes by sets of simultaneous actions;
- sharing of events over arbitrary numbers of processes;
- the particular nature of the composition operator which provides synchronization between processes without removal of the synchronizing events in the resultant behavior.

The behavior of a process may be constrained simply by composing it with another Circal process which represents the constraint. As an example, consider the process $P \in \mathcal{P}_{\{a,b,c\}}$ defined as follows:

$$P < - a B + b A + c P$$
$$A < - a B + c A$$
$$B < - b A + c B$$

Process P generates all the finite strings on the alphabet $\{a, b, c\}$ that consist of alternating occurrences of a and b and arbitrary occurrences of c. Three constraints for process P are processes $C1 \in \mathcal{P}_{\{a,b,c\}}$ and $C2 \in \mathcal{P}_{\{b,c\}}$ and $C3 \in \mathcal{P}_{\{c\}}$ defined as follows

$$C1 < - a S$$
$$S < - a S + b S + c S$$

$$C2 < - b C + c D$$
$$C < - c D$$
$$D < - b C$$

$$C3 < - /\backslash_{\{c\}}$$

Since P and $C1$ have the same sort and at the initial state $C1$ can perform only a the composite process $P * C1$ must perform a as the first action. Then $C1$ evolves to S, which can perform every possible sequence of action. Therefore, process $C1$ constrains the string to start with an occurrence of a with any arbitrary behavior then following. Process $C2$ constrains b and c

to occur in alternation, whereas it does not affect the occurrences of action a, which does not belong to its sort. Process $C3$ has only c in its sort. Thus P can perform c only synchronously with $C3$, but $C3$ terminates immediately without performing any actions. Therefore C constrains P not to perform c.

Example 7.1   An important element in a protocol specification is the *assumptions* about the environment in which the protocol is executed [Holzmann 90]. The constraint-based modeling permits to specify these assumptions within a process that will be composed with the specification of the protocol.

In the protocol verified by Cerone *et al.* [Cerone 96] messages consist of finite sequences of 0 and 1 bits and are encoded by a sender, according to a Manchester encoding scheme, into transitions of the voltage between two levels on the single wire bus connecting the components. Since downgoing transitions take a significant time to change from high to low level, they do not appear to the receiver as edges. So the receiver can observe only upgoing edges and this causes a loss of information during the transmission, which results in an ambiguity in the decoding by the receiver. This ambiguity is overcome by *assuming* that the protocol will always work in an environment that guarantees the following constraints on the input:

- Every message starts with the bit 1;
- Every message either has an odd length or ends with 00.

A sequence of messages is readily modeled in Circal by a nested series of guarded processes where the guards are events consisting of single actions that can describe a bit 0, or a bit 1, or the "end of the message". Different actions are used for input and output message. We represents 0, 1 and "end of the message" in the input by i_0, i_1 and i_e, respectively, and in the output by o_0, o_1 and o_e, respectively. For example the sequence of 2 messages, given by the message 101 followed by the message 1100 is represented in the input by the process

$$M_i = i_1\, i_0\, i_1\, i_e\, i_1\, i_1\, i_0\, i_0\, i_e\, /\backslash$$

and in the output by the process

$$M_o = o_1\, o_0\, o_1\, o_e\, o_1\, o_1\, o_0\, o_0\, o_e\, /\backslash$$

The assumption about the environment is modeled by the process Con defined as follows:

$$Con < - i_1 O_1$$
$$O_0 < - i_0 E_{00} + i_1 E + i_e Con$$
$$O_1 < - i_0 E + i_1 E + i_e Con$$
$$E_{00} < - i_0 O_0 + i_1 O_1 + i_e Con$$
$$E < - i_0 O_0 + i_1 O_1$$

We can notice that the "end of the message" i_e appears only in the states that define an odd length (O_0 and O_1) or an even length with the last two bits equal to 0 (E_{00}).

The constraint-based modeling style supported by the Circal process algebra has been used in other application domains, such as asynchronous hardware [Cerone 97b; Cerone 99] and also allows the modeling of *timing constraints* [Cerone 97c; Cerone 97b]

7.5   A Temporal Logic for Simultaneous Actions

In this section we define, the *Simultaneous Action Unified Branching* Logic (SAUB) [Cerone 00], a branching time temporal logic whose temporal operators are based on actions. With respect to the previous logics based on actions, SAUB has the additional feature of expressing also simultaneity between actions. Therefore it permits to discriminate between *true concurrency* and *non deterministic interleaving*. We give here only a brief introduction to the logic and we refer the reader to the technical report [Cerone 00] for further explanations.

Definition 7.6   The syntax of the *action formulas* on $\mathcal{A}$ is given by

$$AF ::= \epsilon \mid A \mid \neg AF \mid AF \vee AF$$
$$A ::= a \quad \text{for each } a \in \mathcal{A}$$

The set of all the action formulas on $\mathcal{A}$ is denoted by $\mathcal{AF}(\mathcal{A})$.

Definition 7.7 Let $\mathcal{A}$ be a finite, non empty set of actions. Then for each $a \in \mathcal{A}$, $f, f_1, f_2 \in \mathcal{AF}(\mathcal{A})$ and $\mu \in 2^{\mathcal{A}}$

$$
\begin{array}{lll}
\mu, \mathcal{A} \models \epsilon & \text{iff} & \mu = \emptyset \\
\mu, \mathcal{A} \models a & \text{iff} & a \in \mu \\
\mu, \mathcal{A} \models \neg f & \text{iff} & \mu, \mathcal{A} \not\models f \\
\mu, \mathcal{A} \models f_1 \vee f_2 & \text{iff} & \mu, \mathcal{A} \models f_1 \ \text{ or } \ \mu, \mathcal{A} \models f_2
\end{array}
$$

Definition 7.8 For each $f \in \mathcal{AF}(\mathcal{A})$ we define

$$
C_{\mathcal{A}}(f) \stackrel{\text{def}}{=} \{\mu \in 2^{\mathcal{A}} | \mu, \mathcal{A} \models f\}.
$$

Definition 7.9 We define the following derived operators:

$$
\mathbf{1}_{\mathcal{A}} \stackrel{\text{def}}{=} \epsilon \vee \bigvee \mathcal{A}
$$

$$
\mathbf{0}_{\mathcal{A}} \stackrel{\text{def}}{=} \neg \mathbf{1}_{\mathcal{A}}
$$

$$
f_1 \wedge f_2 \stackrel{\text{def}}{=} \neg(\neg f_1 \vee \neg f_2)
$$

$$
f_1 \rightarrow f_2 \stackrel{\text{def}}{=} \neg f_1 \vee f_2
$$

$$
f_1 \leftrightarrow f_2 \stackrel{\text{def}}{=} (f_1 \rightarrow f_2) \wedge (f_1 \rightarrow f_2)
$$

Definition 7.10 For each $\mu \in 2^{\mathcal{A}}$ we define the *characterizing formula* of μ as follows.

$$
f_\mu = \begin{cases} \neg\epsilon \wedge \bigvee_{a \in \mathcal{A} \setminus \mu} \neg a \wedge \bigvee_{a \in \mathcal{A} \setminus \mu} a \text{ if } \mu \neq \emptyset \\ \\ \epsilon \wedge \bigvee_{a \in \mathcal{A}} \neg a \wedge \qquad\qquad\qquad \text{otherwise} \end{cases}
$$

The following theorem shows that f_μ characterizes completely the set $\mu \in 2^{\mathcal{A}}$ It is a simple consequence of Definition 7.8 [Cerone 00].

Theorem 7.1 *For each* $\mu \in 2^{\mathcal{A}}$

$$
C_{\mathcal{A}}(f_\mu) = \{\mu\}.
$$

Definition 7.11 The syntax of *temporal formulas* on $\mathcal{A}$ is given by

$$
\begin{aligned}
F ::= \ & \forall AF \ldots AF \square AF \\
| \ & \exists AF \ldots AF \square AF \\
| \ & \neg F \mid F \vee F \\
| \ & \forall AF \ldots AF \square F \\
| \ & \exists AF \ldots AF \square F
\end{aligned}
$$

The set of all the temporal formulas on $\mathcal{A}$ is denoted by $\mathcal{F}(\mathcal{A})$.

Definition 7.12   Let $\mathcal{T} = \langle \mathcal{S}, \mathcal{A}, \rightarrow, s_0 \rangle$ be a LTS . Then for each $f, f_1, \ldots, f_n \in \mathcal{AF}(\mathcal{A})$ and $F, F_1, F_2 \in \mathcal{F}(\mathcal{A})$

$s_0, \mathcal{T} \models \forall f_1, \ldots, f_n \square f$
   iff   for all $s_1, \ldots, s_n \in \mathcal{S}$ for all $\mu_1, \ldots, \mu_n \in 2^{\mathcal{A}}$
         if $\mu_i, \mathcal{A} \models f_i$, $i = 1, \ldots, n$, and $s_0 \xrightarrow{\mu_1} s_1 \xrightarrow{\mu_2} \ldots s_{n-1} \xrightarrow{\mu_n} s_n$
         then $\mu_i, \mathcal{A} \models f$, $i = 1, \ldots, n$, and
         for all $\rho \in \Pi_{\mathcal{T}}(s_n)$ for all $k \geq 0$ for all $\nu \in 2^{\mathcal{A}}$
         $\rho(k) \xrightarrow{\nu} \rho(k+1) \implies \nu, \mathcal{A} \models f$

$s_0, \mathcal{T} \models \exists f_1, \ldots, f_n \square f$
   iff   there exist $s_1, \ldots, s_n \in \mathcal{S}$ and $\mu_1, \ldots, \mu_n \in 2^{\mathcal{A}}$ such that
         $\mu_i, \mathcal{A} \models f_i$, $i = 1, \ldots, n$, $\mu_i, \mathcal{A} \models f$, $i = 1, \ldots, n$,
         $s_0 \xrightarrow{\mu_1} s_1 \xrightarrow{\mu_2} \ldots s_{n-1} \xrightarrow{\mu_n} s_n$ and
         there exists $\rho \in \Pi_{\mathcal{T}}(s_n)$ such that
         for all $k \geq 0$ for all $\nu \in 2^{\mathcal{A}}$
         $\rho(k) \xrightarrow{\nu} \rho(k+1) \implies \nu, \mathcal{A} \models f$

$s_0, \mathcal{T} \models \neg F$
   iff $s_0, \mathcal{T} \not\models F$

$s_0, \mathcal{T} \models F_1 \vee F_2$
   iff $s_0, \mathcal{T} \models F_1$ or $s_0, \mathcal{T} \models F_2$

$s_0, \mathcal{T} \models \forall f_1, \ldots, f_n \square F$
   iff   for all $s_1, \ldots, s_n \in \mathcal{S}$ for all $\mu_1, \ldots, \mu_n \in 2^{\mathcal{A}}$
         if $\mu_i, \mathcal{A} \models f_i$, $i = 1, \ldots, n$, and $s_0 \xrightarrow{\mu_1} s_1 \xrightarrow{\mu_2} \ldots s_{n-1} \xrightarrow{\mu_n} s_n$
         then for all $\rho \in \Pi_{\mathcal{T}}(s_n)$
         for all $k \geq 0$ $\rho(k), \mathcal{T} \models F$

$s_0, \mathcal{T} \models \exists f_1, \ldots, f_n \square F$
   iff   there exist $s_1, \ldots, s_n \in \mathcal{S}$ and $\mu_1, \ldots, \mu_n \in 2^{\mathcal{A}}$ such that
         $\mu_i, \mathcal{A} \models f_i$, $i = 1, \ldots, n$, and $s_0 \xrightarrow{\mu_1} s_1 \xrightarrow{\mu_2} \ldots s_{n-1} \xrightarrow{\mu_n} s_n$
         and there exists $\rho \in \Pi_{\mathcal{T}}(s_n)$ such that
         for all $k \geq 0$ $\rho(k), \mathcal{T} \models F$

Definition 7.13   Let be $f_1, \ldots, f_n \in \mathcal{AF}(\mathcal{A})$, $F, F_1, F_2 \in \mathcal{F}(\mathcal{A})$ and $\Phi \in \mathcal{AF}(\mathcal{A}) \cup \mathcal{F}(\mathcal{A})$ We define the following derived operators:

$$\top \stackrel{\text{def}}{=} \forall \mathbf{1}_{\mathcal{A}} \square \mathbf{1}_{\mathcal{A}}$$

$$\bot \stackrel{\text{def}}{=} \neg \top$$

$$F_1 \wedge F_2 \stackrel{\text{def}}{=} \neg(\neg F_1 \vee \neg F_2)$$

$$F_1 \rightarrow F_2 \stackrel{\text{def}}{=} \neg F_1 \vee F_2$$

$$\exists f_1, \ldots, f_n \Diamond \Phi \stackrel{\text{def}}{=} \neg \forall f_1, \ldots, f_n \square \neg \Phi$$

$$\forall f_1, \ldots, f_n \Diamond \Phi \stackrel{\text{def}}{=} \neg \exists f_1, \ldots, f_n \square \neg \Phi$$

$$\exists \Diamond \Phi \stackrel{\text{def}}{=} \exists \mathbf{1}_{\mathcal{A}} \Diamond \Phi$$

$$\forall \Diamond \Phi \stackrel{\text{def}}{=} \neg \forall \top \Diamond \Phi$$

$$\forall \square \Phi \stackrel{\text{def}}{=} \neg \exists \Diamond \neg \Phi$$

$$\exists \square \Phi \stackrel{\text{def}}{=} \neg \forall \Diamond \neg \Phi$$

$$\exists X f_1, \ldots, f_n \stackrel{\text{def}}{=} \exists f_1, \ldots, f_n \square \top$$

$$\forall X f_1, \ldots, f_n \stackrel{\text{def}}{=} \neg \exists \neg f_1 \ldots \neg f_n \square \top$$

7.6   The Representation of Properties

A correctness concept that can be readily characterized in Circal is the behavioral equivalence between two processes. The Circal expression $P ==Q$ is the implementation of the equivalence $P \cong Q$.

In verification, however, equivalence is often too strong a property. For certain systems, verifying their correctness consists of determining that certain properties hold, where these properties do not constitute a complete specification. This cannot be done in terms of equivalence, but rather involves the notion of behavioral inclusion.

Let $P \in \mathcal{P}_L$ and $Q \in \mathcal{P}_M$ be such that $L \subseteq M$ and P and Q are deterministic. Then

$$Q - (M \backslash L) \sqsubseteq P$$

if and only if Q can be seen to constrain P and restricts P to behave as Q, that is

$$P * Q \cong P.$$

The Circal expression $P * Q == Q$ characterizes the behavioral inclusion of Q in P.

When Q defines a model of a system, P can be seen as a property that Q must satisfy. However not all temporal properties can be verified through a behavioral equivalence.

A more general approach is the use of processes to *mark* with new *abstract actions* all the paths that satisfy the required property. The property is then defined by a process whose sort consists only of marking actions. By composing the process that defines the model of the system with the marking process and abstracting away all actions apart from the marks, the composite process is equivalent to the process defining the property if and only if the model of the system satisfies the property.

7.6.1 *Formula-Based Characterization*

In this section we define a characterization of a given property of a Circal process by means of an equivalence between processes that involve a representation of the temporal formula that defines the property. We start our characterization with the temporal formulas that do not contain more than one level of temporal operators. Notice that a formula like $\forall f \Box F$, with $F \in \mathcal{F}(\mathcal{A})$, has always more than one level of temporal operators. We will use the following process definitions:

$$TL < - \sum_{\mu \in 2^L} \mu \, TL$$
$$YN < - yYN + nN$$
$$N < - nN$$
$$Y < - yY$$

with $y, n \notin L$. The TL process permits all possible sets of actions to occur anytime. The behavior of the YN process consists of an infinite path labeled by y that has in any point an infinite branch labeled by n.

Theorem 7.2 *The behavior of a process $S \in \mathcal{P}_L$ satisfies the formula*

$$\forall f_1, \ldots, f_r \Box f$$

if and only if

$$S * AL_{f_1, \ldots, f_r} * AGL_f - L \cong Y$$

where

$$AL_{f_1,\ldots,f_r} < - \, AL_{f_1}$$
$$AL_{f_i} < - \sum_{\mu \in C_L(f_i)} \mu \, AL_{f_{i+1}}, \quad i = 1, \ldots, r-1$$
$$AL_{f_r} < - \sum_{\mu \in C_L(f_r)} \mu \, TL$$
$$AGL_f < - \sum_{\mu \in C_L(f)} (\mu \cup \{y\}) \, AGL_f \; + \sum_{\mu \notin C_L(f) \cup \emptyset} (\mu \cup \{n\}) \, N$$

Proof. The $AL_{f_1 \ldots f_r}$ process constrains other processes to start with the occurrence of a sequence of sets of actions such that the i-th set satisfies the temporal formula f_i. The AGL_f process marks with the new action y all the action sets that satisfies f and with the new action n all the other action sets.

Thus, $S * AL_{f_1,\ldots,f_r} * AGL_f - L$ is equivalent to Y

if and only if

$S * AL_{f_1,\ldots,f_r} * AGL_f$ performs only action sets marked by y

if and only if

$S * AL_{f_1,\ldots,f_r}$ performs only action sets that satisfy f

if and only if

S performs only action sets that satisfy the temporal formula f after being constrained to start with the occurrence of a sequence of action sets such that the i-th set satisfies the temporal formula f_i

if and only if

$\mathcal{B}(S)$ satisfies $\forall f_1, \ldots, f_r \square f$. $\qquad\qquad\qquad\qquad\qquad\qquad \square$

Theorem 7.3 *The behavior of a process $S \in \mathcal{P}_L$ satisfies the formula*

$$\exists f_1, \ldots, f_r \square f$$

if and only if

$$S * EGL_f^{f_1,\ldots,f_r} - L \cong YN$$

where

$$EGL_f^{f_1,\ldots,f_r} < -\ EGL_f^{f_1}$$

$$EGL_f^{f_i} < -\ \sum_{\mu \in C_L(f_i) \cap C_L(f)} \mu \cup \{y\} EGL_f^{f_{i+1}} +$$

$$\sum_{\mu \notin C_L(f_i) \cap C_L(f) \backslash \emptyset} \mu \cup \{n\}\, N, \quad i = 1, \ldots, r-1$$

$$EGL_f^{f_r} < -\ \sum_{\mu \in C_L(f_i) \cap C_L(f)} \mu \cup \{y\}\, EGL_f +$$

$$\sum_{\mu \notin C_L(f_i) \cap C_L(f) \backslash \emptyset} \mu \cup \{n\}\, N$$

$$EGL_f < -\ \sum_{\mu \in C_L(f)} (\mu \cup \{y\})\, EGL_f +$$

$$\sum_{\mu \notin C_L(f) \cup \emptyset} (\mu \cup \{n\})\, N$$

Proof. The $EGL_f^{f_1 \cdots f_r}$ process marks with the new action y all the action sets in an initial sequence of action sets such that the i-th set satisfies the temporal formula f_i and the temporal formula f and with the new action n all the other action sets. After marking with n, every $EGL_f^{f_i}$ gives control to the N process, which performs n forever, whereas, after marking with y the last action set of the sequence, $EGL_f^{f_r}$ gives control to the EGL_f process. The EGL_f process marks with y all the action sets that satisfy the temporal formula f until an action set that does not satisfy f is performed. Such an action set and all the following ones are marked with n. Moreover, EGL_f allows at any point the occurrence of an action set containing only n.

Thus, $S * EGL_f^{f_1,\ldots,f_r} - L$ is equivalent to YN

if and only if

$\mathcal{B}(S * EGL_f^{f_1,\ldots,f_r} - L)$ consists of an infinite path labeled by y that has in any point an infinite branch labeled by n

if and only if

$\mathcal{B}(S * EGL_f^{f_1,\ldots,f_r})$ contains at least an infinite path whose action sets contain y and all these infinite paths have in any point an infinite branch whose action sets contain n

if and only if

$\mathcal{B}(S)$ contains a path that starts with a sequences of r action sets such that the i-th set satisfies the temporal formulas f_i and f and that after the r-th action set contains only action sets that satisfy f

if and only if

$\mathcal{B}(S)$ satisfies $\exists f_1, \ldots, f_r \Box f$. $\qquad\qquad\qquad$ □

Formulas consisting of derived temporal operators can be characterized after transforming the derived operators in the primitive ones.

Example 7.2 Let $S \in \mathcal{P}_{\{a,b,c\}}$ be the process defined as follows:

$$S < -\, a\, S + (b\, c)\, S$$

We can notice that S satisfies

$$\forall c \Box (a \vee b) \quad \text{and} \quad \exists c \Box (b \wedge c)$$

but does not satisfy either

$$\forall c \Box b \quad \text{or} \quad \exists c \Box (a \wedge c)$$

In fact

$$S * AL_c * AGL_{a \vee b} - L \quad \text{and} \quad S * EGL_{b \wedge c}^c - L$$

are equivalent to Y and YN, respectively, whereas the behavior of $S * AL_c * AGL_b - L$ is given by

$$S_0 < -\, y\, S_1$$
$$S_1 < -\, y\, S_1 + n\, S_1$$

which is not equivalent to Y, and the behavior of $S * EGL_{a \wedge c}^c - L$ is given by

$$S_0 < -\, y\, S_1$$
$$S_1 < -\, n\, S_1$$

which is not equivalent to YN.

Now we show an example of characterization of a formula containing two levels of temporal operators.

Example 7.3   The formula

$$\forall f_1, \ldots, f_r \Box \forall g_1, \ldots, g_s \Diamond h$$

defines a schema of the important class of liveness properties. The formula is equivalent to

$$\forall f_1, \ldots, f_r \Box \neg \exists g_1, \ldots, g_s \Box \neg h$$

We can notice that the fragment of formula "$\forall f_1, \ldots, f_r$" defines a constraint characterized by the process $AL_{f_1, \ldots, f_r}$. Therefore the behavior of a process $S \in \mathcal{P}_L$ satisfies the formula if and only if

$$S * AL_{f_1, \ldots, f_r} * EGL_h^{g_1, \ldots, g_s} - L \not\cong YN$$

In the protocol defined in Example 7.1, since the receiver can only observe upgoing edges, a sequence 01 encoded by the sender can be decoded by the receiver only when it observes the upgoing edge that encodes the bit 1. The formula $\forall 1_A \Box \forall i_0, i_1 \Diamond d_{01}$ where action d_{01} defines the decoding of the sequence 01 by the receiver. However, the model of the protocol does not satisfy it because the decoding fails when the input message does not respect the constraints defined in Example 7.1.

7.6.2   *Model-Based Characterization*

The following theorem shows an alternative characterization of the formula $\forall f_1, \ldots, f_r \Box f$.

Theorem 7.4   *The behavior of a process $S \in \mathcal{P}_L$ satisfies the formula*

$$\forall f_1, \ldots, f_r \Box f$$

if and only if

$$S * AL_{f_1, \ldots, f_r} * G_f \cong S * AL_{f_1, \ldots, f_r}$$

where

$$G_f < - \sum_{\mu \in C_L(f)} \mu \, G_f$$

Proof. The G_f process constrains other processes to perform only the action sets characterized by f. Thus, $S * AL_{f_1,...,f_r} * G_f$ is equivalent to $S * AL_{f_1,...,f_r}$ if and only if $S * AL_{f_1,...,f_r}$ can perform only action sets satisfying f, that is if and only if S satisfies $\forall f_1, \ldots, f_r \Box f$.   □

In this characterization the property is verified through a behavioral inclusion. This is possible only for safety properties. The approach becomes very interesting when the safety property is characterized in terms of a known model that satisfies it (*model-based characterization*). If process P is the model-based characterization of such a safety property, the equivalence given in Theorem 7.4 becomes

$$S * P \cong S \qquad\qquad (\text{Ex1})$$

Therefore, system S satisfies property P if and only if the behavior of P is included in the behavior of S.

In most cases the correctness of a system depends on the assumptions made about its environment. Thus the process C defining these assumptions must be composed with S, before the verification. Therefore, equivalence (**Ex1**) becomes

$$S * C * P \cong S * C \qquad\qquad (\text{Ex2})$$

This approach exploits the modeling power of a process algebra such as Circal and can overcome the problem of the characterization in terms of a very complex logical formula.

Example 7.4 A typical example that uses the model-based characterization is the correctness proof of a communication protocol. A necessary property for the correctness of a protocol is the following:

> Each sequence of messages that is accepted as an input
> by the protocol is output unchanged by the protocol.

This property is typical of a buffer and the specification of the buffer is well known. If process S describes the protocol and B describes the specification of the buffer, then the protocol satisfies the property if and only if the behavior of B is included in the behavior of S, which is expressed in Circal by

$$S * B \cong S \qquad\qquad (\text{Ex3})$$

In general, the size of the buffer, and therefore the number of its states, depends on the protocol. However, we can be certain that there exists a finite buffer size for each given protocol modeled in Circal, since Circal can describe only finite-state behaviors. Therefore the property can be proved by showing that the above equivalence is true for some finite size of B.

Since the correctness of the protocol defined in Example 7.1 depends on the assumptions defined by process Con, the equivalence to be verified becomes

$$S * Con * B \cong S * Con$$

However this is not yet sufficient to guarantee the correctness of the protocol, since a process that accepts less inputs than the possible inputs that are characterized by Con also satisfies the equivalence above. It is necessary to prove that S accepts at least all the inputs characterized by Con. This is true when the behavior of the restriction of S to the input actions is included in the behavior Con. Such a property is verified by the equivalence

$$Con * (S - O) \cong Con$$

where $O = o_0 \, o_1 \, o_e$ is the list of all output actions.

We can notice that in this case there is a behavioral inclusion of a restriction of the system (to input actions) in the property, which is a very simple liveness property. "The system accepts a class of inputs" means that the system eventually reacts to every input belonging to such a class. In some cases [Cerone 96; Cerone 97a] the two equivalences

$$S * Con * B \cong S * Con \quad \text{and} \quad Con * (S - O) \cong Con$$

are sufficient to verify the correctness of a protocol P. The property characterization is thus entirely model-based.

For a general approach to the verification of liveness properties the recourse to a formula-based characterization is a need. However, in the characterization

$$S * AL_{f_1,\ldots,f_r} * EGL_h^{g_1,\ldots,g_s} - L \not\cong YN$$

of the formula

$$\forall f_1,\ldots,f_r \Box \forall g_1,\ldots,g_s \Diamond h$$

the constraint $AL_{f_1,...,f_r}$ is a very simple assumption about the environment. In practical cases the assumptions about the environment can be very difficult to be characterized in terms of temporal logic formulas. The above characterization still works when $AL_{f_1,...,f_r}$ is replaced by any other constraint. Therefore, we can replace $AL_{f_1,...,f_r}$ by a process C that is a model-based characterization of the assumptions. This is equivalent to verify the constrained system $S * C$ rather than the unconstrained system S. In this way the combination of the formula-based and model-based characterizations increases the power of the verification methodology.

Example 7.5   In the protocol defined in Example 7.1 the assumptions about the environment are modeled by the Con process defined in Example 7.1. Therefore, if $P \in \mathcal{P}_L$ is the process that models the protocol, then $P * Con * EGL_{d_{01}}^{i_0,i_1} - L \not\cong YN$ proves that "when the input satisfies the constraints modeled by Con always a sequence 01 is eventually decoded". Therefore, the composite system $P * Con$ satisfies $\forall 1_A \square \forall i_0, i_1 \Diamond d_{01}$ even if P does not.

The model-based characterization of property has also been applied to the verification of timing constraints [Cerone 97b] and performance properties [Cerone 99] in the domain of asynchronous hardware.

Example 7.6   In an asynchronous micropipelined processor the evaluation of a pipeline stage is governed by local interactions with its neighbors using a request acknowledge handshaking protocol. It is possible that one stage is evaluating while at the same time a stage further on is transferring an instruction to its neighbor. Thus, whilst the performance of a synchronous pipeline is governed entirely by the clock rate that can be achieved with a particular logic design, the performance of an asynchronous pipeline depends as well on the design of the handshaking controls for each stage. In particular, if the asynchronous logic pipeline is to be as fast as the synchronous one it must be possible for all the evaluation of logic stages to overlap as in the synchronous case.

Equivalence **Ex2** has been used in the verification of the simple property that "adjacent stages can never be occupied at the same time" [Cerone 97b; Cerone 99]. This property is verified by exploiting a distinctive feature of the Circal process algebra: simultaneous event guards. A new *abstract action* is introduced in every stage to mark the interval where the stage is full. If we denote by y_i the abstract action introduced in the i-th stage then the process

$$Y_{i,j} < - y_i Y_{i,j} + y_j Y_{i,j}$$

characterizes the property that y_i and y_j never occur simultaneously, that is the i-th and j-th stages "can never be occupied at the same time". Therefore, if S models the handshaking control for the whole micropipeline, then checking for each i

$$S * Y_{i,i+1} \cong S$$

proves that "adjacent stages can never be occupied at the same time".

If such a property holds for adjacent stages, but not for alternate stages then the degree of parallelism achieved by the micropipeline is only 50% of the potential parallelism. If it does not hold for any pair of stages, then adjacent stages may be occupied at the same time. So no upper bound of 50% is given to the degree of parallelism. However, we would like to know whether all stages can be occupied at the same time.

In order to characterize such a property we combine the formula-based and the model-based characterizations. We use the same abstract action y for every stage of the micropipeline [Cerone 99]. Then the process Y given in Section 7.6.1 characterizes the property that y occurs on an infinite path in the behavior of the micropeline. In this case equivalence **Ex2** cannot be applied. If L is list of all actions in the sort of S then

$$(S * Y) - L \cong Y \qquad \textbf{(Ex4)}$$

proves that after abstracting away all the actions in the sort of S from the composition $S * Y$, there is still an infinite sequence of actions y in the resultant behavior. This means that there is a path where all stages are occupied at the same time. Therefore, the whole potential parallelism can be effectively reached [Cerone 99].

7.7 Discussion and Future Work

In this chapter we have developed a methodology for the automatic verification of concurrent systems by using the constraint-based modeling style available within the Circal process algebra. Three distinctive features of the Circal process algebra are the basis of this methodology, namely, simultaneous event guards, sharing of events over arbitrary numbers of processes and the nature of the composition operator which provides synchronization of processes without the removal of the synchronizing events in the resultant behavior.

A temporal property of the system under analysis can be characterized either through a translation of the SAUB formula that defines the property into a set of processes and into the rules to compose these processes with one another (*formula-based* characterization), or by a well-known model that satisfies the property (*model-based* characterization). The formula-based characterization allows the verification of general temporal properties, whereas the model-based characterization can be applied only to the verification of safety properties and of some simple liveness properties. The two characterizations can also be combined together, increasing the power of the verification methodology.

In future work we want to extend the logic with more powerful temporal operators and also would like to add compositionality to SAUB by developing *meta-rules* to combine properties of different processes, which have possibly different sorts, and infer a property of the composite process. This could be a first step towards a decomposition of a global property of the overall system into the local properties of its components, which can be verified on much smaller state spaces.

PART 3

Synthesis Methods for Real-Time Systems

Chapter 8

Verifying Real-Time Systems with Standard Tools

Jonathan S. Ostroff and Hak K. Ng

Abstract: The TTM/RTTL framework allows for the specification, development and verification of discrete real-time properties of reactive systems. Timed transition systems (TTMs) is the underlying computational model, and real-time temporal logic (RTTL) is the requirements specification language. In this paper, we provide a conversion procedure for mapping a timed transition system into a finite state fair transition systems. This means that efficient (untimed) tools for state exploration can be used to check the properties of real-time systems. The procedure has been implemented in the Statetime toolset for the TTM/RTTL framework.

Keywords: Real-time systems, model checking, fair transition system, temporal logic.

8.1 Introduction

In any engineering discipline, no single model fully captures all the physical phenomena under study. Rather models are chosen according to the needs of the design and the types of properties that must be calculated to ensure the safety and adequacy of the design.

The TTM/RTTL framework [Ostroff 89c] was introduced for the specification, development and verification of discrete real-time properties of reactive systems. It has a computational model, specification language and toolset for proving that a system meets its specification. The various parts of the framework are itemized below.

- The framework has a computational model based on TTMs (timed transition models). TTMs are fair transition systems with additional constraints for real time. Concurrent systems are represented by interleaving their transitions with a *tick* transition that updates a master clock t when the tick transition is taken. In a computation, the clock must tick infinitely often. Between any two clock ticks, a sequence of non-tick transitions can be taken, where each such transition takes zero time. Only the tick transition advances time.

  Not only can simulated concurrency via multiprogramming be represented, but also true concurrency, provided atomic transitions are modeled at the right granularity. Real-time programming constructs such as delays, timeouts and interrupts can also be modeled by using appropriate bounds on transitions or clock variables. For models of more complex systems involving dense time domains or continuous variables (hybrid systems), see the hierarchy of models discussed in [Manna 93].

  In the framework, when a transition $\tau[l, u]$ becomes enabled (this is called the *moment of enablement*), it delays for a lower time bound l ticks of the master clock before it can be taken. If, from its moment of enablement, it remains continuously enabled, then it must either be taken or become disabled before the $(u + 1)$-th tick of clock.

  Timed transitions can capture various properties including:

  Spontaneous transitions $\tau[0, \infty]$: The transition τ can be taken at any time or may never be taken, e.g. a device failure.

  Just transitions: A transition τ must eventually be taken if it is continuously enabled, e.g. a process must eventually access its critical region.

  Real-time transitions $\tau[l, u]$: The transition must be taken as specified by the lower and upper time bound requirements, e.g. a traffic light must turn green 50 ticks of the clock after turning red.

- The framework has a requirement specification language called real time temporal logic (RTTL). *Unclocked* properties are standard temporal formulas that do not refer to the master clock, and can be used to assert safety and liveness properties. *Clocked* properties refer to the master clock and can be used to specify bounded response and other timing properties.

- The framework has a set of proof rules that can be used to verify that TTMs satisfy their RTTL properties. For finite state systems there are model checking procedures.

- The framework has a prototype toolset called StateTime which uses a visual language akin to statecharts for representing TTMs. The *Build* tool is used to design TTMs and *execute* or simulate them. The *Verify* tool *model checks* finite state systems for a small but important subset of RTTL properties. The *Develop* tool is used for theorem proving.

  Although StateTime was designed for verifying closed systems that do not interact with their environment, with some minor extensions, compositional verification using TTM modules can also be performed.

The StateTime tool has been used for the design of realistic systems such as a 3-version with majority voting shutdown system for a nuclear reactor. The ability to execute partial systems in the initial phase of the design, and then later to model check or use theorem proving techniques are all vital ingredients that make the treatment of larger systems tractable.

The Verify tool was written in Prolog in 1989, and is slow relative to more modern (untimed) tools that use hash compression or special BDD techniques [Burch 92; Holzmann 90; Holzmann 93; Manna 94]. The current advantages of Verify is that it can verify bounded response properties such as

$$p \Rightarrow \Diamond_{[4,9]} q$$

which is (a) a real time property that is not treated by the untimed tools, and (b) it is unnecessary to supply the bounds (e.g. 4 and 9), as Verify automatically computes the weakest bounds that make the bounded response property valid. The latter advantage is useful in design as changes to system parameters can be made and Verify can then be used to compute what response property is valid.

In this paper we provide a conversion procedure that maps a TTM M

and an RTTL property R into a corresponding fair transition system $\hat{M}$ and unclocked property $\hat{R}$. Efficient untimed tools can then be used to check that $\hat{R} \models \hat{M}$, and that would then automatically entail that the original TTM M satisfies the RTTL property R. These procedures have been implemented in StateTime.

For unclocked RTTL properties that do not involve references to the master clock $\hat{R} = R$. A simple procedure for converting clocked properties R (e.g. bounded response) into an unclocked property $\hat{R}$ is given. However, the converted formula can only be checked efficiently where the time bounds involved are small. For larger time bounds, explicit timers must be introduced as in [Alur 94].

In [Kesten 96] a similar conversion procedure is given for real-time systems with dense time domains. However, the resulting fair transition system is intended for theorem proving and not model-checking (it is not finite state). Also, for simplicity all transitions are disabled after being taken so that stuttering steps (idle transitions) are not permitted, In this paper, we allow stuttering steps which is also important when proving modular properties.

This paper is organized as follows. In Section 8.2, we give an overview of the TTM/RTTL framework. In Section 8.3, the conversion algorithm for TTMs is presented. In section 8.4 a procedure for verifying clocked properties is given. In Section 8.5, a real-time mutual exclusion algorithm is verified using the conversion procedures and the STeP (untimed) model-checker. The paper concludes with Section 8.6.

8.2 Timed Transition Models

TTMs (timed transition systems) are timed extensions of the fair transition systems of [Manna 91]. Transitions have lower and upper bounds that relate to the number of occurrences of a special transition *tick* in a computation of a system. A TTM M is defined as a 4-tuple $M = (V, I, T, J)$ with the following definitions:

- The *system variables* V is a finite set of typed variables that always has two distinguished variables: t (the master clock time) and ε (the event variable). The event variable is useful for specifying when transitions are taken. There may also be *data variables* which range over data domains such as integers. *Activity variables* (also called control variables) are used to indicate progress in the execution of the various concurrent threads or process of the TTM. Each variable $v \in V$ has an associated range of values $type(v)$, e.g. $type(t) = \{0, 1, 2, \ldots\}$.

A state s of the TTM is a mapping that assigns to each variable $v \in V$ a value in $type(v)$. The set of all states is denoted by Σ.

- The *initial condition* I is a boolean valued expression in the variables set that characterizes the states at which the execution of the TTM can begin. A state s satisfying I, i.e. $s \models I$, is called an *initial state*.

- T is a finite set of transitions which includes the distinguished transition *tick*. Each transition τ in T is a function $\tau : \Sigma \to 2^{\Sigma}$ that maps a state s in Σ to a (possibly empty) set of τ-*successor* states $\tau(s)$ which are obtained when τ is taken. Each state s' in the set $\tau(s)$ is defined to be a τ-*successor* of s.

  A transition relation $\rho(V, V')$ relates the state s to its τ-successor $s' \in \tau(s)$ by referring to both unprimed and primed system variables. An unprimed variable v is evaluated in s while the corresponding primed variable v' is evaluated in the successor state s'. Assuming $V = \{x, y, t, \epsilon\}$, some examples of transition relations are:

  - $\rho_{tick}(V, V')$: $x' = x \wedge y' = y \wedge t' = t + 1 \wedge \epsilon' = tick$.
    When a *tick* transition is taken, then the only variables that change are the global time t (which is incremented by one), and the event variable ϵ which is updated to indicate which transition has just been taken.
  - $\rho_{\alpha}(V, V')$: $x \geq y \wedge x' = x + y \wedge y' = y \wedge t' = t \wedge \epsilon' = \alpha$.
    When the non-tick transition α is taken, the global time remains the same. The assertion $x \geq y$ in the unprimed variables is the *enabling condition* e_{α} of transition α, i.e. α can only be taken if x is at least as large as y. The *transformation function* $h_{\alpha} = \{x : x + y, \epsilon : \alpha\}$ is used to denote those variables that change when the transition is taken (the variables that are unchanged are by convention not included in the transformation function).

In addition to its enabling condition e_{τ} and transformation function h_τ, each transition $\tau \in (T - \{tick\})$ also has a *lower time bound* l_τ (a nonnegative integer constant), and an *upper time bound* u_τ so that $u_\tau \geq l_\tau$. It is possible for l_τ to be zero and for u_τ to be infinity.

For a set of variables $U \subseteq V$ we define the predicate

$$same(U) = (\forall u \in U : u' = u)$$

If $U = \{v_1, v_2\}$ we write $same(v_1, v_2)$ instead of the more precise $same(\{v_1, v_2\})$. This predicate can be used to describe the transitions that are preserved when taking a transition. We require that

$$\rho_{tick}(V, V') \equiv (t' = t + 1 \wedge \epsilon' = tick) \wedge same(V - \{t, \epsilon\})$$

and for all non-tick transition τ,

$$\rho_\tau(V, V') \rightarrow same(t)$$

- $J \subseteq T$ is a set of *just* transitions. If a transition $\tau \in J$ is continually enabled it must eventually be taken. Justice conditions are only imposed on transitions τ where $u_\tau = \infty$. A transition with a finite upper time bound is automatically just; it will be constrained in the sequel to satisfy an even stronger constraint than justice, viz. that the transition must be taken or disabled by u_τ ticks from its moment of enablement.

The enabling condition e_τ of transition τ can be formally defined from its transition relation by $e_\tau \equiv (\exists V' : \rho_\tau(V, V')$. A transition τ is *enabled* in a state s if $s \models e_\tau$ (i.e. if $\tau(s) \neq \emptyset$) — otherwise τ is said to be *disabled*.

8.2.1 *TTM Semantics*

A *trajectory* of a TTM $M = (V, I, T, J)$ is any infinite sequence of states:

$$\sigma = s_0 \xrightarrow{\tau_0} s_1 \xrightarrow{\tau_1} s_2 \xrightarrow{\tau_2} \ldots$$

with $\tau_0, \tau_1, \tau_2 \ldots$ elements of T, so that the following three requirements are satisfied:

(1) **Initialization:** The first state of the trajectory satisfies the initial condition, i.e. $s_0 \models I$.

(2) **Succession:** For all positions i in the trajectory, $s_{i+1} \in \tau_i(s_i)$, i.e. state s_{i+1} is a τ_i-successor of state s_i. This means that $s_i \models e_{\tau_i}$. Also, $s_{i+1} \models (\epsilon = \tau_i)$, and we say that τ_i is *taken* at position i in the trajectory σ.

(3) **Justice:** For each τ in the justice set, it is not the case that τ is continually enabled beyond some position in the trajectory, but taken at only finitely many positions in the trajectory.

The above three requirements are standard in fair transition systems. In order to obtain the real-time semantics of TTMs, we add three additional requirements:

- **Ticking:** The clock ticks infinitely often in the trajectory σ. In standard temporal logic the ticking requirement is written: $\Box\Diamond(\varepsilon = tick)$. Thus, tick transitions are interleaved with non-tick transitions. Only the tick transition advances the master clock by one unit of time. Between any two ticks of the clock a finite sequence of non-tick transitions can be taken, each transition in the sequence taking zero time.

- **Lower bound:** For every transition τ with lower time bound l_τ, if τ is taken at position j of the trajectory, then there must exist a position $i \leq j$ so that $s_i(t) + l_\tau \leq s_j(t)$, and τ is enabled on the states $s_i, \ldots, s_j$. This means that τ must be enabled for at least l_τ units of time before it is taken.

- **Upper bound:** For every transition τ with upper time bound u_τ, if τ is enabled at position j, there exists a position $k \geq j$, with $s_j(t) + u_\tau \geq s_k(t)$, such that either τ is disabled on s_k or τ is taken at position $j - 1$. Thus τ cannot be continuously enabled for more than u_τ ticks of the clock without being taken.

If a trajectory of a TTM M satisfies the additional real-time requirements of ticking and lower and upper time bounds, then the trajectory is said to be a *legal trajectory* (or computation) of M.

In a legal trajectory, there are infinitely many ticks of the master clock. Between any two clock ticks, zero or a finite sequence of non-tick transitions can be taken. Each transition in the sequence takes zero time (does not change the master clock) as only the *tick* transition "advances time".

Transitions "mature" together as time advances but execute separately in an interleaving manner. Once a transition τ becomes enabled at position

i (this is called the moment of enablement $moe(\tau, i)$ [Ostroff 90a]) it begins
to mature but cannot be taken until its lower time bound number of ticks
have been taken, at which point the transition becomes "eligible" or "ripe"
for execution. If the transition has been continuously enabled from its
moment of enablement then it can be taken any time after it becomes
eligible, but it must be taken or become disabled before the upper time
bound number of ticks has expired (from its moment of enablement).

Fair transitions systems can model truly concurrent systems by impos-
ing the appropriate fairness constraints at the right granularity of atomicity.
Similarly, TTMs can model true concurrency if the right grain of atomicity
is chosen.

Unfortunately, not every TTM is guaranteed to satisfy both the ticking
and the bound requirements. If there is any *immediate* transition $\tau[0, 0]$
that is a self-loop, then τ is taken an infinite number of times before a tick
transition. This is called a *Zeno computation*. Any cycle whose elements are
all immediate may also create Zeno computations. Whenever a system has
cycles of immediate transitions, the ticking requirement should be checked
for explicitly so as to ensure that there are no Zeno computations.

The model of TTMs presented above is expressive enough to capture
most of the features specific to real time programs including delays, timeouts, preemptions and interrupts (see e.g. [Ostroff 89c] for the use of TTMs
to model the constructs of the Ada-like language Conic).

8.2.2   Real-Time Temporal Logic

The standard temporal logic of Manna and Pnueli ([Manna 91]) uses temporal connectives such as □ (henceforth), ◇ (eventually) and $\mathcal{U}$ (until) to
represent quantitative temporal properties.

Most proposals for real-time temporal logics extend the standard operators with new connectives such as $\diamond_{\leq 5}$ (eventually within 5 ticks of the
clock) [Henzinger 94a]. Thus a bounded response property may be written:

$$p \Rightarrow \diamond_{\leq 5} q$$

which asserts that every occurrence of a p-state is followed within 5 clock
ticks by a q-state (a state satisfying q).

However, using unextended temporal logic as in [Ostroff 89c], the above bounded response property is an abbreviation for:

$$(p \wedge t = t_0) \Rightarrow \Diamond(q \wedge (t \leq t_0 + 5))$$

where the master clock t is a *flexible* variable (may change from state to state in a computation), whereas t_0 is a *rigid* variable (has the same nonnegative integer value throughout the computation). By using unextended temporal logic, we can re-use many of the tools and methods developed for untimed systems.

We may use additional clock variables to capture transition bounds or to check the bounded response property above. These clock variables can refer to the master clock or any other system variables. These additional clock variables increase uniformly whenever the tick transition is taken, and may be reset to measure the end of a period of interest. The master clock variable t is never reset.

8.2.3 *An Example of a TTM*

Figure 8.1 presents a TTM with several transitions, some spontaneous, others just and some bounded. Let x be the activity variable with $type(x) = \{0, a, b, c, d, e, f, g\}$. Let transition ω be in the justice set J, the following properties are valid (satisfied in all computations):

- $(\epsilon = \text{start}) \Rightarrow \Diamond_{[1,8]}(x = c)$
  The above property is valid because of the bound requirements. The shortest path between locations a and c is $\alpha \cdots \beta$ $(1 + 0 = 0)$ and the longest path is $\alpha \cdots \gamma \cdots \delta$ $(3 + 1 + 4 = 8)$. In a fair transition system that ignores the time bounds, this property is invalid. This formula is called a *clocked* property because it refers to the master clock t.
- $(x = c) \Rightarrow \Diamond(x = f)$.
  This property is valid because ω is a *just* transition. This formula is called an *unclocked* property because it does not refer to the master clock t.
- $\Box \neg(\epsilon = \lambda)$
  λ will never be taken since its lower bound is less than the upper bound of δ (i.e. δ will always be taken before λ). This is an unclocked property that is valid only because of the time bound requirements. In a fair transition system that ignores time bounds, this property is invalid.

For the TTM of Figure 8.1 the property

$$\Box\Diamond(\epsilon = tick) \qquad\qquad (\textbf{Ex1})$$

is *invalid* because there is a cycle $\tau \cdots \rho \cdots \phi$ of immediate events.

The TTM of Figure 8.1 can be entered as a chart in the Build tool. The conversion procedures of the next section have been implemented in Build. This means that Build will output a file that the untimed STeP tool [Manna 94] can process directly. All the above formulas are then model checked and shown to be valid. The tool yields a counterexample in the case of the formula in equation (**Ex1**), indicating that the cycle of immediate transitions produces Zeno behavior.

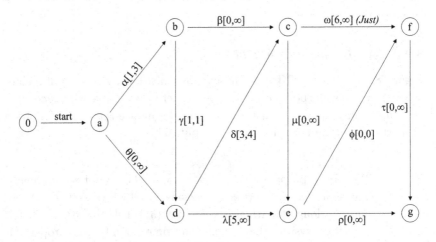

Fig. 8.1   A TTM example

8.3   Translating Timed into Fair Systems

Untimed model checking tools such as SPIN [Holzmann 90; Holzmann 93], SMV [Burch 92] and STeP [Manna 94], use effective hashing or BDD state reduction techniques to deal with systems of millions of reachable states efficiently. These tools can all implement fair transition systems (FTS) as defined in Section 8.2.1.

For example, in STeP, transitions can be written almost directly as described in Section 8.2.1, and the declaration *Just, Compassionate* or *No-fairness* can be assigned to each transition. In SPIN, each transition can be declared as an *atomic active* process.

We would like a conversion procedure that maps a TTM M and an RTTL property R into a corresponding fair transition system $\hat{M}$ and un-clocked property $\hat{R}$. The abovementioned tools can then be used to check that $\hat{M} \models \hat{R}$, and that would then automatically entail that the original TTM M satisfies the RTTL property R.

As mentioned in Section 8.2.3, unclocked RTTL properties do not involve references to the master clock t. The conversion procedure is not needed for unclocked RTTL requirements R as $\hat{R} = R$ in this case.

A simple procedure for converting clocked properties R (e.g. bounded response) into an unclocked property $\hat{R}$ will also be given. However, the converted formula can only be checked efficiently where the time bounds involved are small. For larger time bounds, explicit timers must be introduced as in [Alur 94].

The original Verify tool [Ostroff 89c] for the TTM/RTTL framework essentially used a timer for each transition to compute the global reachability graph [Ostroff 90a]. In a similar fashion, for each non-tick transition τ, we will introduce a *clock* variables c_τ where $type(c_\tau) = \{0, 1, 2, \cdots, u_\tau\}$. When the clock variable reaches its upper bound u_τ, the tick is disabled from occurring until τ is taken or becomes disabled. Not all transitions will need clock variables. For example, a spontaneous transition $\tau[0, \infty]$ does not have any timing constraints. Let C be the set of all new clock variables, and let T_{clock} be the set of all transitions that have associated clock variables.

Initially, each clock variable is set to zero ($c_\tau = 0$). When the transition *tick* is taken (time progresses), and transition τ is enabled, clock variable c_τ is incremented by one. A non-*tick* transition τ can only occur when it is enabled and the corresponding clock variable is within the lower and upper time bounds (i.e. $l_\tau \leq c_\tau \leq u_\tau$). When a transition τ is taken, the clock c_τ is reset to zero.

A new transition *reset* is also introduced. Its enabling condition is given by $e_{reset} = res$ where *res* is a boolean variable. The transition relation for *reset* is given by:

$$\rho_{reset} : \; res \wedge res' = false \wedge \epsilon' = reset \wedge same(V - \{\epsilon\})$$

$$\wedge zero(C) \wedge nonzero(C)$$

where

$$zero(C) = (\forall \tau \in T_{clock} : \neg e_\tau \to c'_\tau = 0)$$

$$nonzero(C) = (\forall \tau \in T_{clock} : e_\tau \to c'_\tau = c_\tau)$$

The transition *reset* thus sets all clock variables of disabled transitions to zero. The need for this is explained in the sequel.

Thus, given a non-tick transition such as $\tau[3,5]$, the new transition relation is

$$\rho_{\hat\tau} : \quad \rho_\tau \wedge (3 \leq c_\tau \leq 5) \wedge \neg res \wedge c'_\tau = 0 \wedge res' = true$$

where ρ_τ is the original transition relation of transition τ in the TTM.

When a transition is taken it may change data variables which may have the effect of disabling other transitions. By the lower and upper time bound requirements, the clock variables of these newly disabled transitions must be reset to zero. This is because, transitions have to be continuously enabled (as measured by the original enabling conditions e_τ) for the lower time bound number of ticks before becoming eligible for execution. Thus, after every occurrence of a transition, all transitions are disabled via the *res* bit, until the *reset* transition is taken.

When the clock of τ reaches the upper time bound (i.e $c_\tau = u_\tau$), transition τ becomes a *must* transition, i.e. *tick* cannot happen until either τ is taken or disabled. Hence, a *tick* can only occur when there is no *must* transition, i.e. $c_\tau < u_\tau$. The *tick* transition increments all clock variables of enabled transitions by one. The transition relation for *tick* is thus:

$$\rho_{tick} : \quad \neg res \wedge (\forall \tau \in T_{clock} : \neg e_\tau \vee c_\tau < u_\tau)$$
$$\wedge inc(C) \wedge noninc(C) \wedge \epsilon' = tick \wedge same(V - \{\epsilon\})$$

where

$$inc(C) = (\forall \tau \in T_{clock} : e_\tau \to c'_\tau = c_\tau + 1)$$

$$noninc(C) = (\forall \tau \in T_{clock} : \neg e_\tau \to c'_\tau = c_\tau)$$

By the above transition relation, the *tick* transition is not allowed to occur if there is a *must* transition. Thus, the clock variable c_τ will never be incremented to more than the upper time bound u_τ.

For transitions with $u_\tau = \infty$, there is no need to increment c_τ beyond the lower time bound. Since we have not included the master clock, the resulting fair transition system is finite state. The types of the clock variables are thus:

- $type(c_\tau) = \{0, 1, 2, \ldots, l_\tau\}$ if $u_\tau = \infty$
- $type(c_\tau) = \{0, 1, 2, \ldots, u_\tau\}$ if $u_\tau < \infty$.

We noted above that no clock variables are needed for spontaneous transitions $\tau[0, \infty]$. Immediate transitions also do not need clock variables. The four cases are thus:

Case 1: $\tau[0, 0]$: τ is immediately a *must* transition and is taken before the first tick of the clock. No clock variable is needed. The tick transition cannot be taken when τ is enabled.

Case 2: $\tau[0, \infty]$: If τ is *spontaneous* no clock variable is necessary. It is allowed to be taken any time after it is enabled. Since the clock will never reach the upper time bound, which is infinity, tick is allowed to occur freely.

Case 3: $\tau[m, n]$: If m is some integer (which could be zero), and $n < \infty$, a clock variable is introduced. Tick is allowed to happen only when τ is not a *must* transition.

Case 4: $\tau[m, \infty]$: If m is some non-zero number, a clock variable should be introduced since τ can only occur when it has been enabled for at least m ticks of the clock. Tick is allowed to happen since $n_\tau = \infty$.

8.3.1 *The Conversion Procedure*

Given a TTM $M = (V, I, T, J)$ where $T = \{\tau_0, \cdots, \tau_k, tick\}$ the output of the procedure will be a FTS $\hat{M} = (\hat{V}, \hat{I}, \hat{T}, \hat{J})$.

- $\hat{V} := V \cup C \cup \{res\}$ where $C = \{c_\tau : \neg((l_\tau = 0 \wedge u_\tau = 0) \vee (l_\tau = 0 \wedge u_\tau = \infty))\}$
  The FTS variables set consists of the original variables together with the clock variables (Cases 3 and 4).

- $\hat{I} := I \wedge (\forall c_\tau \in C : c_\tau = 0) \wedge (res = false)$
- $\hat{T} = \{\hat{\tau}_0, \cdots, \hat{\tau}_k, \hat{tick}, reset\}$

   where the $\hat{\tau}$ transitions are obtained from the original transition τ according to the discussion in Section 8.3.

- $\hat{J} = J$. The justice set does not change.

The function below is used to increment the clock variable up to either the lower bound (in Case 4, $limit = l_\tau$) or the upper time bound (in Case 3, $limit = u_\tau$).

Definition: Bounded increment

$$Inc(e_\tau, c_\tau, limit) = \begin{cases} c_\tau + 1 & \text{if } e_\tau = \text{true} \wedge c_\tau < limit \\ c_\tau & \text{otherwise} \end{cases}$$

Definition: Reset to Zero

$$Rto0(e_\tau, c_\tau) = \begin{cases} 0 & \text{if } \neg e_\tau \\ c_\tau & \text{otherwise} \end{cases}$$

The above function is used in the *reset* transition to set the clock variables of disabled transitions to zero.

A transition $\hat{\tau}$ in a FTS is described by its transition relation $\rho_{\hat{\tau}}$. As mentioned in Section 8.2, we can obtain the enabling condition $e_{\hat{\tau}}$ and the transformation function $h_{\hat{\tau}}$ from the transition relation. In the conversion procedure, we will refer to the transition $\hat{\tau}$ via a 3-tuple:

$\hat{\tau} = (e_{\hat{\tau}}, h_{\hat{\tau}}, mode)$ where $mode = (\text{if } \hat{\tau} \in \hat{J} \text{ then } Just \text{ else } Spon)$.

8.4   Verifying Clocked Properties

We provide below some examples of how to convert clocked properties into unclocked properties. Since the transformed formulas are difficult to get right, the Build tool allows the user to enter the formulas as clocked expressions, and then transforms the formula into the appropriate unclocked expression.

The converted formulas count the number of tick events that occur. Thus, the size of the formulas grow according to the bounds that must be checked. Since the cost of checking a linear time formula is exponential in the size of the formula, these procedures are only useful for small bounds. For larger bounds we may use explicit clock variables that are reset at the end of the period of interest similar to [Alur 94]. These clock variables progress in lockstep with the tick transition.

- $\Diamond_{=t}P$

  Consider the simple case: $\Diamond_{=1}p$. We can translate this into the unclocked formula: $\bigcirc(\neg\varepsilon = tick\ \mathrm{U}\ (\varepsilon = tick \wedge \bigcirc(\neg\varepsilon = tick\ \mathrm{U}\ p)))$. In general, for the RTTL formula: $\Diamond_{=t}P$, the transformed formula is:

  $\underbrace{\bigcirc(\neg\varepsilon = tick\mathcal{U}(\varepsilon = tick \wedge \ldots \bigcirc(\neg\varepsilon = tick\mathcal{U}(\varepsilon = tick \wedge \bigcirc(\neg\varepsilon =}_{t-1}$

  $tick\mathcal{U}p))) \underbrace{\ldots)}_{t-1}$.

- $\Diamond_{\leq t}p$

  If $t = 1$, the unclocked formula is:
  $\neg\varepsilon = tick\mathcal{U}(p \vee (\varepsilon = tick \wedge \bigcirc(\neg\varepsilon = tick\mathcal{U}p)))$. For general t, the transformed formula is:

  $\underbrace{(\varepsilon = tick \wedge \bigcirc(\neg\varepsilon = tick\mathcal{U}(p \vee \ldots}_{t-1}$

  $(\varepsilon = tick \wedge \bigcirc(\neg\varepsilon = tick\mathcal{U}p)) \underbrace{\overbrace{)))}\ldots\overbrace{)))}}_{t-1}$.

- $\Box_{\leq t}p$

  When $t = 1$, the transformed formula is:

  $$p\mathcal{U}(\varepsilon = tick \wedge p \wedge \bigcirc(p\mathcal{U}\varepsilon = tick))$$

  For general t:
  $p\mathcal{U}(\varepsilon = tick \wedge p \wedge \underbrace{\bigcirc(p\mathbf{U}(\varepsilon = tick \wedge p \wedge \ldots}_{t-1}$

  $\underbrace{\bigcirc(p\mathcal{U}\varepsilon = tick)))\ldots))}_{t-1}\ldots)))$.

8.5   A Real-Time Mutual Exclusion Protocol Example

We now show how a real-time system can be converted by the algorithm. The Fischer mutual exclusion problem will be used as an example. It uses time bounds on its actions to ensure conformance to the protocol. The kernel of each process P_i (where $i \in \{1, 2\}$ executes the following code:

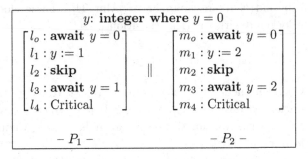

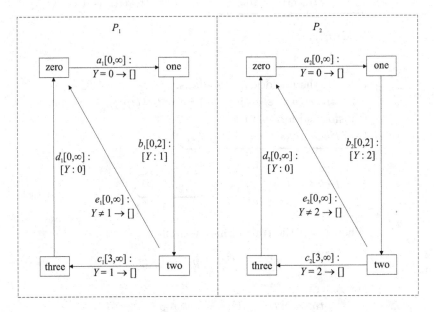

Fig. 8.2   TTM Fischer mutual exclusion

In Figure 8.2, we provide a TTM chart from the Build tool that refines the kernel. It also represents the behavior of the the processes when they exit from their critical regions (location "three" in the figure). The Build tool allows us to annotate transitions with time bounds as shown in the figure. Mutual exclusion is ensured because $l_{c_1} > u_{b_2}$.

The dotted lines around the processes P_1 and P_2 respectively indicate that these two processes are running in parallel. Each P_i has activity variable X_i which ranges from {zero,one,two,three}. The mutual exclusion property therefore is:

$$\Box\neg(X_1 = \text{three} \wedge X_2 = \text{three})$$

By using the conversion procedure, we can convert this into a fair transition system. Untimed tools can be used to do the verification.

We use STeP [Manna 94] below to illustrate the procedure. The input to STeP consists of two parts: a *transition file* and a *specification file*. The transition file models the system by declaring all the variables, macros, constants and transformations. For each transition, there is an **enable** field for the enabling condition and an **assign** field for transformations. Fairness can be asserted for each transition.

In STeP, we have to enumerate all the activities and transitions. Variables are declared as **local** while constants are declared in a **macro**. Values of constants or variables can be initialized in the declaration.

An converter for STeP has been implemented in the Build tool, which automatically generates the appropriate transition file. A template for the transition file is:

```
Transition System
macro c:n where c=v
```

> *declare a constant c of type n with value v*

```
local x:n
```

> *declares variable x with either type or range n*

```
Initially
```

> *initial condition*

```
Transition t Just/NoFairness
```

> **enable** *enabling condition*
> **assign** *assignment statements*

Some of the declarations for the mutual exclusion protocol are shown below. The activity variable X_1 is declared as:

```
local X1 : [0..3]
```

The enabling condition of transition b_1 is declared in a macro:

```
macro e_b_1:bool where e_b_1= (X1=one)
```

The lower time bound and clock variable of c_1 are:

```
macro l_c_1:int where l_c_1 = 3
macro c_c_1:int where c_c_1 = 0
```

The new enabling condition of transition b_2 $(\hat{e}_{b_2})$ is:

```
macro e_hat_b_2:bool where e_hat_b_2 =
(e_b_2 /\ (c_b_2 >= l_b_2) /\ !res )
```

The initial condition is declared as:

```
Initially
(Event = start /\ X1=zero /\ X2=zero /\ Y=0)
```

The functions *Inc* and *RtoO* for transitions *tick* and *reset* are declared as macros:

```
macro Inc:bool*int*int-->int where Inc(e,c,l)= if e /\ c<l then c+1
else c
```

```
macro RtoO:bool*int-->int where RtoO(e,c)=
if !e then 0 else c
```

The transition b_2 with an upper bound $(\neq \infty)$ is declared *Just*. The *res* bit is set to true so that only *reset* can occur. Transition c_1 has an infinite upper bound and is not in the justice set J, so it is declared as NoFairness.

```
Transition B_2 Just:
enable     e_hat_b_2
assign     res:=true, Event:=b_2 , X2:=two , Y:=2, c_b_2:=0
```

```
Transition C_1 NoFairness:
enable     e_hat_c_1
assign     res:=true, Event:=c_1, X1:=three , c_c_1:=0
```

The *tick* transition increments all the clock variables using the function Inc. The *reset* transition will reset the clock variables of all disabled transitions, using the function Rto0.

```
Transition TICK Just:
enable     e_hat_tick
assign     Event:=tick, c_b_1:=Inc(e_b_1,c_b_1,u_b_1),
c_b_2:=Inc(e_b_2,c_b_2,u_b_2),
c_c_1:=Inc(e_c_1,c_c_1,l_c_1), c_c_2:=Inc(e_c_2,c_c_2,l_c_2)

Transition RESET Just:
enable     e_hat_reset
assign     Event:=reset, res:=false,
c_b_1:=Rto0(e_b_1,c_b_1), c_b_2:=Rto0(e_b_2,c_b_2),
c_c_1:=Rto0(e_c_1,c_c_1), c_c_2:=Rto0(e_c_2,c_c_2)
```

In order to check the mutual exclusion property, the complete transition system file is loaded into STeP. The goal:

```
[] ~ ( X1 = three /\ X2 = three )
```

is entered directly in STeP or as a *specification file*. By using the model checking feature in STeP, the above property can be verified for all possible computations.

If the upper time bound of b_i is changed from 2 to 3, STeP provides a counterexample.

8.6 Conclusion

A procedure was presented to convert timed transition systems into fair transitions systems. This allows the use of efficient untimed model checking tools to be used for verifying timed systems.

The procedure has been implemented in the Build tool that automatically converts timed systems into fair transition systems that STeP can model check. The Build tool with its converter has been used on larger systems than shown here. Preliminary data indicates that SPIN [Holzmann 90] can verify larger systems than STeP. On the other hand, we can use STeP's theorem proving capabilities as well as its model-checking facilities for larger systems.

Table 8.1   Conversion procedure

(1) Initially: $\hat{T} := \{\}; e_{t\hat{i}ck} := \neg res;$
    $h_{t\hat{i}ck} := \{\}; res := false; e_{re\hat{s}et} := res; h_{re\hat{s}et} := \{res : false\}$

(2) **FOR all** $\tau \in (T - \{tick\})$ **do**

        case $l_\tau = 0 \wedge u_\tau = 0$ CASE 1

            do $e_{\hat{\tau}} := e_\tau \wedge \neg res$
                $h_{\hat{\tau}} := h_\tau \cup \{res : true\}$
                $\hat{T} := \hat{T} \cup \{(e_{\hat{\tau}}, h_{\hat{\tau}}, Just)\}$
                $e_{t\hat{i}ck} := e_{t\hat{i}ck} \wedge \neg e_\tau$

        case $l_\tau = 0 \wedge u_\tau = \infty$ CASE 2

            do $e_{\hat{\tau}} := e_{\hat{\tau}} \wedge \neg res$
                $h_{\hat{\tau}} := h_\tau \cup \{res : true\}$
            if $\tau \in J$
                then $\hat{T} := \hat{T} \cup \{(e_{\hat{\tau}}, h_{\hat{\tau}}, Just)\}$
                else $\hat{T} := \hat{T} \cup \{(e_{\hat{\tau}}, h_{\hat{\tau}}, Spon)\}$

        case $u_\tau \neq \infty$ CASE 3

            do introduce c_τ and set $c_\tau = 0$
                $e_{\hat{\tau}} := e_\tau \wedge c_\tau \geq l_\tau \wedge \neg res$
                $h_{\hat{\tau}} := h_\tau \cup \{c_\tau : 0\} \cup \{res : true\}$
                $\hat{T} := \{(e_{\hat{\tau}}, h_{\hat{\tau}}, Just)\}$
                $h_{re\hat{s}et} := h_{re\hat{s}et} \cup \{c_\tau : Rto0(e_\tau, c_\tau)\}$
                $e_{t\hat{i}ck} := e_{t\hat{i}ck} \wedge (\neg e_\tau \vee c_\tau < u_\tau)$
                $h_{t\hat{i}ck} := h_{t\hat{i}ck} \cup \{c_\tau : Inc(e_\tau, c_\tau, u_\tau)\}$

        case $l_\tau \neq 0 \wedge u_\tau = \infty$ CASE 4

            do introduce c_τ and set $c_\tau = 0$
                $e_{\hat{\tau}} := e_\tau \wedge c_\tau \geq l_\tau \wedge \neg res$
                $h_{\hat{\tau}} := h_\tau \cup \{c_\tau : 0\} \cup \{res : true\}$
            if $\tau \in J$
                then $\hat{T} := \{(e_{\hat{\tau}}, h_{\hat{\tau}}, Just)\}$
                else $\hat{T} := \{(e_{\hat{\tau}}, h_{\hat{\tau}}, Spon)\}$
                $h_{re\hat{s}et} := h_{re\hat{s}et} \cup \{c_\tau : Rto0(e_\tau, c_\tau)\}$
                $h_{t\hat{i}ck} := h_{t\hat{i}ck} \cup \{c_\tau : Inc(e_\tau, c_\tau, l_\tau)\}$

(3) $\hat{T} := \hat{T} \cup \{(e_{t\hat{i}ck}, h_{t\hat{i}ck}, Just)\}$

(4) $\hat{T} := \hat{T} \cup \{(e_{re\hat{s}et}, h_{re\hat{s}et}, Just)\}$

Chapter 9

Beyond the Verification Approach: The Synthesis Approach

Michel Barbeau and Richard St-Denis

Abstract: Synthesis approaches involve deriving a program from a high-level specification. This can be accomplished by using synthesis algorithms that are well adapted to a particular application domain. Efficiency of synthesis algorithms may be demonstrated by experiments done in different settings. Such experiments help to bridge the gap between empirical practices and formal methods. We present an academic experiment that constitutes a first step toward the performance study of synthesis algorithms that allow verification of properties while generating controllers for discrete-event systems. The goal of this experiment is to show the limitations of synthesis algorithms and compare algorithms between them.

9.1 Introduction

Current software development processes used in the software industry provide guidelines to produce programs by following an *analytical* approach that is mainly based on developer intuition and experience. Whenever a version of the program is available, a verification step is necessary to detect errors and show that the results conform to the requirements specification.

This work has been partially supported by the Natural Sciences and Engineering Research Council of Canada and the Fonds pour la formation de chercheurs et l'aide à la recherche (FCAR).

Part of this task can be achieved with formal verification tools based on *model-checking*. In this framework, the verification of a program (generally consisting of coordinating processes running in parallel) consists in satisfying a temporal logic formula f on a state transition model $\mathcal{P}$ that represents the program (*i.e.*, verifying that $\mathcal{P} \models f$) [Kurshan 95]. If the formula is not satisfied, then the program has to be modified and verified again. This cycle is repeated while errors are detected.

Nevertheless, developers can break the *modification and verification* cycle by using a synthesis procedure that generates the code or a mathematical structure of the program. This schema is particular to the *synthesis* approach. Given state transition models $\mathcal{M}_1, \ldots, \mathcal{M}_n$ that represent the unrestrained behaviors of n processes and a temporal logic formula f that represents constraints on the behaviors of parallel processes, a program $\mathcal{P}$ that satisfies f is derived (*i.e.*, deriving $\mathcal{P}$ from $\langle \mathcal{M}_1, \ldots, \mathcal{M}_n, f \rangle$ such that $\mathcal{P} \models f$). Because our synthesis approach is mainly based on *Supervisory Control Theory* [Ramadge 89b], programs are controllers for discrete-event systems given in the form of transition structures and feedback functions.

In the simplest case, the synthesis of a controller consists in, on the one hand, verifying that the legal language (admissible event sequences according to f) is controllable with respect to $G := \|_{i=1}^{n} \mathcal{M}_i$ (the global state transition model obtained from the synchronous composition of $\mathcal{M}_1, \ldots, \mathcal{M}_n$) and Σ_u (the set of uncontrollable events), and, on the other hand, deriving a controller, that is, a feedback function φ that disables some controllable events according to the current sequence of events generated by G. In contrast to the verification approach, the negative outcome is also handled. Indeed, if the legal language is uncontrollable, then the supremal controllable sublanguage included in the legal language is calculated in the form of a transition structure S that records the observable and controllable behavior of G. The final result is a closed-loop system C/G in which the processes and controller $C := \langle S, \varphi \rangle$ evolve concurrently.

The synthesis of controllers for discrete-event systems and formal verification share the same mathematical foundations and their underlying theoretical concepts are well-mature. In addition, both fields offer formal representations of systems and have their own algorithms. Like verification procedures, the computational complexity of synthesis algorithms grows exponentially with problem size. Hence, computational complexity and expressiveness of formal specification languages constitute an impediment to the application of these techniques in an industrial setting.

Supervisory Control Theory and verification of concurrent processes differ, however, on several points. First, *Supervisory Control Theory* gives special attention to the enunciation of conditions for the solvability of different control problems. These conditions are formulated, for example, in terms of *controllability*, *observability*, *normality*, *nonblocking*, and *nonconflicting*. Second, there are very few real control applications based on this theory reported in the literature [Balemi 93; Brandin 94a]. To the best of our knowledge, most synthesis algorithms have not been yet implemented so that they can be used efficiently on real problems. Much work remains to be done before we can truly claim that synthesis of control systems is feasible on a large scale. Finally, as mentioned earlier, the synthesis approach tackles a different class of problems, with larger state spaces, that are solved with their own software development process close to automatic programming. These characteristics suggest that this approach requires more experimentation.

An experiment was conducted to compare two families of synthesis algorithms. The algorithms used in this experiment deal with safety properties, which is a practical rather than theoretical limitation. The reason for conducting such an experiment is of an application-oriented nature. Before attempting to design a software development environment based on *Supervisory Control Theory*, it would be useful to know what features would be efficient in the implementation of synthesis algorithms and valuable to engineers in the construction of controllers.

Section 9.2 reviews some basic concepts of *Supervisory Control Theory* and outlines the main characteristics of synthesis algorithms. Section 9.3 briefly describes the synthesis algorithms that we have retained for this experiment and shows how they work in a short example. Section 9.4 fixes experimental parameters and describes the problems and the tool used. Section 9.5 provides the main results of the experiment. Section 9.6 concludes with comments that indicate to what extent the experiment is conclusive.

9.2 Supervisory Control Theory

The objective of *Supervisory Control Theory* is the supervision of discrete-event systems (DES), which are characterized by a discrete state space and an event-driven dynamics. This theory has been described in three survey papers [Cassandras 95; Ramadge 89b; Thistle 96] and one book

[Kumar 95]. We recall only the underlying concepts and results, related to the control under full observation, that are necessary to understand how our experiment unfolds.

9.2.1 *Preliminaries*

In the context of automaton-based models, a DES is represented by a deterministic automaton $G = (X, \Sigma, \delta, x_0)$, where X is a finite set of states, Σ is a finite set of events, $\delta : \Sigma \times X \rightarrow X$ is a transition function, and $x_0 \in X$ is an initial state. Let Σ^* and Σ^ω be the set of finite words and the set of infinite words over Σ, respectively. We extend the transition function δ to apply to a word and a state as in the usual way. A DES modeled by an automaton G generates a $*$-language $L(G) \subseteq \Sigma^*$ defined as

$$L(G) := \{w \in \Sigma^* : \delta(w, x_0) \text{ is defined}\}.$$

A second language can be defined from a DES if we introduce an acceptance condition for G which is a pair (X_m, Θ), where $X_m \subseteq X$ is a set of marker states and Θ is a predicate on sequences of states that belong to X. A trajectory of G on an ω-word $w = w[0]w[1]\ldots$ is an infinite sequence of states $\tau = x[0], x[1], \ldots$ such that $x[0] = x_0$ and $x[i+1] = \delta(w[i], x[i])$. For a natural number n, $\tau[0..n]$ is the finite sequence of states $x[0], x[1], \ldots, x[n]$. The set of trajectories of G is denoted by $T^\omega(G)$ and the set of finite sequences of states of G is denoted by $T^*(G)$.

We give two examples of sequences of states accepted by G with respect to (X_m, Θ) (other examples are given by Maler *et al.* [Maler 95]):

$$\mathcal{S}(G, X_m, \dashv) := \{\tau[0..n] \in T^*(G) : x[n] \in X_m\} \text{ and} \qquad (\textbf{Ex1})$$
$$\mathcal{S}(G, X_m, \Box\Diamond) := \{\tau \in T^\omega(G) : Inf(\tau) \cap X_m \neq \emptyset\}, \qquad (\textbf{Ex2})$$

where $Inf(\tau)$, the infinity set of τ, denotes the set of all states appearing in τ infinitely many times (*i.e.*, $Inf(\tau) := \{x \in X \mid (\exists^\omega i)(x[i] = x)\}$). According to (**Ex1**), where $\Theta = \dashv$, a sequence of states is accepted as long as it ends with a marker state. This case corresponds to classical finite automata. According to (**Ex2**), where $\Theta = \Box\Diamond$, a trajectory is accepted as long as it infinitely often contains at least one marker state. This case corresponds to Büchi automata.

If we consider the finite behaviors of G, then $L(G)$ is the *closed* behavior of G and

$$L_m(G) := \{w \in \Sigma^* : (\exists \tau \in T^*(G) \text{ on } w)(\tau \in \mathcal{S}(G, X_m, \dashv))\}$$

is a $*$-language that defines the *marked* behavior of G [Ramadge 87]. In that case, the role of X_m is to record the complete tasks of G. If we consider the infinite behaviors of G, then $L(G)$ is the *transient* behavior of G and

$$L_p(G) := \{w \in \Sigma^\omega : (\exists \tau \in T^\omega(G) \text{ on } w)(\tau \in \mathcal{S}(G, X_m, \square \Diamond))\}$$

is an ω-language that represents the *persistent* behavior of G [Ramadge 89a].

The use of $*$-languages or ω-languages in modeling discrete-event systems depends on the types of constraints included in the control requirements. Whereas safety properties can be expressed as conditions on finite sequences of states, liveness properties refer to infinite behaviors and thus can only be formulated by considering infinite sequences of states [Manna 91].

Let $\Sigma^\infty := \Sigma^* \cup \Sigma^\omega$ and $V \subseteq \Sigma^\infty$. The prefixes of V, noted $\text{pre}(V)$, is the set $\{u \in \Sigma^* \mid (\exists v \in V)(u \text{ is a prefix of } v)\}$. It should be noted that $\text{pre}(L_m(G)) \subseteq L(G)$ and $\text{pre}(L_p(G)) \subseteq L(G)$. If $\text{pre}(L_m(G)) = L(G)$ or $\text{pre}(L_p(G)) = L(G)$, then G is nonblocking.

Consider modifying a DES such that Σ is partitioned into two fixed disjoint subsets Σ_c and Σ_u, the set of *controllable* events and set of *uncontrollable* events, respectively. The new model is called a *controlled* DES.

A *supervisor* for a controlled DES G is a function $s : L(G) \to 2^{\Sigma_c}$ that maps each finite sequence of events to a set of disabled events. Given a controlled DES G and a supervisor s, the closed-loop system consisting of s controlling G is denoted s/G. Its closed behavior is the language $L(s/G) \subseteq L(G)$ defined recursively as i) $\epsilon \in L(s/G)$ and ii) for all $w \in \Sigma^*$ and $\sigma \in \Sigma$, $w\sigma \in L(s/G)$ iff $w \in L(s/G)$, $w\sigma \in L(G)$, and $\sigma \notin s(w)$. If the acceptance condition for G is $(X_m, \dashv)$, then the marked behavior of s/G is the language $L_m(s/G) := L(s/G) \cap L_m(G)$. If the acceptance condition for G is $(X_m, \square \Diamond)$, then the persistent behavior of s/G is the language $L_p(s/G) := \lim(L(s/G)) \cap L_p(G)$, where $\lim(K) := \{w \in \Sigma^\omega : \text{pre}(\{w\}) \subseteq K\}$ (*i.e.*, the set of infinite words having their prefixes in K). A supervisor s is said nonblocking for G if $\text{pre}(L_m(s/G)) = L(s/G)$ or $\text{pre}(L_p(s/G)) = L(s/G)$.

In addition to a DES G, a control problem includes a language L that represents its legal behavior or the control requirements. The control problem addressed hereinafter is now formulated in a general form as follows:

> Given a controlled DES G and a legal language L, find a nonblocking supervisor s such that the behavior of the closed-loop system s/G is restrained to the greatest number of admissible event sequences included in L and possible in G.

In the sequel, we concentrate on the case of finite behaviors. The reader must, however, keep in mind that the concepts and results presented hereinafter have been extended to the case of infinite behaviors [Thistle 94b].

Let a language $K \subseteq \Sigma^*$. The expression $\overline{K}$ denotes the *prefix closure* of K. A language $K \subseteq \Sigma^*$ is **-controllable* with respect to G if $\overline{K}\Sigma_u \cap L(G) \subseteq \overline{K}$. Let E be a language included in Σ^*; the set of **-controllable sublanguages of E with respect to G is $\mathcal{C}(E) := \{K \subseteq E \mid K$ is **-controllable w.r.t. $G\}$. This set is nonempty and closed under set union. Thus, it contains a unique supremal element called the *supremal *-controllable sublanguage* of E. Let us consider under what conditions there exists a solution to the nonblocking supervisory control (NSC) problem [Wonham 94].

Theorem 9.1   *Let $L \subseteq L_m(G)$, $L \neq \emptyset$. There exists a nonblocking supervisory control s for G such that $L_m(s/G) = L$ iff L is **-controllable with respect to G and L is $L_m(G)$-closed, that is, $L = \overline{L} \cap L_m(G)$.*

If $L \subseteq L_m(G)$, then it is always the case that $L \subseteq \overline{L} \cap L_m(G)$ since $L \subseteq \overline{L}$. If $L \supseteq \overline{L} \cap L_m(G)$, then the language L is said $L_m(G)$-marked. This means that every complete task of G that is a prefix of a word in L must belong to L (*i.e.*, L agrees about the complete tasks of G). Since the legal language L is not generally **-controllable, the closed-loop system is restricted to the supremal **-controllable sublanguage of L.

Theorem 9.2   *Let $L \subseteq \Sigma^*$ be $L_m(G)$-marked and let $K = sup\mathcal{C}(L \cap L_m(G))$. If $K \neq \emptyset$, there exists a nonblocking supervisory control s for G such that $L_m(s/G) = K$.*

In the case of finite behaviors, if L is $L_m(G)$-marked, then $sup\mathcal{C}(L \cap L_m(G))$ is $L_m(G)$-closed [Wonham 94]. If this condition is not satisfied, then we may consider the *marking nonblocking supervisory control* (MNSC) problem in which the controller detects the complete tasks instead of G.

The two previous theorems can be applied to the MNSC problem except that the conditions $L_m(G)$-closed and $L_m(G)$-marked are irrelevant. We have a similar situation in the case of infinite behaviors. There are control problems in which the supremal ω-controllable sublanguage of $L \subseteq L_p(G)$ is not ω-closed with respect to $L_p(G)$. This means that there are cycles that do not satisfy the liveness properties. In some conditions, a family of useful supervisors can, however, be generated by unwinding the bad cycles a finite number of times [Barbeau 98]. An example is given in Sec. 9.3.2 to illustrate this point.

9.2.2 *Synthesis Procedures*

In addition to theoretical results, several synthesis procedures have been proposed and may be classified into different categories according to the following criteria:

- *The control problem to be solved.* Most control problems have been formulated and studied in the perspective of control under full observation, control under partial observation, modular control, decentralized control, hierarchical control, on-line control, control of timed discrete-event systems, and control of vector discrete-event systems.
- *The underlying semantic models.* Synthesis procedures have been initially developed in the context of automaton-based models. Petri net-based models have also been used [Holloway 97]. In the past, ω-automata [Thistle 94a] and temporal logics [Barbeau 98] have been exploited to model infinite behaviors of systems and express liveness and real-time properties.
- *The algorithm approach.* There are many ways to translate a synthesis procedure into a program. On the one hand, one can implement mathematical operators or formulas explicitly into the code. The algorithms resulting from this approach are based on a fixpoint [Maler 95; Wonham 87], algebraic [Wonham 94], or linear integer mathematical programming [Li 94] calculation. On the other hand, one can adopt various search space techniques and heuristics in the area of artificial intelligence [Barbeau 98; Ben Hadj-Alouane 94; Ben Hadj-Alouane 96]. The algorithms resulting from this approach are based on a forward search with backtracking operations.

- *The implementation aspects.* The choice of data structures impacts on the efficiency of algorithms. For example, binary decision diagrams can be used to store and manipulate legal languages with significantly less computation than an explicit representation [Balemi 93]. Symmetry specifications can be used to avoid an exhaustive search of the state space [Makungu 96]. Symbolic representations can be used to facilitate the debugging of the possible solutions.

The synthesis procedures that we consider accept as inputs a DES G that defines the unrestrained behavior of the system, a set of uncontrollable events, and a legal language given in the form of an automaton $H = (Y, \Sigma, \xi, y_0, Y_m)$ or a temporal logic formula f formalizing the properties of the control requirements. They produce as output a *controller C*, that is a realization of a supervisor, implemented as a transition structure $S := (Z, \Sigma, \gamma, z_0, Z_m)$ and a feedback function $\varphi : Z \to 2^{\Sigma - \Sigma_u}$. The behavior of the closed-loop system is defined by $(X \times Z, \Sigma, \delta \times \gamma, (x_0, z_0))$, where the function $\delta \times \gamma : \Sigma \times X \times Z \to X \times Z$ is defined as $(\delta \times \gamma)(\sigma, (x, z)) = (\delta(\sigma, x), \gamma(\sigma, z))$ if $\delta(\sigma, x)$ is defined, $\gamma(\sigma, z)$ is defined, and $\sigma \notin \varphi(z)$. In contrast to a supervisor s, which is applied to an event sequence $w \in L(G)$, a feedback function is applied to a state $z \in Z$ (*i.e.*, $\varphi(\gamma(w, z_0)) = s(w)$).

9.3   Synthesis Algorithms for Totally Observed DES

We overview the synthesis algorithms that are used in this experiment and illustrate how they work on a *cat and mouse* example (adapted from an example taken from Ramadge and Wonham [Ramadge 89b]). A cat and a mouse move in a maze that have eight rooms accessible through several doors. The configuration of the maze is pictured in Fig. 9.1.

Each door is unidirectional and is either for the exclusive use of the cat $(c_0, \ldots, c_{10})$ or for the exclusive use of the mouse $(m_1, \ldots, m_6)$. Doors c_7, c_8, and c_9 are always open, while others can be opened or closed. Two constraints must be insured by a controller. The cat and the mouse must never occupy the same room simultaneously and must be able to return to their initial room. We assume that initially the cat is in room 2 and the mouse is in room 4. The behavior of the cat and the mouse are modeled by two automata in which a state represents a room and a transition the

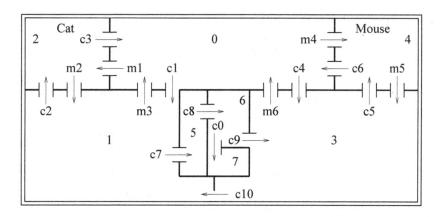

Fig. 9.1   Maze for cat and mouse

movement from an exit room to an entry room through a particular door. Figure 9.2 shows the solution for this problem calculated by the algorithms in Secs 9.3.1 and 9.3.3. Each state is an ordered pair of room numbers giving the current positions of the cat and mouse. The sequence of events $c_3 c_1 m_5$ that is possible in G is prohibited by the controller because event m_5 is disabled at state $(1\ 4)$. If it was not the case, the mouse would be able to move from room 4 to room 3 on event m_5 and then the cat would be able to move from room 1 to room 3 on the sequence of uncontrollable events $c_7 c_8 c_9$. The cat and the mouse would unfortunately be in the same room!

9.3.1   *Wonham and Ramadge Synthesis Algorithm*

The Wonham and Ramadge algorithm [Ramadge 87] is characterized by the following operator:

$$\Omega(K) = L \cap L_m(G) \cap \sup\{T \subseteq \Sigma^* \mid T = \overline{T}, T\Sigma_u \cap L(G) \subseteq \overline{K}\}. \quad \textbf{(Ex3)}$$

Starting with $K_0 = L \cap L_m(G)$ and calculating $K_{i+1} = \Omega(K_i)$, $i \geq 0$, the supremal *-controllable sublanguage of the legal language is the largest fixpoint of Ω. The sets $K_0, K_1, \ldots$, defined by Eq. (**Ex3**), can be straightforwardly computed by an iterative algorithm. The code is given in Fig 9.3.

This algorithm works on the product transition structure $\langle S, h \rangle := G \times H$ that represents the admissible event sequences that are possible in G.

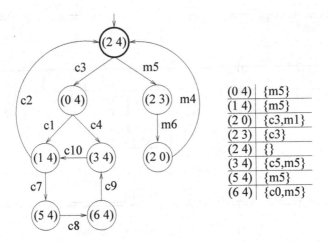

(0 4)	{m5}
(1 4)	{m5}
(2 0)	{c3,m1}
(2 3)	{c3}
(2 4)	{}
(3 4)	{c5,m5}
(5 4)	{m5}
(6 4)	{c0,m5}

Fig. 9.2   The controller for the *cat and mouse* example

Automaton S *refines* G and h is the *correspondence function* between states of S and states of G. Two states are in correspondence if they represent the same event sequences. Furthermore, the product of G by H ensures that $K_0 = L \cap L_m(G)$. The controllability property expressed as $T\Sigma_u \cap L(G) \subseteq \overline{K}$ in Eq. (**Ex3**) is implemented at lines 3–10. The expression $\Sigma_u(z)$ at line 5 denotes the *active set* of state z and is defined by $\{\sigma \mid \sigma \in \Sigma_u \text{ and } \gamma(\sigma, z) \text{ is defined}\}$. The nonblocking property, which is reflected by the expression $T = \overline{T}$ in Eq. (**Ex3**), is implemented at line 11 by a call to the procedure *Trim*, which keeps only reachable and coreachable* states of S. Thus, the algorithm calculates the automaton of the controller by repetitively pruning states of S. At each iteration, each state of S is compared with the corresponding state of G. If a state of S does not comprise an outgoing transition on an uncontrollable but physically possible event in G, then it is eliminated as well as non-coreachable states that cause blocking. This process ends when no state of S can be removed. Lines 13–15 compute the feedback function. Given a state $z \in Z$, the feedback function assigns to z the set of events that cannot occur from x in G, where $x = h(z)$.

The execution of this algorithm in the *cat and mouse* example is summarized in Table 9.1. For each iteration, the table indicates the states

---

*A state z is coreachable if there exists a word that leads to a marker state from z.

```
1  function Derive_Controller(in G, H, Σ_u, out ⟨S, φ⟩)

2    ⟨S, h⟩ ← G × H; /* S = (Z, Σ, γ, z_0, Z_m) */

3    repeat
4        Z' ← Z;   γ' ← γ;
5        Z ← {z | z ∈ Z' and Σ_u(h(z)) ⊆ Σ_u(z)};
6        for each (σ, z) in Σ × Z do
7            if γ'(σ, z) ∈ Z then
8                γ(σ, z) ← γ'(σ, z);
9            else
10                γ(σ, z) is undefined;

11       Trim(S);
12   until Z = Z';

13   for each z in Z do
14       for each σ in Σ − Σ_u do
15           if not γ(σ, z)! then φ(z) ← φ(z) ∪ {σ};
16 end.
```

Fig. 9.3   Wonham and Ramadge synthesis algorithm

that are removed depending on the property (controllability, nonblocking, or reachability) that is violated. The number of states and the number of transitions in G are 40 and 97, respectively. Initially, S has 33 states and 65 transitions. The algorithm performed four iterations to find the solution.

Table 9.1   Trace of the execution of the Wonham and Ramadge algorithm in the *cat and mouse* example

Iteration	Controllability	Nonblocking	Reachability
1	(6 3)	(7 0), (7 1), (7 2), (7 3), (7 4)	
2	(5 3)		
3	(1 3)	(0 3)	(0 1), (0 2), (1 0), (1 2), (3 0), (3 1), (3 2), (4 0), (4 1), (4 2), (5 0), (5 1), (5 2), (6 0), (6 1), (6 2)
4			

9.3.2   *Barbeau, Kabanza, and St-Denis Synthesis Algorithm*

The algorithm proposed by Barbeau *et al.* [Barbeau 98] is more general than the previous algorithm because it allows synthesis from control requirements that may include not only safety properties, but also liveness and real-time properties. The admissible event sequences are expressed by an MTL (metric temporal logic) formula and the nonterminating behavior of the system is modeled by a timed transition graph which is like a Büchi automaton, but with the following particularities: i) $L_p(G) := \lim(L(G))$, ii) events have time duration, and iii) states are labeled by propositional symbols. This algorithm produces a controller by using a forward search technique instead of a fixpoint calculation. More precisely, it simultaneously performs the following operations:

- Incremental exploration of the state space from $\mathcal{M}_1, \ldots, \mathcal{M}_n$ (instead of G) while verifying formula f over trajectories of G to detect bad states (violations of safety properties) or bad cycles (violations of liveness properties). The result is a finite labeled directed graph that represents a combination of f and some trajectories of G.
- Use of a control-directed backtracking technique that goes back over an uncontrollable path of arbitrary but finite length (instead of length 1), from bad states or states that close bad cycles, to prune the search space more efficiently. Most of the states on these paths are not expanded further.
- Incremental creation of the state space of the controller (instead of extracting S from $G \times H$) and calculation of the feedback function by incrementally determining states at which controllable events must be disabled.

Compared with the Wonham and Ramadge algorithm, which works on the structure $G \times H$, our algorithm computes the expression $\mathcal{M}_1 \parallel \cdots \parallel \mathcal{M}_n$ *on-the-fly* and assigns to each generated state: n ordered propositional symbols (one per process), a formula, and a set of unbounded-time eventualities. A state $z = \langle (p_1, \ldots, p_n), g, E \rangle$ generated by the algorithm is interpreted as follows: propositional symbols $p_1, \ldots, p_n$ hold at z, formula g would have to be satisfied by sequences of states starting at z in order for the entire sequences from the initial state to satisfy f, and the set E contains the unbounded-time eventualities that would have to be eventually satisfied along cycles in order to satisfy liveness properties in f. Thus, the transition function ξ of H is replaced by a mechanism of formula progression and the states of H are replaced by temporal formulas that result from the progression of f through trajectories of G. In addition, sets of unbounded-time eventualities are also progressed to take into account liveness properties that can only be violated by infinite trajectories or cycles [Kabanza 97]. In the Wonham and Ramadge algorithm, the number of generated states is the maximum of $|X|$ and $|Z|$ (the number of states in $G \times H$). In the Barbeau *et al.* algorithm, the number of generated states is less than or equal to $|X| \times |\mathcal{F}| \times |\mathcal{E}|$, where $\mathcal{F}$ is the set of different possible subformulas of f and $\mathcal{E}$ is the set of different possible sets of unbounded-time eventualities obtained from subformulas of f.

For the *cat and mouse* example, $f = (\wedge_{i=0}^{4} \Box \neg(i\ i)) \wedge (\Box \Diamond(2\ 4))$. The first subformula of f expresses the safety property that the cat and mouse must never be in the same room. The second subformula states that it is always the case that the cat and mouse will be eventually in room $(2\ 4)$ whatever their current position. This is a liveness property. Figure 9.4 illustrates a part of the expansion of the state space. In this figure, $g = f \wedge \Diamond(2\ 4)$. The progression of f from state $\langle(2\ 3), f, \{\}\rangle$ on event m_6 is g. This means that the present part of f, which is $\wedge_{i=0}^{4} \neg(i\ i)$, is satisfied at $\langle(2\ 3), f, \{\}\rangle$ and the future part of f, which is formula g, would have to be satisfied from $\langle(2\ 0), g, \{\}\rangle$. The progression of the empty set of unbounded-time eventualities from state $\langle(1\ 4), g, \{\}\rangle$ on event c_7 is $\{(2\ 4)\}$ because g contains a conjunct (*i.e.*, $\Diamond(2\ 4)$) that represents an eventuality to be satisfied. The progression of the set of unbounded-time eventualities $\{(2\ 4)\}$ from state $\langle(2\ 4), g, \{(2\ 4)\}\rangle$ on event m_5 is the empty set because the eventuality $(2\ 4)$ holds at $\langle(2\ 4), g, \{(2\ 4)\}\rangle$. Thus, the eventuality $(2\ 4)$ is removed from the set of unbounded-time eventualities.

In Fig. 9.4, solid lines represent the controller (the feedback function is indicated to the right of good states). Dashed lines represent trajectories that have been explored then rejected because they lead to bad states (states labeled *false*) or states that do not close a cycle (states that cause blocking). Dotted lines represent a bad cycle (a cycle that does not contain an empty set of unbounded-time eventualities). A bad cycle corresponds to the situation in which the cat runs clockwise infinitely through rooms 1, 5, 6, and 3 without ever returning to room 2. Since event c_7 is uncontrollable, the controller can only prevent this situation from occurring at state $\langle(0\ 4), f, \{\}\rangle$ by disabling the controllable event c_1, Unfortunately, this state is blocking. Thus, the controller must disable controllable event c_3 at state

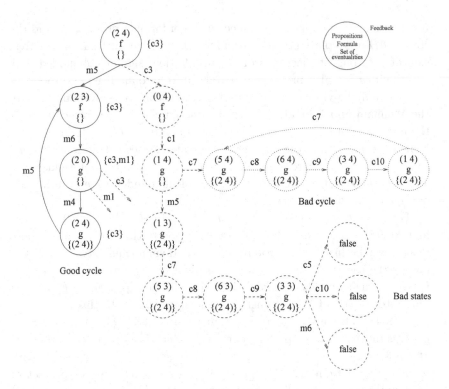

Fig. 9.4 Expansion of the state space for the *cat and mouse* example

$\langle(2\ 4), f, \{\}\rangle$. If event c_7 were controllable, then it would be possible to generate a useful (not maximally permissive) controller by unwinding the bad cycle a finite number of times.

One may observe that this controller is more restrictive than the controller in Fig. 9.2. This is essentially due to the liveness property in f. In the case of finite behaviors, synthesis procedures allow cycles of unmarked states with transitions going out of the cycles. The system is accountable for leaving cycles to complete a task.

9.3.3 *Barbeau, Kabanza, and St-Denis Synthesis Algorithm (Safety Properties)*

The algorithm described in Sec. 9.3.2 can be adapted to situations in which control requirements include only safety properties and instantaneous events. We obtain a forward search based algorithm that works on the untimed transition structure $(\mathcal{M}_1 \parallel \cdots \parallel \mathcal{M}_n) \times H^\dagger$ and solve the same problems as the Wonham and Ramadge algorithm [Barbeau 97]. This is the version of the algorithm that was used in the experiment. Table 9.2 gives, in part, a trace of its execution in the *cat and mouse* example.

Table 9.2 Trace of the execution of the Barbeau *et al.* algorithm in the *cat and mouse* example

Step	Expanded	Generated	Controllability	Nonblocking
1	(2 4)	(0 4), (2 3)		(2 4)
2	(2 3)	(0 3), (2 0)		
3	(2 0)	*(2 4)*		(2 0), (2 3)
4	(0 3)	(1 3)		
5	(1 3)	(5 3), (1 0) *(2 3)*		(1 3), (0 3)
6	(1 0)	(5 0), (1 2), (1 4) *(2 0)*		(1 0)
7	(1 4)	(5 4) *(2 4),(1 3)*		(1 4)
8	(5 4)	(6 4), *(5 3)*		
9	(6 4)	(7 4), (3 4), (6 3)		
10	(6 3)	(7 3)	(6 3)	
11	(3 4)	*(1 4)*		(3 4), (6 4), (5 4)
⋮				
31	(5 3)		(5 3), (1 3)	
32	(0 4)	*(1 4),(3 4),(0 3)*		(0 4)

For each step, the table indicates the states that violate the controllability property and states that are nonblocking. The algorithm generated 33 states and expanded 32 of them. The states appearing in italics have been already generated, but were visited during the expansion of states. Note that an uncontrollable path of length greater than 1 has been eliminated in a single step (see step 31). In contrast, the Wonham and Ramadge algorithm requires two iterations to obtain the same result.

9.4 Description of the Experiment

This experiment is academic in nature and comprises two main objectives. Firstly, it seeks to show the limitations of the synthesis approach as well

---

†The expression $\mathcal{M}_1 \parallel \cdots \parallel \mathcal{M}_n$ is always calculated on-the-fly.

Table 9.3   Characteristics of DES and control requirements

	G		H		Type of
Example	State	Transitions	State	Transitions	Structure
maze (5 rooms)	25	70	18	38	irregular
maze (8 rooms)	40	97	33	65	irregular
2 users	9	18	9	14	symmetrical
3 users	27	81	31	57	symmetrical
4 users	81	324	129	252	symmetrical
factory (3)	27	108	32	248	symmetrical
factory (4)	27	108	40	316	symmetrical
factory (5)	27	108	48	384	symmetrical
factory (10)	27	108	88	724	symmetrical
2 trains	10^2	2×10^2	70	120	symmetrical
3 trains	10^3	3×10^3	150	300	symmetrical
4 trains	10^4	4×10^4	100	160	symmetrical

as the efficiency (or inefficiency) of the tool used. Secondly, it aims to evaluate and compare synthesis algorithms. Thus, a number of examples — obtained from four basic problems — have been analyzed during this experiment. They consist of tens to several thousands of states.

The first three problems are taken from a paper by Ramadge and Wonham [Ramadge 89b]: the maze problem (already presented in Sec. 9.3), the problem of sharing a single resource by l users, and the factory problem in which two machines feed a buffer and another takes parts from the buffer. The fourth problem was initially suggested by Jensen [Jensen 92], then reconsidered by Makungu *et al.* [Makungu 94] in the framework of the *Supervisory Control Theory*, where the DES is represented by a colored Petri net. It consists in synthesizing a controller that orders m trains on a circular railway composed of n sections, where $m \leq (n-2) \div 2$[‡]. Tables 9.3 and 9.4 give the complexity of each example with respect to the size of input automata G and H, and output automaton S, respectively.

During the experiment, it is important to solve problems that have different size and structure characteristics. The structure may be symmetrical or irregular. The size of a problem is defined in terms of the number of states in G (*i.e.*, $|X|$), the number of states in H (*i.e.*, $|Y|$), and the number of states in S (*i.e.*, $|Z|$). The aforementioned problems have the following characteristics:

[‡] The trains must be separated by at least one section, two contiguous free sections are required to move a train, and the entry into any two contiguous sections is controllable.

Table 9.4 Characteristics of controllers

Example	S	
	States	Transitions
maze (5 rooms)	6	9
maze (8 rooms)	8	11
2 users	9	14
3 users	31	57
4 users	129	252
factory (3)	96	302
factory (4)	126	408
factory (5)	156	514
factory (10)	306	1044
2 trains	60	100
3 trains	90	150
4 trains	40	40

- The maze problem has an irregular structure (while the other three have symmetrical structures). Its complexity depends on maze configuration. In this problem, $|X| > |Y| > |Z|$.
- The problem of sharing a single resource by l users is such that $|X| = 3^l$ (three states are used to model the behavior of a user) and $|Y|$ is on the order of $l!$ (since FIFO service is specified in the control requirements, we must take into account the order in which the requests are made). If l is not too large, then the size of G and H are comparable, but generally, $|X| \ll |Y|$. Furthermore, in this problem, the legal language is controllable for any value of l (*i.e.*, $|Y| = |Z|$). It is solely a case of verification.
- The factory problem depends on the length of the buffer, which represents a constraint imposed on the processes. Since the factory has always three machines (*i.e.*, $|X|$ is fixed), $|X| < |Y| < |Z|$.
- The problem of the m trains differs from the other three in that the train movements are more and more limited proportionally to the number of trains that circulate on a ten-section track ($n = 10$). In this problem, $|X| = n^m$ and $|X| \gg |Y| > |Z|$.

The controllers are calculated using our own tool. It implements different synthesis algorithms, among others, for full [Barbeau 97; Wonham 87] and partial observation [Barbeau 95] of events. It is written in the *C++* programming language. To insure code portability, two compilers were used during its development: *gnu* and *ObjectCenter*. Presently, our tool comprises eight specific classes and five generic classes (*templates*), totaling approximately 15,000 lines of code. This small number of lines of code results in an intensive use of generic classes. For example, in controller synthesis, one frequently finds feedback, correspondence, and mask functions. The latter is useful in synthesis problems with partial observation when events are erased or observed differently. The feedback function type is declared using the following statements:

```
typedef Set<Event> SetOfEvents and
typedef Map<State,SetOfEvents> Feedback.
```

The other functions are defined in a similar manner. A state of an automaton is built from atomic states. Its size depends on the size of its atomic states. For example, the state (idle, working), made of two atomic states, occupies 69 bytes. This number is quite high, but this representation allows an implementation in which attributes (*e.g.*, a cost) can be attached to each state. Each transition occupies 12 bytes.

States and transitions are represented in symbolic form, which allows a very high degree of traceability between inputs and outputs. For example, consider the following entry of the feedback function for the *factory* problem:

```
( down idle idle buffer3 repair1 notrepair3 )  :  { feed2 }
```

This entry is interpreted as follows. The controller prevents *machine 2* from feeding the buffer, if *machine 1* is down, *machine 2* and *machine 3* are idle, the number of parts in the buffer is 3 (*i.e.*, the buffer is full), *machine 1* is under repair, and *machine 3* is not under repair.

The experiment was carried out using our tool compiled without optimization with the *gnu* compiler, then executed on a *Sun Microsystems SPARCstation 5* computer with 32 megabytes of main memory. The size of the program, without system functions that are loaded dynamically during the execution of the program, is 315 Kbytes. Data are allocated dynamically.

The algorithm presented in Sec. 9.3.1 was implemented with a slight modification. In the code of Fig. 9.3, the bad states detected at line 5 are removed at the end of the repeat-until loop just before the statement at line 11, but they can be removed immediately when they are identified as bad states. The algorithm presented in Sec. 9.3.3 was implemented as described in a companion paper [Barbeau 97] except that no priority was given to uncontrollable transitions.

9.5 Performance Study

In the performance study, we considered eight measures:

(1) the run time (denoted t_1) of a synthesis algorithm without inputs and outputs in seconds;

(2) the total run time (denoted t_2) of the program in seconds (the time spent in execution of the command according to *UNIX*);

(3) the elapsed time (denoted t_3) in seconds from the beginning to the end of the program (the elapsed time during the command according to *UNIX*);

(4) the number of generated states as discussed in Sec. 9.3.2;

(5) the number of expanded states, only for the Barbeau *et al.* algorithm;

(6) the number of inspected states to verify solely the controllability property, only for the Wonham and Ramadge algorithm;

(7) the number of iterations (denoted n), only for the Wonham and Ramadge algorithm; and

(8) the number of exercised transitions (denoted T) in the automaton G to verify solely the controllability property.

Measures do not take into account the effort for problem preparation. In general, files produced by users are small compared to files for systems and legal languages. The latter are generated automatically from basic files provided by users. The problem of memory space was not initially a concern. This aspect of the experiment was confirmed in the sequel, since we have had no difficulties.

Tables 9.5 and 9.6 present the obtained measures resulting from the execution of synthesis algorithms. For each example, the values of variables t_1, t_2, and t_3 are the average of measures of times observed during five executions of the tool. By examining the tables, one observes that run times of synthesis algorithms (t_1) are small with respect to the total run times of the program (t_2). This is due to the fact that reading and validation of data provided in input consume time. For example, the file size of the automaton G in the example of *4 trains* is about two megabytes (compared to 516 bytes for the file size of the automaton modeling the behavior of one train). One also notices that there are few variations in run times (t_1) according to the algorithms used. This can be explained as follows. Firstly, the algorithms use the same base classes. Secondly, in the given examples, the length of uncontrollable paths proceeded through backtracking (and consequently the number of states pruned) in the Barbeau *et al.* algorithm is generally small compared to the overhead due to expand states on-the-fly (this can be easily verified by examining line by line the second column of Table 9.4 and the fifth and sixth columns of Table 9.6). Note, nevertheless, an exception. In the example of *4 trains*, the run time obtained with the Wonham and Ramadge algorithm is higher.

Table 9.5   Measures for the Wonham and Ramadge algorithm

Example	t_1	t_2	t_3	Generated	Inspected	n	T
maze (5 rooms)	0.03	0.28	0.45	25	24	2	66
maze (8 rooms)	0.07	0.38	0.51	40	94	4	247
2 users	0.02	0.20	0.51	9	9	1	18
3 users	0.07	0.41	0.56	31	31	1	93
4 users	0.48	1.66	1.94	129	129	1	516
factory (3)	0.50	1.19	1.43	120	315	3	1164
factory (4)	0.67	1.48	1.70	150	405	3	1518
factory (5)	0.86	1.77	2.06	180	495	3	1872
factory (10)	2.07	3.62	4.04	330	945	3	3642
2 trains	0.14	0.67	0.96	100	130	2	255
3 trains	0.45	5.24	5.84	1000	240	2	649
4 trains	0.86	167.29	170.11	10000	140	2	430

Figure 9.5 allows further discrimination of the two algorithms. For the *users* and *factory* problems, there is no significant gain in total run times for either algorithm. It should be noted, however, that the total run time grows exponentially with the number of users for the *users* problem. If the number of users were larger, it seems that the Barbeau *et al.* algorithm would have a certain advantage over the Wonham and Ramadge algorithm. For the *factory* problem, the total run time grows linearly with the size of the buffer. For the *trains* problem, the Barbeau *et al.* algorithm performs better. This is partially due to huge files handled in the implementation of the Wonham and Ramadge algorithm.

Measures (4) to (8) reproduce, in a sense, internal processing of algorithms. Because the Wonham and Ramadge algorithm is an iterative

Table 9.6 Measures for the Barbeau *et al.* algorithm

Example	t_1	t_2	t_3	Generated	Expanded	T
maze (5 rooms)	0.02	0.21	0.42	8	8	21
maze (8 rooms)	0.05	0.26	0.42	33	32	82
2 users	0.01	0.17	0.33	9	9	18
3 users	0.07	0.30	0.45	31	31	93
4 users	0.56	1.21	1.49	129	129	516
factory (3)	0.54	1.02	1.26	114	111	397
factory (4)	0.78	1.38	1.63	144	141	520
factory (5)	1.02	1.71	2.04	173	170	636
factory (10)	2.49	3.66	4.09	324	321	1215
2 trains	0.16	0.48	0.66	70	70	135
3 trains	0.50	1.12	1.46	145	135	355
4 trains	0.24	0.74	1.08	75	60	210

algorithm, these measures are greater for this algorithm. Nevertheless, in all cases, this is not reflected as a significant gain in run times. One observes that they are all identical for the *users* problem because the legal language is controllable.

9.6 Conclusion

The experiment described in this chapter is interesting from several points of view. Firstly, it focuses on problems having their own specific characteristics.

Secondly, the chosen examples show that we have not yet reached the size limit of processable problems. The run times that we obtained are small considering the size of some of the examples. Nevertheless, it should be noted that the size of automata accepting the legal languages, and consequently that of automata of the controllers, are small. In addition, in most of our examples, times for reading and validating input files are significant.

Thirdly, the fact that run times obtained with the Barbeau *et al.* algorithm (a special case of a more general algorithm handling also liveness and real-time properties) are comparable to the Wonham and Ramadge algorithm is promising. Indeed, this observation shows that the first algorithm does not introduce, to a certain extent, overhead compared to the other. If the Barbeau *et al.* general algorithm described in Sec. 9.3.2 were used on problems that include only safety properties, run times comparable to those of other synthesis algorithms would be achieved. In addition, it is

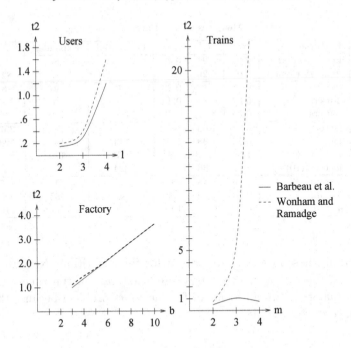

Fig. 9.5   Comparison of total run times

worth mentioning that the Barbeau *et al.* algorithm is adapted to *on-line* calculation of controllers that operate in dynamic environments.

Finally, for some examples, the definition of the legal language is tedious since one proceeds by extension (enumeration of state transitions). The Barbeau *et al.* general algorithm allows us to specify properties in comprehension (formulation of predicates over state transitions). This facilitates the task of controller developers.

Extensions to Formal Languages

Chapter 10

Testing Semantics for Urgent Timed Process Algebras

Luis F. Llana-Díaz, David de Frutos-Escrig and Manuel Núñez

10.1 Introduction

Process algebras have been widely used as high level languages for specifying concurrent systems, for example [Hoare 85; Milner 89; Bergstra 84]. Nevertheless, time is an important aspect of the description of a concurrent system that cannot be directly represented by such process algebras. The introduction of time aspects has received much attention, and there have been many proposals [Reed 86; Ortega-Mallén 91; Yi 91; Baeten 93].

Hennessy and Regan [Hennessy 95] present a testing semantics for a timed process algebra, where there is a simple notion of time: it is expressed by introducing a special action σ. The execution of this action by a process suggests that it is idling until the next clock cycle. In this chapter we present a testing semantics for a process algebra in which time is introduced in a more general way. We have transitions labeled with timed actions similar to those in [Yi 91; Baeten 93; Quemada 93; Schneider 95]. Nevertheless, all our results can be easily adapted to a process algebra with timed transitions and action transitions, as those proposed in [Nicollin 91; de Frutos 94; E-L 97].

The main aim of this paper is to characterize in an explicit way (that is, without using tests) the testing semantics (as in [De Nicola 84;

This research has been partially supported by the CICYT project TIC97-0669-C03-01.

Hennessy 88]) for a timed process algebra in which internal actions are *urgent*. We consider an operational semantics in which transitions are of the form $P \xrightarrow{et} P'$, meaning that the process P performs the event e at time t and becomes P'. Under this operational semantics, internal actions (denoted by i) are considered to be urgent, so we have

$$P \xrightarrow{it} P' \implies \forall\, e, t' > t : P \xrightarrow{et'} \!\!\!\!\not\rightarrow$$

In this chapter we consider a discrete time domain T. Actually, we could also assume a dense time domain for our simple language, but if the language is enriched with other operators, this could be no longer true. For such a language, using a dense time domain, we could define processes that make an infinite number of actions in a finite amount of time. We could also distinguish among processes that are undefined at time 1, just before time 1, or just after time 1, and thus, we should have to consider a rather more complicated model.

The rest of the chapter is structured as follows: In Section 10.2 we give the syntax of our language. In Section 10.3 we present the operational semantics, which is urgent with respect to internal actions, and in Section 10.4 we define the *must* testing semantics. The main section is Section 10.5, where an operational characterization of the *must* testing semantics is given. As *must* testing semantics is not a congruence with respect to + operator, in Section 10.6, we give the characterization of the weakest congruence stronger than must testing equivalence. Finally, in Section 10.7 we present our conclusions and some lines for future work.

10.2   Syntax

In this section we present the syntax of our language. In order to concentrate ourselves on the main characteristics and problems of timed algebras, we introduce a simple timed process algebra which, however, contains the operators that usually characterize such an algebra. In this language time is introduced via the prefix operator; actions must be executed at the indicated time. We will work with a discrete time domain T. We consider a finite set of actions Act, and an internal event $i \notin Act$; then, we consider the sets of events $\mathcal{E} = Act \cup \{i\}$. We denote by $\mathcal{P}$ the set of terms generated by the following BNF expression:

$$P ::= \text{STOP} \mid \text{DIV} \mid et\,; P \mid P_1 + P_2 \mid P \,\|_A\, Q \mid P \setminus A \mid x \mid \text{rec}\, x.P$$

where x denotes a variable process, $A \subseteq Act$, $e \in \mathcal{E}$, and $t \in \mathcal{T}$. A *process* is a closed term generated by the previous grammar. We denote the set of processes by $\mathcal{CP}$. In order to define our operational semantics we need an auxiliary function $Age(t, P)$, which represents the pass of t units of time on P.

Definition 10.1 We inductively define the function $Age(\cdot, \cdot) : \mathcal{T} \times \mathcal{P} \longmapsto \mathcal{P}$, as:

$$Age(t, P) = \begin{cases} P & \text{if } P = \texttt{STOP} \text{ or } P = \texttt{DIV} \\ \texttt{STOP} & \text{if } P = et' \, ; P_1 \text{ and } t' < t \\ e(t' - t) \, ; P_1 & \text{if } P = et' \, ; P_1 \text{ and } t' \geq t \\ Age(t, P_1) \, op \, Age(t, P_2) & \text{if } P = P_1 \, op \, P_2, \; op \in \{+, \|_A\} \\ Age(t, P_1) \setminus A & \text{if } P = P_1 \setminus A \\ \texttt{DIV} & \text{if } P = x \\ Age(t, P_1) & \text{if } P = \texttt{rec} \, x.P_1 \end{cases}$$

where $P[Q/x]$ indicates the syntactical substitution of the free occurrences of x in P by Q. Looking at the operational semantics, we can observe that the function $Age(P, t)$ is only used when $\forall t' < t : P \xrightarrow{it'} \!\!\!\!\!\! /$, so the definition of $Age(t, it' \, ; P)$ when $t' < t$ is not important, and it is included for the sake of completeness. Processes with unguarded recursion are considered undefined (or divergent). This is the reason of the definition of the function $Age(P, t)$ in the last two cases.

10.3 Operational Semantics

The operational semantics of $\mathcal{CP}$ (set of processes) is given by the relation $\longrightarrow \subseteq \mathcal{CP} \times (\mathcal{E} \times \mathcal{T}) \times \mathcal{CP}$ defined by the rules given in Table 10.1. Since some rules in Table 10.1 have negative premises we have to provide a way to guarantee that the transition system is consistent. Following [Groote 93], we consider the following *stratification*: $f(P \xrightarrow{et} P') = t$. This function is indeed a stratification, because we are considering a discrete time domain.

Internal actions are urgent, as the following proposition states. Nevertheless, internal actions have not greater priority than observable actions to be executed at the same time (although, as in the untimed case, the execution of these internal actions could preclude, in a nondeterministic way, the execution of those observable actions). Finally, those observable actions which are executed before some internal action are not affected by the existence of such an internal action.

Table 10.1   Operational Semantics

[DIV] $\mathrm{DIV} \xrightarrow{i0} \mathrm{DIV}$

[PRE] $et\,;P \xrightarrow{et} P$

[CH]
$$\dfrac{P \xrightarrow{et} P', \quad Q \xrightarrow{it'} \!\!\!\!\!\!/ \;\; t' < t}{P+Q \xrightarrow{et} P'} \qquad\qquad \dfrac{P \xrightarrow{et} P', \quad Q \xrightarrow{it'} \!\!\!\!\!\!/ \;\; t' < t}{Q+P \xrightarrow{et} P'}$$

[INT]
$$\dfrac{P \xrightarrow{et} P', \quad Q \xrightarrow{it'} \!\!\!\!\!\!/ \;\; t' < t}{P \,\|_A\, Q \xrightarrow{et} P' \,\|_A\, Age(t,Q)}\; e \notin A \qquad \dfrac{P \xrightarrow{et} P', \quad Q \xrightarrow{it'} \!\!\!\!\!\!/ \;\; t' < t}{Q \,\|_A\, P \xrightarrow{et} Age(t,Q) \,\|_A\, P'}\; e \notin A$$

[SYN]
$$\dfrac{P \xrightarrow{at} P', \quad Q \xrightarrow{at} Q'}{P \,\|_A\, Q \xrightarrow{at} P' \,\|_A\, Q'}\; a \in A$$

[HD1]
$$\dfrac{P \xrightarrow{et} P', \quad P \xrightarrow{at'} \!\!\!\!\!\!/ \;\; t' < t,\; a \in A}{P \setminus A \xrightarrow{et} P' \setminus A}\; e \notin A$$

[HD2]
$$\dfrac{P \xrightarrow{at} P', \quad P \xrightarrow{a't'} \!\!\!\!\!\!/ \;\; t' < t,\; a' \in A}{P \setminus A \xrightarrow{it} P' \setminus A}\; a \in A$$

[REC]
$$\dfrac{P[\mathbf{rec}\,x.P/x] \xrightarrow{et} P'}{\mathbf{rec}\,x.P \xrightarrow{et} P'}$$

Proposition 10.1   *Urgency If* $P \xrightarrow{it} P'$ *then* $P \xrightarrow{et'} \!\!\!\!\!\!/$ *for any* $e \in \mathcal{E}$ *and* $t' > t$.

Another important fact is that our operational semantics is *finite branching*. In an untimed process algebra this property could be set as: *for a given process P there exist a finite number of transitions that P can execute.* This property is satisfied by the timed process algebra we have presented but, given that we want to extend the results of this chapter to a more general timed process algebra, we have modified this property. For instance, if we could have time intervals for the prefix operator such as $a[0..\infty]\,; P$, then the above property is no longer true. Instead, the property that we need is:

Proposition 10.2   *Let* $e \in \mathcal{E}$ *and* $t \in \mathcal{T}$. *Then, the set* $\{P' \mid P \xrightarrow{et} P'\}$ *is finite.*

10.4   Testing Semantics

In this section we define the testing semantics induced by the operational semantics previously defined. First, we introduce the concept of *weak and strong convergence*. Weak convergence is just an auxiliary predicate which is introduced to define strong convergence.

Definition 10.2 We define the *weak convergence* predicate over $\mathcal{P}$ (denoted by $\downarrow$) as the least predicate verifying:

- STOP $\downarrow$.
- For any $t \in \mathcal{T}$, and $e \in \mathcal{E}$ we have $et\,;P \downarrow$.
- If $P \downarrow$ and $Q \downarrow$ then $P \setminus A \downarrow$, $\mathtt{rec}\,x.P \downarrow$, $P\,op\,Q \downarrow$, $op \in \{\|_A, +\}$.

Definition 10.3 We define the *strong convergence*, or simply *convergence*, predicate over $\mathcal{CP}$ (denoted by $\Downarrow$) as the least predicate satisfying:

$$P \Downarrow \iff P \downarrow \text{ and } \forall P'(P \xrightarrow{i0} P' \implies P' \Downarrow)$$

We will say that a process P diverges, which is denoted by $P \Uparrow$, if $P \Downarrow$ does not hold. Note that a process only diverges due either to the occurrence of an unguarded recursion, or to the occurrence of an infinite computation of internal actions executed instantaneously, that is, at time 0.

Tests are just finite processes (recursive processes could also be considered, but they have not been since they would not add any additional semantic information) but defined by the extended grammar where we add a new process, OK, which expresses that the test has been successfully passed. More exactly, tests are generated by the following BNF expression:

$$T ::= \mathtt{STOP} \mid \mathtt{OK} \mid et\,;T \mid T_1 + T_2 \mid T_1 \|_A T_2 \mid T \setminus a$$

The operational semantics of tests is defined in the same way as for plain processes, but adding a new rule for the test OK*:

$$[\mathbf{OK}] \quad \mathtt{OK} \xrightarrow{OK\,0} \mathtt{STOP}$$

Finally, we define the composition of a test and a process as:

$$P \mid T = (P \|_{Act} T) \setminus Act$$

Definition 10.4 Given a computation of $P \mid T$

$$P \mid T = P_1 \mid T_1 \xrightarrow{it_1} P_2 \mid T_2 \cdots P_k \mid T_k \xrightarrow{it_k} P_{k+1} \mid T_{k+1} \cdots$$

we say that it is

- *Complete* if it is finite and blocked (no more steps are possible), or infinite.
- *Successful* if there exists some k such that $T_k \xrightarrow{OK\,0}$ and for all $j < k$ we have $P_j \Downarrow$.

---

*To be exact, we should extend the definition of the operational semantics of both processes and tests to mixed terms defining their composition, since these mixed terms are neither processes nor tests, but since this extension is immediate we have preferred to avoid this formal definition.

Definition 10.5

- We say that P *must pass* the test T (denoted by P must T) iff any complete computation of $P \mid T$ is successful.
- We write $P \sqsubseteq_{\sim} Q$ iff whenever P must T we also have Q must T.

10.5 Operational Characterization

In this section we present an alternative characterization of the (must) testing semantics defined in the previous section. In order to define this characterization we will consider some kind of sets of timed actions which we call *states*. These states will represent any of the possible *local configurations* of a process.

10.5.1 *Sets of States*

A state includes the set of offered timed actions that are offered at some instant, as well as the time, if any, at which the process becomes undefined, i.e. divergent. In order to capture divergence (or equivalently undefinition) with a simple notation, we introduce a new element $\Omega \notin Act$, that represents an undefined substate. Then we consider the sets $Act_{\Omega} = Act \cup \{\Omega\}$, $TAct = Act \times \mathcal{T}$ and $TAct_{\Omega} = Act_{\Omega} \times \mathcal{T}$.

Definition 10.6 We say that $A \subseteq TAct_{\Omega}$ is a *state* if:

- There is at most a single $\Omega t \in A$, i.e., Ωt, $\Omega t' \in A \implies t = t'$.
- If $\Omega t \in A$ then t is the maximum time in A, i.e., Ωt, $at' \in A \implies t' < t$.

We will denote by $\mathcal{ST}$ the set of all the states. Let us illustrate this definition by means of a simple example.

Example 10.1 Let $P = (a1;\text{STOP}) + i2;((i1;b0;\text{STOP}) + i1;(c0;\text{STOP} + i1;\text{DIV}))$. This process is graphically represented in Figure 10.5.1. Initially, action a at time 1 cannot be rejected, i.e., if the environment wants to execute it the process cannot deny it. After 2 units of time we get the process $(i1;b0;\text{STOP}) + (i1;(c0;\text{STOP} + i1;\text{DIV}))$ so, after 1 unit of time more, an internal action i is executed. This execution involves a non-deterministic choice between $b0;\text{STOP}$ and $c0;\text{STOP} + i1;\text{DIV}$, what means their both initial actions in these processes can be either rejected or executed. Finally, in the second process, if time passes one more unit, the process becomes DIV, i.e. undefined. These ideas are captured by the fact that P has two states: $\{a1, b3\}$ and $\{a1, c3, \Omega4\}$.   □

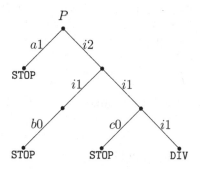

Fig. 10.1

Next we give some auxiliary definitions:

Definition 10.7

- We define the function $nd : \mathcal{ST} \mapsto \mathcal{T} \cup \{\infty\}$, which gives us the time at which a state becomes undefined, as $nd(A) = t$ if $\Omega t \in A$ and $nd(A) = \infty$ otherwise.
- Given a state $A \in \mathcal{ST}$ and a time $t \in \mathcal{T}$, we define:
  - The state $A + t$ as: $A + t = \{a(t + t') \mid at' \in A\}$.
  - The state $A \rceil t$ as: $A \rceil t = \{at' \mid at' \in A \text{ and } t' < t\}$.
- If $A \in \mathcal{ST}$, we define its *set of timed actions* as $TAct(A) = A \rceil nd(A)$.
- If $A \subseteq TAct$ and $t \in \mathcal{T}$, we say that $A < t$ (resp. $A \le t$) iff for all $at' \in A$ we have $t' < t$ (resp. $t' \le t$).

10.5.2 *States of a Process*

In order to define the set of states of a process, first we have to define the initial set of timed actions that a process P can execute, which is given by

$$S(P) = \left\{ at \mid P \xrightarrow{at}, \ a \in Act \right\}$$

To define the states of a process we will generalize the procedure followed in Example 10.1. We observe that a state includes the actions that a process can execute after the execution of a *finite* number of internal actions. Besides, we find a very important difference with respect to untimed process algebras: a process P can execute an infinite sequence of internal actions without diverging; take for instance, the process $P = \mathbf{rec}\, x.i1 \, ; \, x$.

Definition 10.8   Given a process P, the set $\mathcal{A}(P)$ is the set of states $A \in \mathcal{ST}$ which can be generated as described below from a *complete* computation (that is, it is either infinite, or there exists a final process such that either no internal action can be executed, or it diverges)

$$P = P_1 \xrightarrow{it_1} P_2 \xrightarrow{it_2} \cdots P_k \xrightarrow{it_k} P_{k+1} \cdots$$

where if the computation is finite we denote by P_n the final process and we take $t^i = \sum_{j=1}^{i-1} t_j$. Note that $P_i \Downarrow$ for any $i < n$. Then:

- For each such infinite computation, if for each $i \in \mathbb{N}$ we take the set $A_i = S(P_i) \rceil t_i$, we have $\bigcup_{i \in \mathbb{N}} (A_i + t^i) \in \mathcal{A}(P)$.

- For each such finite computation, let $A_i = S(P_i) \rceil t_i$, for any $i \le n-1$, and let $A_n = S(P_n)$ if $P_n \Downarrow$, and $A_n = \{\Omega 0\}$ otherwise. Then we have $\bigcup_{i=1}^{n} (A_i + t^i) \in \mathcal{A}(P)$.

10.5.3   *Barbs*

A barb is a generalization of an acceptance [Hennessy 88], but additional care must be taken about the actions that the process offers *before* any action has been executed. First, we introduce the concept of *b-trace*, which is a generalization of the notion of trace. A b-trace, usually denoted by bs, is a sequence $A_1 a_1 t_1 A_2 a_2 t_2 \cdots A_n a_n t_n$, that represents the execution of the sequence of timed actions $a_1 t_1 a_2 t_2 \cdots a_n t_n$, where the timed actions included in A_i were offered before accepting $a_i t_i$. Then, a *barb* is a b-trace followed by a state; this state represents a configuration of the process after executing the b-trace.

To illustrate these concepts let us recall Example 10.1. There we have that P may execute b at time 3, but a at time 1 is always possible. So we have that P can execute the b-trace $\{a1\}b3$, to become STOP. Urgency is the reason why we have to keep the information about the actions that the process could have executed *before* any other. In this example, if the environment could synchronize in action a at time 1, the process should execute it, and then the action b at time 3 would be no longer possible. The full set of barbs of P is the following

$$Barb(P) = \Big\{ \{a1, b3\}, \{a1, c3, \Omega 4\}, \emptyset a1\emptyset, \{a1\}b3\emptyset, \{a1\}c3\emptyset \Big\}$$

Definition 10.9

- We say that a *b-trace* is a finite sequence, $bs = A_1 a_1 t_1 \cdots A_n a_n t_n$, where $n \geq 0$, $a_i t_i \in TAct$, $A_i \subseteq TAct$, and $A_i < t_i$. We say that $length(b) = n$. If $n = 0$ we have the empty b-trace, which is denoted by ϵ.
- A *barb* b is a sequence $b = bs \cdot A$ where bs is a b-trace and A is a state. We will write the barb $\epsilon \cdot A$ as A, so we consider any state A as a barb.

To define the barbs of a process first we need the some auxiliary definitions.

Definition 10.10   Given $t \in T$, a b-trace $bs = A_1 a_1 t_1 \cdot bs_1$, and a set of timed actions $A \subseteq TAct$, such that $A < t$, we define the b-trace $(A, t) \sqcup bs$ as:

$$(A, t) \sqcup bs = (A \cup (A_1 + t))a(t_1 + t) \cdot bs_1$$

Definition 10.11   Let P, P' be processes and bs be a b-trace. We define the relation $P \stackrel{bs}{\Longrightarrow} P'$ as follows:

- $P \stackrel{\epsilon}{\Longrightarrow} P$.
- If $P \stackrel{it}{\longrightarrow} P_1$ and $P_1 \stackrel{bs'}{\Longrightarrow} P'$, with $bs \neq \epsilon$, then $P \xrightarrow{(S(P)\upharpoonright t, t) \sqcup bs'} P'$.
- If $P \stackrel{at}{\longrightarrow} P_1$, and $P_1 \stackrel{bs'}{\Longrightarrow} P'$ then $P \xrightarrow{(S(P)\upharpoonright t)at \cdot bs'} P'$.

Definition 10.12   Let $b = bs \cdot A$ be a barb and P be a process. We say that b is a *barb* of P (denoted by $b \in Barb(P)$) iff there exists a process P' such that $P \stackrel{bs}{\Longrightarrow} P'$ and $A \in \mathcal{A}(P')$.

We will use barbs to characterize our testing semantics. This will be done by defining a preorder between sets of barbs. In order to define this preorder, we need the following ordering relations.

Definition 10.13   We define the relation $\ll$:

- between b-traces $\ll$ as the least relation satisfying:

  (1) $\epsilon \ll \epsilon$.
  (2) if $bs' \ll bs$ and $A' \subseteq A$ then $A'at \cdot bs' \ll Aat \cdot bs$.

- between barbs as the least relation satisfying:

  (1) if bs, bs' are b-traces such that $bs' \ll bs$ and A, A' are states such that $nd(A') \leq nd(A)$ and $TAct(A') \subseteq A$, then $bs' \cdot A' \ll bs \cdot A$.
  (2) if A' is a state, $b = A_1 a_1 t_1 \cdot b'$ is a barb such that $nd(A') \leq t_1$ and $TAct(A') \subseteq A_1$, and $bs' \ll bs$ then $bs' \cdot A' \ll bs \cdot (A_1 a_1 t_1 \cdot b')$.

Note that the symbol $\ll$ is overloaded: It is used for barbs, set of barbs, and will be used for processes. Intuitively, a b-trace bs is *worse* than bs' if the actions appearing in both b-traces are the same, and the intermediate sets A_i included in bs are *smaller* than the corresponding ones A_i' appearing in bs'. For barbs, we must notice that whenever a process is in an undefined state, that is $nd(A) < \infty$, it cannot pass any test *after* that time. We extend the preorder $\ll$ to sets of barbs as follows:

$$B' \ll B \quad \textbf{iff} \quad (\forall b \in B \ \exists b' \in B' \text{ s.t. } b' \ll b)$$

The relation $\ll$ between sets of barbs induces a relation between processes, i.e., $P \ll Q$ iff $Barb(P) \ll Barb(Q)$. To illustrate the above definitions let us consider the following example.

Example 10.2 Let P and Q as follows:

$$P = (i0 \,;\, \texttt{STOP}) + (i0 \,;\, (a1 \,;\, \texttt{STOP} + b2 \,;\, \texttt{STOP}))$$
$$Q = (i0 \,;\, \texttt{STOP}) + (i0 \,;\, (a1 \,;\, \texttt{STOP} + b2 \,;\, \texttt{STOP})) + (i0 \,;\, b2 \,;\, \texttt{STOP})$$

Their sets of barbs are given respectively by:

$$Barb(P) = \left\{ \begin{array}{l} \varnothing,\ \{a1, b2\}, \\ \varnothing a1\varnothing,\ \{a1\}b2\varnothing \end{array} \right\} \quad Barb(Q) = \left\{ \begin{array}{l} \varnothing,\ \{b2\}, \{a1, b2\}, \\ \varnothing a1\varnothing,\ \varnothing b2\varnothing,\ \{a1\}b2\varnothing \end{array} \right\}$$

We have $Q \ll P$, but for $b = \varnothing b_2\varnothing \in Barb(Q)$ there is no barb $b' \in Barb(P)$ such that $b \ll b'$, so we have $P \not\ll Q$. In $Barb(P)$, b at time 2 is *always offered* together with a at time 1. If P can synchronize with a test that offers a at time 1, then b at time 2 is never executed; oppositely, in Q, b at time 2 may be executed. In fact, if we consider the test

$$T = (a1 \,;\, \texttt{OK}) + (i2 \,;\, \texttt{OK}) + (b2 \,;\, \texttt{STOP})$$

it is easy to check that P must T while Q does not, so $P \not\sqsubseteq Q$. □

The rest of the section is devoted to prove the desired characterization, i.e.

$$P \sqsubseteq Q \iff P \ll Q$$

Lemma 10.1 *Let P be a process such that $P \Downarrow$ and $P \xrightarrow{it'} \!\!\!\!\!/ \ $ for $t' < t$. Then we have:*

- $S(P) = (S(P){\upharpoonright}t) \cup (S(Age(P,t)) + t)$.
- $A \in \mathcal{A}\big(Age(P,t)\big)$ *iff* $(S(P){\upharpoonright}t) \cup (A + t) \in \mathcal{A}(P)$.
- *If $bs \neq \epsilon$ then $Age(P,t) \xRightarrow{bs} P'$ iff $P \xRightarrow{(S(P){\upharpoonright}t,t)\sqcup bs} P'$.*

Proof. By structural induction we have $Age(P,t) \xrightarrow{et'} P'$ iff $P \xrightarrow{e(t'+t)} P'$, and then the result is immediate. □

Lemma 10.2 *For any process P and for each test T, we have*

- *Let $bs = A_1 a_1 t_1 \cdots A_n a_n t_n$ and $bs' = A_1' a_1 t_1 \cdots A_n' a_n t_n$ be b-traces such that $A_i \cap A_i' = \emptyset$. If $T \overset{bs}{\Longrightarrow} T'$ and $P \overset{bs'}{\Longrightarrow} P'$ then there exists a computation from $P \mid T$ to $P' \mid T'$.*
- *Let $A \in \mathcal{A}(P)$, and let us suppose that T has a computation*

$$T = T_1 \xrightarrow{it_1} T_2 \xrightarrow{it_2} T_3 \cdots$$

such that $A \cap ((S(T_i){\restriction}t_i) + t^i) = \emptyset$, where $t^i = \sum_{j=1}^{i-1} t_i$. Then we have:

  - *If $t^i < nd(A)$ then there exists a process P_i such that there is a computation from $P \mid T$ to $P_i \mid T_i$.*
  - *If $t^i < nd(A)$ and $t^{i+1} \geq nd(A)$ then there exists a process P' and a test T' such that $P' \Uparrow$, $T' = Age(T_i, t')$ for some $t' \geq 0$, and there exists a computation from $P \mid T$ to $P' \mid T'$.*

Proof. We apply the previous lemma and the following facts:

- If $P \xrightarrow{at} P'$, $T \xrightarrow{at} T'$ and $(S(P){\restriction}t) \cap (S(T){\restriction}t) = \emptyset$ then we have $P \mid T \xrightarrow{at} P' \mid T'$.
- If $P \xrightarrow{it} P'$, $T \overset{it'}{\nrightarrow}$, with $t' < t$, and $(S(P){\restriction}t) \cap S(T) = \emptyset$ then we have $P \mid T \xrightarrow{it} P' \mid Age(T, t)$.
- If $T \xrightarrow{it} T'$, $P \overset{it'}{\nrightarrow}$, with $t' < t$, and $(S(T){\restriction}t) \cap S(P) = \emptyset$ then we have $P \mid T \xrightarrow{it} Age(P, t) \mid T'$.

$\square$

Now we can already prove the right to left side of our characterization.

Theorem 10.1 *If $P \ll Q$ then $P \sqsubseteq_{\overline{\leftarrow}} Q$.*

Proof. Let T be a test such that P must T. In order to check that Q must T, let us consider any complete computation of $Q \mid T$:

$$Q \mid T = Q_0 \mid T_0 \xrightarrow{it_1} Q_1 \mid T_1' \cdots \xrightarrow{it_k} Q_k' \mid T_k' \cdots$$

This computation may be unzipped into a computation of Q

$$Q = Q_{11} \xrightarrow{it_{11}^Q} \cdots Q_{1\,m_1-1} \xrightarrow{it_{1\,m_1-1}^Q} Q_{1m_1} \xrightarrow{a_1 t_{1m_1}^Q} Q_{21} \cdots$$

and a computation of T

$$T = T_{11} \xrightarrow{it_{11}^T} \cdots T_{1\,n_1-1} \xrightarrow{it_{1\,n_1-1}^T} T_{1n_1} \xrightarrow{a_1 t_{1n_1}^T} T_{21} \cdots$$

where $t_i = \sum_{j=1}^{m_i} t_{ij}^Q = \sum_{j=1}^{n_i} t_{ij}^T$. From the computations of Q and T we can get a sequence of b-traces of Q and T:

$$bs_i^Q = A_1^Q a_1 t_1 \cdots A_i^Q a_i t_i, \qquad bs_i^T = A_1^T a_1 t_1 \cdots A_i^T a_i t_i,$$

such that $Q \xrightarrow{bs_i^Q} Q_{(i+1)1}$, and $T \xrightarrow{bs_i^T} T_{(i+1)1}$, where

$$A_j^Q = \bigcup_{k=1}^{m_j} \left((S(Q_{jk}) \rceil t_{jk}^Q) + \sum_{l=1}^{k-1} t_{jl}^Q \right), \quad A_j^T = \bigcup_{k=1}^{n_j} \left((S(T_{jk}) \rceil t_{jk}^T) + \sum_{l=1}^{k-1} t_{jl}^T \right)$$

Given that the computation of P and T is possible, we have $A_j^Q \cap A_j^T = \emptyset$. Now, given the b-trace bs_i^Q, there exists a state A such that $b_i = bs_i^Q \cdot A \in Barb(Q)$, and so there exists $b = bs \cdot A \in Barb(P)$ such that $b \ll b_i$. If $length(b) < length(b_i)$, by applying the previous lemma we could find an unsuccessful computation of $P \mid T$, which contradicts our hypothesis. So we have $length(b) = length(b_i)$, and then there exists a process P_{i+1} such that there exists a computation from $P \mid T$ to $P_{i+1} \mid T_{(i+1)1}$.

Let us suppose that the sequence of b-traces is infinite. Then, for any $k \in \mathbb{N}$ there exists a process P_k such that there exists a computation from $P \mid T$ to $P_k \mid T_{k1}$. As the operational semantics is finite branching, by applying Köning's Lemma, we have that there exists an infinite computation, in which all the T_{ij}'s appears. As P must T we have that there exists T_{ij} such that $T_{ij} \xrightarrow{OK\,0}$, so the computation of $Q \mid T$ is successful.

Now, let us suppose that there exists a *last* b-trace bs_k^Q. Then, there exists a state A^Q such that

$$A^Q \rceil t^{Qj} = \bigcup_{i=1}^{j-1} \left((S(Q_{(k+1)i}) \rceil t_{(k+1)\,i}^Q) + \sum_{l=1}^{i-1} t^{Q\,i} \right) \quad \text{where} \quad t^{Q\,i} = \sum_{l=1}^{i-1} t_{(k+1)l}^Q$$

and $b^Q = bs_k^Q \cdot A^Q \in Barb(Q)$. As $P \ll Q$, there exists some $b^P = bs^P \cdot A^P \in Barb(P)$ such that $b^P \ll b^Q$. Let us suppose that $P \xrightarrow{bs^P} P'$ and $A^P \in \mathcal{A}(P')$. If $length(b^P) < length(b^Q)$, by applying the previous lemma we can find an unsuccessful computation of $P \mid T$, which contradicts our hypothesis. So we necessarily have $length(b^P) = length(b^Q)$. Let us consider $t^{T,i} = \sum_{j=1}^{i-1} t_{(k+1)j}^T$. Then, for any $t^{T,i} < nd(A^P)$, there exists a computation from $P' \mid T_{(k+1)1}$ to $P_i \mid T_{(k+1)i}$, for some P_i. If either $nd(A^P) < \infty$ or the collection of tests is finite, as P must T there must be some test T_{ij} such that $T_{ij} \xrightarrow{OK\,0}$, so we have that the computation of $Q \mid T$ is successful. If $nd(A^P) = \infty$ and the collection of tests is infinite, as the operational semantics is finite branching, by applying Köning's lemma, we have that there must be some infinite computation, in which all the T_{ij}'s appear. As P must T we have that there exists T_{ij} such that $T_{ij} \xrightarrow{OK\,0}$, so the computation of $Q \mid T$ is successful. $\qquad\square$

Now we have to prove that $P \sqsubseteq_{\mathcal{C}} Q$ implies $P \ll Q$. For it, let us assume that $P \not\ll Q$. Then, by definition, there exists some $b \in Barb(Q)$ such that there does not exist any $b' \in Barb(P)$ such that $b' \ll b$. To find a test T such that P must T and Q m$\not$ust T we will generalize the procedure described in Example 10.2. First, we need some auxiliary definitions.

Definition 10.14 Let B be a set of barbs and bs be a b-trace. We define the set of barbs of B *after* bs as: $Barb(B, bs) = \{b \mid bs \cdot b \in B\}$.

Definition 10.15 Given a barb b and a set of barbs B such that there does not exist $b' \in B$ such that $b' \ll b$, we say that a test T is *well formed with respect to B and b* when it can be derived by applying the following rules:

- If $b = A$, we take a finite set $A_1 \subseteq TAct$ such that for any $A' \in B$ such that $nd(A') \leq nd(A)$, we have $A_1 \cap A' \neq \emptyset$. Then, taking

$$T_1 = \begin{cases} it \text{ ; OK } & nd(A) = t < \infty \\ \text{STOP} & \text{otherwise} \end{cases} \quad T_2 = \begin{cases} \displaystyle\sum_{at \in A_1} at \text{ ; OK } & A_1 \neq \emptyset \\ \text{STOP} & \text{otherwise} \end{cases}$$

  we have that $T = T_1 + T_2$ is *well formed with respect to B and b*.

- If $b = Aat \cdot b_1$, we consider a finite set $A_1 \subseteq TAct$ such that $A_1 \cap A = \emptyset$, and a barb $A'at \cdot b_1' \in B$ satisfying either $A' \cap A \neq \emptyset$ or $b_1' \not\ll b_1$. Then, we consider the test

$$T_2 = \begin{cases} \displaystyle\sum_{at \in A_1 \setminus A} at \text{ ; OK } & A_1 \setminus A \neq \emptyset \\ \text{STOP} & \text{otherwise} \end{cases}$$

  and the set of barbs $B_1 = \{b' \mid A' \subseteq A \text{ and } A'at \cdot b' \in B\}$. Then, the test $T = T_1 + T_2 + it$; OK is a *well formed test with respect to B and b*, where if $B_1 \neq \emptyset$ then T_1 can be any well formed test with respect to B_1 and b_1, and if $B_1 = \emptyset$ then we take $T_1 = \text{STOP}$.

It is possible that for an arbitrary set of barbs B and a barb b, there does not exist any well formed test T with respect to B and b, because it might not exist the finite set A_1 required in the definition. But, as the operational semantics is finite branching, we have that if $B = Barb(P)$, for a process P, and $b \in Barb(Q)$, for a process Q, such that there does not exist $b' \in B$ such that $b' \ll b$, then, there must exists a well formed test T with respect to B and b. So, we have the following result.

Proposition 10.3   *Let T be a well formed test with respect to a set of barbs B and a barb b. Then:*

- *If $b \in Barb(Q)$ then Q does not must T.*
- *If $B = Barb(P)$ and there is no $b' \in B$ such that $b' \ll b$, then P must T.*

As a corollary of the previous proposition we have that the right to left implication of the characterization holds

Theorem 10.2   *If $P \sqsubseteq Q$ then $P \ll Q$.*

Proof. We will make the proof by the contrapositive. Let us suppose that $P \not\ll Q$. Then, there exists a barb $b \in Barb(Q)$ such that there does not exist $b' \in Barb(P)$ verifying $b' \ll b$, so we can find a well formed test T with respect to $Barb(P)$ and b. Then, by the previous proposition, we have P must T while Q does not, and so $P \not\sqsubseteq Q$.   □

10.6   Congruence

As we will show, our testing semantics is not a congruence. In this section we will deal with the weakest congruence stronger than the relation $\sqsubseteq$. For this new relation we will present an alternative characterization. First, we extend the set of actions Act with a new action c (c from congruency), and we consider the set $Act^C = Act \cup \{c\}$.

Proposition 10.4   *The equivalence between processes is a congruence with respect to all the operators of our language except the operator $+$.*

The problems caused by the operator $+$ are the usual ones when dealing with a *CCS*-like choice operator and internal actions.

Example 10.3   Consider $P = a3$; STOP and $Q = i1$; $a2$; STOP. Both processes are equivalent under testing, but if we consider the process $R = b2$; STOP and the test $T = b2$; OK, we have that $P + R$ must T while $Q + R$ does not.   □

Now we will define the previously announced congruence based on the testing relation $\sqsubseteq$, and an auxiliary function which will be used in order to characterize this congruence.

Definition 10.16   We write $P \sqsubseteq^C Q$ iff for any context $C[\ ]$ we have $C[P] \sqsubseteq C[Q]$.

Definition 10.17   We define the function $T : \mathcal{CP} \mapsto \mathcal{T} \cup \{\infty\}$ by $T(P) = t$ if $P \xrightarrow{it} P'$ and $T(P)$ otherwise.

Note that by Proposition 10.1 we have that if $P \xrightarrow{it_1} P_1$ and $P \xrightarrow{it_2} P_2$ then $t_1 = t_2$, so, the previous definition makes sense. Finally, we have the theorem which presents an alternative characterization of the largest congruence included in the testing semantics.

Theorem 10.3 *The following conditions are equivalent:*

(1) $P \mathrel{\rotatebox[origin=c]{180}{$\sqsubseteq$}}^C Q$.

(2) *For any* R, $P + R \mathrel{\rotatebox[origin=c]{180}{$\sqsubseteq$}} Q + R$.

(3) *For any* $t \in \mathcal{T}$, $P + ct\,;\,\mathtt{STOP} \mathrel{\rotatebox[origin=c]{180}{$\sqsubseteq$}} Q + ct\,;\,\mathtt{STOP}$.

(4) $P \mathrel{\rotatebox[origin=c]{180}{$\sqsubseteq$}} Q$ *and* $T(P) = T(Q)$.

10.7 Conclusions and Future Work

In this chapter we have studied the testing semantics for a timed process algebra. The results of this chapter can be easily adapted to any process algebra having two basic properties: urgent internal actions, and finite branching operational semantics, i.e., for a fixed action and time there exists only a finite number of transitions with the indicated action and time.

The operational characterization we have found is a basis to define fully abstract denotational semantics with respect to the must testing semantics. As the + operator is not congruent, it is not possible to give a proper value to this operator in a denotational semantics, so we have to *enrich* the information included in a barb by adding some information about the time at which is executed an internal action. This could be done by introducing the concept of t-barb, a pair (t, b) such that $t \in \mathcal{T}$ and b is a barb. In [Llana-Díaz 97], a denotational semantics for a CSP–like language, where all operators are congruent, has been defined using the ideas of this chapter.

It is possible to enrich barbs, and extend the results of this chapter in order to support a dense time domain. In this chapter divergence at a certain instant t is captured by checking if Ωt belongs to a state. If we want to support a dense time domain, we have to distinguish among three different kinds of divergence: Just before the instant t, just at the instant t, and just after the instant t. In order to achieve this we could add a *label* to the instant in which a state becomes undefined: we would have that Ωt^- (resp. Ωt, Ωt^+) is a state if it becomes undefined just before (resp. just at, just after) time t.

Chapter 11

Compositional Model for Formal Development of Real-Time Systems Design

F. Vazquez and S. Rotenstreich

11.1 Introduction

RTS are complex systems that are difficult to represent due to the complexity of the real world in which these systems operate. The environment for RTS can be diverse, dynamic and unpredictable. Components fail at random, communications are corrupted, interruptions occur when they are most inappropriate. This complexity is mirrored in the size and structure of real-time software. The software for the Advance Automation System [Vazquez 92] consists of millions of lines of Ada code and is supposed to control the operation and the traffic of the airplanes. It has been developed by programming teams consisting of thousands of people. In spite of this, there is a steadily growing demand for even more complex systems.

A RTS consists of processing, data, control and timing. The behavior of RTS depends on the control signals that interact with the system. It could be a very complicate diagram if we try to mix processing, data, control and timing on a single diagram. [Hatley 87] suggested to divide the representation into pure process and pure control. The paper of [Dillon 94] uses interval diagrams to represent the time and [Mealy 71] and [Moore 56] use state transition diagrams to explain behavior of the system.

Current approaches to formal design of RTS are inappropriate to satisfy the high expectations of actual systems. The challenge is to develop new approaches for dealing with this problem. Several RTS models [France 92] have been developed to formalize the design of RTS, but in real life they have not been successful. These models almost guarantee error-free development, but their use normally involves an unreasonable amount of time and effort. Successful use of formal methods for the design of RTS requires the development of tools for faster and easier development of RTS. This requires tools with graphical representation and the power of the formal techniques. Real Time Extensions to Structure Analysis techniques are similar to structured analysis and add notational and conventions to accommodate control and timing [Woodman 88]. Real Time Temporary Analysis techniques are related to Real Time Temporal Logic [Lamport 94a] and in some cases incorporate elements of structured analysis to explain RTS. There are many varieties of approaches for this technique like The Interval Logic for RTS from Melliar-Smith [Melliar-Smith 88]. Real Time Algebraic Specifications are not very common but some authors like France [France 92] expresses RTS design with algebraic specifications. Initial Algebra, Final Algebras, sorts and operations are used to analyze and design RTS [Feijs 92]. Formal Specification Languages like VDM, Z, CCS, CSP and LOTOS have an elaborate notation that can be used to give denotational description of RTS as well as of programming languages [Semmens 92]. Z, CCS, CSP and LOTOS have generated formal extensions for RTS [Semmens 92]. These extensions include time as a part of the language.

This chapter consists of seven sections. Section 11.2 introduces the graphical temporal representation of the model. Section 11.3 provides the graphical interprocess communication of the model. Section 11.4 describes the composition of temporal representation and interprocess communication modeling. Section 11.5 describes Time Extended LOTOS and provides the rules of conversion from the Compositional Model to Time Extended LOTOS . Related work is described in Section 11.6 and conclusions and future work is presented in Section 11.7.

11.2   Graphical Temporal Representation

A process will be represented by a circle labeled by a unique name. Temporal relations among processes are depicted by directed edges that represent the temporal relationships. Edges are labeled with partial order relationships.

We define the Graphical Temporal Real Time System (GTRTS) as a partially ordered set $(P, <_t, N)$, where P is the set of Processes, $<_t$ is an

Table 11.1   Relations between P and Q.

P relation Q	Pb ...... Pe Qb ...... Qe
Before (P,Q, $<_t$)	$P_e <_t Q_b$
After (P,Q, $<_t$)	$Q_e <_t P_b$
Inside (P,Q,$<_{tt'}$)	$Q_b <_t P_b \wedge P_e <_{t'} Q_e$
Outside (P, Q, $<_{tt'}$)	$P_b <_t Q_b \wedge Q_e <_{t'} P_e$
Overlap (P, Q, $<_{tt't''}$)	$(P_b <_t Q_b \wedge Q_b <_{t'} P_e \wedge$ $P_e <_{t''} Q_e) \vee$ $(Q_b <_t P_b \wedge P_b <_{t'} Q_e \wedge)$ $Q_e <_{t''} P_e)$
Lasted (P, Q, $<_t$)	$P_b <_t P_e \wedge Q_e = P_e$
Starts (P, Q, $<_t$)	$P_b <_t P_e \wedge Q_b = P_b$
Until (P, Q, $<_t$)	$P_b <_t P_e \wedge Q_b = P_e$
Since (P, Q, $<_t$)	$P_b <_t P_e \wedge P_b = Q_e$

irreflexive and transitive relation on N called the at most relation and N is the set of natural numbers. Every process $P \in \mathbf{P}$ has a start time P_b and an end time P_e and we have the following relation:

$$\exists P_e (\forall P_b \in N \wedge P_e \in N(P_b < P_e))$$

There are several temporal operators that represent relational constraints specified between processes, such as Before, After, Inside, Outside, Overlap, Lasted, Starts, Until and Since. A relation constraint for two processes P and Q consists of one of the following simple relations shown in Table 11.1. The intuitive meaning of these operators is as follows: Before (P,Q, $<_t$) means that a process P ends at most t time units before a process Q begins. Inside (P,Q,$<_{tt'}$) means that a process P begins after a process Q began, Q began at most t time units before a process P begins and a process P finished before a process Q finished at most t' time units. Until (P, Q, $<_t$) means that a process P happens until a process Q begins. Lasted (P, Q, $<_t$) means that a process P lasted until a process Q finished. The meaning of After, Outside, Since and Starts is symmetrical to Before, Inside, Until and Lasted respectively. Overlap (P, Q, $<_{tt't''}$) means that a process P begins before a process Q at most t time units, a process Q begins at most t' time units before a process P ends and a process P finishes before a process Q finished at most t" time units or a process Q begins before a process P at most t time units, a process P begins at most t' time units before a process Q ends and a process Q finishes before a process P finished at most t" time units.

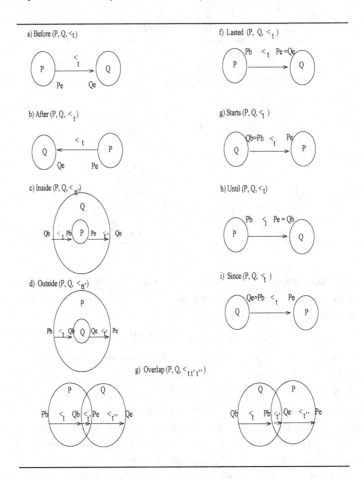

Fig. 11.1   Graphical representation of temporal operators

From the above definitions, the graphical representations derived for the temporal operators are shown in Figure 11.1.

11.3   Interprocess Communication

Processes can execute sequentially one after the other, choice among processes can be made possibly based on a condition, a set of processes can execute in parallel and asynchronous and synchronous communication between processes can take place.

11.3.1 *Interprocess I/O Operators*

The I/O Operators for processes are defined as follows:

- Conjunction Operator: $I_1 \bullet I_2 \ldots I_n \mathbf{P}$
- Disjunction Operator: $I_1 \circ I_2 \ldots I_n \mathbf{P}$
- Exclusive Disjunction Operator: $I_1 \otimes I_2 \ldots I_n \mathbf{P}$

where I_i is an input variable and $\mathbf{P}$ is a process. The conjunction operator states that the inputs $(I_1, I_2, I_3, \ldots)$ are required for a process $\mathbf{P}$ to execute correctly. The disjunction operator states that at least one of the inputs $(I_1, I_2, I_3, \ldots)$ is required for a process $\mathbf{P}$ to execute correctly. The exclusive disjunction operator states that only one input is required for a process $\mathbf{P}$ to execute correctly. Similar relations exist for the outputs (Oi) of a process $\mathbf{P}$.

11.3.2 *Interprocess Composition Operators*

Interactions of the processes can be described by the interprocess composition operators. Temporal rules define a relation between processes and the time domain. A binary relation between a process and time is represented by: For example, $P :<_t$ means that process P will be completed sometime in the interval (0, t). The interprocess composition operators are sequence, choice, parallel, guard and loop. The sequence operator; in $P_1 :<_t; P_2 :<_{t'}; P_3$ means that processes (P_1, P_2, P_3) are executed one after the other. The choice operator $[]$ in $P_1 :<_t []P_2 :<_{t'}$ means that one of the processes $P_1 or P_2$ is selected. The parallel operator $\|$ means that the processes are full synchronized. The guard operator "if B then $P_1 :<_t else P_2$" means that if the Boolean expression B is true then Process P_1 is executed otherwise process P_2 is executed. The loop operator for process P in "Loop P until B" defines the execution of process P until the Boolean expression B is true. The graphical representations are shown in Figure 11.2.

11.3.3 *Synchronous and Asynchronous Operators*

A synchronous data flow is one that requires the sender process and the receiver process to rendezvous in order for the communication to take place. The behavior of a synchronous data flow is implicit in the specification of the synchronous communication between its senders and receivers.

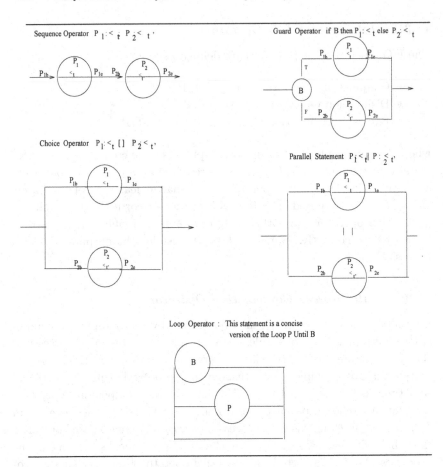

Fig. 11.2   Graphical representation of intreprocess composition operators

An asynchronous data flow is one that does not require its sender and receivers to synchronize by a shared signal, proceeding independently. Asynchronous behavior is modeled by the data flow associated with a message queue and two actions: send and receive. The receive action places data transmitted by the generator process onto the back of the queue, while the send action transmits data from the top of the queue to the receivers. A data flow associated with a queue is called a queued flow.

Let f be a flow, v a variable, and receiveflow and waitreceiveflow are functions that map flows to variables, sendflow and waitsendflow are functions that map data to flow and a signal represents a change in the com-

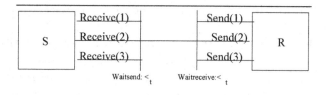

Fig. 11.3 Synchronous data flow representation

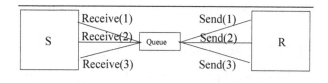

Fig. 11.4 Asynchronous data flow representation

munication between the receiver and the sender; a signal is represented as a Boolean. The definitions to characterize the above actions are:

(1) receive(v) ≡ Receiveflow(f,v)
(2) waitreceive:$<_t$ (v) ≡ Waitreceiveflow:$<_t$ (f,v)
(3) send(d) ≡ Sendflow(f,d)
(4) waitsend:$<_t$ (d) ≡ Waitsendflow:$<_t$ (f,d)
(5) signal(f)=true ≡ Sendflow(f)

In Definition 1, a receive function, receive(v), means that a receive action places data transmitted through flow f into variable v. For Definition 2, a waitreceive function, waitreceive:$<_t$ (v), means that a receive action places data transmitted through flow f into a variable v sometime in the interval (0,t). In Definition 3, a send function, send(d), means that data d is sent over flow f. For Definition 4, a waitsend function, waitsend:$<_t$ (d), means that the data d is sent over flow f and $<_t$ is the time that the sender waits before sending the data. Finally, for Definition 5, when a signal to send is true a flow f is sent. Synchronous data flow is represented in Figure 11.3 and asynchronous data flow is represented in Figure 11.4.

11.4   Composition of Temporal and Interprocess Models

We provide a framework with two views; one is a description with a graphical representation and the other is a formal representation provided by the semantics of the graphical representation. The formal description can generate a partial formal specification, or represent specific parts of the formal representation.

The formal representation technique is based on algebra specifications to describe the interprocess relations of the system and temporal logic to describe the time constraints of the system. This dual representation of the system allows us to visualize RTS formal specifications in an easier way.

11.4.1   *Syntax of the Compositional Model*

The compositional model provides means to express a process as a procedure. Every procedure P steps through the following phases

- P accepted (instantiated)
- P is not enabled because P requires resources not available at this time
- P enabled
- P enabled but preempted by another procedure acceptations
- P starts
- P is active
- P terminates

We define the syntax of the Composition Model as a combination of the temporal model and the interprocess model in the following way:

$< Module >$ ::= Module $< name >$ is $< exprs >$ end of module

$< exprs >$:= [Include Formal module Specifications]

[Introduce
     [Sorts Sortlist]
     [Variables Variablelist]
     [Procedures Procedurelist]]
[Asserts Equations Equationlist]

where the nonterminal symbols have the following meaning

$< name >$: Name of the module

< *module* > : Definition of a name for a module specification.

< *exprs* > : Explicit presentation of a module specification or parts of it.

Procedures are of the form

$$P(in : Sort_1, \ldots, Sort_n; out : Sort_1, \ldots, Sort_n)$$

procedures can have several states that are defined as follow:
Let (par1 , ..., parm) = parameter list then the state procedures for P_i are defined as

nil
AcceptPi (par1, ... ,parm)
WaitPi (par1, ... ,parm)
EnablePi (par1, ... ,parm)
ReadyPi (par1, ... ,parm)
StartPi (par1, ... ,parm)
ExecPi (par1, ... ,parm)
TermPi (par1, ... ,parm)

where nil means that nothing is happening.

AcceptPi means that the procedure Pi has been accepted.
WaitPi means that the procedure Pi is not enabled for a period of time.
EnablePi means that the procedure Pi has been enabled.
ReadyPi means that the procedure Pi is enabled or preempted for a period of time.
StartPi means that the procedure Pi begins to execute.
ExecPi means that the procedure Pi is executing for a period of time.
TermPi means that the procedure Pi is terminated.

and the equations that define these states are defined by

- The operators $\neg, \wedge, \vee, \Rightarrow, \bigcirc, \square, \Diamond$ where

  - P $\bigcirc$: P holds in the next state
  - P $\square$: P holds in all coming states
  - P $\Diamond$: P holds in some coming states

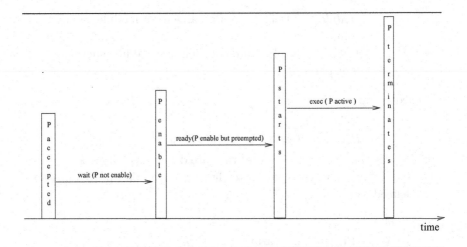

Fig. 11.5   States in the compositional model

- Temporal operators: Before $(P,Q, <_t)$,   After $(P,Q, <_t)$,   Inside $(P,Q,<_{tt'})$, Outside$(P, Q, <_{tt'})$,Overlap$(P, Q, <_{tt't''})$, Lasted$(P, Q, <_t)$, Starts$(P, Q, <_t)$, Until$(P, Q, <_t)$ and Since$(P, Q, <_t)$ as defined in section 11.2.
- The interprocess composition operators: Sequence Operator $(P_1; P_2)$, Choice Operator $(P_1 [] P_2)$, Parallel Operator $(P_1 \| P_2)$, Guard Operator (If B then P_1 else P_2), Loop Operator (Loop P Until B) as defined in Section 11.3.2, and the synchronous and asynchronous operators Receive (v), Send(d), Waitreceive:$<_t$ (v) and Waitsend:$<_t$ (d) as defined in Section 11.3.3.

A graphic notation with the states is shown in Figure 11.5.

11.4.2   *Temporal Semantics of the Compositional Model*

We now discuss the temporal semantic rules for the Compositional Model. The temporal meaning of the operators depend on the temporal attributes of the processes. The temporal attributes of the processes are expressed with the temporal rules. The temporal rules described below define a relation between processes and the time domain. The Actions are composed of temporal operators and interprocess communication operators. These rules consist of expressions with relations above the line and below the line. These rules are to be read as follow: When relation(s) processes above the line can be considered, we can infer the actions below the line. The temporal meaning of these expressions is divided into sequential processing, parallel processing and periodicity. For the sequential processing "Before $(P_1, P_2, <_t)$", the sequential completion of P_1 and P_2 will be at most the completion time of P_1 plus the completion time of P_2 plus t (rule **Ex1**). In "Until $(P_1, P_2, <_t)$", the sequential completion of P_1 and P_2 will be the completion time of P_1 plus the completion time of P_2 (rule **Ex3**). For rule **Ex2**, P_2; P_1 has the same completion time that rule **Ex1** and for rule **Ex4**, P_2; P_1 has the same completion time that rule **Ex3**. For the parallel processing; In "Starts $(P_1, P_2, <_t)$", the parallel processing of P_1 and P_2 will be completed when both processes are completed (rule **Ex5**. In "Inside$(P_1, P_2, <_{tt'})$", the parallel processing of P_1 and P_2 will be completed when P_2 is completed (rule **Ex7**). In "Outside$(P_1, P_2, <_{tt'})$"; the parallel processing of P_1 and P_2 will be completed when P_1 is completed (rule **Ex8**). When process P_1 begins at most t time units before process P_2 and process P_1 finished at most t' time units after process P_2 begins and Process P_2 finished at most t" time units after process P_1 finished, the parallel processing of P_1 and P_2 will be completed in at most $(t + t' + t'')$ units (rule **Ex9**). Rule **Ex6**, and rule **Ex10** have the same completion time that rules **Ex5**, and **Ex9** respectively. For a periodic process P that repeats over and over until a certain condition B is true, the completion time is unbounded (Rule **Ex11**).

Sequential-Actions:

$$\frac{Before(P_1, P_2, <_t)P_1 :<_{t_1} P_2 :<_{t_2}}{(P_1, P_2) :< (t_1 + t + t_2)} \tag{Ex1}$$

$$\frac{After(P_1, P_2, <_t)P_1 :<_{t_1} P_2 :<_{t_2}}{(P_1, P_2) :< (t_2 + t + t_1)} \tag{Ex2}$$

$$\frac{Until(P_1, P_2, <_t)P_2 :<_{t_2}}{(P_1, P_2) :< (t + t_1)} \tag{Ex3}$$

$$\frac{Since(P_1, P_2, <_t)P_2 :<_{t_2}}{(P_1, P_2) :< (t_2 + t)} \tag{Ex4}$$

Parallel-Actions:

$$\frac{Starts(P_1, P_2, <_t)P_2 :<_{t_2}}{(P_1 \| P_2) : Max(t + t_2)} \tag{Ex5}$$

$$\frac{Lasted(P_1, P_2, <_t)P_2 :<_{t_2}}{(P_1 \| P_2) : Max(t + t_2)} \quad \textbf{(Ex6)}$$

$$\frac{Inside(P_1, P_2, <_{tt'})P_2 :<_{t_1}}{(P_1 \| P_2) :< (t + t_1 + t')} \quad \textbf{(Ex7)}$$

$$\frac{Outside(P_1, P_2, <_{tt'})P_2 :<_{t_2}}{(P_1 \| P_2) :< (t + t_2 + t')} \quad \textbf{(Ex8)}$$

$$\frac{P_{1b} <_t P_{2b} \wedge P_{2b} <_{t'} P_{1e} \wedge P_{1e} <_{t''} P_{2e}}{(P_1 \| P_2) : (t + t' + t'')} \quad \textbf{(Ex9)}$$

$$\frac{P_{2b} <_t P_{1b} \wedge P_{1b} <_{t'} P_{2e} \wedge P_{2e} <_{t''} P_{1e}}{(P_1 \| P_2) : (t + t' + t'')} \quad \textbf{(Ex10)}$$

Periodicity-structures:

$$\frac{P :<_t}{if \neg B then P :<_t, \ldots, if \neg B then P :<_t, if B then < stop >:< \infty} \quad \textbf{(Ex11)}$$

11.4.3   *Operational Semantics of the Compositional Model*

The operational semantic rules for the Compositional Model give meaning to the operational operators. The operational operators describe the relation among the processes. The notation $P - a \rightarrow P'$ means that process P behaves like process P' after performing action a. $P - a \nrightarrow$ means that process P is not ready. These rules are to be read as follow: If the transition(s) above can be inferred, then we can infer the transition below the line. For rules **Ex12** and **Ex13**, a sequential composition "$P_1; P_2$", P_1 can engage in actions before P_2 begins and P_2 can engage in actions after P_1 is completed. For rule **Ex14** and **Ex15**, only the selected process P_1 or P_2 can engage in an action. For rules **Ex16**, **Ex17** and **Ex18**, in a parallel processing "$P_1 \| P_2$", P_1 or P_2 or both can engage in actions. For rule **Ex19**, a periodic process can engage in a periodic action. Finally, for rules **Ex20** and **Ex21**, in a conditional process, only the selected process can engage in an action. The shutdown of the system (process P_2) after all the users connected to the system (process P_1) logoff (action), is an example of rule **Ex12**.

Sequence:

$$\frac{P_1 - a \rightarrow P_1'}{P_1; P_2 \rightarrow P_1'; P_2} \quad \textbf{(Ex12)}$$

Fig. 11.6   Graphical representation of the inspection station

Choice:

$$\frac{P_2 - a \to P_2'}{P_1; P_2 \to P_1; P_2'} \tag{Ex13}$$

$$\frac{P_1 - a \to P_1'}{P_1; P_2 [] P_1'; P_2} \tag{Ex14}$$

$$\frac{P_2 - a \to P_2'}{P_1; P_2 [] P_1; P_2'} \tag{Ex15}$$

Parallel:

$$\frac{P_1 - a \to P_1' \; P_2 - a \not\to}{P_1 \| P_2 - a \to P_1' \| P_2} \tag{Ex16}$$

$$\frac{P_2 - a \to P_2' \; P_1 - a \not\to}{P_1 \| P_2 - a \to P_1 \| P_2'} \tag{Ex17}$$

$$\frac{P_1 - a \to P_1' \; P_2 - a \to P_2'}{P_1 \| P_2 - a \to P_1' \| P_2'} \tag{Ex18}$$

Periodicity:

$$\frac{P - a \to P'}{LoopPUntilB - a \to LoopP'UntilB} \tag{Ex19}$$

If Structure:

$$\frac{B = trueP_1 - a \to P_1'}{if B then P_1 else P_2 - a \to P_1'} \tag{Ex20}$$

$$\frac{B = falseP_2 - a \to P_2'}{if B then P_1 else P_2 - a \to P_2'} \tag{Ex21}$$

11.4.4   *The Simulation of an Inspection Station*

In order to illustrate our model we provide the following example. Consider an inspection station as defined in Figure 11.6. There are two inspection stations A and B and two lines L_1, L_2 in which cars are waiting for inspection. The number of cars that each line can hold is finite. Cars in L_1 are inspected by A, cars in L_2 are inspected by B; cars in L_1 can be inspected by B if L_2 is empty and cars in L_2 can be inspected in A if L_1 is empty. Every station can inspect only one car at a time.

We can simulate the operating of this inspection station by a module with two procedures: $inspect_1$ and $inspect_2$ that represent the complete inspection event with lining up in L_1 and L_2 respectively. Each of the procedures has one input parameter and a unique identification of its different states (accept, wait, start, exec, term). The lines are represented by queues whose definition is not shown and the graphical representation for the inspection station is shown below. The temporal relations among states are represented with graphical temporal operators described in Section 11.2, and the relations among the processes are represented by graphical representations of interprocess composition operators given in Section 11.3.2. The equations without graphical representation are shown inside bars ($\|\|$).

The entry of a car (c) in a Line (queue L_1 or queue L_2) is only possible if the Line (queue) is not full. We assume a queue with the functions: append, rest, isfull and top of the queue. The equations that represent these actions are represented inside bars. The notation used in the equations is explained in Section 11.4.1.

A car (c) is accepted for inspection only if the queue (line) is not full. If the queue is not full the car is added to the queue (Line)

/*Comment: lining up in queues L_1 and L_2 */

$$\left| \begin{array}{l} acceptinspect_1(c) \to \neg isfull(L_1) \land L = L_1 \to \bigcirc(L = append(L_1, c)) \\ acceptinspect_2(c) \to \neg isfull(L_2) \land L = L_2 \to \bigcirc(L = append(L_2, c)) \end{array} \right|$$

After the car has been accepted to inspection, the car must wait on Line. This temporal relation is represented by Since (Wait, Accept, $<_t$). The graphical representation is shown below:

/* Comment: waiting for inspection */

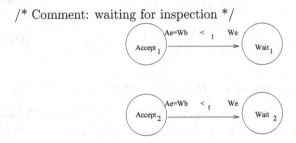

After the car has been waiting on line, when the inspection station is ready for the car (c), the car is withdraw from the top of the queue.

/*Comment: leaving the line*/

$$\begin{vmatrix} startinspect_1(c) \rightarrow c = top(L_1) \land L = L_1 \rightarrow \bigcirc(L = rest(L_1, c)) \\ startinspect_2(c) \rightarrow c = top(L_2) \land L = L_2 \rightarrow \bigcirc(L = rest(L_2, c)) \end{vmatrix}$$

The execution of the inspection is represented by Until (Exec, Term, $<_t$). The graphical representation is shown below.

/*Comment: execution of inspection */

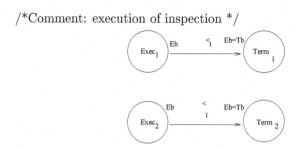

A car (c) can be inspected in station A or station B and the steps are: Start the inspection, inspect (execute) and terminate the inspection. The graphical representation is shown below:

/*Comment: Car Inspection */

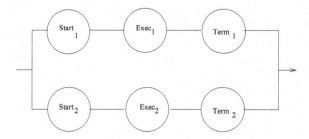

The serving strategy is more difficult to represent in a graphic form. We use equations combined with the graphical representation After (Start, Exec, $<_t$) that are shown in a box. The strategy means that a car can start the inspection in its respective inspection station (A or B) or in the other inspection station if there is not car waiting. The representation is shown below:

/*Comment: Serving strategy */
$|startinspect_1(c) \rightarrow (\neg isempty(L_2) \wedge isempty(L_1) \vee \neg isempty(L_2)|$

$|startinspect_2(c) \rightarrow (\neg isempty(L_2) \wedge isempty(L_2) \vee \neg isempty(L_1)|$

The module for the inspection station is

Module InspectionStation (car) is
Include : Queue (car)
Introduce
variables : L, L_1, L_2 queue
procedures : $inspect_1$(in: car) $inspect_2$(in: car)
Asserts
Comment: lining up in queues L_1 L_2 and L_3
$acceptinspect_1(c) \rightarrow \neg isfull(L_1) \wedge L = L_1 \rightarrow \bigcirc(L = \text{append}(L_1, c))$
$acceptinspect_2(c) \rightarrow \neg isfull(L_2) \wedge L = L_2 \rightarrow \bigcirc (L = \text{append}(L_2, c))$
Comment: waiting for inspection
$Since(waitinspect_1(c), acceptinspect_1(c), <_t)$
$Since(waitinspect_2(c), acceptinspect_2(c), <_t)$
Comment: leaving the line
$startinspect_1(c) \rightarrow c = \text{top}(L_1) \wedge L = L_1 \rightarrow \bigcirc (L = \text{rest}(L_1,c))$
$startinspect_2(c) \rightarrow c = \text{top}(L_2) \wedge L = L_2 \rightarrow \bigcirc (L = \text{rest}(L_2,c))$
Comment: execution of inspection
$Until(execinspect_1(c), terminspect_1(c), <_t)$
$Until(execinspect_2(c), terminspect_2(c), <_t)$
Comment: car inspection
$startinspect_1(c) ; execinspect_1(c) ; terminspect_1(c)$ []
$startinspect_2(c); execinspect_2(c) ; terminspect_2(c)$
Comment: Serving strategy
$startinspect_1(c) \rightarrow isempty(L_2) \wedge \neg isempty(L_1) \vee \neg isempty(L_2)$
$\rightarrow After(execinspect_1(c), startinspect_1(c), <_t)$
$startinspect_2(c) \rightarrow isempty(L_2) \wedge \neg isempty(L_2) \vee \neg isempty(L_1)$
$\rightarrow After(execinspect_2(c), startinspect_2, <_t)$
End of Module

The lining up formula describes the entry of a car in a line that is only possible if this line is not full. The next formulas (waiting for inspection, leaving the line and execution of the inspection) are obvious. The car inspection describes that a car can be inspected on station A or B; the remaining formulas express the serving strategy. The first of them means a car that leaves line L_1 is inspected in station 1 or a car in line L_1 can be inspected in station 2 if there is not car waiting in L_2. The serving strategy produces analogous formulas for line L_2.

11.5   Time Extended LOTOS

Several versions of Timed LOTOS exist. Some of them are similar to Timed Petri Nets [Bolognesi 90] others offer a Process Algebra with timed interaction approach [Bolognesi 91]. Our approach, called Time Extended LO-TOS , was inspired by Quemada [Quemada 93]. This approach allows an acceptable definition of timed systems. Every event has an explicit time restriction. The interleaving events are merged according to their occurrence in time. The Untimed Full LOTOS calculus is a subcalculus of Time Extended LOTOS. As in Full LOTOS, only the emission of indistinguishable signals through gates is observable. A gate is denoted by a name. Full LOTOS [Turner 93] also considers internal actions that are not observable from outside, but whose execution can change the state of the process and therefore its future observable behavior. In addition, time can be observed at each action, with respect to a discrete scale of time. The set of natural numbers represents the domain for time.

11.5.1   *Operational Semantics of Time Extended LOTOS*

The operational semantics of the calculus is defined by a labeled transition system that is defined as follows:

The transition system of B, denoted as $(\mathbf{B}, D, TR, B)$, where $\mathbf{B}$ is the set of the system states, D is the set of natural numbers, B is the initial state, and TR is the set of labeled transitions derived from applying the rules described below. These rules are to be read as follows: if the transitions(s) above the line can be inferred, then we can infer the transitions below the line. A special case in when there is nothing above the line. In this case, the transition below the line can be inferred unconditionally. The notation

$B - d \rightarrow B'$ means that the behavior expression B evolves into behavior expression B' after d units of time.

A one step derivation system is used to define the transition system of a given timed behavior i. Where i is an internal action, $d \in D$, g, g' range over G where G is the set of gate names, $[t'/t]$ B is a syntactic substitution function which substitutes any occurrence of t in B by t', P is a predicate. According to rule **Ex22**, an internal action i, that executes in a time interval (d'+d, d"+d), will executes in the time interval (d', d") after d time units have been consumed and the time dependent actions in the behavior expression B will be adjusted to reflect the d time units consumed. Rules **Ex23** and **Ex24** describe that the execution of a selected behavior expression will consume d units of time. Rule **Ex25** describes the execution of a behavior expression, if the predicate is true, consuming d time units. Rule **Ex26** says that a waiting time can be considered for any behavior expression. Rule **Ex27** describes the parallel execution of two time dependent behavior expression; only full synchronization is considered (i.e. both expressions occur at the same time).

Internal Action-Prefix:

$$\overline{i(t \in (d' + d, d'' + d)); B - d \rightarrow i(t \in (d', d'')); ((t + d)/d)B} \qquad \textbf{(Ex22)}$$

Choice:

$$\frac{B_1 - d \rightarrow B_1'}{B_1[]B_2 - d \rightarrow B_1'} \qquad \textbf{(Ex23)}$$

$$\frac{B_2 - d \rightarrow B_2'}{B_1[]B_2 - d \rightarrow B_2'} \qquad \textbf{(Ex24)}$$

Guard:

$$\frac{B - d \rightarrow B'}{[P] \rightarrow B - d \rightarrow B'} \qquad \textbf{(Ex25)}$$

Wait:

$$\frac{B - d \rightarrow B'}{[P] \rightarrow B - d \rightarrow B'} \qquad \textbf{(Ex26)}$$

Parallel Composition:

$$\frac{B_1 - d \rightarrow B_1', B_2 - d \rightarrow B_2'}{B_1[|G|]B_2 - d \rightarrow B_1'[|G|]B_2'} \qquad \textbf{(Ex27)}$$

11.5.2 *Conversion Rules among LOTOS Operands and Interprocess Composition Operands*

Time Extended LOTOS introduces time constraints to actions and introduces a wait operator. LOLA [Quemada 93] accepts as input full LOTOS. Consequently, in order to represent Timed Extended LOTOS, auxiliary gates (time and wait) are required and the certain procedures have to be follow:

- The time domain is defined as a data type from the library time-nat.lot which must be included in the specification (i.e. Library time Endlib).

- Time attributes are defined as time intervals that constraint the instant of time when an event can happen. In "bank ! borrow {0 .. 4}", borrow is the event and 0..4 the time interval.

- Time variables can be used to register the instant of occurrence of events and are treated as any other variable in LOTOS. {i.e. y in 0 .. 4; where y is the time variable}

- An interval is unbounded if it ranges from 0 to ∞ {i.e. $0 \ldots \infty$ is an unbounded interval}.

- Bounded intervals are represented following the next two steps:

  - Add a special gate named time to the gate lists of the specification wherever needed (specifications and process declarations/instantiations).

  - Prefix every time constrained action with the special gate time and offer a list that will be translated into the time constraints of that action. The offer list may contain a variable of sort time, and two value expressions (i.e. bank ! borrow { 0 .. 4 } is represented by time ! 0 !4; bank ! borrow).

- The introduction of the wait operator consists of the following steps:

  - It is necessary to introduce a special gate named wait in the gate lists of the specification and processes and wherever it will be used.

  - Prefix the behavior you need to delay with the special gate wait with one offer (a value expression) (i.e. wait(t);B is represented by wait ! t ; B).

- The interleaved expansion is not supported.

Table 11.2　Conversion between models

Interprocess Operator	Timed LOTOS Operator
Sequence Operator	Action Prefix
Choice Operator	Choice
Guard Operator	Guards
Parallel Operator	Parallel
Loop Operator	Recursion

The conversion rules among Time Extended LOTOS Operands and Interprocess Compositional Operands are straightforward. The relationship among operators is shown in the Table 11.2, Tables 11.3 show the conversion rules for the main module, Table 11.4 show conversion rules for interprocess composition operands and The conversion rules for temporal operators are explained in [Vazquez 98].

Table 11.3　Conversion rules for the main module

Input Compositional Model Code	Output Time Extended LOTOS Code
/*Rule for Modules */ Module CMId is <exprs> End of Module CMId	Specification CMId [Gatelist]: noexit := <exprs> end spec
/*Rule for General Structure */ Include <formal module specifications>	Library <formal module specifications> EndLib
Introduce [*Sorts* :<*sortname*> , <*sortname*>]	*Type* < *sortname1* > ... . . . *Type* < *sortnamen* > ... Behavior MID[Gatelist](...) where *ProcessMID*[*Gatelist*](<*var_name1* >:< *sortname1* >,
[*Variables* :< *var_name* > {,< *var_name* >}]	. . . < *var_namem* >:< *sortnamem* >) : *noexit* := *Translationof* < *equationlist* >
[*Procedures* :< *Proc_name* > , < *Proc_name* >]	where *ProcessAccept* < *Proc_name1* > [*gatelist*] : *exit* := < *exprs* > end proc
[*Asserts* < *equationlist* >]	. . . *ProcessTerm* < *Proc_name1* > [*gatelist*] : *exit* := < *exprs* > end proc *ProcessAccept* < *Proc_name2* > [*gatelist*] : *exit* := < *exprs* > end proc . . . endproc

Table 11.4   Conversion rules for interprocess composition operators

Input Compositional Model Code	Output Time Extended LOTOS Code
/*Rule for Sequential Processing */ $< process > \{; < process > \}$	$< process >\{; < process >\}$
/*Rule for Choice Processing */ $< process > \{ \; [] \; < process > \}$	$< process >\{[] < process >\}$
/*Rule for Parallel processing */ $< process > \{ \; \|\| \; < process > \}$	$< process >\{\|\| < process >\}$

/*Rule for Conditional Statements */
if $< bool_e xpr >$ then
$< process1 >$
else
$< process2 >$
	$[< bool_e xpr >] \rightarrow$
	$< process1 >$
	$[not < bool_e xpr >] \rightarrow$
	$< process2 >$

/* Rule for repetition */ LOOP $< process > \ldots$ END LOOP	LOOP [Gatelist] where process LOOP[Gatelist] : noexit:= $< process >$ (LOOP[Gatelist]) endproc
/*process restricted by time */	$< process >:<_t< process >$[Gatelist,time] ... where process $< process >$ [Gatelist,time] : exit:= time !x !x+t; gd1...dn [SP]; exit endproc

- The list of LOTOS gates (gatelist) are computed from the list of activities found in each module of the Compositional Model. We can not describe the computation, because is application dependent.
- Translation of types from the Compositional Model to LOTOS is straightforward and consists of arrangements of the elements of the Compositional Model to configure LOTOS type structure.

11.5.3   *The Conversion of the Inspection Station Example*

We applied the rules described above to the example of the inspection station.

The temporal operators Since and Until are translated from the Compositional Model to LOTOS by the conversion rules. For example, the equation

$$Since(waitinspect1(c), acceptinspect1(c), <_t)$$

is translated to LOTOS as

```
acceptinspect1 [c,time]
  ≫
waitinspect1 [c,time]
WHERE
PROCESS acceptinspect1 [c,time] : exit :=
  time !0 of nat; c; exit
ENDPROC
PROCESS waitinspect1[c,time] : exit :=
  time !0 of nat !t of nat; c; exit
ENDPROC
```

and the equation

$$Until(execinspect1(c), terminspect1(c), <_t)$$

is translated to LOTOS as

```
execinspect1 [c,time]
  ≫
terminspect1 [c,time]
WHERE
PROCESS execinspect1[c,time] : exit :=
  time !t of nat !t of nat + 1 of nat; c; exit
ENDPROC
PROCESS terminspect1[c,time] : exit :=
  time ! t of nat + 1 of nat; c; exit
ENDPROC
```

A similar translation is done for the other temporal operators. The equation

```
startinspect1 (c); execinspect1 (c);
  terminspect1 (c) [] startinspect2 (c);
  execinspect2 (c); terminspect2 (c)
```

is translated to LOTOS as

```
(

        startinspect1[c,time]
          ≫
        execinspect1 [c,time]
          ≫
        terminspect1[c,time]

    )
  [] (

        startinspect2 [c,time]
          ≫
        execinspect2 [c,time]
          ≫
        terminspect2[c,time]

    )
```

After the translation of the other constraints from the Compositional Model to LOTOS the specification for the inspection station is shown below:

SPECIFICATION InspectionStation [c,time] : noexit
LIBRARY Queue, Boolean, NaturalNumber, time ENDLIB
BEHAVIOR

    time!0 of nat;
    c ? car1 : Element ?car2 : Element;
    InsStation[c,time](append (empty of Queue, car1) of Queue,
      append (empty of Queue, car2) of Queue)

WHERE
PROCESS InsStation[c,time](L1, L2 : Queue) : noexit :=

    $([not(isfull(L1))] \rightarrow$

        ((c ? car : Element;exit(car))
            $\gg$
            accept car : Element in
            (
            acceptinspect1 [c,time]
            $\gg$
            waitinspect1 [c,time]
            $\gg$
            InsStation[c,time] (append (L1,
              car), L2)
)

)

      []

      $[not(isfull(L2))] \rightarrow$

          ((c ? car : Element;exit(car))
             $\gg$

              $\ddots$

)
    []
    (

      $[not(isempty(L1))] \rightarrow$
      (c ! top(L1);
      startinspect1[c,time]
      $\gg$
      execinspect1 [c,time]
      $\gg$
      terminspect1 [c,time]
      $\gg$
      InsStation[c,time] (rest(L1), L2)
)

    []

      $[not(isempty(L1))and(isempty(L2))] \rightarrow$
      (c ! top(L1);
      startinspect1[c,time]
      $\gg$

        execinspect1 [c,time]
           ≫
        terminspect1[c,time]
           ≫
        InsStation[c,time] (rest(L1), L2)
)

[]

        [*not(isempty(L2))*] →
        (c ! top(L2);

           ⋱

)

[]

        [*not(isempty(L2))and(isempty(L1))*] →
        (c ! top(L2);

           ⋱

)

)
WHERE

        PROCESS acceptinspect1 [c,time] : exit :=
           time !0 of nat; c; exit
        ENDPROC
        PROCESS waitinspect1[c,time] : exit :=
           time !0 of nat !3 of nat; c; exit
        ENDPROC
        PROCESS startinspect1[c,time] : exit :=
           time !4 of nat; c; exit
        ENDPROC
        PROCESS execinspect1[c,time] : exit :=
           time !5 of nat !5 of nat + 1 of nat; c; exit
        ENDPROC
        PROCESS terminspect1[c,time] : exit :=
           time !5 of nat + 1 of nat; c; exit
        ENDPROC

           ⋱

    ENDPROC

    ENDSPEC

This example shows the conversion of the behavior of the system. The Compositional Model describes the problem from a higher design than does LOTOS and the graphical representation of the Compositional Model makes this model more suitable in RTS Design than LOTOS. GLOTOS does not consider time representations as the Compositional Model does.

11.6   Related Work

DART (Diagrams to represent process relations) [Sanchez-Allende 94] is a visual language that represents LOTOS and its use in communication system definition. G-LOTOS [Bolognesi 91] is a graphical language for concurrent systems. It provides a better readability and more intuitive understanding of formal specifications than textual LOTOS. A graphical interval logic that is the foundation of a toolset to support formal specifications and verification of concurrent software systems is presented in [Dillon 92] [Dillon 94] [Ramakrishna 93]. TIMELOGIC [Koomen 87] is an interval-based forward-chaining inference engine that provides a facility for storing, retrieving and inferring temporal constraints between intervals. Lamport [Lamport 94b] describes the predicate-action diagrams, which are similar to standard state-transition diagrams and are interpreted as formulas of temporal logic of actions.

11.7   Conclusions and Further Work

This chapter described a temporal model, an interprocess model and the composition of temporal and interprocess models. It gives conversion rules between the Compositional Model and Time Extended LOTOS. We have developed a Real Time System Design Tool (RTSDT) that allows the implementation of the Graphical Temporal Operators and the Interprocess Composition Operators. Nowadays, we are working in a graphical user interface that will replace the RTSDT system and it will be able to implement the complete graphical representation of the Compositional Model for RTS Design.

PART 5

Tools for Real-Time Systems

Chapter 12

RALE: An Environment for Simulation and Transformations

Miquel Bertran, Miquel Nicolau, Francesc Oller, Jordi Forga Felipe Alvarez-Cuevas, Albert Duran and Miquel Porta

Abstract: The Ramon Llull Environment (RALE), a development environment for parallel-distributed (PD) and real-time (RT) software, is reported. It has been developed with didactic and industrial concerns, and with integrating and unifying aims. This effort has resulted in a novel language, PADD, and in an integrated set of tools for both teaching concurrency and parallelism, and for developing real-life systems. The explicit character of parallelism in PADD allows the definition of hardware high-level models in addition to software. Extensive application of tree-like schemes for the user interface and to represent PADD programs, the introduction and usage for system refinement of the concept of Communication-extended Abstract Types (CATs), monitor elimination and communication elimination transformations, and their integration with simulation, allocation-mapping, and documentation generation tools are amongst the elements integrated within the environment. Its cooperation with well established specification and verification environments for concurrent programs is under investigation.

12.1 Introduction

12.1.1 *Motivation*

The current trend towards specialization has lead to a situation where there exist methods and tools tailored to many phases and activities of PD

265

and RT software development: requirements, specification, modeling and simulation, design, verification, coding, testing, maintenance. However, an integration suitable for the whole development process, such that redundant work is avoided is hard to find. It is common that in order to use methods and tools for the distinct phases, translation between different notations (languages) has to be made, often manually. This is the main cause of redundant work which increases cost and decreases reliability. Usually, this artificial complexity is the result of the influences of many groups and of political factors. Clearly, there is a need for simplification and for global perspective. Furthermore, if applications have to emerge, this has to occur within a scientific-engineering framework. The pure formal mathematical approach would be too specialized. The RALE project aims towards the attainment of the above simplification in PD and RT software development.

12.1.2 *Didactic and Industrial Objectives*

Both the understanding of the nature of parallelism and of integration tools, such that the development effort is reduced, are the aims of this chapter. Parallelism is expressed explicitly in PADD, using a notation scheme close to the environment. PADD is a tree-schema introducing an intuitive notation very much needed in the understanding of parallel processes. It also provides a framework for clarity of expression.

Integration in the same development environment, and with a unifying notation, of formal transformation with simulation based methods and tools is pursued. The main aims are the investigation of the complementarity in their application and the reduction of costs through reuse of common activities in distinct development stages. The following are amongst the questions to be investigated within the PADD/RALE project framework: How can a schema-based formal notation, for programming-in-the-small and in-the-large, simplify the whole development process? Which are the requirements to be imposed upon proof construction tools and formal object databases in order to make formal transformation tractable from an engineering standpoint? In this context, which is a useful set of practical proof construction procedures and strategies? Up to what degree and how can modeling and simulation effort, for both testing and evaluation, be reduced if formal transformations are used? Can some of the documentation effort be reused in design, and some of the design effort be reused in coding?

12.1.3 Scope and Limitations of this Work

The purpose of this work is to give an overall picture of the environment and of its notation. The detailed coverage and mathematical justification of the methods and tools can not be undertaken here. In some cases, the reader is referred to other published works which cover some of the topics in greater detail. In other cases, published material does not exist yet.

RALE is in constant evolution. Some of its tools are quite complete and stable. This is the case, for instance, of the event driven simulation, documentation, and mapping tools. On the contrary, the user interface and the formal program transformation tools are changing. This has to be kept in mind when reading this work.

12.1.4 Overview of the Environment

RALE is built around a software development database (SDDB) which integrates in an orderly manner projects, project phases, documents, theories, proofs, programs, maps, results, data, and many other objects arising in software development. The tools are accessed from specific points of the existing SDDB views. Some of the activities supported by the tools are the following:

(*a*) SDDB browsing and editing.

(*b*) Tree-Schema editing. For entering documentation, specifications, models, designs, programs, and allocation-maps.

(*c*) Pretty printing of documentation tree-schemas.

(*d*) Design Specification standard ANSI/IEEE software quality document generation from tree-schemas.

(*e*) Formal proof user interactive construction.

(*f*) Event-driven simulation. For both testing and statistical evaluation.

(*g*) Process distribution over the two most common real-time multiprocessor multitasking platforms. Guided by allocation-map schemas.

(*h*) C code and VHDL code generation from tree-schemas, for mapping PADD into programs, into hardware, or into both in codesign.

12.1.4.1 Overview of the PADD notation

(g) Introduction

Notation, or language, is important for integration and design. As a matter of fact, it is the most important tool. Think, for instance, about arithmetic:

the roman notation for numbers compared to the positional decimal notation which is used today. The notation of the environment is PADD. It stands for Parallelism and Abstraction in Dimensional Design (DD). DD is a tree representation technique introduced in reference [Witty 81], reference [Bertran 88] gives a formalization and some applications. PADD programs are expressed as PADD schemas, a specific interpretation of DD. Some of the characteristic features of PADD, as well as an introductory example are covered next.

(h)   Mathematical semantics

PADD is a formal notation for specification, modeling, and programming. Its semantics is specified with a parallel communicating program algebra. Its laws constitute the base for program transformations.

(i)   Explicit parallelism and communication

The construct

$$\textbf{Parbegin} \dots \textbf{ParEnd}$$

is available in schematic form, horizontal connection of processes under symbol '||'. Also, communication between processes through conceptual connections. The availability of communicating parallel processes, with simple synchronized rendez-vous over connections, puts PADD in the same family of explicit parallelism notations such as OCCAM and ADA. Therefore loosely coupled, devoid of shared storage, multiprocessors can be modeled.

(j)   Parametric abstract types and monitors

They are available within the type definition system of PADD. This puts PADD in the family of languages such as CLU [Liskov 86]. As it will be covered below, an extended form of abstract type, referred to as CAT, is being incorporated into the environment. Monitors [Hoare 74; Buhr 95], as a generalization of semaphores, are viewed as abstract types which use process synchronization and scheduling operations (condition variables). PADD provides a library so that monitors can be programmed. Thus closely coupled multiprocessors, with shared store, can be modeled, in addition to loosely coupled multiprocessors.

DeLine
  Structural expression of a three register delay line.
  int
    res —————— **par**
      []out: ElType   *<>in: ElType*
  alg
    var
      Variables modeling register store.
        s0, s1, s2: ElType
  con
    c0, c1: ElType
    Global input-output synchronization connection.
      Sync: Nil
  | |

  P1 ————————— *P2* ————————— *P3*
  Output register   Internal register   Input register
    * ∞   * ∞   * ∞
      []out:=s0   *[]c0:= s1*   *[]c1:= s2*
      s0:= <>c0   *s1:= <>c1*   *s2:= <>in*
      []Sync   *<>Sync*

(k) DD schema embedded documentation

Readability and clarity of programs are made easier with PADD. A formal hierarchical structure can be constructed, where the diagonal dimension denotes refinement of description. This amounts to a formalization of the informal indentation of structured programming. Trees of annotations with precisely defined scopes, their diagonal lower subschemas, can be edited. An example is shown above. Standard design specification documentation is extracted automatically from PADD schemas with a RALE tool.

(l) An example

The PADD procedure in the above figure, which models a three register delay line as a parallel system of communicating processes, will introduce and illustrate the notation. An equivalent expression in indented form would be as follows:

DeLine
Structural expression of a three register delay line
   interface
      results [] out : ElType
      parameters $\diamond$ in : ElType
   algorithm
   var
      Variables modeling register storage.
      s0, s1, s2: ElType
   connections c0, c1: ElType; Sync:Nil;
   parallel
      P1:
         Output register
         do forever
            [] out := s0
            s0:= $\diamond$ c0
            []*Sync*
      P2:
         Internal register
         do forever
            [] $c0$:= s1
            s1:= $\diamond$ c1
      P3:
         Input register
         do forever
            [] $c1$:= s2
            s2:= $\diamond$ in
            $\diamond$ *Sync*

The delay line is modeled as a procedure devoid of proper parameters (variables) and results. Three communicating processes exist. This corresponds to a *structural* model, in other words involving parallelism. It has a single input (in) and a single output (out) connection. These global connections are declared in the interface (**int**) section. Input connections are prefixed with the symbol '$<>$', and output connections with '[ ]'. Connections represent logical half-duplex communication points between two processes for simple rendez-vous communication, $c0$, $c1$, and *Sync* are used as connections internal to the system, declared within a **con(...)** construct. They are hidden to an external observer. Input and output *offers* are expressed as an assignment ('$:=$') between connections and variables. Also, offers may be nil typed, as the ones over *Sync* in the example, then no assignment symbol is needed. A communication *event* takes place when the two processes actually synchronize and communicate over a connection. The operator '$\|$' denotes parallel process composition. Indefinite repetition or iteration is expressed by the unary operator ' $*\infty$ '. Type *ElType* is assumed to be visible.

12.1.5 *Ramon Llull*

RALE has been named after this universal catalan, born in Mallorca about 1233. He died in 1316, and wrote more than four hundred books covering most of the knowledge of his time, from which only about twelve have reached us. He taught at the University in Paris departing from the scholastic approach.

Among many other activities, he was after a system to derive "all truths", described in his *Ars Magna*. Reference [Gardner 58] elaborates on this. He was a predecessor of Leibnitz and Descartes, who had the same goal in mind. For greater information, refer to [Yates 82; Hillgarth 71] and [Bonner 97; Sales 97].

Ramon Llull is a predecessor of modern researchers such as Georges Bool and Götlieb Frege in the search for formal logic systems. Since such systems constitute the basis of formal transformations, naming our system after him was obvious.

12.1.6 *Prior Usage*

PADD and its various environments have been used extensively in both industry and academy. It is taught at three university schools now. A consulting company has PADD over RALE as the environment which provides its framework for the development of high quality multiprocessor projects, including hard real-time systems. Various industry departments have also adopted PADD for the same reason. One of the real-time applications was a digital telephone voice compression and packetization interface for a packet switching network. Reference [Alvarez-Cuevas 93] reports on it. A number of report publications and presentations in international conferences exist, see references [Bertran 89; Bertran 93; Bertran 94].

12.2 Some System Forms and Transformations

12.2.1 *Introduction*

In a formal design process, programs representing systems are transformed but remaining equivalent in some sense. This section introduces some typical system forms which are going to appear later in this article. Some simple transformations are also covered. The exact meaning of the equivalences will be covered in next section.

12.2.2　*Sequential (SQ) Form*

Sequential (also functional) Form. Programs in this form are purely sequential. They involve neither inner parallelism nor communications connections, neither internal nor external. The data that they need is located in storage. The results that they generate are left in storage also. The symbolism

$$r:= SQ(d)$$

will be used to denote a purely sequential system form with d denoting all the data which is needed in order to compute result r. Multiple values will correspond to a product typed d or r.

12.2.3　*Communicating Sequential (CS) Form*

A program whose data and results are communicated through connections with other processes composed in parallel, and whose algorithm is sequential. The symbolism:

$$[]out := CS(\Diamond in)$$

will denote a program in this form.

12.2.4　*To Connections Interface Transformation (T_{ci})*

Transforms a program whose parameter data and results are storage variables into an equivalent program in CS form with the same functionality. For example, a program in SQ form can be transformed into an equivalent program in CS form by the transformation T_{ci}.

$$
\begin{aligned}
&T_{ci} \left(\; r:= SQ(d) \; \right) \; \triangleq \\
&\quad \textbf{var} \; (vr: \text{Typer}; \; vd: \text{Typed}) \\
&\quad vd:= \; \Diamond d \\
&\quad vr:= SQ(vd) \\
&\quad []r := vr
\end{aligned}
$$

12.2.5   *Simple Cyclic (SC) Form*

A program in this form has a global indefinite iteration whose body is in CS form:

$$\textbf{do forever}$$
$$[]out := \text{CS}(\;\Diamond\,in\;)$$

12.2.6   *Structural (ST) Form*

A program having parallelism and whose processes may communicate with one another through connections. The program *DeLine* given above is an example of ST form.

12.2.7   *To Communicating Process Transformation (T_{cp})*

Given a program in SQ form, this transformation obtains an equivalent program where the sequential is transformed into a parallel composition, and the necessary connection communications are introduced for the conservation of functionality. More specifically, let the original program be

$$\text{r}:= \text{SQ0(d)} \;\triangleq$$
$$\textbf{var } \text{t:Typet}$$
$$\text{t}:= \text{SQ1(d)}$$
$$\text{r}:= \text{SQ2(t)}$$

which has two subprograms composed sequentially. Then, the resulting structural program form will be

$$\text{r}:= \text{ST(d)} \;\triangleq$$
$$\textbf{con } \text{t:Typet}$$
$$\textbf{parallel}$$
$$\quad \text{P1:}$$
$$\qquad \textbf{var } \text{vt: Typet}$$
$$\qquad \text{vt}:= \text{SQ1(d)}$$
$$\qquad []t := \text{vt}$$
$$\quad \text{P2:}$$
$$\qquad \textbf{var } \text{vt: Typet}$$
$$\qquad \text{vt}:= \;\Diamond\,t$$
$$\qquad \text{r}:= \text{SQ2(vt)}$$

And the following may be written

$$\text{r}:= \text{ST(d)} =_f T_{cp}(\text{ r}:= \text{SQ0(d) })$$

This transformation is based on the application of a sequence of laws of the algebra.

12.3   Communication-Extended Abstract Types

A Communications-extended AT (CAT) is an abstract type but including
also *send* and *receive* operations to communicate values of that type. The
specific structure of the implied communication is hidden from the user
program, only a connection typed with the abstract type is seen. Implementations of a CAT may specify a more detailed communications structure
of the send and receive operations. For instance, two implementations of
CAT complex number may correspond either to communications of the real
and imaginary parts in series through a connection of type real, or in parallel through two such connections. Thus, a CAT implementation has *two*
representations, the usual storage representation, and the communications
representation.

   The CAT syntactic construct has as objective the collection of all the
implementations of an abstract type under their common specification, so
that reuse of structures of the specification is possible, avoiding unnecessary
text typing and inconsistency errors, but without impairing clarity. Also,
selection of a specific refinement is made easier. The global structure of a
CAT is the following:

> **cat** *cat_name*
> **specification**
> *Specification body*
> **implementations**
> *Sequential implementations*
> *Structural implementations*
> *Other implementations*

The specification body, which is shared by all the implementations of
the CAT, has the following form:

> **specification**
> **results**
> *Operation names, their interfaces and signatures*
> **parameters**
> *Constants, types, functions*
> **preconditions**
> *Conditions on parameters*
> **postconditions**
> *Algebraic specification laws*

   The results of a CAT are its operations, which depend on the parameters of the CAT, and are constrained by the classical algebraic
specification laws which have here a natural place as postconditions,

involving operations and parameters. The parameters may be types (CATs), constants, and procedures (functions). References [Bertran 93; Bertran 97b] provide further details and examples of CATs, and its application to refinement.

12.4 Algebraic Framework

12.4.1 *Introduction*

The algebraic laws associated to the PADD notation constitute the base for the definition of most of the transformations. Essentially, they are used in two directions: formal parallelization and communication simplification. Formal parallelization is a refinement process, some parallelized version of an initial sequential program is obtained. Suitable transformations are applied in order to bring the program to a desired parallelized form. Communication simplification is the opposite process and it will be covered below. Both processes have at their ends two functionally equivalent programs, a simple or short one, and a more complicated one involving parallel communicating processes.

At present the environment does not contemplate specification and verification. These activities would take place in a well established environment such as the Stanford Temporal Prover (STeP), [Manna 91; Manna 95], which is reported in this volume. A tool could translate programs in PADD into SPL, the notation of STeP. The simple forms associated to some of the ends of the formal parallelization and simplification processes are the candidates for verification. RALE could complement environments such as STeP by either refining verified programs or verifying programs simplified within RALE.

12.4.2 *Equivalences for Parallel Communicating Processes*

Functional equivalence

Given a bag (a set admitting copies of its elements) of input or parameter values, a process computes a resulting bag of values. Such a process may be connected in parallel with other processes. Values may be passed (or left) in storage common to processes, state, before (or after) the execution of the process. But also values may be exchanged by communication operations with other processes connected in parallel. Therefore, the input and output bags of values, denoted *ParValues* and *ResValues* respectively, encompass both values passed through storage and values communicated via connections with neighbour parallel processes.

In the sequel, two programs are considered to be *functionally equivalent* if, for the same input bag of values, the same output bag of values is generated by both. The order among the values is irrelevant for functional equivalence. Event and communication offering order does not matter. This may be expressed as follows:

$$P_1 =_f P_2 \iff \forall d \ in \ ParValues . \{ResValues(P_1(d)) = ResValues(P_2(d))\}$$

Order equivalence

Two programs P_1 and P_2 are *order equivalent*, denoted by

$$P_1 =_o P_2$$

with respect to a given subset of their events, if the partial orders of events, belonging to the given subset, are the same in all their corresponding executions. The given subset of events may contain both internal events and value passing communication events, with other programs (processes) connected in parallel with P_1 and P_2.

12.4.3 *Algebraic Semantics of Communications*

A linear-textual presentation of programs is used in this section for convenience. The symbols O_c and $\hat{O}_c$ will denote complementary communication operations over connection c. The symbols ';' and '||' will stand for sequential and parallel composition respectively. Both are associative and only parallel composition is commutative. Process *Nil* is the unity for both. The equivalence which is used in laws is *order* equivalence ($=_o$). First, some basic cases which are deadlock (*Stop()*) configurations are given.

Law 12.4.1   (Isolated communication offering) The following holds

$$\mathbf{con} \ c \ O_c =_o \mathbf{con} \ c \ \hat{O}_c =_o Stop()$$

Law 12.4.2   (Unmatching communication) One has that

$$\mathbf{con} \ c \ (\ O_c \ || \ O_c \ ) =_o Stop()$$
$$\mathbf{con} \ c \ (\ \hat{O}_c \ || \ \hat{O}_c \ ) =_o Stop()$$

The following are some of the laws needed to eliminate, or to introduce, communication and parallelism.

Law 12.4.3 (Matching communication) The following holds for nil typed connections:

$$\textbf{con } c \left(O_c \parallel \hat{O}_c \right) =_o c$$

where event c is equivalent to *Nil*.

For typed connections, a value is passed from a variable v_{out} in the output side into another variable v_{in} in the input side, and the assignment $v_{in} := v_{out}$ replaces c in the right hand side of the equivalence. Here is is the corresponding law:

Law 12.4.4 (Matching variable communication) One has that

$$\textbf{con } c \left(v_{in} := \diamondsuit c \parallel []c := v_{out} \right) =_o v_{in} := v_{out}$$

The following laws capture the synchronization implicit in simple rendez-vous communication. Their analogues involving variable communications would be obtained as before.

Law 12.4.5 (Parallel post-communication) Let H_1 and H_2 not involve any communication operation over c. Then:

$$\textbf{con } c \left(H_1 ; O_c ; T_1 \parallel H_2 ; \hat{O}_c ; T_2 \right)$$
$$=_o$$
$$\textbf{con } c \left\{ \left(H_1 ; O_c \parallel H_2 ; \hat{O}_c \right) ; \left(T_1 \parallel T_2 \right) \right\}$$

Law 12.4.6 (Parallel pre-communication) One has that

$$\textbf{con } c \left(H_1 ; O_c ; T_1 \parallel H_2 ; \hat{O}_c ; T_2 \right)$$
$$=_o$$
$$\textbf{con } c \left\{ \left(H_1 \parallel H_2 \right) ; \left(O_c ; T_1 \parallel \hat{O}_c ; T_2 \right) \right\}$$

All these laws stand as axioms used in communication simplification and other types of proofs, together with other laws in the algebra.

12.4.4 *Time Interval Algebra*

Time is modeled with intervals. Let $\tau(t_{min}, t_{max})$ denote a time interval with minimum and maximum execution times. Then, the following are some of the laws:

$$\tau(t_0, t_1) \; ; \; \tau(t_2, t_3) \; = \; \tau(t_0 + t_2, t_1 + t_3)$$

$$\tau(t_0, t_1) \parallel \tau(t_2, t_3) \; = \; \tau(max(t_0, t_2), max(t_1, t_3))$$

$$\tau(t_0, t_1) \; ? \; \tau(t_2, t_3) \; = \; \tau(min(t_0, t_2), max(t_1, t_3))$$

for sequential, parallel, and selection composition. Where $t_0 \leq t_1$ and $t_2 \leq t_3$.

Let $delay(t) \stackrel{\triangle}{=} \tau(t, t)$. Then

$$(delay(t_0) \; ; \; delay(t_1)) \; = \; delay(t_0 + t_1)$$

$$(delay(t_0) \parallel delay(t_1)) \; = \; delay(max(t_0, t_1))$$

$$(delay(t_0) \; ? \; delay(t_1)) \; = \; \tau(min(t_0, t_1), max(t_0, t_1))$$

In order to model time, τ's and *delay*'s are inserted at appropriate points of programs, and the above laws are used to compute or propagate time within communications simplification transformation processes.

12.5 Methods and Tools

12.5.1 *Documentation*

The lack of documentation, and (when existing) its lack of coherency with the system which is being documented are quite usual facts in practice. It is time consuming to maintain coherency. The environment supports a method for overcoming this problem.

Specifications and programs are expressed as tree-schemas. There is place for annotations whose scope is precisely defined. An annotation is at a node of the schema and should describe its diagonal subtree. Schema editors are used to construct programs and specifications. Sets of parallel communicating processes may be entered with a block diagram editor. Hence, schemas constitute the first documentation.

RALE helps in fulfilling the requirements of ANSI-IEEE quality software development standards. The Design Specification document is automatically extracted from PADD schemas containing annotations. A tool which works on top of LaTeX is available for that. This reduces the cost of documentation and the incoherency risks between design documentation and the program which is being documented.

In addition, LaTeX templates of ANSI-IEEE documents are given by default and the user has to fill in the text concerning his project, without having to define sections, chapters, and other constant features of the documents. The templates contain summaries of the norm at the appropriate places, guiding the user about what should be described at each point.

12.5.2 *Purely Communicating System Modeling and Specification*

This refers to a technique where a concurrent program is modeled as a set of parallel communicating processes over nil typed connections. No storage variables exist in these models. This simplification facilitates the analysis of concurrency properties. Only a subset of PADD is needed to model systems at this level. Animation of specifications is available. The corresponding detailed program may be obtained by reusing its specification, adding variables and operations in the algebra framework. A tool will transform a detailed program into its purely communicating model.

12.5.3 *Simulation*

Event-driven simulation is available, for both testing and performance evaluation. The event-driven simulation method departs from the familiar one based on a central event queue. In this respect the Simula approach, as introduced in references [Dahl 68; Dahl 72], is followed. Time modeling and statistics collection procedures are available, and plots of the resulting statistics can be specified by the user, with popular office tools.

12.5.4 *Allocation-Mapping Transformation*

Simulation and transformations take place at a conceptual level. The actual real-time software, to work in a concrete platform, is obtained from programs by allocation mapping tools. They are guided by schemas edited by the designer and defining where in the base real-time platform should each conceptual (PADD) process be allocated.

A base platform is defined in terms of processors, tasks, and threads. Two base platforms are available, corresponding to two widely used networks. Therefore PADD processes will be transformed into tasks residing at some processor or threads within some task within a processor. An equivalent program in C is obtained for each of the tasks. In this context, mapping to VHDL for hardware design is under development.

12.5.5   *Communications Simplification*

The laws introduced in section 12.4.3 are used with all the rest in order to try to eliminate internal communication and parallelism. Three outcomes are possible in this attempt:

(*a*) An equivalent system having no internal communication results.

(*b*) The process stops with a system where internal communications remain, and can not be eliminated.

(*c*) The proof does not end.

In the first case, the relation between the initial and the simplified programs depends on the laws which have been used in the process. Normally, functionality is preserved and deadlock-freeness is inferred. As a consequence, simulation effort may be reduced by replacing structural parts of the program to be simulated by their simplified forms. In the second case a design error may be inferred. In the last case nothing can be said.

A simple example of the first case follows.   The simplified form which is equivalent to the structural delay line introduced earlier in this work, resulting from a communications simplification proof is the following program:

```
A_DeLine
      Equivalent SC form for DeLine.
         interface
            results  []out : ElType
            parameters  ◇ in : ElType
         algorithm
            var
               Variables modeling register storage.
               s0, s1, s2: ElType
            do forever
               []out := s0
               s0:= s1
               s1:= s2
               s2:=  ◇ in
```

Since this equivalence preserves the order of external offers, and an equivalent form without internal communication has been reached, this means that the original structural delay line does not deadlock, and that both forms are equivalent as far as interaction with other parallel processes is concerned.

The environment has a proof editing tool for the construction of proofs, integrated in the environment. Sets of laws (theories) and proofs can be stored in the environment data base. A more powerful proof construction tool will be integrated in the near future. Laws may have applicability conditions and the designer can define procedures for automatic construction of parts of a proof. They are referred to as *transformation procedures*. Some elementary ones are the following:

ToSelPar. Conversion of a given parallel construct, whose subprocesses contain selections, into a selection whose alternatives are parallel constructs.

FndFrsCm. Finds the *first* pair of communication operations over a given connection, and within a parallel construct. This is invoked before the next one, which tries to eliminate the corresponding communications operation.

ComElimi. Given a suitable pair of communication operations over the same connection, and within a given parallel construct, this strategy tries to obtain the equivalent program where both communication operations are eliminated and an equivalent assignment is left.

12.5.6 *System Refinement Based on CATs*

Refinement here is understood as the introduction of more *structural* detail in a program. Structural means parallelism and communication.

One way to achieve this is to change the implementation of a CAT which is typing some of the connections of the program to be refined. The change replaces a sequential by a structural implementation.

As an example, consider CAT complex number. The abstract implementation which we are interested in will have complex multiplication in CS form. The structural implementation has parallel communication of the real and imaginary parts of a complex value, and its operations will have processes such as addition and multiplication of reals connected in parallel to compute the complex multiplication. Thus, changing a CAT implementation amounts to deciding for a specific communications structure. More detail is given in [Bertran 97b].

12.5.7 *Proper Monitor Elimination Transformation (T_{me})*

The transformations covered so far apply to parallel processes communicating through connections, which model well distributed storage systems.

Shared storage systems are modeled very naturally with monitors. In order to bring the latter systems into the transformation approach based on parallel connection communicating systems a transformation is needed.

```
var m:MonClass;
   parallel
      P1:
         . . . r:= op2(m) . . . op1(m) . . .
      P2:
         . . . op1(m) . . .
      . . .
      . . .
      Pp:
         . . . op3(p,m) . . .
```

This transformation obtains a purely communicating program which is order equivalent to the program involving a shared storage monitor, whose structure is detailed above. It has p parallel processes. *MonClass* denotes this monitor with n operations: *op1, op2, ..., opn* .

Some monitor operation invocations have been made explicit. Without loss of generality, assume that operation i is invoked at more than one location in the above program, namely at n_i locations. The parallel processes are synchronized at their monitor operation invocations. Within monitor operations, processes may be suspended until certain condition holds. For each monitor invocation, the start s and end e events are important for the order semantics, since the monitor amounts to a scheduler of the p processes. The two forms of monitors have thus to be order equivalent. Event s occurs at the invocation instant and event e at the return instant of operations, respectively. The monitor releases the calling process at the e event. Thus the transformed program has to use connection communications for this synchronization. Two connection arrays

$$s(1..n)(1..max(n_i)), \ and \ e(1..n)(1..max(n_i))$$

where the maximum is taken over $i = 1 \cdots n$, will represent the start and end events of the kth instance of the ith operation (in general some of the connections may not be actually used). The overall schema of the purely communicating parallel processes obtained by the transformation, equivalent to the above program schema, is the following:

Structure of an equivalent program without the proper monitor
con s(1..n)(1..maxni), e(1..n)(1..maxni): Nil
parallel
    MonProcess
        The process acting as the proper monitor

. . .

    parallel
        Q1:

. . .

        Q2:

. . .

        . . .
        . . .
        Qp:

. . .

The Q_i processes correspond to the P_i ones. Each Q_i is obtained by applying a suitable transformation to its corresponding P_i. This transformation replaces each operation invocation by a sequential composition of the start and end events associated to the operation instance,

$$
\begin{array}{l}
\cdot\,\cdot\,\cdot \\
[]e(i)(k) \\
\diamondsuit s(i)(k) \\
\cdot\,\cdot\,\cdot
\end{array}
$$

Process *MonProcess* simulates the proper monitor, it is constructed in such a way that the execution order of the start and end events of all invocation operation instances is the same as in the starting parallel program involving the proper monitor. The algorithm form of *MonProcess*, which is the result of the transformation, guarantees that. More detail is available in reference [Bertran 97a].

12.6 Conclusion and Future Work

A global picture of an environment for distributed and real-time system development has been given. The environment and its notation support both shared storage and distributed storage systems.

Shared storage systems are modeled using monitors. A transformation has been outlined to take these systems to the order equivalent distributed storage form, introducing a new process and new connections.

Distributed storage systems may be simplified by eliminating inner communication and parallelism in trying to reach an equivalent sequential externally communicating form. The verification of the equivalent form will be done in well established specification and verification environments, such as STeP. Also, these systems may be refined by introducing internal parallelism and communication and with the transformation which involves the change of implementation of a Communication-extended Abstract Type. This concept has been summarized above.

Simulation of the systems under design is also undertaken, in cooperation with the transformation approach. Allocation-mapping tools exist for generation of C processes implementing the distributed system. A VHDL generator is under construction and it will permit to experiment the generation of hardware defined in the PADD notation.

RALE is fully operational as far as editing, documentation generation, simulation, proof editing, and allocation mapping to a set of C programs to run in two well established networks. It is used to teach parallelism and to simulate computer architectures at the university.

The following are other envisioned future lines of work: the integration of an interactive proof construction tool equipped with transformation procedures for proof acceleration, the completion of the integration of CATs and its refinement transformation capabilities, and the monitor elimination transformation. Further investigation of high-level hardware design from PADD models will be continued with the VHDL generator. This will result in the possibility of software and hardware codesign support by PADD/RALE.

Chapter 13

Analysis of Real-Time Systems Using OSA

J. M. DuBois and S. N. Woodfield

13.1 Introduction

The advent of object-oriented programming and the subsequent development of object-oriented design has greatly improved the quality of software development. Until the late 1980's, however, there were no object-oriented analysis techniques to complement design and coding. In the late 1980's we tried to fill that vacuum. We didn't want to modify existing techniques but wanted to build a new analysis model based on sound principles [Embley 92].

One of our fundamental principles was that analysis was a process of discovering and recording knowledge. Thus, an analysis technique should facilitate knowledge acquisition. We have observed that many of the so-called structured and object-oriented analysis techniques are really specification techniques [Embley 95]. They have been implicitly or explicitly designed to describe systems that can be easily implemented using current object-oriented programming languages. Their techniques require the analyst to consider implementation concerns in addition to acquiring knowledge. Since they are implementation biased their modeling concepts are not as expressively powerful as they could be. With our technique, Object-oriented Systems Analysis (OSA), we wanted to create a model that was expressive and allowed the analyst to think more in terms of the real world.

A second fundamental principle of OSA is being "Model Driven" rather than "Method Driven". With a model-driven technique there is a well defined analysis model. As the analyst acquires knowledge it is recorded in terms of the model. As knowledge is recorded, the structure of the model helps the analyst consider information that may have been overlooked. There are many means of discovery and the analyst is free to choose the means deemed best.

With a method-driven technique the emphasis is on a set of steps. There is only one prescribed manner in which analysis can be performed which is often informally defined. If the analyst deviates from the approach then they are likely to get lost. Since the underlying model is usually poorly-defined it cannot easily be used to help in decision making.

The difference between model-driven and method-driven techniques is similar to the difference between using a map to find an address and using directions. When using a map we use our understanding of maps and geography to come up with a route to an address. There may be more than one way to get there but different people using the same map will get to the right location. If they get lost, travelers can use the map to create a new route to their goal. If we only use directions we must follow them precisely. With just one mistake we will be lost and there is little chance we will arrive at our destination on time if at all.

Another fundamental principle of our analysis technique was the need for a formal definition. We found many of the existing techniques hard to understand because there was no underlying formal definition. OSA is formally defined using a temporal, first-order logic. Using the formal definition of OSA, the semantics of any expression can unambiguously be determined. When great precision is needed in a model, OSA supports it. Since OSA is based on a temporal logic, it provides both expressive power and semantic clarity for the analysis of real-time systems.

The OSA model has three main sub-models. The first is an information-structure model called the Object-Relationship Model (ORM). This allows information about objects, such as a "Person has a Name" to be recorded. ORMs are similar in nature to ER models [Chen 76]. The second model is called the Object-Behavior Model (OBM) and is represented by state nets. State nets are an enhanced state-transition model. The third type of model is the Object-Interaction Model (OIM). The interaction model describes the origin and destination of events as well as the source and destination of information transfer.

In this chapter, we will describe the principal features and uses of the three sub-models of OSA and particularly how they address the needs of real-time system analysis.

13.2   Object-Interaction Models

There are many ways to approach analysis. In database systems we usually start by building an ORM. With real-time systems we often start by identifying all of the external events a system must respond to. In OSA these events are represented by interactions. Interactions show the source and destination of events and information.

The data flow diagram from Structured Analysis [Yourdon 89] is the primary interaction model used by many analysis techniques. Even one of the most famous object-oriented analysis models, OMT [Rumbaugh 91], uses data flow diagrams as its primary interaction model. Data flow diagrams have several problems, however. First, they are not object-oriented. They show only the interaction between processes and not between objects or object sets. Next, they show only data flow. Data flow diagrams required so called "real-time extensions" [Ward 91a; Ward 91b; Ward 91c] to represent the transmission and reception of events. This resulted in a bifurcated model that did not mix event and information flow. While the real time extensions allowed continuous data flow and allowed us to represent when and why events may be generated, we still could not indicate when and why information is generated and under what conditions it may be rejected by the receiver. Because data flow diagrams were not well defined it is not known whether they represented synchronous communication or asynchronous communication. Also, it was not possible to show the broadcast of information, multi-way interactions, or describe timing constraints.

The interaction model of OSA solves all of these problems. The basic one-way interaction is shown in Figure 13.1. The interaction has a name and represents an event which in this case is "temperature fell below 70 degrees". The interaction shows the source of an event, a thermostat, and the destination of the event, a heating system. This form of interaction is asynchronous. That is, if the heating system is not in a state to acknowledge the event generated by the thermostat, then the communication is lost. To represent synchronous communication we use two-way interactions as shown in Figure 13.2. In this case the thermostat will attempt to interact with the heating system until it has received an acknowledgement.

We believe that in the real world, all interactions take some amount of time. To limit the duration of an interaction we allow timing constraints. These constraints are especially useful when dealing with synchronous com-

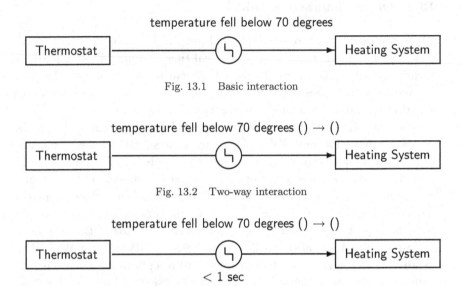

Fig. 13.1   Basic interaction

Fig. 13.2   Two-way interaction

Fig. 13.3   Timing constraint on an interaction

munication. As shown in Figure 13.3, they allow us to limit the amount of time an entity will try to synchronize with another entity.

There are other forms of constraints in the OSA interaction model. The formal semantics of Figure 13.3 indicate that any furnace can respond to the event generated by any thermostat. If there is only one heating system for a particular thermostat then we may wish to indicate it as shown in Figure 13.4. The "TO:" clause allows us to restrict the set of objects which can actually respond to a particular event. While not used as often, we can use a "FROM:" clause to restrict the set of objects able to send a particular interaction.

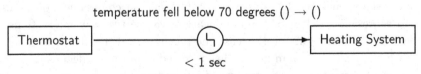

Fig. 13.4   Interaction with a constraint on the recipient

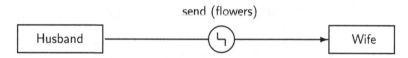

Fig. 13.5   Interaction with information passed

Fig. 13.6   Interaction without an event identifier

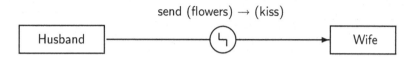

Fig. 13.7   Synchronous interaction with returned information

Many times we not only want to represent the transmission of events but also the transmission of information. The information transmitted from source to destination is represented by parameters inside the parenthesis of the interaction. Figure 13.5 gives an example. In this case, the thermostat not only signals the heating system but also provides the current temperature. When it is primarily the information flow we want to represent and not the event, we use the form in Figure 13.6 where the name of the interaction is omitted. This form is still asynchronous. Figure 13.7 shows that while it is not required, synchronous communication allows the return of information. While these examples show single units of information, the information in parenthesis can be represented by a comma separated list of parameters.

Notice that these forms of interactions allow us to naturally mix descriptions of events and data interactions using a single form. Many other techniques use one form to represent event interactions (e.g. the dashed line in extended data flow diagrams) and another form to represent data flow (e.g. the solid line of data flow diagrams).

In the examples presented so far, each interaction has an origin and destination. While this is often the case, there are times when we want to show interactions that originate or have a destination outside the scope of

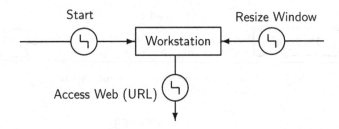

Fig. 13.8   Interactions to and from outside the analysis model

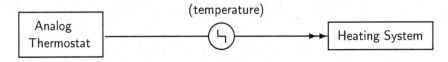

Fig. 13.9   Continuous interaction

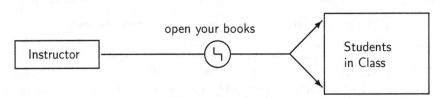

Fig. 13.10   Broadcast interaction

analysis. In this case the interaction arrow need only have a destination or origin. Figure 13.8 shows an example. This form is often used when describing the logical interface of a system.

Like real-time extensions to structured analysis, OSA provides a means to represent continuous interactions. Figure 13.9 shows an example. OSA's interaction model provides other constructs as well. It can show broadcast interactions as shown in Figure 13.10. In this case the event or information is sent to all members of an object class. At a higher level of abstraction we can show not only two way interaction but multi-way interaction as in Figure 13.11. At lower-levels of abstraction we can show when interactions are triggered and when an object may respond to an interaction as in Figure 13.12. In the latter case we connect parts of the behavior model (to be presented in more detail in the next section) with interactions. With these connections we can describe when an interaction is generated and

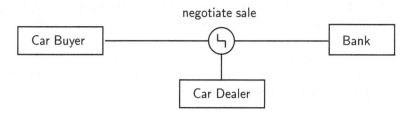

Fig. 13.11 Multi-way interaction

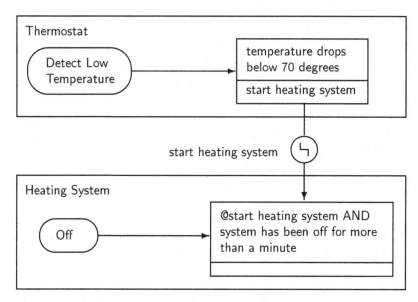

Fig. 13.12 Interaction triggered in a specific transition which fires a specific transition in another object set

when a receiving object may respond to the interaction. For instance, in Figure 13.12, we see that the thermostat only interacts with the heating system when it is in the "Detect Low Temperature" state and the temperature drops below 70 degrees. The heating system will only respond to the thermostat if it has been in the "Off" state for 1 minute or more. In this scenario it is possible for the temperature to drop below 70 degrees and for the heating system to ignore the event. It is ignored because the event, which is considered to be instantaneous in OSA, can occur when the heating system will not respond. This may not be the intended behavior.

With a formal model this situation is easier to detect and correct. It is also easier to discuss because we can point to a part of a model instance* and ask whether what is written represents what was intended. Many other analysis models are informal and the true semantics of what is written is never clearly understood. Without clear understanding it is difficult to detect or discuss semantic errors.

13.3 Object-Behavior Models

When developing OSA we considered using one of several existing behavior models including pseudo-code, finite-state machines, Harel charts [Harel 87], and Petri nets [Peterson 81]. We found problems with each model. Many models lacked forms of concurrency. Other models did not support real-time constraints. Some did not allow the analyst to describe exceptional behavior. Few behavior models provided any form of higher-level abstraction. Most of the models were not formally defined and thus were ambiguous. Those that were formal, such as Petri nets, made unrealistic assumptions (e.g. all transitions are instantaneous). We thus attempted to develop a better Object Behavior Model (OBM) represented by what are called "State Nets".

A state net is a sophisticated state-transition model. Each state net is associated with an object class and defines the behavior of members of the class. Figure 13.13 shows a simple transition from a state net for a person.

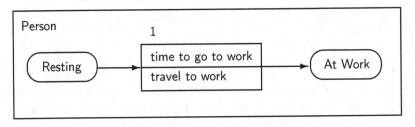

Fig. 13.13 Simple transition

*When discussing analysis there can be confusion between the concept of a specific model (e.g. the model of a flight control system) and the meta-models used to define valid specific models (e.g. OSA). In this chapter we use the term "model instance" to mean a specific model of reality and the word "model" when referring to meta-models.

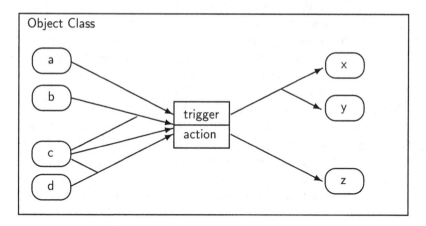

Fig. 13.14   General transition with prior- and subsequent-state conjunctions

The transition is the box with a horizontal line through the middle and is labeled with the number "1". The top half of the transition contains the transition trigger and the bottom half of the transition contains the transition body or action. This transition represents the fact that when a person is in the "Resting" state and it is "time to go to work" then a person will leave the "Resting" state, travel to work, and enter the "At Work" state. The transition from "Resting" to "At Work" may take time. Also, at any time an object can be in one or more concurrent states which are said to be "true".

Figure 13.14 shows a general transition. Each transition may have 0 or more prior-state conjunctions entering the transition. A prior-state conjunction is a set of 1 or more states which are connected to the transition by an arrow. The arrow has a single head on the transition and a tail on each of the prior states. Similarly, a transition may have 0 or more subsequent-state conjunctions leaving the transition. Each subsequent-state conjunction is also a set of states connected to the transition by an arrow with a single tail on the transition and a head on each of the subsequent states. In Figure 13.13, transition 1 has one prior-state conjunction which contains a single state and has one subsequent-state conjunction which also has a single state. Figure 13.13 is typical of many transitions.

A transition is considered enabled if all of the states in at least one prior-state conjunction are true. If a transition is enabled and the trigger is true then the transition fires. When a transition fires all of the states in the enabling prior-state conjunction become false. If there are more then one enabling prior-state conjunction then one conjunction is arbitrarily selected to be turned off. When the transition is finished firing then one of its subsequent-state conjunctions is arbitrarily selected and all of the states of the conjunction become true. The semantics of multiple prior- and subsequent state conjunctions allows us to represent non-determinism which is not found in all behavior models. It is also possible to assign priorities to prior-state conjunctions and probabilities to subsequent-state conjunctions. This allows us to better model reality. This capability is found in few behavior models.

In many models, transitions are only triggered by events. If conditions are present they are considered guards to the event. In OSA a trigger may have an event, condition, or both. Figure 13.15 shows an example of a transition with a single event. In this case, if a person is in their office and its "5:00 o'clock", then they leave work. An event is true at only one instant in time. If a transition contains a single event then the transition can only fire at that point in time when the transition is enabled and the event is true. If the transition is enabled just after the event occurs then the transition does not fire. For instance, according to Figure 13.15, if a person enters their office at one second after 5:00 then they will not go home. While we do need to be able to model events in real-time systems, it was not appropriate to model the intended behavior of Figure 13.15 with an event. We can correct this problem by using a condition rather than an event for the trigger as shown in Figure 13.16. In this case, if a person enters the office after 5:00 they will still go home. None of the existing object-oriented models that we are aware of support this feature. At best they allow a conjunction of events and conditions.

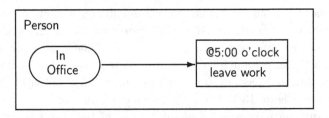

Fig. 13.15 Transition fired by an event

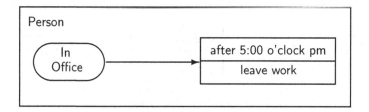

Fig. 13.16 Transition fired by a condition

All object-oriented analysis models support inter-object concurrency. That is, the objects in a model instance are assumed to act concurrently with respect to one another. Few object-oriented analysis models, however, support intra-object concurrency (OMT supports a limited form of intra-object concurrency). We have talked to authors of other techniques who insist that it is not needed because they can model intra-object concurrency in one of two ways. They can break an object into two smaller objects; each acting concurrently. Or they can simulate concurrency by using a context switching technique; they rapidly switch back and forth between two threads of control. We found both forms unacceptable for modeling reality. For instance, if we wished to model a person who is both driving a car and talking on the telephone we need to either create two people, or, have the person quickly switch back and forth between driving and talking. In OSA we support intra-object concurrency by allowing an object to have an arbitrary number of threads of control. N new threads are created when taking a subsequent-state conjunction that contains $N + 1$ states. Each of these threads are independent of any other thread. We can reduce the number of concurrent threads in one of two ways. First, we can use prior-state conjunctions with multiple-states to combine multiple threads into a single thread. Or, we can use a transition with no subsequent state conjunctions to eliminate threads. Figure 13.17 shows one way of modeling the driver who is talking on the phone. Figure 13.18 shows a better way of producing multiple threads of control. In this case, the "Driving" state is an enabling state of the transition, but when the transition fires we do not leave the "Driving" state. After the transition there are two threads of control.

To accurately model real-time systems we need to be able to constrain the time it takes to perform various actions or respond to different stimuli.

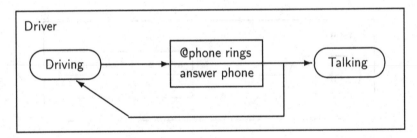

Fig. 13.17   Transition which creates two threads of control, one in the talking state and the other in the driving state

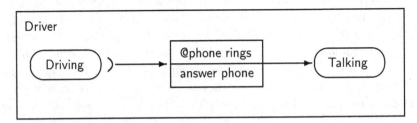

Fig. 13.18   Transition which goes to the talking state, leaving a new thread of control in the driving state

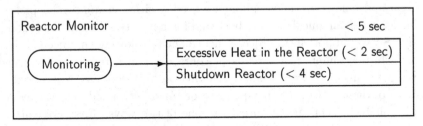

Fig. 13.19   Transition showing real-time constraints on total duration of transition, time to start the transition and time to complete the action

Figure 13.19 shows how, in OSA, we can constrain the time it takes to transition from one state to another. The note above the transition constrains the total time it takes to transition from state to state. The note inside the trigger constrains the amount of time it takes to start performing an action once the transition has been triggered. The note inside the body of the transition constrains the amount of time it takes to perform the action described in the body. Figure 13.20 shows another means of expressing

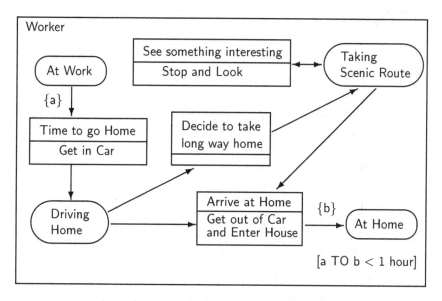

Fig. 13.20 Real-time constraint on a path within the state net

timing constraints. In OSA we can place named path markers on prior-
and subsequent-state conjunctions. We can then write general real-time
constraints in terms of these markers. Figure 13.20 shows that drivers who
decide to take the scenic route home must take less than 1 hour.

In OSA we felt it important to model the difference between hard errors
and soft errors. A hard error means that the model has entered a state
that is inconsistent with our view of reality. In general it means that an
executing model instance must be terminated. A soft error is an error
that can be handled by the system. Systems are considered robust if they
can handle many or all soft errors. In OSA, soft errors are represented
by exceptions. Figure 13.21 shows an example of exceptional behavior.
In this case a person is "Procrastinating" and on April 15 starts to do
their taxes. We consider it an error to not find a "W-2" form but we
don't want this real-world situation to invalidate the model instance. If the
W-2 form is lost, then an exception is taken and we file for an extension.
Our representation of exceptions define both the exception and what is to
be done when the exception occurs. Whenever an exception occurs, the
transition is terminated immediately, even if it is not finished performing
the action. Notice the use of general constraints in Figure 13.21 to indicate

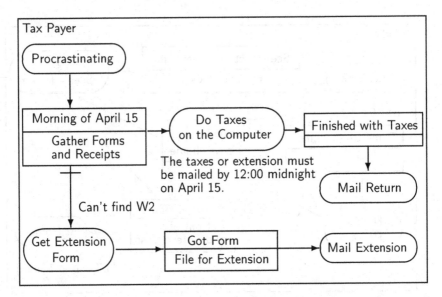

Fig. 13.21   State net with an exception transition

that in any case we must have mailed in our forms by 12:00 midnight on the evening of April 15. Figure 13.21 showed an example of an exception taken while transitioning from state to state. It is also possible to be in a state and have an exceptional condition arise. Figure 13.22 shows that while doing taxes, the computer disk crashes. In this case we take the exceptional transition and start performing taxes by hand.

We have found that in most cases our OSA model instances become so large that some form of abstraction is needed to manage the large amounts of detail. OSA provides behavior abstraction in terms of high-level states and high-level transitions. High-level states and transitions are fully reified in OSA. That is, you can treat a high-level state like any other state and treat a high-level transition like any other transition. Many other behavior models have no abstraction mechanisms and those that do provide abstraction mechanisms are not fully reified. Harel charts are the only other behavior models we are aware of that provide a similar form of state or transition abstraction.

Figure 13.23 shows the behavior of a ceiling fan in terms of a high-level state. A fan can be in an off, slow, medium, or fast state. We transition between these states by pulling a chain. If the ceiling fan is in the slow, medium, or fast state then it is also considered to be in the on state. The

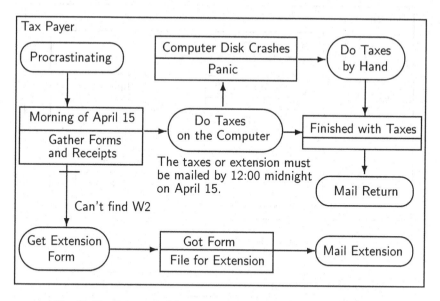

Fig. 13.22   State net with a transition on an exceptional condition

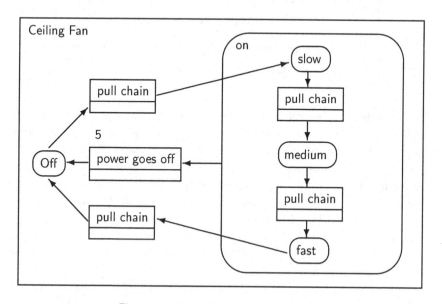

Fig. 13.23   High-level state in a state net

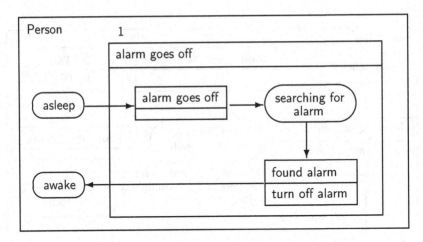

Fig. 13.24   High-level transition in a state net

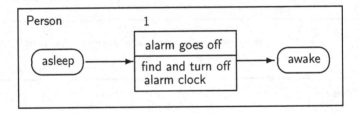

Fig. 13.25   Imploded high-level transition

on state is a high-level state. It acts exactly like any other state. In Figure 13.23, transition 5 treats the on as a normal state. If the power goes off we leave the on state and enter the off state. When leaving the on state using transition 5, all sub-states of the on state that are on are also turned off. A common example of high-level transitions is shown in Figure 13.24. In this case a person transitions from the asleep state to the awake state. The details of the waking up are shown inside high-level transition 1. Figure 13.25 shows how we implode a high-level transition to make it look like a normal transition. Similar representations are available for imploded high-level states.

There are more details to behavior models in OSA, but we believe that state nets can describe real-world and real-time behaviors better than any other object-oriented behavior model.

13.4 Object-Relationship Model

Real-time modeling is provided primarily by the interaction and behavior models of OSA. We believe that real-time modeling is a subset of "real-world" modeling. The Object-Relationship Model (ORM) of OSA is a structural or information model and thus does not provide real-time modeling concepts. However, it does support better real-world modeling concepts when compared to other object-oriented techniques. There are several problems found in other techniques that we have tried to solve in OSA. Some techniques confuse the notions of objects and object sets. Others define object sets as if they were programming language classes. While this provides an easier transition from analysis to implementation, it can confuse developers and users of analysis models. Many object-oriented techniques only allow information to be recorded in terms of binary relations. We have found that "real-world" model instances are much easier to produce if relations of arbitrary arity can be used. As with behavior models, we found that high-level abstractions are needed to represent real systems. Many analysis models have no high-level abstraction mechanisms, or, at best have limited mechanisms.

The concept of an object and a set of objects is essential to an object-oriented analysis technique. Some techniques introduce confusion by either omitting objects from the model or by calling object sets objects. In OSA, we represent an object by a solid dot and an object set by a square box with the object set name on the inside as in Figure 13.26. An object set represents a set of objects with common properties. The common properties can be either interactions, behavior, or relations. In OSA, relations are represented by relationship sets. An example is shown in Figure 13.27. In this case a Person can own a Car. The numbers by the object sets are

●

George Washington

USA President

Fig. 13.26 Singleton object and object set

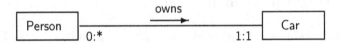

Fig. 13.27   Object sets participating in a relationship set

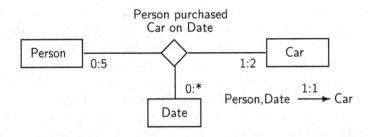

Fig. 13.28   Object sets participating in a ternary relationship set with a co-occurrence constraint

called participation constraints and constrain the number of times an object in an object set can participate in the relationship set. The participation constraint next to the object set Person states that a person may participate 0 or more times. The other participation constraint states that a car must participate once and only once. In other words, a person may own an arbitrary number of cars but a car must be owned by exactly one person. Figure 13.28 shows a ternary relationship set with participation constraints. This relationship set states that a person can purchase from 0 to 5 cars, that a car must be purchased by 1 or 2 people, and that any number of cars can be purchased on any date. Figure 13.28 shows another form of constraint, the co-occurrence constraint, that is not found in any other analysis model. It is useful when further constraining relationship sets of arity 3 and above. In this case it states that a person can purchase at most one car on a given date.

OSA's use of participation constraints allows them to be used with relationship sets of any arity. Other models use another form of cardinality constraint that works only with binary relationship sets. Because of this, and the belief that relationship sets of arity greater than two are extremely rare, other models fully support only binary relationships. We find this to be restricting and forces analysts to produce models that are harder to understand in terms of the real world.

Many other modeling techniques support the notion of attributes. They enable object sets created during analysis to look like classes found in object-oriented programming languages. While attributes are needed when doing design, they are not needed during analysis. Any attribute can be represented as a relationship set. Thus the attribute mechanism is redundant. Its presence can cause problems. In most models attributes are considered values and not objects. As such they cannot participate in relationship sets. Thus, if a person has an attribute "Birthdate", we cannot relate birth dates to anything. For instance, we cannot relate a birthdate to a "Historical Event" that occurred on that date. When attributes are present in analysis there is great temptation to make design decisions, especially whether a piece of information should be an attribute or represented by a relationship set. Thus attributes encourage design when a person should be doing analysis. These and other problems occur when attributes are present in analysis models. For these reasons OSA does not support attributes at the analysis level.

There is a need for abstraction mechanisms in any information model. OSA, like most other object-oriented techniques, provides means for representing aggregation and generalization/specialization. OSA also provides high-level object sets and relationship sets. These high-level constructs are not found in other techniques but are essential. Any real-world model instance soon becomes so big that it can't be dealt with as a flat model. High-level constructs allow us to organize the details and view them from arbitrary levels of abstraction. To do this, high-level object sets must have all of the properties of normal object sets and allow us to define lower-level details. Similarly, high-level relationship sets must have all the properties of relationship sets and provide means of representing lower-level details. Figure 13.29 shows a high-level object set in its imploded and exploded forms. In this case the Name and Address are grouped inside the high-level object set Person. The analyst has decided that when viewing the model instance from a more abstract level, the Person object set can be imploded so that extraneous detail can be hidden.

Notice that high-level object sets provide the grouping mechanism of choice to be used in the absence of attributes in OSA. Figure 13.30 shows a high-level relationship set. It shows that the notion of "Person owns House" really is an abstraction of "Person pays Bank" and "Bank possess

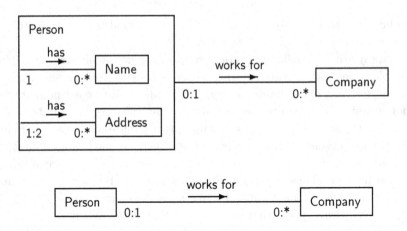

Fig. 13.29   Detail in the high-level object set *Person* can be explicitly shown or hidden

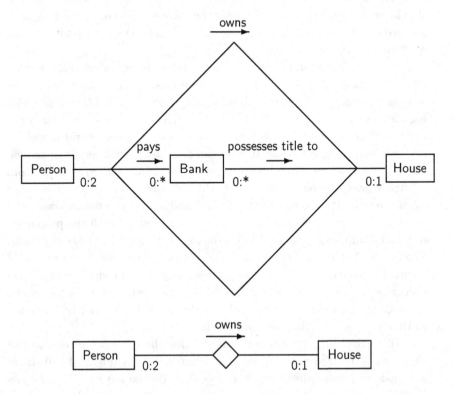

Fig. 13.30   Detail in the high-level relationship set *owns* can be explicitly shown or hidden

title to House". When presented at a more abstract level we can choose to implode the relationship and present it as a normal relationship set.

There are many other aspects of ORMs but the ones presented here illustrate that OSA is better able to model real-world systems than other analysis techniques.

13.5 Tunable Formalism

Most analysis models have no formal definition. In most cases they are defined using English prose and examples. This can lead to incompleteness, imprecision and contradictions. For instance, OMT is described in [Rumbaugh 91]. On page 85 of the book it is stated that events have no duration. However, on page 96 events are described that do have duration. Many examples of these types of problems are present in all informally defined models. To overcome these problems requires that a technique have an underlying formal model.

Some analysis techniques are formal and still have problems. Z is a classic example [Spivey 88]. Such models require so much rigor and precision that it makes it difficult to model real-world situations. It is almost impossible for an untrained person to understand the model instance. Most clients of analysts who use Z cannot read or understand the produced model instance.

We believe that "Tunable Formalism" [Clyde 92] can provide a solution to both problems. It requires that a complete and formal definition of the model exists. However most users of the analysis technique will model things informally. Typically the structure of a particular model instance, like the ORM, satisfies the formal definition of the technique. Many of the triggers, constraints, and actions, however, are expressed informally. Those desiring a more precise model instance can refine the informal instance by replacing informal statements with formal expressions. At some point the final model instance becomes fully formal, unambiguous, and is executable in a prototyping tool.

OSA satisfies these requirements. OSA is defined in terms of a temporal, first-order logic. Frequently many triggers, actions, and constraints are expressed informally. Most of the examples in this chapter have informal components. For these informal components we can not determine exactly what they mean. We can only do that for the parts of the system that are

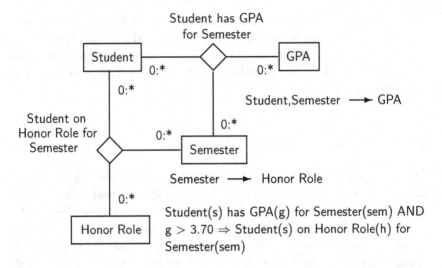

Fig. 13.31 ORM with precise constraints

defined formally. Figure 13.31 shows an OSA model instance in which the constraints are precisely defined. Such a model instance can be executed.

We have found in practice that laymen can quickly learn to read and understand OSA model instances and that the information presented informally in a model instance greatly enhances expressive power and understanding while maintaining a formal foundation.

13.6 State of OSA

Although OSA is not a commercial product, it has been used successfully in real projects by corporations and consultants. For example, Hewlett–Packard used it in a medical environment [de Champeaux 92]. We have used it to analyze the information needed to upgrade the information processing system for the Division of Family Services of the State of Utah. In addition, support for drawing OSA models is currently included in several commercial tools and is being added to others.

We have created a few tools ourselves. One is a graphical editor for creating and editing OSA model instances which was used to create the figures in this chapter. Currently it runs on HP, and Sun workstations and is considered a prototype system. We have also completed a generation of the tool which runs on Windows platforms. The new generation tool features an intelligent assistant technology to aide in the creation of good models and the generation of object-relational databases. We have also created a prototype generator that takes an OSA model instance and allows users to create executable prototypes.

We have also designed a lexical representation of OSA and have produced a parser for the representation. We have created a lexical representation because we have found the graphical forms to be useful for presentations but cumbersome when trying to capture information. Lexical forms seem better suited to information gathering in larger scale project environments.

We have done research into moving from an OSA model instance to specification and design. OSA was designed to be a powerful analysis tool. We wanted to make it as easy as possible to model real-world systems. Because of that power it is difficult to directly map OSA to any of the current object-oriented programming languages. For instance, OSA assumes the existence of inter- and intra-object concurrency. None of the popular object-oriented languages support non-deterministic intra-object concurrency. Thus, we are trying to determine how to map these powerful modeling concepts into implementations. The first part of the effort will develop a specification model that will allow us to transform an OSA model instance into an object-oriented specification. The main emphasis in this research is on interface definition and modeling. The next phase will deal with design and especially with modularization and optimization. We have had some success in doing this for database systems, which has resulted in a book by Embley [Embley 97], and hope to do it for real-time systems.

13.7 Conclusion

We have presented the three sub-models of OSA and their principal features with a particular focus on their application to the analysis and modeling of real-time systems. We have also pointed out some of the strengths of OSA as compared to other modeling systems that make it better suited to real-time analysis such as OSA's model-driven technique with a formal foundation rather than an informal, method-driven technique. Continuous, time constrained, and broadcast interactions between object sets are other examples of features not found in other systems.

While no analysis technique is perfect, we believe OSA provides many new ideas that can improve our analysis capabilities, especially when modeling real-time systems. We hope that many will investigate our model and use those ideas that will be of most benefit to them.

Chapter 14

Algebraic Implementation of Model Checking Algorithms

Theodor Rus and Erick Van Wyk

14.1 Introduction

An algebraic compiler $\mathcal{C} : L_s \to L_t$ is a *language-to-language* translator that uses an algorithm for homomorphism computation to embed a source language L_s into a target language L_t. We have developed a methodology and its supporting tools that allow us to automatically generate such compilers from algebraic specifications of the source and target languages [Rus 91]. Although algebraic compilers are typically used for program translation, many other computations can be easily implemented within this framework. In this chapter, we describe the application of this methodology to generate algebraic implementations of model checking algorithms.

Model checking is a formal technique [Clarke 86] used to verify the correctness of concurrent and distributed programs according to some correctness specification. Programs are represented as labeled finite state transition systems called *Kripke models* [Kripke 63] or simply *models*, and correctness properties are described by formulas written in a temporal logic, which acts as a correctness specification language. In this chapter, we use CTL, Computational Tree Logic [Clarke 86], a propositional, branching-time temporal logic. A model checking algorithm determines which states in a model satisfy a given temporal logic formula. For example, the behavior of two concurrent processes competing for access to a critical section can be represented as a model and the mutual exclusion and absence of starvation requirements can be expressed as temporal logic formulas. Given a model describing the processes and a formula describing mutual exclusion, the model checker can then determine which states of the model satisfy the mutual exclusion property. If all states in the model satisfy the formula, then the program satisfies the mutual exclusion property.

Formally, a model M is a tuple $M = \langle S, E, P{:}T \rightarrow 2^S \rangle$, where S is a finite set of states, $S = \{s_1, s_2, \ldots, s_m\}$, and E is a binary relation on S, $E \subseteq S \times S$, such that $\forall s \in S, \exists t \in S, (s, t) \in E$, that is, every state in the graph of M has a successor. For each $s \in S$ we use the notation $successors(s) = \{s' \in S | (s, s') \in E\}$. A *path* is an infinite sequence of states $(s_0, s_1, s_2, \ldots)$ such that $\forall i, i \geq 0, (s_i, s_{i+1}) \in E$. T is a finite set of *atomic propositions*, $T = \{p_1, p_2, \ldots, p_n\}$, and is a subset of AP, the set of all possible atomic propositions. P is a proposition labeling function that maps an *atomic proposition* in T to the set of states in S on which that proposition is *true*. Figure 14.1 shows a model [Clarke 86] for two processes

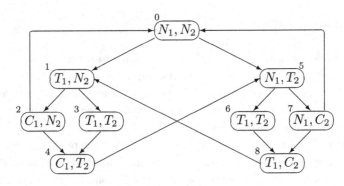

Fig. 14.1   Model example

competing for entrance into a critical section. The atomic propositions T_i, N_i, and C_i denote process $i, 1 \leq i \leq 2$, trying to enter the critical section, not trying to enter the critical section, and executing in the critical section, respectively.

The set of well-formed CTL formulas is described by the following rules [Clarke 86]:

(1) The logical constants, *true* and *false* are CTL formulas.
(2) Every atomic proposition, $p \in AP$, is a CTL formula.
(3) If f_1 and f_2 are CTL formulas, then so are $\neg f_1$, $f_1 \wedge f_2$, $AX f_1$, $EX f_1$, $A[f_1 U f_2]$, and $E[f_1 U f_2]$.

As in [Clarke 86], we define the satisfaction relation, $\models$, of a formula $f \in CTL$ on a state s in the model M, denoted $s \models f$ or $M, s \models f$ and read "s satisfies f". The satisfaction of logical constants is defined as $\forall s \in S, s \models true$ and $\neg \exists s \in S, s \models false$. The relation $\models$ is defined as follows:

$$
\begin{aligned}
s &\models p & \text{iff} \quad & s \in P(p) \\
s &\models \neg f & \text{iff} \quad & not\ s \models f \\
s &\models f_1 \wedge f_2 & \text{iff} \quad & s \models f_1 \text{ and } s \models f_2 \\
s &\models AX\ f_1 & \text{iff} \quad & \forall (s,t) \in E, t \models f_1 \\
s &\models EX\ f_1 & \text{iff} \quad & \exists (s,t) \in E, t \models f_1 \\
s &\models A[f_1\ U\ f_2] & \text{iff} \quad & \forall\ paths\ (s_0, s_1, s_2, \ldots),\ s = s_0 \text{ and} \\
& & & \exists i[i \geq 0 \wedge s_i \models f_2 \wedge \forall j[0 \leq j < i \Rightarrow s_j \models f_1]] \\
s &\models E[f_1\ U\ f_2] & \text{iff} \quad & \exists\ a\ path\ (s_0, s_1, s_2, \ldots),\ s = s_0 \text{ and} \\
& & & \exists i[i \geq 0 \wedge s_i \models f_2 \wedge \forall j[0 \leq j < i \Rightarrow s_j \models f_1]]
\end{aligned}
$$

The set of states $\{s \in S \mid M, s \models f\}$ is called the *satisfiability set* of the formula f for model M. For the model in Figure 14.1, we can express the mutual exclusion property that both processes should not be in the critical section at the same time by the CTL formula $\neg(C_1 \wedge C_2)$. The absence of starvation property, which states that if a process is trying to enter the critical section it will eventually be able to do so, is described for process i by the formula $\neg T_i \vee A[true\ U\ C_i]$. The model checker would verify that both of these properties hold on all states in the model; thus, the program satisfies both properties.

Clarke, Emerson, and Sistla [Clarke 86] developed a model checking algorithm that, when given a CTL formula f and a model M, labels each state of M with all sub-formulas of f which the state satisfies. This is accomplished by converting the CTL formula to a prefix form and then working from the end of the prefix formula. During each step towards the front of the formula, all sub-formulas of the sub-formula being checked have been labeled on the states on which they are true. Thus, upon completion, the formula f holds on a particular state, s, if the state s is labeled with the formula f.

We present in this chapter a simple algorithm that implements a model checker based on the algorithm for homomorphism computation used by an algebraic compiler [Rus 91]. To implement a model checker as an algebraic compiler $\mathcal{C} : L_s \rightarrow L_t$ we take the source language L_s to be the language of CTL formulas for a given model M and the target language L_t to be a language describing the subsets of the states of the model M. The algebraic compiler $\mathcal{C}$ translates a CTL formula f, to the set of states, S', on which the formula f holds. That is, $\mathcal{C}(f) = S'$ where $S' = \{s \in S | M, s \models f\}$. A significant advantage of using this methodology is that this algorithm is automatically generated from its specifications by our existing TICS (Technology for Implementing Computer Software) tools [Rus 97a]. Hence, the implementation of our algorithm does not require any programming activity other than the algebraic specification of the CTL language, the structuring of the model M as an algebra, and the definition of appropriate macro operations associated with the specification rules of the CTL language that embed CTL into the states of M. Consequently, this algorithm does not require any preprocessing of the formula and provides a clean simple algebraic solution to the model checking problem. Another significant advantage of our approach is that since the homomorphism computation used by an algebraic compiler is a parallel algorithm, the generated model checker is also a parallel algorithm.

The chapter is structured as follows: Section 14.2 describes the algebraic structure of the CTL logic and the model M. Section 14.3 describes the algebraic algorithm implementing the model checker and gives the the algebraic specification used to generate the model checker program. Section 14.4 provides some conclusions. Appendix A contains the complete specification of the algebraic CTL model checker.

14.2   Algebraic Specification of CTL

The source and target languages of an algebraic compiler are defined as Ω-languages [Rus 91]. This formalism defines a language as a tuple $L = \langle Sem,\ Syn,\ \mathcal{L} : Sem \to Syn \rangle$ where Sem is the language semantics specified by a universal algebra of a given class of similarity, Syn is the language syntax specified by the word algebra of that same class of similarity, and $\mathcal{L}$ is a partial mapping, called the language learning function. There also exists a homomorphism $\mathcal{E} : Syn \to Sem$, called the language evaluation function, such that $\mathcal{E}(\mathcal{L}(\alpha)) = \alpha$ whenever $\mathcal{L}(\alpha)$ is defined. That is, $\mathcal{L}$ maps computations, or semantics, in the semantics algebra to their expressions in the syntax algebra and $\mathcal{E}$ maps expressions in the syntax algebra to their computations, or semantics, in the semantics algebra. $\mathcal{L}$ and $\mathcal{E}$ are related by a Galois connection [Mac Lane 71]. In this section, we describe the CTL formulas and the satisfiability sets of a model M as Ω-languages.

Let us consider first the class of similarity $C(\Omega^9)$ defined by the signature $\Omega^9 = \langle 0, 0, 1, 2, 2, 1, 1, 2, 2 \rangle$ and an unspecified set of axioms. The nine non-negative integer values in the signature define the arity of the nine operations in algebras of this class. We define CTL as the Ω^9-language $L_{ctl} = \langle \mathcal{A}_M, \mathcal{A}_{ctl}^w, \mathcal{L}_{ctl} \colon \mathcal{A}_M \to \mathcal{A}_{ctl}^w \rangle$. Here $\mathcal{A}_{ctl}^w$ is the word (term) algebra of the class $C(\Omega^9)$ generated by the operator scheme $\Omega_{ctl}^9 = \{true, false,$ $\neg, \wedge, \vee, AX, EX, AU, EU\}$ and a finite set of variables from AP. $\mathcal{A}_M$ is a CTL semantic algebra of type Ω^9 defined on the satisfiability sets of the CTL formulas and determined by some model M. In other words, since the meaning of a CTL formula is dependent upon the model M, the CTL semantic algebra is also dependent upon the model M. $\mathcal{L}_{ctl}$ is a mapping that associates satisfiability sets in $\mathcal{A}_M$ with the CTL expressions in $\mathcal{A}_{ctl}^w$ that satisfy them, and $\mathcal{E}_{ctl}$ is a homomorphism that evaluates CTL expressions in $\mathcal{A}_{ctl}^w$ to their satisfiability sets in $\mathcal{A}_M$.

The word algebra $\mathcal{A}_{ctl}^w$ is unique, up to homomorphism, in the class $C(\Omega^9)$ and is independent of any model. The carrier set F of this algebra is the collection of expressions, also called *words* or *terms*, built by the juxtaposition of operator symbols in Ω_{ctl}^9 and variables in AP by the usual rules shown in Figure 14.2, where "D" stands for domain, and "R" stands

Operator	D		R	Description
$true$:	$\emptyset$	$\to$	F	$true \in F$
$false$:	$\emptyset$	$\to$	F	$false \in F$
not :	F	$\to$	F	if $f \in F$ then $\neg f \in F$
and :	$F \times F$	$\to$	F	if $f_1, f_2 \in F$ then $f_1 \wedge f_2 \in F$
or :	$F \times F$	$\to$	F	if $f_1, f_2 \in F$ then $f_1 \vee f_2 \in F$
AX :	F	$\to$	F	if $f \in F$ then $AX\ f \in F$
EX :	F	$\to$	F	if $f \in F$ then $EX\ f \in F$
AU :	$F \times F$	$\to$	F	if $f_1, f_2 \in F$ then $A[f_1\ U\ f_2] \in F$
EU :	$F \times F$	$\to$	F	if $f_1, f_2 \in F$ then $E[f_1\ U\ f_2] \in F$

Fig. 14.2   The operator scheme of $\mathcal{A}_{ctl}^w$

for range. The constants *true* and *false* form the set of nullary operators, $\Omega_{ctl_0} = \{true, false\}$, and thus are the free generators of the ground terms of $\mathcal{A}_{ctl}^w$. In other words, the carrier set F of the word algebra $\mathcal{A}_{ctl}^w$ is constructed in the usual way by the following rules:

(i) if $f \in AP \cup \Omega_{ctl_0}^9$ then $f \in F$
(ii) if $f_1, \ldots, f_n \in F$ and $\omega \in \Omega_{ctl_n}^9$, then the "string" $\omega(f_1, \ldots, f_n) \in F$

where $\Omega^9_{ctl_n}$ is the set of operators in Ω^9_{ctl} of arity n [Burris 80; Cohn 81]. Note, however, that the CTL formulas are usually written using an infix notation instead of the prefix notation given above.

The CTL semantic algebra $\mathcal{A}_M$ has the same signature Ω^9, but uses the operator scheme $\Omega^9_{sem} = \{S, \emptyset, \mathcal{C} \cap, \cup, Next_{all}, Next_{some}, lfp_{all}, lfp_{some}\}$. For a model M the carrier set of $\mathcal{A}_M$ is $S_M = 2^S$, the set of subsets of the states S in the model M. These are the satisfiability sets of the formulas in $\mathcal{A}^w_{ctl}$. Since $\mathcal{A}^w_{ctl}$ and $\mathcal{A}_M$ are similar, each operator in Ω^9_{ctl} corresponds to an operator of the same arity in Ω^9_{sem}. However, while the operators in Ω^9_{ctl} are used to construct well-formed CTL expressions, the operators in Ω^9_{sem} are used to construct satisfiability sets of well-formed CTL expressions. Therefore we use different symbols to denote these operators. That is, the operators $true, false, \neg, \wedge, \vee, AX, EX, AU,$ and EU in Ω^9_{ctl} correspond, respectively, to the operators $S, \emptyset, \mathcal{C}, \cap, \cup, Next_{all}, Next_{some}, lfp_{all},$ and lfp_{some} in Ω^9_{sem} whose actions in S_M are defined as follows:

- S is the constant set of all states in M.
- $\emptyset$ is the constant empty set.
- $\mathcal{C}$ is the unary operator that produces the complement in S of its argument.
- $\cap$ and $\cup$ are the binary set union and intersection operators.
- For $\alpha \in S_M$ the unary operators $Next_{all}(\alpha)$ and $Next_{some}(\alpha)$ are defined by the equalities $Next_{all}(\alpha) = \{s \in S | successors(s) \subseteq \alpha\}$ and, $Next_{some}(\alpha) = \{s \in S | successors(s) \cap \alpha \neq \emptyset\}$, respectively, where $successors(s)$ denotes the successors of the state s in the model M.
- lfp_{all} and lfp_{some} are inspired by the Y operator for fixed point construction [Gordon 88]. For $\alpha, \beta \in 2^S$, $lfp_{all}(\alpha, \beta)$ computes the least fixed point of the equation $Z = \beta \cup \{s \in \alpha | successors(s) \subseteq Z\}$ and $lfp_{some}(\alpha, \beta)$ computes the least fixed point of the equation $Z = \beta \cup \{s \in \alpha | (successors(s) \cap Z) \neq \emptyset\}$ [Clarke 86].

Although the algebra $\mathcal{A}_M$ exists, it is not used directly in the model checking process. It is only used to explain CTL as an Ω-language.

The CTL model checker defined as an algebraic compiler maps expressions in the CTL syntax algebra $\mathcal{A}^w_{ctl}$ into *set expressions* of a *set expression language* determined by the model M while preserving the satisfiability semantics of the CTL expressions. Thus, we need to organize the model as an Ω-language whose syntax is the set of *set expressions* and whose semantics is 2^S where S is the set of states of the model. For that we consider the class of algebras $C(\Omega^4)$ defined by the signature $\Omega^4 = \langle 0, 2, 2, 2 \rangle$ and an unspecified set of axioms. Further, we define the model M as the Ω^4-language $L_M = \langle \mathcal{A}_{sets}, \mathcal{A}^w_{sets}, \mathcal{L}_{sets} \colon \mathcal{A}_{sets} \to \mathcal{A}^w_{sets} \rangle$. Here $\mathcal{A}^w_{sets}$ is the word (term) algebra of the class $C(\Omega^4)$ generated by the operator scheme $\Omega^4_{sets} = \{\emptyset, \cup, \cap, \setminus\}$ and a finite set of variables. The ground terms of $\mathcal{A}^w_{sets}$ are the set expressions generated without any variables, i.e., set expressions which evaluate to the empty set. It is only with variables specified by some model that meaningful set expressions can be written. Therefore the set of variables for this word algebra includes the set of atomic propositions AP, the states in S, and the variable S. In a set expression containing these variables, a variable p in AP represents the set of states which satisfy p, a variable s in S represents the singleton set $\{s\}$, and the variable S represents the full set of states of a model M. Given this interpretation, the evaluation function $\mathcal{E}_{sets}$ can evaluate any expression in $\mathcal{A}^w_{sets}$ to produce the set of states in $\mathcal{A}_{sets}$ which the expression describes. This underscores the fact that the meaning of a CTL formula can only be defined for a specified model. The *set expressions*, i.e. the elements of A^w_{sets}, are created by the same rules forming the expressions in $\mathcal{A}^w_{ctl}$ with Ω^4_{sets} replacing Ω^9_{ctl}.

$\mathcal{A}_{sets}$ is a set algebra of the class of similarity Ω^4 such that there is the homomorphism $\mathcal{E}_{sets} \colon \mathcal{A}^w_{sets} \to \mathcal{A}_{sets}$ and $\mathcal{E}_{sets}(\mathcal{L}_{sets}(\alpha)) = \alpha$ whenever $\mathcal{L}_{sets}(\alpha)$ is defined. The operator scheme for $\mathcal{A}_{sets}$ is given in Figure 14.3.

Operator	D		R	Description
$\emptyset$:	$\emptyset$	$\to$	S_M	$\emptyset \in S_M$
$\cap$:	$S_M \times S_M$	$\to$	S_M	*if* $S_1, S_2 \in S_M$ *then* $S_1 \cap S_2 \in S_M$
$\cup$:	$S_M \times S_M$	$\to$	S_M	*if* $S_1, S_2 \in S_M$ *then* $S_1 \cup S_2 \in S_M$
$\setminus$:	$S_M \times S_M$	$\to$	S_M	*if* $S_1, S_2 \in S_M$ *then* $S_1 \setminus S_2 \in S_M$

Fig. 14.3   The operator scheme of $\mathcal{A}_{sets}$ and $\mathcal{A}^w_{sets}$

Now we can define the CTL model checker as an algebraic compiler $\mathcal{MC}_M \colon L_{ctl} \to L_M$, by an embedding morphism H_{MC} from A^w_{ctl} to A^w_{sets}, which maps from the word algebra of CTL formulas $\mathcal{A}^w_{ctl}$ to the word algebra of sets $\mathcal{A}^w_{sets}$. This morphism will map a CTL formula f to the set expression that evaluates to the set of states in the model M which satisfy the formula f. In other words, the CTL model checker can be defined as a tuple $\mathcal{MC}_M = \langle \mathcal{I}, H_{MC} \rangle$, where $\mathcal{I} : 2^S \to 2^S$ is the identity map on the carrier sets of the

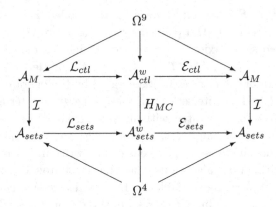

Fig. 14.4　Ω-languages L_{ctl}, and L_M, and the model checker $\mathcal{MC}_M = \mathcal{E}_{sets} \circ H_{MC}$

algebras $\mathcal{A}_M$ and $\mathcal{A}_{sets}$, and $H_{MC} : \mathcal{A}^w_{ctl} \to \mathcal{A}^w_{sets}$ is an embedding of $\mathcal{A}^w_{ctl}$ into $\mathcal{A}^w_{sets}$ such that the diagram in Figure 14.4 is commutative.

The commutativity of this diagram ensures that the mapping H_{MC} preserves the meaning of formulas in $\mathcal{A}^w_{ctl}$ when mapping them to set expressions in $\mathcal{A}^w_{sets}$. Since the model checker should evaluate CTL formulas to produce sets, not set expressions, the model checker, $\mathcal{MC}_M$ is implemented as $H_{MC} \circ \mathcal{E}_{sets}$, the composition of H_{MC} and the set language evaluation function $\mathcal{E}_{sets}$. Thus, for a CTL formula f in $\mathcal{A}^w_{ctl}$,
$$\mathcal{MC}(f) = (H_{MC} \circ \mathcal{E}_{sets})(f) = \mathcal{E}_{sets}(H_{MC}(f)) = \{s \in S \mid M, s \models f\}.$$

Since $\mathcal{A}^w_{ctl}$ and $\mathcal{A}^w_{sets}$ are not similar, the mapping $H_{MC} \colon \mathcal{A}^w_{ctl} \to \mathcal{A}^w_{sets}$ is not a homomorphism, rather it is an embedding morphism. This embedding is implemented by creating a subalgebra $\mathcal{A}^w_{sctl}$ of $\mathcal{A}^w_{sets}$ similar to the algebra $\mathcal{A}^w_{ctl}$ and then constructing the monomorphism $H_{MC} : \mathcal{A}^w_{ctl} \to \mathcal{A}^w_{sctl}$. The subalgebra $\mathcal{A}^w_{sctl}$ has the same carrier set as the algebra $\mathcal{A}^w_{sets}$. Its operations are however those of similarity class Ω^9 and are defined as derived operations [Burstall 69; Cohn 81; Rus 91] in terms of the existing operations in Ω^4_{sets}. Hence, on the one hand this subalgebra will be similar to $\mathcal{A}^w_{ctl}$ and thus $H_{MC} : \mathcal{A}^w_{ctl} \to \mathcal{A}^w_{sctl}$ can be implemented as a homomorphism, and on the other hand $\mathcal{A}^w_{sctl}$ is a subalgebra of $\mathcal{A}^w_{sets}$ and thus the images of elements in $\mathcal{A}^w_{ctl}$ by H_{MC} are computable set-expressions whose values are sets of states of the model M. The commutativity of the diagram in

Figure 14.4 ensures that the values of these set-expressions are precisely the satisfiability sets of the CTL expressions taken as arguments by H_{MC}.

In order to define the derived operations that implement the operations in Ω_{ctl}^9 in the algebra $\mathcal{A}_{sets}^w$ we need some *meta-variables*, that run over the carrier set of $\mathcal{A}_{set}^w$. That is, the values taken by these meta variables are set-expressions. Further, we consider for each operation $\omega \in \Omega_{ctl}^9$ a parameterized macro operations denoted by $d(\omega)$, whose name is ω, whose parameters are meta variables denoted by $@_i$, $1 \leq i \leq arity(\omega)$, and whose bodies are defined as well-formed words in the word algebra over operations in Ω_{sets}^4 and meta variables $@_i$. The variable $@_i$ used as a parameter in the macro operation $d(\omega)$ take as values set-expressions in $\mathcal{A}_{sets}^w$ that are images of argument i of the CTL expressions constructed by the operator ω. In other words, if $arity(\omega) = n$ and ω is the function $\omega: A_1 \times A_2 \times \ldots \times A_n \to A_0$, which defines CTL expressions of syntax category A_0 in terms of CTL expressions of syntax categories A_i, $1 \leq i \leq n$ then $@_i$ is the meta variable that take as values set-expressions that are images of the CTL expressions of syntax category A_i, $1 \leq i \leq n$.

Now the morphism H_{MC} can be constructed by the following rules:

(1) Define the macro operations for the generators of the $\mathcal{A}_{ctl}^w$. This is done by setting $d(true) = S$, $d(false) = \emptyset$, and $d(p) = p$ for each $p \in AP$.

(2) Embed the generators of the algebra $\mathcal{A}_{ctl}^w$ in the algebra $\mathcal{A}_{sets}^w$ by the function: $H_{MC}(true) = d(true)$, $H_{MC}(false) = d(false)$, and $\forall p \in AP.H_{MC}(p) = d(p)$

(3) Extend the function defined at (2) above to the entire algebra $\mathcal{A}_{sets}^w$ by the equality: for each $w \in \mathcal{A}_{ctl}^w$ such that $w = \omega(f_1, f_2, \ldots, f_n)$ define $H_{MC}(w) = d(\omega)(H_{MC}(f_1), H_{MC}(f_2), \ldots, H_{MC}(f_n))$

Since H_{MC} is the unique extension of the function (2) to a homomorphism H_{MC} is well defined.

To improve the efficiency of the model checker it is possible to interpret the derived operations, $d(\omega), \omega \in \Omega_{ctl}^9$ as operations over sets in $\mathcal{A}_{sets}$ instead of as operations over set expressions in $\mathcal{A}_{sets}^w$. Thus, instead of mapping a formula in $\mathcal{A}_{ctl}^w$ to a set expression in $\mathcal{A}_{sets}^w$ and then evaluating the set expression to a set in $\mathcal{A}_{sets}$, we can map the formula directly into the set algebra $\mathcal{A}_{sets}$. This is accomplished by modifying the *macro processor* portion of the algebraic compiler and is discussed in the following section.

14.3　Algebraic Implementation of a Model Checker

The behavior of a model checking algorithm consists of identifying the set of states of the model M that satisfy each sub-formula of a given CTL formula f and constructing from these sets, the set of states that satisfy the formula f. This is precisely the behavior of the algorithm for homomorphism computation performed by an algebraic compiler; it evaluates an expression by repeatedly identifying its generating sub-expressions and replacing them with their values. In the case of a model checker, the sub-expressions are CTL sub-formulas and their values are the sets of states in the model which satisfy the sub-formulas. Hence, to understand the algebraic implementation of the model checking algorithm, we describe first the structure of an algebraic compiler and then show its relationship with a model checker.

14.3.1　*Structure of an Algebraic Compiler*

The syntax of the source language of an algebraic compiler is specified by a finite set, R, of BNF specification rules. Each rule $r \in R$ corresponds to an operation in the source language syntax algebra and is an equation of the form $A_0 ::= t_0 A_1 t_1 \ldots t_{n-1} A_n t_n$ where, for each $i, 0 \leq i \leq n$, t_i is a string (possibly empty) of *terminal symbols* and each A_i is a variable called a *nonterminal symbol*. We use the notation $lhs(r)$ to denote the left-hand side of the rule r, that is, $lhs(r) = A_0$, and $rhs(r)$ to denote the right-hand side of the rule r, that is, $rhs(r) = t_0 A_1 t_1 \ldots t_{n-1} A_n t_n$. As an example, in an algebraic model checker, the $\mathcal{A}_{ctl}^w$ operation $\wedge \colon F \times F \to F$ could be represented as the BNF rule $F ::= F$ and F.

An algebraic compiler is specified by associating each source language specification rule $r \in R$, $r \colon A_0 ::= t_0 A_1 t_1 \ldots t_{n-1} A_n t_n$, with a target macro operation, $macro(r)$. This forms a *compiler specification* $CS = \{\langle r, macro(r) \rangle \mid r \in R\}$. Typically, the macro operation $macro(r)$ is a parameterized target language representation of the computation expressed by the source language construct specified by r. In a Pascal to C language translator for example, the macro operation associated with a rule specifying a Pascal `for` loop would describe, in C, the equivalent C `for` loop. That is, $macro(r)$ is defined by the compiler implementor by expressing in the target language the meaning of the source language computation specified by r in terms of the target language images of the components of the source expression. The components of the source language construct specified by

$r : A_0 ::= t_0 A_1 t_1 \ldots t_{n-1} A_n t_n$ are source language constructs of syntax categories $A_1, A_2, \ldots, A_n$. Hence, the formal parameters of $macro(r)$ are the nonterminals $A_1, A_2, \ldots, A_n$ and the actual parameters are target language images of the source language constructs of syntax categories $A_1, A_2, \ldots, A_n$. The body of $macro(r)$ expresses the computation denoted by the constructs specified by r as a valid target construct in the target language called the target image; this target image is composed from the target images of the components of the construct specified by r. As in Section 14.2 we use the symbol @, with indices, to denote the target images of the components of constructs specified by r. That is, the actual parameters of the macro operation $macro(r)$ are the target images, denoted $@_1, @_2, \ldots, @_n$, of the source language constructs of syntax categories $A_1, A_2, \ldots, A_n$. For example, in the algebraic specification of a model checker, the macro operation associated with the rule $F ::= F$ and F must express, in the target language of sets, the set of states on which a formula specified by this rule holds. This set of states is the intersection of the two sets of states which satisfy the two sub-formulas of any formula specified by this rule. This macro operation implements the $\wedge$ operator in the source language by the $\cap$ operator in the target language. This operation may be defined by the expression $@_1 \cap @_2$ which would be associated with the rule $F ::= F$ and F in the compiler specification.

An algebraic compiler is implemented by three components $\mathcal{R}, \mathcal{I}$, and $\mathcal{M}$. $\mathcal{R}$ is a pattern-matching parser recognizing valid constructs in the source language. $\mathcal{M}$ is a target language *macro processor* which expands target language macro operations associated with the specification rules used by $\mathcal{R}$ to produce valid target language constructs called *images*. $\mathcal{I}$ provides an interface between $\mathcal{R}$ and $\mathcal{M}$. Let $r : A_0 = t_0 A_1 t_1 \ldots t_{n-1} A_n t_n$ be a specification rule, in R, used by $\mathcal{R}$ to recognize valid constructs specified by r in the input text. When $\mathcal{R}$ recognizes a portion of the input text specified by r, it calls $\mathcal{I}$, giving it as parameters the rule r and the portion of input text matched by the right hand side of rule r. $\mathcal{I}$ identifies the macro operation $macro(r)$ associated with r and uses the text matched by $rhs(r)$ to identify the previously computed target images $@_1, @_2, \ldots, @_n$ of the components of the construct recognized by $\mathcal{R}$. These target images are associated with the construct components which belong respectively to syntax categories $A_1, A_2, \ldots, A_n$. $\mathcal{I}$ packages these target images into the list $macro(r), (@_1, @_2, \ldots, @_n)$ which it passes to the the macro processor $\mathcal{M}$. The macro processor $\mathcal{M}$ expands the macro operation $macro(r)$ taking

$@_1$, $@_2$, ..., $@_n$ as parameters in order to construct the target image $@_0$ of the portion of input text matched by $rhs(r)$ of syntax category A_0. This target image is passed back to $\mathcal{I}$ which associates it with the left hand side of the rule r, $lhs(r)$, i.e., with A_0, thus constructing the tuple $(lhs(r), @_0)$. This tuple then replaces the portion of the text matched by $rhs(r)$ in the input. This process is illustrated in Figure 14.5. In the case where an alge-

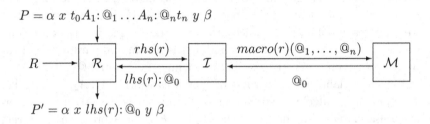

$$P = \alpha \, x \, t_0 A_1\!:@_1 \ldots A_n\!:@_n t_n \, y \, \beta$$

$$P' = \alpha \, x \, lhs(r)\!:@_0 \, y \, \beta$$

Fig. 14.5   The integration of the components of an algebraic compiler

braic compiler $\langle \mathcal{R}, \mathcal{I}, \mathcal{M} \rangle$ implements a model checker, the source language is the language of CTL formulas and the target language is a language of sets of a model. Thus, the source language constructs recognized by $\mathcal{R}$ are sub-formulas of CTL formulas, the target images produced by $\mathcal{M}$ are the satisfiability sets of the sub-formulas recognized by $\mathcal{R}$, and $\mathcal{I}$ is the interface between them. The components $\mathcal{R}$, $\mathcal{I}$, and $\mathcal{M}$ are generated by the TICS compiler generation tools from specifications of the source and target languages.

The compilation process performed by the algebraic compiler is a sequence of transformations of the input text during which source language constructs specified by the rules $r \in R$ are discovered in the input text, their target images $@_{lhs(r)}$ are constructed by expanding their associated macros, $macro(r)$, and the portions of the input text representing such constructs are replaced by records of the form $lhs(r)\!:@_{lhs(r)}$. Suppose that after a number of transformations the input text has the form

$$P = \alpha \, x \, t_0 \, A_1\!:@_1 \, t_1 \ldots A_n\!:@_n \, t_n \, y \, \beta$$

where α, β, x, and y are text strings, and the tuple $A_i\!:@_i$, $1 \le i \le n$, shows that a source language construct of syntax category A_i has been discovered by $\mathcal{R}$ as a valid component of the input and its target image constructed by $\mathcal{M}$ is $@_i$. The next transformation of P by the algebraic compiler is performed by the following three steps.

(1) For each $\langle r, macro(r) \rangle \in CS$, $\mathcal{R}$ interprets $rhs(r) = t_0 A_1 t_1 \ldots A_n t_n$ as a pattern to search for in P. $\mathcal{R}$ ignores the target images embedded in P. When an occurrence of the $rhs(r)$ is discovered in P by $\mathcal{R}$ the context [Rus 94] (x, y) is checked against the pre-computed *context* and *non-context* sets associated with r. If (x, y) is in the context set of rule r then the $rhs(r)$ can be replaced by the $lhs(r)$ preserving the syntactic validity of P, i.e., P is transformed into $P' = \alpha \; x \; lhs(r) \; y \; \beta$. If (x, y) is in the non-context set of rule r then the $rhs(r)$ can not be replaced by the $lhs(r)$ because r was not used to generate the text specified by $rhs(r)$.

(2) For each $\langle r, macro(r) \rangle \in CS$, $\mathcal{I}$ interprets $rhs(r) = t_0 A_1 t_1 \ldots A_n t_n$ as the name of the macro operation $macro(r)$. Therefore, when $\mathcal{R}$ determines that a portion of the input can be replaced by the $lhs(r)$, $\mathcal{I}$ identifies the macro operation $macro(r)$, extracts the actual parameters $@_1, \ldots, @_n$ from the portion of the input $t_0 \; A_1 \colon @_1 \; t_1 \ldots \; A_n \colon @_n \; t_n$ matched by $\mathcal{R}$ and calls the macro processor $\mathcal{M}$ to expand the macro operation $macro(r)$ with parameters $(@_1, \ldots, @_n)$. $@_0$ denotes the construct thus generated by $\mathcal{M}$. Then $\mathcal{I}$ associates the parameter $@_0$ with the $lhs(r)$ creating the record $lhs(r) \colon @_0$.

(3) When $\mathcal{I}$ calls the macro processor $\mathcal{M}$ and passes it the parameters $macro(r)$ and $@_1, \ldots, @_n$, $\mathcal{M}$ builds a target image $@_0$ from the component target images $@_1, \ldots, @_n$ according to the macro $macro(r)$. The macro specifies how the macro processor will build the target image $@_0$ from the components $@_1, \ldots, @_n$. The relationship between components $\mathcal{R}$, $\mathcal{I}$, and $\mathcal{M}$ of the algebraic compiler while performing a transformation of the input text is shown in Figure 14.5.[Rus 97b]

14.3.2   *The Macro Processor Generating Satisfiability Sets*

Although the components $\mathcal{R}$ and $\mathcal{I}$ of an algebraic compiler depend only on the specification rules R, $\mathcal{M}$ depends on the macro operations and the target language in which these macro operations are expanded. Hence, algebraic compilers with different target languages use different macro processors to generate target images. A macro processor used for generating assembly language programs is not appropriate for generating the sets of states in a model which satisfy CTL formulas since the macro processor used by the CTL model checker generates the sets of states which satisfy CTL formulas. It builds the target image set $@_0$ for a CTL formula, f, from target image sets $@_1, \ldots, @_n$ which satisfy the sub-formulas of f. The macros processed by this macro processor specify how to construct the set $@_0$ from the parameter sets $@_1, \ldots, @_n$. Each macro processor works in a different target algebra and thus defines an appropriate language in which the macros it processes are written. While both assembly macro processors and CTL macro processors construct target images from component target images as instructed by macro operations, the macro operations are specific to the target language. Thus, when specifying an algebraic compiler, we must be sure that an appropriate macro processor exists for the target language. To adapt the general algebraic compiler methodology to model checking, a new macro processor, named $\mathcal{M}_{\mathcal{A}_{sets}}$, must be created to compute the sets of states in the model.

The macro operations discussed in Section 14.2 provide a mechanism for specifying *parameterized* set expressions which define operations in the word algebra $\mathcal{A}_{ctl}^{w}$. These macro operations take as parameters valid set expressions and generate valid set expressions. For example, if $@_i \cup @_j$ is a parameterized set expression and $@_i$ and $@_j$ are valid set expressions then, $@_i \cup @_j$ evaluates to a valid set expression whenever $@_i$ and $@_j$ are substituted into $@_i \cup @_j$. These same parameterized set expressions can also define operations in the set algebra $\mathcal{A}_{sets}$ which take sets as parameters and evaluate to sets. Considering the nature of our problem, we design a macro processor which implements the macro operations in the set domain of $\mathcal{A}_{sets}$ instead of the set expressions domain of $\mathcal{A}_{sets}^{w}$.

The language in which the macro operations processed by $\mathcal{M}_{\mathcal{A}_{sets}}$ are written is a simple imperative language that allows us to construct satisfiability sets using set operations $(\cap, \cup, \backslash)$ over the given generator sets of $\mathcal{A}_{sets}$ and set variables over the carrier set of $\mathcal{A}_{sets}$, denoted by $@i$, $i = 0, 1, \ldots, n$. Specifically, since our macros expand into the satisfiability sets of CTL formulas specified by BNF rules, r, of the form $A_0 ::= t_0 A_1 t_1 \ldots t_{n-1} A_n t_n$, the variables $@i$, $1 \leq i \leq n$, stand for the satisfiability sets of the CTL components of syntax categories A_i, $1 \leq i \leq n$, and $@_0$ stands for the satisfiability set of the CTL formula matched by rule r. This language has been extended with the conditional set construction operator denoted by $\{s \in S | < condition\ on\ s >\}$. There are also macro assignment statements and while loops which are used to control the application of the target language algebra operations. Boolean expressions over sets using the subset and equivalence relations are also available. These provide a convenient mechanism to write macros to express complex derived operations in the target language algebra of sets. The implementation of this macro processor, $\mathcal{M}_{\mathcal{A}_{sets}}$ is discussed below in 14.3.4.

14.3.3 Generating a Model Checker Program

Here we develop the implementation of $\mathcal{MC}_M$ using the methodology of the algebraic compiler. The essential element here is the embedding of the source algebra $\mathcal{A}_{ctl}^w$ into the target algebra $\mathcal{A}_{sets}$ by derived (macro) operations. In this section we show the BNF rules, R, which specify $\mathcal{A}_{ctl}^w$ and the macro operations that map the CTL formulas into $\mathcal{A}_{sets}$ thus embedding $\mathcal{A}_{ctl}^w$ into $\mathcal{A}_{sets}$. The model checking program is automatically generated from these specifications.

The set of BNF rules that directly specify the source syntax algebra may be ambiguous, which is the case with $\mathcal{A}_{ctl}^w$. Therefore, we split the carrier set F of $\mathcal{A}_{ctl}^w$ on the layers of generation $Factor$, $Term$, and $Expression$ and write BNF rules that provide a non-ambiguous specification of $\mathcal{A}_{ctl}^w$. This yields the three syntax categories F_f, F_t, and F_e. The complete specification, with the associated macro operations, can be seen in Appendix A. To increase the readability of this specification we discuss a few of the rules and their macro operations and show an example compilation below. In the specification rule

$$r: \qquad F_t ::= F_t \text{ and } F_f \ ;$$
$$macro(r): \qquad @_0 := @_1 \cap @_2 \ ;$$

as described above, the macro operation implements the source algebra $\wedge$ operation as the target algebra $\cap$ operation. In the following,

$$r: \qquad F_f ::= \text{p} \ ;$$
$$macro(r): \qquad @_0 := P(p) \ ;$$

the generator $P(p)$ gives the set of states on which the proposition p holds. The macro operation in

$$r: \qquad F_f ::= \text{ax } F_f \ ;$$
$$macro(r): \qquad @_0 := \{s \in S | successors(s) \subseteq @_1\} \ ;$$

finds all states s such that all successors of s are in the set $@_1$. In

$$r: \qquad F_f ::= \text{a } [\ F_e \text{ u } F_e \ ] \ ;$$

$macro(r)$:   let Z, Z' be sets;
$$Z := \emptyset \; ; \; Z' := @_2 \; ;$$
while ($Z \neq Z'$) do
$$Z := Z' \; ;$$
$$Z' := Z' \cup \{s \in S | s \in @_1 \wedge successors(s) \subseteq Z\} \; ;$$
end while
$$@_0 := Z \; ;$$

the macro operation uses set variables Z and Z' to implement a least fixed point solution to the equation $Z = @_2 \cup \{s \in @_1 | successors(s) \subseteq Z\}$.

By applying the TICS compiler generation tools to the complete specification in Appendix A we obtain a program that implements a CTL model checking algorithm. As described in Section 3.2, when this program is run on a CTL formula and a model M it gives as the result the set of states of M which satisfy the given formula. We should also note that although we have stated that the model M dictates the creation of the algebras $\mathcal{A}^w_{sets}$ and $\mathcal{A}_{sets}$, the same model checker program can be used to find the satisfiability set of any CTL formula on any given model M. When M changes, the model checker algorithm works correctly by simply updating the generator sets of the new $\mathcal{A}^w_{ctl}$ and $\mathcal{A}_{sets}$ algebras.

As an example, consider the CTL formula *not* (C_1 *and* C_2) checked against the model in Figure 14.1. The $rhs(r)$ of the rule $F_f ::= $ p will match atomic propositions C_1 and C_2 since "p" matches names of atomic propositions. The macro processor is called, once for each proposition matched, to execute the macro $@_0 := P(p)$, generating, respectively, the sets $\{2, 4\}$ and $\{6, 8\}$ since $2 \models C_1$, $4 \models C_1$, $6 \models C_2$, and $8 \models C_2$. The *lhs* symbol, F_f, and the target set images replace the respective propositions in the CTL formula to yield

$$\text{not (} F_f \text{:} \{2, 4\} \text{ and } F_f \text{:} \{6, 8\} \text{)}$$

Next, the rule $F_t ::= F_f$ will match the first sub-formula. (The second sub-formula textually matches $rhs(r)$, but the context set of the rule does not include the tuple $\langle$ *and,* $\rangle$ $\rangle$, so this occurrence is not matched. This parsing method is explained fully in [Rus 91; Rus 90; Knaack 94]). The macro associated with the rule $F_t ::= F_f$ is $@_0 := @_1$ and consequently only copies the target image from the first parameter yielding

$$\text{not (} F_t \text{:} \{2, 4\} \text{ and } F_f \text{:} \{6, 8\} \text{)}$$

Now the *rhs* of rule $F_t ::= F_t$ and F_f will match the pattern "F_t and F_f."
The associated macro, $@_0 := @_1 \cap @_2$, will take the set intersection of the
parameter sets, which in this case results in the empty set. The empty set
is associated with F_t and placed in the formula to yield

$$\text{not } (\ F_t \colon \emptyset\ )$$

After application of the copy rules $F_e ::= F_t$ and $F_f ::= (\ F_e\ )$, we are left
with

$$\text{, } \quad \text{not } F_f \colon \emptyset$$

The *rhs* of the rule $F_f ::= \text{not } F_f$ now matches the text and the associated
macro $@_0 := S \setminus @_1$ is applied with $@_1 = \emptyset$ to yield

$$F_f \colon \{0, 1, 2, 3, 4, 5, 6, 7, 8\}$$

After the application of the copy rules $F_t ::= F_f$ and $F_e ::= F_t$ we are left
with the final form

$$F_e \colon \{0, 1, 2, 3, 4, 5, 6, 7, 8\}.$$

Since no more rules in R have a *rhs(r)* which match any portion of the
CTL formula text, the process is complete. Thus, this process shows that
the formula $not(C_1 \text{ and } C_2)$ is satisfied on all states in the model and thus
mutual exclusion is assured.

14.3.4 *Implementing the Macro Processor* $\mathcal{M}_{\mathcal{A}_{sets}}$

The implementation of the macro processor $\mathcal{M}_{\mathcal{A}_{sets}}$ is necessary to generate model checking algorithms from their algebraic specifications. As
stated before, the macro operations are written in a macro language for
sets which specifies the target algebra operations to be performed to build
the satisfiability sets for the CTL formulas constructed by the BNF rules.
The macro processor $\mathcal{M}_{\mathcal{A}_{sets}}$ interprets the macro operations as collections
of operations on sets. At the time when the model checker program is
generated from its specifications, the macro operations, which are essentially code fragments written in the macro language, are translated into
C language code fragments which are compiled and linked to the rest of
the model checker program. These C language statements perform the operations specified by the macro operations. This translation is done by a

macro *pre-processor* which translates each macro operation into a C language function which is executed when a CTL formula is being verified to construct the satisfiability set specified by the macro operation. For example, the macro operation $@_0 := @_1 \cap @_2$ associated with the rule $F_e ::= F_e$ and F_t is translated by the macro pre-processor into the C language function shown in Figure 14.6. (Since this rule appears as the third rule in the

```
void macro_3 ( image_struct_ptr LHS, image_struct_ptr RHS[2] )
  { set_copy ( LHS->image,
        set_intersection ( RHS[1]->image, RHS[2]->image ) ) ; }
```

Fig. 14.6   C language function implementing a macro operation

specification the function name is `macro_3`.) The functions `set_copy` and `set_intersection` belong to a library of set functions which are also linked to the model checker program.

The macro pre-processor which translates the macros to C language functions is itself implemented as an algebraic compiler generated by the same TICS tools used to generate the model checker. This compiler has the macro language as its source language and C as its target language. Like any algebraic compiler, it is automatically built from the algebraic specification of its source and target languages. Thus, building the macro pre-processor is not a difficult task.

14.4   Conclusions

The complexity of the original model checker algorithm presented by Clarke, Emerson, and Sistla [Clarke 86] is $\mathcal{O}(length(f) \times (card(S) + card(E)))$. Having in view that the recognizer $\mathcal{R}$ is linear in the length of the input text f, and that macro expansion could be polynomial in the size of the model, the worst case behavior of the model checker algorithm presented in this chapter is $\mathcal{O}(length(f) \times (card(S)^2 + card(E))$. However, this is not inherent in the use of the algebraic methodology and one can write target language macros that are linear, therefore obtaining the same complexity. A distinct advantage of using a homomorphism computation is that the generated model checker can be easily implemented by a parallel algorithm. The process performed by $\mathcal{R}$, $\mathcal{I}$, and $\mathcal{M}$ can be replicated to work on different parts of the input text at the same time, thus executing in parallel.

Another significant advantage of our methodology is that all components $\mathcal{R}$, $\mathcal{I}$, and $\mathcal{M}$ of the model checker are automatically generated from their specifications. Thus, human programming errors are avoided. If the specifications are correct, then the generated program is correct. This ensures the correctness of the model checker. This does require the implementor to understand the model checker in the algebraic framework presented above and be able to specify it as a homomorphism between algebras. However, the universality of the homomorphism computation makes various algebraic frameworks implementable by this same approach. There is very little, if any, traditional programming required by this implementation framework; the program is automatically generated. The re-usability of previous work allowing the extension of the algorithm is another advantage of using an algebraic framework. By extending the algebraic specification the implementor can change the generated program such that its behavior fits new requirements [Rus 97d].

Finally, we want to observe that the application of the algebraic model checker expands beyond the usual field of interest. We are involved in a project to use CTL model checking to identify and exploit implicit parallelism in sequential programs [Rus 97c; Rus 97e]. The program text is analyzed by a usual recognizer and a macro processor generates a model describing its flow of data and control. A CTL model checker uses this model and CTL formulas describing opportunities for parallelism or parallelism properties to identify states where implicit parallelism exists or to verify that an appropriate amount of parallelism in the original program has been exploited. Other CTL formulas can verify that certain optimality conditions have been satisfied.

Acknowledgments

We thank the NASA Jet Propulsion Laboratory for supporting this research.

PART 6

Industrial Applications of Real-Time Systems

Chapter 15

An Automaton Based Algebra for Specifying Robotic Agents

Jana Košecká and Hanêne Ben-Abdallah

15.1 Introduction

Robotic agents are often complex systems that reside in dynamically changing environments. In order for robotic agents to operate robustly and reliably in a real world environment, they are equipped with several sensors and actuators that constantly monitor the environment and act upon observed changes, according to a prespecified strategy. In other words, robotic agents consist of several components that interact with their environments and with one another. In addition, since most applications of robotic agents are typically costly and safety critical, it is crucial that the design of these systems be within a structured methodology that supports analysis. Furthermore, to make the design process manageable, it is essential that the methodology allows modular specification and exploits the inherent architectures of these systems.

Within the area of intelligent control and flexible manufacturing systems, a significant progress has been made on automaton (or finite state machine) based methodologies for the specification and verification of control systems (e.g., [Lygeros 94; Weinberg 95]). In some cases these methodologies have been successfully used in the synthesis problem where a controller is automatically constructed from a given specification [Ostroff 89a; Ramadge 89b]. These methodologies, however, focus more on verification and synthesis of the controller and offer mainly two types of operations to compose a large system from the finite state machines of its components: parallel and sequential composition. This in turn limits the notion of modularity in the design process. For example, one cannot compose two components such that one interrupts or disables the other. Such an operation is essential for robotic applications where, for example, a robot must be able to interrupt the execution of another to avoid a collision.

Within the area of concurrent systems, which include robotic applications, several process algebraic formalisms have been developed to specify and analyze communicating, concurrently executing systems, for example, CCS [Milner 89], CSP [Hoare 85], ACSR [Lee 94]. One aspect that makes these formalisms attractive is their support of various operators for constructing a complex system from simpler systems.

In this chapter, we propose a framework that combines the conveniences of finite state machines with operators borrowed from process algebras. That is, a complex system in this framework can be described in terms of its elementary components and a set of operators to describe their interactions. Our framework is based on finite state machines and thus can benefit from methodologies for automatic controller synthesis and analysis. Its set of operators adapts several operators from process algebras to the finite state model, e.g., the sequential composition of CSP [Hoare 85] and the notion of exception in ACSR [Lee 94]. The operators are adapted using common techniques for defining sequential and parallel composition of finite state machines. In addition, the set of operators in this framework reflect typical strategies of composing the various elementary components in robotic agent applications.

Section 15.2 briefly reviews relevant formalisms that have been applied to robotic agents. Section 15.3 informally describes an example of a task of robotic agents that is used throughout the chapter to illustrate our formalism. Section 15.4 first describes a typical system architecture of robotic agents and then presents our formalism. Section 15.5 briefly describes how the composition operator can be used to define a supervisor process. The chapter is summarized in Section 15.6.

15.2   Related Work

Significant progress has been accomplished in formally specifying and analyzing concurrent, communicating systems. The developed formalisms often addressed different motivations, e.g., applicability to a specific problem

Example 333

domain, ease of representation, and computational complexity associated with the verification process. We next review relevant formalisms that were applied to the area of robotics.

Petri Nets [Lefebvre 92; Freedman 91] and Supervisory Control Theory of Discrete Event Systems [Ramadge 89b] have been successfully applied to robotic systems in the manufacturing domain (e.g., [Brandin 93]), controller synthesis (e.g., [Antoniotti 95]) and modeling of visually guided mobile robots (e.g. [Košecká 94]). These formalisms are based on the intuitive notation of transition diagrams. They however offer few composition operators.

In the domain of autonomous mobile agents, temporal automata (defined in [Shoham 90]) were used to demonstrate some simple examples that concentrated mainly on the design specification issues as opposed to verification and analysis of the system.

Lyons [Lyons 90] adopted a process algebraic approach and proposed the formal *Robot Schemas* ($\mathcal{RS}$) model which is well suited for sensory based robotic applications. The $\mathcal{RS}$ model has the power of a full procedural programming language. It however abandoned the intuitive state diagram representation in favor of procedural description in terms of $\mathcal{RS}$.

Among the approaches which tackle the hybrid system issues of modeling robotic agents are Constraint Nets [Zhang 94] and Hybrid Automata [Alur 93a]. These models capture both continuous and discrete phenomena of the design but did not emphasize modularity which is important for specifying a variety of tasks. More applications using synchronous programming languages such as Lustre, Esterel were reported in the domains of visual servoing and mobile robotics [Rives 95; Espiau 95].

15.3 Example

The system task consists of navigating two mobile robots together towards a prespecified goal location while avoiding obstacles. Figure 15.1 illustrates the task. Each robot is equipped with cameras that detect the obstacles in the field of view of the robot. The fields of view of the two robots overlap. In Figure 15.1, the rhomboid areas I., II., and III. correspond to the birdeye view of the fields of view of robot A, B, and the common field of view, respectively.

The two robots must reach the goal location autonomously, i.e., without any intervention from a human supervisor. For this, the robots need to coordinate their activities (or goals), exchange the information about the obstacles in their respective fields of view, and in case of failure, interrupt each other so that no one proceeds without the other. Throughout the task accomplishment, several concurrent processes extract the sensory information from the environment, generate the motion commands to the individual robots, and react to any unexpected presence of obstacles.

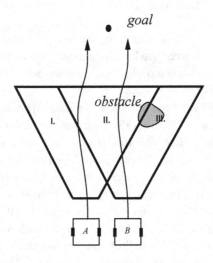

Fig. 15.1   Two mobile robots system

We will revisit this example in the following sections to illustrate how we can model it within the proposed formalism.

15.4   Our Framework

A robotic agent typically consists of a finite set of sensors and actuators. Each sensor has a set of data extraction and processing strategies. Each actuator has a set of control strategies. The agent sensors and actuators execute in parallel to achieve a specific task (or objective), e.g., locate and avoid an obstacle in the environment.

On a lower level of abstraction, each sensor and actuator is in charge of invoking its strategies in a specific logical and temporal order to achieve the overall task of the agent. This may require interactions with other sensors and actuators of the agent. Interactions are modeled through communication events that are broadcasted. In addition, global variables can be used to exchange system state information. Figure 15.2 describes the architecture of a robotic agent, where each sensor and each actuator have a set of elementary strategies, ES_i's, associated with it.

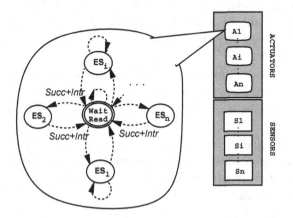

Fig. 15.2   Architecture of a robotic agent

In our framework, each sensor and actuator strategy is represented by a finite state machine (FSM) model, called *elementary process*. An elementary process can be viewed as a server for the sensor or actuator that encapsulates the low level protocol of the device and a specific strategy for generating motion commands or extracting sensory data. Each sensor and actuator is described by combining, e.g., in sequence or parallel, various elementary processes. We call the resulting FSM model of the sensor or actuator a *process*. A robotic agent can be represented by the parallel composition of the processes of its sensors and actuators. This modular specification can be carried to a higher level of abstraction, where multiple agent processes can be combined to describe more complex systems of interactive agents.

We next describe elementary processes which are the basic notion of a component in our framework. We then describe the various composition operators which allow us to describe more complex components in an intuitive way.

15.4.1   *Elementary Processes*

An elementary process has an FSM model that describes an elementary control or perceptual strategy. The transitions between the states of the FSM model are labeled with *events* that describe initiation, termination, interruption of, or communication with another process. Communication is modeled via shared events; that is, if two parallel processes share an event, a communication link is established between them. Furthermore, communication in our model is broadcast based. In other words, more than two processes activated in parallel can share a communication link at any time instant.

A state of the FSM model represents execution modes such as data processing, control mode, and idling mode. The set of final states of an elementary process is partitioned into a set of *successful* and *unsuccessful* final states.

We assume that each elementary process can access global variables and use them inside predicates to express the goals the mobile agent should achieve, maintain or prevent from happening. In this paper, however, we do not model variables.

Definition 1   An elementary process is defined as a generator
$\mathcal{G} = (Q, \Sigma, \delta, q_0, F)$, where:

Q is the set of states;
Σ is the set of communication events such that $\epsilon \in \Sigma$;
q_0 is the initial state;
$F \subseteq Q$ is a set of "marked" states, such that $F = F_s \cup F_u$ where $F_s \cap F_u = \emptyset$,
$\qquad F_u \neq \emptyset$, F_s is a set of successful final states, and F_u is a set of
$\qquad$ unsuccessful final states;
$\delta \subseteq (Q \times \Sigma \times Q)$ is the transition relation such that $\forall (q, e, q') \in \delta . q \notin F$.

Figure 15.3 shows two elementary processes, *GoTo* and *DetObs*, from our robotic example. Process *GoTo* describes an elementary strategy of the mobile base actuator. The process starts in state 1 where the agent waits for the event *goto* which indicates that a destination location was set. In state 2, the proportional control law to compute the next command for the mobile base is continuously applied until the goal location is reached (event $succ_{GT}$), or either an unexpected failure (event $fail_{GT}$) or an external interrupt (event $intrpt_{GT}$) occurs. In state 2 the goal can be reset (event *goal*), and information about the obstacles can be provided (event *obst*).

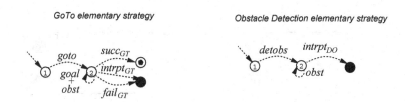

Fig. 15.3   Example of elementary processes: *GoTo* (left) and *DetObs* (right)

The process *DetObs* describes an elementary strategy for a stereo vision sensor. It starts in state 1, and moves to state 2 when the obstacle detection process starts (event *detobs*). In state 2, the process continuously acquires images from the stereo vision sensor. After filtering the image data and applying the appropriate mapping, the process broadcasts the information about the obstacles in the field of view of the mobile robot (event *obst*) until an external interrupt (event *intrpt$_{DO}$*) occurs.

We will revisit this example to show how to combine the two processes in parallel to define a specific strategy for a robot.

15.4.2   *Composition Operators*

As mentioned earlier, elementary processes can be composed to describe various strategies of a sensor and actuator. The resulting FSM models, or *processes*, of sensors and actuators can be further combined to describe the task of the robotic agent. Furthermore, the same operators can be used to describe a system with multiple robotic agents that interact with one another.

The choice of operators in our framework is motivated by execution scenarios and system architectures that are common within the domain of robotic agents. The set of operators we describe next is by no means exhaustive. It however illustrates how to define essential, primitive operators that can be used to define others.

Let P, R and S range over the set of processes and $\sigma_1, \cdots, \sigma_n$ range over the set of events. The syntax of a process in our framework is defined by the following grammar:

$$P ::= R; S \mid R : S \mid R \| S \mid R \natural_{\{\sigma_1, \cdots, \sigma_n\}} S \mid R :; S \mid R :: S$$

Sequential composition: $P = R; S$. Process P behaves like the process R until R terminates at which time P starts behaving like S. The process

R   S

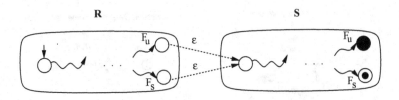

Fig. 15.4   Sequential composition

P terminates when S terminates and has the same termination status as S, i.e., being in a successful or unsuccessful state. In terms of the FSM model, sequential composition of processes R and S is achieved by connecting *each* final state of R with the initial state of S by an ϵ-transition, and making the final states of S those of P and the initial state of R the initial state of P. Figure 15.4 depicts the sequential composition of two processes. Note that regular minimization algorithms can be applied to eliminate the ϵ transitions from the resulting finite state machine.

As an example, consider the following sequential composition:

$$GoTo\,;GoTo$$

It specifies that the mobile agent must execute the *GoTo* strategy twice, consecutively. The objective for the robot is to navigate to two different locations one after another. The locations are determined by global system variables. Note that in this composition, even if the first process terminates unsuccessfully, i.e., the first process did not accomplish its task of reaching the first location, the second process is initiated and an attempt is made to reach the second location.

Conditional composition: $P = R : S$. Process P behaves like the process R until R terminates successfully at which time P starts behaving like the process S. If R fails, the conditional composition also fails. If R terminates successfully, the termination status of P is that of S. If R terminates unsuccessfully, then so does P. In terms of the FSM model, P is obtained by connecting each *successful* state in the FSM model of R to the initial state of the FSM model of S.

Conditional composition can be used to describe a process that monitors a certain condition to be true, e.g., a landmark is found, a goal location is reached, a target is detected. The condition is required for initiating a second process. Once the condition is reached the first process successfully terminates and the second process is started.

As an example, consider the following process:

$$LocLand : Navigate$$

where a robot must first detect and locate a landmark (process *LocLand*). The successful termination of detecting and locating a landmark is a precondition for instantiating the *Navigate* process which will move the robot towards the landmark, the new goal location, while avoiding obstacles. The process *Navigate* is a composite process that will be described shortly. The conditional composition process is part of our robotic example where the *LocLand* process is used to determine an initial goal location that is used when starting the *GoTo* process to move the robot.

Parallel composition: $P = R \,\|\, S$. Process P behaves like the processes R and S running in parallel. P terminates with the termination status of the process which terminates *last*. Parallel composition is formed as a modified version of a *synchronous product* of the participating FSM's; that is, both R and S must agree on the transitions labeled with the (non-ϵ) events they share, i.e., a shared event can be asserted only when both processes can make a transition on that event. The processes R and S however proceed independently on unshared events, i.e., unshared events can be asserted in an interleaved fashion in P.

Informally, the FSM model of P is obtained from a restricted version of the synchronous product of the FSM models of R and S. Transitions on unshared events are interleaved, while transitions on shared events must be synchronized to produce a single transition in P that is labeled with the shared event. The initial state of P is composed of the initial states of R and S. The final states of P are states composed of the final states of R and S. The successful (unsuccessful) final states of P are those states where the last substate (i.e., state from R or S) that changed is a successful (unsuccessful) state. In addition, the unsuccessful states of P also include those states that are reached through a synchronous transition to an unsuccessful state in one process (e.g., R) and to a successful state in the other (e.g., S). In practice, if R and S synchronize on an event right before terminating, then they should terminate with a *consistent* status. Appendix A contains the formal definition of the FSM model of the parallel composition.

As an example, consider the process in charge of navigating a robot while avoiding obstacles. Process *Navigate* can be specified as follows:

$$GoTo \,\|\, DetObs$$

where the processes *GoTo* and *DetObs* are the elementary processes of

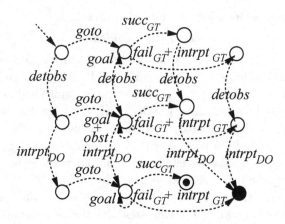

Fig. 15.5   Parallel Composition of GoTo and DetObs

Figure 15.3. The FSM model of the parallel composition of the two processes is shown in Figure 15.5.

Disabling composition: $P = R \sharp_{\{\sigma_1, \cdots, \sigma_n\}} S$. Disabling composition is similar to the parallel composition with the difference in the way transitions on the *disabling* events $\sigma_1, \cdots, \sigma_n$ are handled. First, transitions on any of the specified disabling events need not be synchronized, even when the event is shared between R and S. Second, the first process that can assert a disabling event, terminates the participation of the second process in the parallel composition; that is, P behaves from that point on like the process which first asserted a disabling event. The transitions in P from that point on are those of the process which asserted a disabling event first and the termination status of P is that of this latter process.

A particular application of the disabling operator is when the set of the disabling events consists of all the events leading to final states in R and S. In this case, the disabling composition describes a process where R and S are executed in parallel and P terminates when either process terminates.

In our robotic example, the two robots are required to navigate together. However, it is sometimes necessary to make one follow the other, for instance, to move through a narrow space. The corresponding process can be described as follows:

$$GoTo_A \sharp_D Follow_B$$

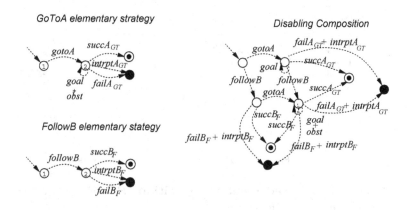

Fig. 15.6 Disabling composition

where the set

$$D = \{succA_{GT}, intrptA_{GT}, failA_{GT}, succB_F, failB_F, intrptB_F\}.$$

Both agents (processes) proceed in parallel until one of them terminates, which interrupts and disables the other process. The termination status is the status of the process which terminates first. Figure 15.6 shows the disabling composition of the two elementary processes $GoTo_A$ and $Follow_B$.

The next two operators use the earlier ones to describe recursive instantiation of elementary strategies.

Synchronous Recurrent Composition: $P = R :; S$. This can be recursively defined as follows:

$$R :; S = R(S ; (R :; S)) \quad .$$

Once process R successfully terminates process S is initiated. Upon completion of S, process R is again initiated and so on so forth. The sequential initiations terminate with the failure of process R, otherwise the process P has a recursive, non-terminating behavior. Figure 15.7 depicts the synchronous recurrent composition operation.

As an example, consider the task of looking for moving targets and tracking them upon request. This can be described by the following process:

$$DetectIndMotion :; Track$$

where the process $DetectIndMotion$ detects independently a moving target and the process $Track$ then locks on it and tries to keep the target in center of the field of view. If the target is lost or the tracking process can not function any more, the motion detection process is invoked again.

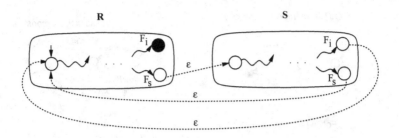

Fig. 15.7   Synchronous recurrent composition

Asynchronous Recurrent Composition: $P = R :: S$. This can be recursively defined as follows:

$$R :: S = R : (S \,\|\, (R :: S)) \quad .$$

Once the process R successfully terminates, the process S is instantiated with a new copy of the process $R :: S$. This means that R is asynchronously "forking" instances of S. The forking process terminates with the failure of the process R. The fact that this composition operator creates multiple copies of process S brings some subtleties to the finite state machine representation and cannot be clearly represented pictorially.

As an example, consider an observer agent that sits at a home station and monitors a working area with multiple mobile agents. The goal of the observer agent is to keep track of the destinations which still have to be visited by the team of mobile agents. When a mobile agent A satisfies a given goal, it comes back to the home station. Upon detecting agent A, the observer agent sends it to an unvisited destination. The whole process terminates if all destinations are visited or the observer agent fails to detect a mobile agent. The system can be described by the following process:

$$ObserverAgent :: GoTo_A \; .$$

15.5   Synthesis Example

During the specification of our mobile robotic example, the composition operators facilitate the specification of the *desired behavior* of the mobile robot. Having the FSM model of the desired behavior and the model of the plant, which in our case corresponds to the sensor and actuator processes activated in parallel, we can formulate the control of the mobile robot as a Supervisory Control Theory Problem [Ramadge 87]. This allows us to synthesize a supervisor process if one exists, which in turn guarantees the *desired* behavior of the system. The supervisor process is then executed in parallel with the elementary strategies (i.e., elementary processes) of the system sensors and actuators. It serves as a run-time monitor and scheduler of the elementary strategies.

Consider the navigation task in our mobile robotic example. Each robot has copies of the *GoTo* and *DetObs* elementary processes associated with its actuators and sensors. Navigation is accomplished through the possibly repeated executions of these elementary processes. However, to achieve the overall system task of moving the robots together while avoiding obstacles, the execution of the elementary processes must not be random. For this, we construct a *supervisor* process that describes the desired behavior of the system as a whole unit.

The specification of the desired behavior is constructed in a bottom-up fashion by first combining the elementary processes into more complicated processes. In our robotic example, each of the two robots A and B has a navigation process which is described as the disabling composition of the *GoTo* and *DetObs* processes. This guarantees that the termination of either process, terminates the second process. (This is to be contrasted with the previous definition of the navigation task where the obstacle detection process and the motion process did not interrupt one another.) The two robot navigation processes are then combined to describe the navigation task of the overall coupled system. The two processes are combined using the disabling composition to allow the two robots to march in parallel and collaborate in such a way that the task will not proceed unless both mobile agents are progressing successfully. The overall system navigation task is described by the following process:

$$Navigate \quad = NavPhase1 :; Navigate$$
$$NavPhase1 = (GoTo_A \natural_{D1} DetObs_A) \ \natural_{D2} \ (GoTo_B \natural_{D3} DetObs_B)$$

where

$$D1 = \{succA_{GT}, intrA_{GT}, failA_{GT}, intrA_{DO}\}$$
$$D3 = \{succB_{GT}, intrB_{GT}, failB_{GT}, intrB_{DO}\}$$
$$D2 = D1 \cup D2$$

The system navigation task is a recursive process that stops if a failure occurs in the process $NavPhase1$.

15.6   Conclusion

We have illustrated a way to enrich a finite state machine based model with a set of operators that allow modular description of robotic systems. The FSM model is chosen due its intuitive notation and provides suitable abstraction of the sensing and control strategies which could be described in terms of differential equations. The proposed representation allows our formalism to benefit from available synthesis and verification methodologies. The set of operators has been chosen to reflect common execution scenarios in robotic applications and, thus, provides an intuitive way of describing such applications.

We have used the presented formalism to formally specify the presented robotic example. The robotic system currently consists of seven elementary processes for each mobile agent. We found the composition operators a helpful mechanism in structuring a supervisor process for the example. They allowed us to describe various supervisors for different system tasks in a modular and intuitive way. A detailed description of the implementation and the workings of the individual strategies can be found in [Košecká 95].

Chapter 16

A Three-Level Analysis of a Simple Acceleration Maneuver, with Uncertainties

Nancy Lynch

16.1 Introduction

In this chapter, we give a three-level analysis of a toy vehicle acceleration maneuver. The goal of the maneuver is to cause a vehicle, starting at velocity 0 at time 0, to attain a velocity of b (or as close to b as possible) at a later time a. The vehicle is assumed to provide accurate sampled data every d time units. The vehicle is assumed to be capable of receiving control signals, one immediately after each vehicle data output. Each control signal can set an "acceleration variable", acc, to an arbitrary real number. However, the actual acceleration exhibited by the vehicle need not be exactly equal to acc — instead, we assume that it is defined by an integrable function whose values are always in the range $[acc - \epsilon, acc]$.* We can think of this uncertainty as representing, say, uncertainty in the performance of the vehicle's propulsion system.

The vehicle interacts with a controller, presumably a computer. In this chapter, we describe a particular controller and analyze the behavior of the combination of the vehicle and controller. One conclusion we draw is that the velocity of the vehicle at time a is in the range $[b - \epsilon d, b]$. That is, the uncertainty in setting acc combines multiplicatively with the sampling

---

*We could also have included some uncertainty in the upper bound, but that would not add any interesting features to the example.

period to yield the uncertainty in the final velocity of the vehicle. More strongly, we obtain a range for the velocity of the vehicle at each time in the interval $[0, a]$.

We prove this fact using invariants and levels of abstraction (in particular, simulation methods), based on a new hybrid I/O automaton model of Lynch, Segala, Vaandrager and Weinberg [Lynch 96]. Invariants and levels of abstraction are standard methods used in computer science for reasoning about discrete systems. Many of the pieces of the proofs use standard continuous methods, such as solving algebraic and differential equations. The entire proof represents a smooth combination of discrete and continuous methods.

The point of this exercise is to demonstrate some simple uses of levels of abstraction in reasoning about hybrid control problems. We use levels of abstraction here for two purposes: (a) to express the relationship between a derivative-based description of a system and an explicit description, and (b) to express the relationship between a system in which corrections are made at discrete sampling points and a system in which corrections are made continuously. The uncertainty in the acceleration is treated at all three levels of our example, and is integrated throughout the presentation.

We do not contribute anything new in the way of techniques for continuous mathematics; for example, we use standard methods of solving differential equations. Our contributions lie, rather, in the smooth combination of discrete and continuous methods within a single mathematical framework, and in the application of standard methods of discrete analysis (in particular, invariants and levels of abstraction) to hybrid systems. Our methods are particularly good at handling uncertainties and other forms of system nondeterminism.

16.2 Hybrid Input/Output Automata

We use the Lynch-Segala-Vaandrager-Weinberg hybrid input/output automaton (HIOA) model [Lynch 96], and refer the reader to [Lynch 96] for the details. We give a rough summary here.

A *hybrid I/O automaton* (HIOA) is a state machine having a (not necessarily finite) set of *states* with a subset distinguished as the *start states*, a set of *discrete actions* partitioned into *input*, *output* and *internal actions*, and a set of *variables*, similarly partitioned into *input*, *output* and *internal variables*. The states are simply combinations of values for the variables. An HIOA also has a set of *discrete steps*, which are state transitions labelled by discrete actions, plus a set of *trajectories*, which are mappings from a left-closed interval of $R^{\geq 0}$ with left endpoint 0 to states. A trajectory shows how the state evolves during an interval of time. An HIOA must satisfy a collection of axioms describing restrictions on the behavior of input actions and variables, closure properties of trajectories, etc.

The operation of an HIOA is described by *hybrid execution fragments*, each being a finite or infinite alternating sequence, $\alpha = w_0 \pi_1 w_1 \pi_2 w_2 \cdots$, of trajectories and discrete actions, where successive states match up properly. A *hybrid execution* is a hybrid execution fragment that begins with a start state. A state is defined to be *reachable* if it is the final state of some finite hybrid execution.

The externally-visible behavior of an HIOA is defined using the notion of a *hybrid trace*. The *hybrid trace* of any hybrid execution fragment α is obtained from α by projecting all trajectories onto external (input and output) variables, removing all internal actions, concatenating all consecutive trajectories for which states match up properly, and inserting a special placeholder symbol τ between consecutive trajectories for which states do not match up.

The levels of abstraction that we referred to in the introduction are captured by means of mappings called *simulations*. A *simulation* from HIOA A to HIOA B with the same external actions and the same external variables is a relation R from $states(A)$ to $states(B)$ satisfying the following conditions:

(1) For every start state of A, there is an R-related start state of B.
(2) For every discrete step (s_A, π, s'_A) of A with s_A a reachable state, and every reachable state s_B of B that is R-related to s_A, there is a finite hybrid execution fragment of B that starts with s_B, ends with some s'_B that is R-related to s'_A, and has the same hybrid trace as the given step.
(3) For every right-closed trajectory w_A of A starting with a reachable state, and every reachable state s_B that is R-related to the first state of w_A, there is a finite hybrid execution fragment of B that starts with s_B, ends with some s'_B that is R-related to the last state of w_A, and has the same hybrid trace as w_A.

The important fact about a simulation is:

Theorem 16.1   *If there is a simulation from A to B, and if α_A is any hybrid execution of A, then there is a hybrid execution α_B of B having the same hybrid trace.*

HIOAs come equipped with a *composition* operation, based on identifying actions with the same name and variables with the same name in different automata. HIOAs also have *hiding* operations, which simply reclassify some output actions or output variables as internal. All definitions and results are given in [Lynch 96].

16.3   Mathematical Preliminaries

16.3.1   *Assumptions about the Constants*

In the informal description in the introduction, we mentioned several constants: a, b, d and ϵ. All are assumed to be positive real-valued. We assume only that d divides evenly into a.

16.3.2   *Some Useful Functions*

16.3.2.1   *Function f*

The following function $f : [0, a] \to \mathsf{R}$ will be used in the analysis:

$$f(t) = \begin{cases} \frac{bt}{a} + \epsilon(a - t)\log(\frac{a-t}{a}) & \text{if } t \in [0, a), \\ b & \text{if } t = a. \end{cases}$$

In particular, $f(0) = 0$ and $f(a) = b$. Function f is continuous over $[0, a]$, since $\lim_{t \to a} f(t) = f(a)$. Function f satisfies:

$$\dot{f}(t) = \frac{b}{a} - \epsilon \log\left(\frac{a - t}{a}\right) - \epsilon = \frac{b - f(t)}{a - t} - \epsilon,$$

for all $t \in (0, a)$. Moreover, f has a right derivative of $\frac{b}{a} - \epsilon$ at 0, while at a, f's left derivative is undefined. (It approaches $+\infty$.)

Function f describes the behavior of a continuous process that starts at time 0 at value 0, always "tries to" set its derivative so as to point to the graph point (a, b), but consistently "misses low" by exactly ϵ. That is, f is a solution to the differential equation

$$\dot{f}(t) = \frac{b - f(t)}{a - t} - \epsilon,$$

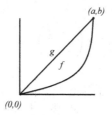

Fig. 16.1 Functions f and g

where $t \in [0, a)$, with the boundary condition $f(0) = 0$. Function f is depicted in Figure 16.1.

16.3.2.2 *Function g*

We also define the function $g : [0, a] \to [0, b]$, by

$$g(t) = \frac{bt}{a}.$$

Then $g(0) = 0$ and $g(a) = b$, and g is continuous over $[0, a]$. Function g satisfies:

$$\dot{g}(t) = \frac{b}{a} = \frac{b - g(t)}{a - t}$$

for all $t \in (0, a)$. Moreover, g has a right derivative of $\frac{b}{a}$ at 0 and a left derivative, also of $\frac{b}{a}$ at a. Function g is a solution to the differential equation

$$\dot{g}(t) = \frac{b - g(t)}{a - t},$$

where $t \in [0, a)$, with the boundary condition $g(0) = 0$. Function g is also depicted in Figure 16.1.

16.3.2.3 *Function f_1*

The following function $f_1 : [0, a] \to \mathbb{R}$ is like f, but it uses the goal of $(a, b - \epsilon d)$ instead of (a, b).

$$f_1(t) = \begin{cases} \frac{(b - \epsilon d)t}{a} + \epsilon(a - t)\log(\frac{a - t}{a}) & \text{if } t \in [0, a), \\ b - \epsilon d & \text{if } t = a. \end{cases}$$

In particular, $f_1(0) = 0$ and $f_1(a) = b - \epsilon d$. Function f_1 is continuous over

$[0, a]$. Function f_1 satisfies:

$$\dot{f}_1(t) = \frac{b - \epsilon d}{a} - \epsilon \log\left(\frac{a - t}{a}\right) - \epsilon = \frac{b - \epsilon d - f_1(t)}{a - t} - \epsilon,$$

for all $t \in (0, a)$. Moreover, f_1 has a right derivative of $\frac{b - \epsilon d}{a} - \epsilon$ at 0, while at a, f_1's left derivative is undefined. (It approaches $+\infty$.) Function f_1 is a solution to the differential equation

$$\dot{f}(t) = \frac{b - \epsilon d - f(t)}{a - t} - \epsilon,$$

where $t \in [0, a)$, with the boundary condition $f(0) = 0$. The function f_1 is depicted in Figure 16.2.

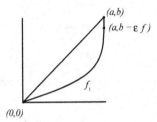

Fig. 16.2   Function f_1

16.3.2.4   *Function h*

Finally, we consider the function $h : [0, a] \to [0, b - \epsilon a]$, where

$$h(t) = \frac{bt}{a} - \epsilon t.$$

In particular, $h(0) = 0$ and $h(a) = b - \epsilon a$. Also,

$$\dot{h}(t) = \frac{b}{a} - \epsilon$$

for all $t \in (0, a)$, and the half derivatives at the endpoints are also equal to $\frac{b}{a} - \epsilon$. Function h satisfies:

$$\dot{h}(t) \leq \frac{b - h(t)}{a - t} - \epsilon$$

for all $t \in [0, a)$.

16.4 High Level Specification *V*

We begin with a high-level system specification. This will not be our final version of the high-level specification — this preliminary version includes only the effects of the uncertainty in the acceleration, but not the effects of sampling delays. We add those later, in V_1, in Section 16.6.1.

16.4.1 *Overview*

Our highest-level system description consists of constraints on the vehicle velocity, embodied in an HIOA *V*. *V* simply constrains the vehicle velocity *v* to be anywhere within a given region bounded by the continuous functions *f* and *g*. This region is represented by the area under the line and over the curve in Figure 16.1 above. Note that this region is determined by the parameters *a*, *b* and ϵ; in particular, it depends on the uncertainty of acceleration, ϵ.

We imagine that this region delineates the "acceptable" vehicle velocities at various times. These limitations on velocities might be used to prove some properties of a system containing the vehicle. This description places no limitations on, say, vehicle acceleration; for example, it permits the vehicle to accelerate arbitrarily quickly, as long as the velocity remains within the given region.[†]

We think that it is reasonable to use such region descriptions to express system requirements. It might not matter *how* a system ensures that the controlled entity remains within the required region — just the region restriction itself might be enough to ensure that the system behaves as required. For example, an air traffic control system might operate by allocating regions in space-time to airplanes. As long as the allocated regions are disjoint, planes can fly without danger of collision. It should not matter how the system ensures that the planes remain within their regions.

In Section 16.5, we will give a lower-level description of the system, in terms of $\dot{v}$, the derivative of the velocity. We think of the derivative-based description as a way of implementing the region description.

[†]Of course, in a practical context, there might also be limitations on acceleration, imposed, for example, by passenger comfort requirements or physical laws. In such a case, the high-level specification would be different from what we give here, including restrictions on acceleration as well as velocity.

16.4.2   *Formal Description*

We define a single HIOA V. Automaton V has no discrete actions (except for a dummy *environment action e* required as a technicality by the formal model). It has the following variables:

Input:	Internal:
none	*none*
Output:	
$now \in [0, a]$, initially 0	
$v \in \mathsf{R}$, initially 0	

The only discrete steps are dummy *e*-steps that cause no state change. The trajectories of V are all the mappings w from left-closed subintervals I of $[0, a]$ to states of V such that:

(1) For all $t \in I$, the following conditions hold in state $w(t)$.

 (a) $now = w(0).now + t$.

 (b) $v \in [f(now), g(now)]$.

Condition (a) says that the value of *now* just increases along with the real time — the difference is that t is a relative time measure, which starts at 0 in each trajectory, while *now* is an absolute time measure, which starts at 0 at the beginning of an entire hybrid execution. Condition (b) describes the envelope for v. The *now* variable allows us to express the second condition just in terms of the automaton state, a useful style for invariant and simulation proofs.

We do not require any other assumptions. For instance, continuity of v is not required at this level, although it will be guaranteed by any real implementation. We believe that the continuity condition for v is not important for using this specification, but only in reasoning about implementations.

Note that our description at this level does not involve any controller. At the highest level, it is probably appropriate to consider just the behavior of the controlled system, regarding the controller as a part of the implementation.

In general, we follow the philosophy of using the maximum possible nondeterminism in our specifications — in particular, we do not include assumptions such as continuity or bounds on acceleration until we need them in the proof of some result.

We give a trivial invariant of V:

Lemma 16.1   *In every reachable state of V, it is the case that $v \in [f(now), g(now)]$.*

Proof.   The proof (as usual for invariants of HIOAs) is by induction on the length, that is, the number of trajectories and discrete steps, in a finite hybrid execution that leads to the state in question. Here (as usual for such proofs), we must show three things: that the property is true in every initial state, that it is preserved by every discrete step, and that it is preserved by every right-closed trajectory. (Note that we need consider only right-closed trajectories, and that we need show only that the property holds in the last state of the trajectory, assuming that it holds in the first state. We do not need to show anything about the intermediate states in the trajectory.)

In this case, all of these are easy to see. In the unique start state of V, we have $v = 0$, $now = 0$, and $f(0) = g(0) = 0$, so that $v \in [0, 0]$, which is what is needed. The only discrete steps are the dummy e-steps, which obviously preserve this property. And trajectories are defined explicitly so as to preserve this property.   □

Note that Lemma 16.1 implies that, in every reachable state of V in which $now = a$, it must be that $v = b$.

16.5   Derivative Automaton D

In Section 16.4, we gave a high-level specification HIOA V, describing a region that contains the allowed values of the velocity v at all times. Now we give a lower-level description in terms of constraints on the derivative of the velocity, $\dot{v}$; this description is given as another HIOA D. Again, there is no controller.

After defining D, we prove some basic properties of its behavior, and then show that D implements V, in the sense of hybrid trace inclusion. Finally, we give an example to show how similar results could be proved for cases where the differential equations do not have known solutions.

16.5.1   *Formal Description*

HIOA D includes a variable acc, which is assumed to always "point to" the goal point (a, b). For this section, we include no uncertainty in the value of acc — we assume that it is set completely accurately. However, there is uncertainty in the actual acceleration $\dot{v}$ — we assume that the value of $\dot{v}$ is in the interval $[acc - \epsilon, acc]$. The actual velocity v is derived from the actual acceleration $\dot{v}$ using integration.

Formally, HIOA D has a single discrete action (besides the dummy environment action e) — an internal *reset* action that simply resets $\dot{v}$ arbitrarily, as long as it preserves the required relationship between $\dot{v}$ and acc.

The discrete actions of D are:

Input: Internal:
   e, the environment action   *reset*
Output:
   none

D has the following variables:

Input: Internal:
   none $acc \in \mathsf{R}$, initially $\frac{b}{a}$
Output: $\dot{v} \in \mathsf{R}$, initially any value in $[\frac{b}{a} - \epsilon, \frac{b}{a}]$
   $now \in [0, a]$, initially 0
   $v \in \mathsf{R}$, initially 0

The e steps cause no state change, while the non-e discrete steps are all of the form:

reset
   Precondition:
      true
   Effect:
      $\dot{v} :=$ any value in $[acc - \epsilon, acc]$

The trajectories of D are all the mappings w from left-closed subintervals I of $[0, a]$ to states of D such that:

(1) $\dot{v}$ is an integrable function in w.[‡]

(2) For all $t \in I$, the following conditions hold in state $w(t)$.
   (a) $now = w(0).now + t$.
   (b) If $now \neq a$ then $acc = \frac{b-v}{a-now}$. (Otherwise, acc is arbitrary).
   (c) If $now \neq a$ then $\dot{v} \in [acc - \epsilon, acc]$.
   (d) $v = w(0).v + \int_0^t w(x).\dot{v}dx$.

In D, acc points directly at the "goal" (a, b), but $\dot{v}$ reflects an uncertainty of ϵ. The quantity v is simply derived from $\dot{v}$, using integration.

[‡]More precisely, this means that $w(t).\dot{v}$ is an integrable function of t, where t ranges over the interval I.

16.5.2 *Some Properties of D*

Lemma 16.2 *Let w be any trajectory of D. Then v is a continuous function in w.*[§]

The following are some obvious invariants.

Lemma 16.3 *In every reachable state of D, the following are true.*

(1) *If $now \neq a$ then $acc = \frac{b-v}{a-now}$.*

(2) *If $now \neq a$ then $\dot{v} \in [acc - \epsilon, acc]$.*

Proof. These follow easily from the definition of D. $\square$

The following invariant is a little less obvious, but is an easy consequence of Lemma 16.3. The functions f and g used in this lemma are as defined in Section 16.3.2.

Lemma 16.4 *In every reachable state of D in which $now \neq a$, the following are true.*

(1) $\frac{v - f(now)}{a - now} \geq \dot{f}(now) - \dot{v}$.

(2) $\frac{g(now) - v}{a - now} \geq \dot{v} - \dot{g}(now)$.

Proof.

(1) By definition of f, we have that:
$$\dot{f}(now) = \frac{b - f(now)}{a - now} - \epsilon.$$
By Lemma 16.3, we have that:
$$\dot{v} \geq acc - \epsilon = \frac{b - v}{a - now} - \epsilon.$$
Therefore,
$$\dot{f}(now) - \dot{v} \leq \frac{b - f(now)}{a - now} - \epsilon - \left(\frac{b - v}{a - now} - \epsilon\right) = \frac{v - f(now)}{a - now}.$$
This is as needed.

(2) By definition of g, we have that:
$$\dot{g}(now) = \frac{b - g(now)}{a - now}.$$
By Lemma 16.3, we have that:
$$\dot{v} \leq acc = \frac{b - v}{a - now}.$$

[§] This means continuous in the time argument of w.

Therefore,

$$\dot{v} - \dot{g}(now) \le \frac{b - v}{a - now} - \frac{b - g(now)}{a - now} = \frac{g(now) - v}{a - now}.$$

This is as needed.

$\square$

The following are limitations on the rate of change of the velocity in D (for contrast, recall there were no such limitations in V):

Lemma 16.5   *Let w be any (right-closed or right-open) trajectory of D whose now values do not include a, and that starts from a reachable state of D. Then:*

(1) *The ratio $\frac{v - f(now)}{a - now}$ is monotone nondecreasing in w.*¶

(2) *The ratio $\frac{g(now) - v}{a - now}$ is monotone nondecreasing in w.*

This says that v cannot increase too slowly — its distance from f, weighted by the time remaining, cannot decrease. Likewise, v cannot increase too fast — its distance from g, weighted by the time remaining, cannot decrease.

Proof.   In each case, it suffices to show that the first derivative of the ratio is always nonnegative.

(1) The first derivative of the ratio is:

$$\frac{(a - now)(\dot{v} - \dot{f}(now)) - (v - f(now))(-1)}{(a - now)^2}$$

$$= \frac{(a - now)(\dot{v} - \dot{f}(now)) + (v - f(now))}{(a - now)^2}.$$

(Here we are using the fact that $\dot{v}$ is the derivative of v — this is justified formally by the integral definition of the variable v.)
Since the denominator is always positive, it suffices to show that:

$$(a - now)(\dot{v} - \dot{f}(now)) + (v - f(now)) \ge 0$$

in all states of w. This is equivalent to saying that:

$$\frac{v - f(now)}{a - now} \ge \dot{f}(now) - \dot{v},$$

in all states of w. But this follows immediately from Lemma 16.4 (using the fact that w starts in a reachable state of D, so all its states are reachable).

¶This means monotone nondecreasing in the time argument of w.

(2) The derivative of the ratio is:

$$\frac{(a - now)(\dot{g}(now) - \dot{v}) - (g(now) - v)(-1)}{(a - now)^2}$$

$$= \frac{(a - now)(\dot{g}(now) - \dot{v}) + (g(now) - v)}{(a - now)^2}.$$

Since the denominator is always positive, it suffices to show that:

$$(a - now)(\dot{g}(now) - \dot{v}) + (g(now) - v) \geq 0$$

in all states of w. But this is equivalent to saying that:

$$\frac{g(now) - v}{a - now} \geq \dot{v} - \dot{g}(now)$$

in all states of w. This follows from Lemma 16.4.

$\square$

16.5.3 *D Implements V*

The main result that we want to show about D is the following:

Theorem 16.2 *If α_D is a hybrid execution of D, then there is a hybrid execution α_V of V having the same hybrid trace.*

Note that the hybrid trace of each of V and D includes just the *now* and v values. Theorem 16.2 implies that the changes in *now* and v that are exhibited by D are allowed, according to the constraints expressed by V. The correspondence does not mention the implementation variables *acc* and $\dot{v}$. We prove Theorem 16.2 using a simulation, as defined informally in Section 16.2. We define a relation *fsim* from states of D to states of V as follows. If s_D is a state of D and s_V is a state of V, then we say that $(s_D, s_V) \in$ *fsim* provided that the following hold.

(1) $s_D.now = s_V.now$.

(2) $s_D.v = s_V.v$.

We show:

Lemma 16.6 *fsim is a simulation from D to V.*

Proof. We show the three conditions in the definition of a simulation. The start condition is straightforward: If s_D is any start state of D and s_V is the unique start state of V, then both states have *now* $= 0$ and $v = 0$. It follows that $(s_D, s_V) \in$ *fsim*.

Next, we consider discrete steps. Suppose that (s_D, π, s_D') is any discrete step of D, and that $(s_D, s_V) \in$ *fsim*. Then let the hybrid execution fragment corresponding to this step consist of the trivial trajectory containing exactly one state and no steps. Then both the discrete step and the corresponding fragment have the same hybrid trace, consisting of the values of *now* and v that appear in s_D. It suffices to show that $(s'_D, s_V) \in \textit{fsim}$. But this is immediate, because π (a *reset* or e action) does not modify either *now* or v. Now we consider trajectories. Suppose that w_D is an I-trajectory of D, where I is right-closed, and suppose that the first state, s_D, of w_D is reachable in D. Suppose that s_V is a reachable state of V such that $(s_D, s_V) \in \textit{fsim}$. Then let the corresponding hybrid execution fragment of V consists of a single trajectory w_V, where $w_V(t).now = w_D(t).now$ and $w_V(t).v = w_D(t).v$ for all t in the domain of I. It is obvious that the two trajectories have the same hybrid trace. The only interesting thing to show is that w_V is in fact a trajectory of V. By the definition of a trajectory of V, what we must show is that

(1) For all $t \in I$, the following conditions hold in state $w(t)$.
  (a) $now = w(0).now + t$.
  (b) $v \in [f(now), g(now)]$.

(We must verify these conditions throughout the trajectory, not just at the beginning and end.) The first condition follows immediately from the same condition for w_D and the definition of w_V in terms of w_D. The second condition has two parts, a lower bound and an upper bound.

For the lower bound, since s_V is a reachable state of V, Lemma 16.1 implies that, in s_V, $v \geq f(now)$. By Lemma 16.5 and the definition of w_V in terms of w_D, we know that the ratio $\frac{v - f(now)}{a - now}$ is monotone nondecreasing in w_V, except possibly at the right endpoint of w_V if $now = a$ there. It follows that $v \geq f(now)$ throughout w_V, except possibly at the right endpoint if $now = a$ there. But since $f(now)$ and v are continuous functions of the time argument of w_V, this inequality must hold at the right endpoint as well.

The upper bound argument is analogous. Since s_V is reachable, Lemma 16.1 implies that, in s_V, $v \leq g(now)$. By Lemma 16.5 and the definition of w_V in terms of w_D, we know that the ratio $\frac{g(now) - v}{a - now}$ is monotone nondecreasing in w_V, except possibly at the right endpoint of w_V if $now = a$ there. It follows that $v \leq g(now)$ throughout w_V, exept possibly at the right endpoint if $now = a$ there. But since $g(now)$ and v are continuous functions of the time argument of w_V, this inequality must hold at the right endpoint as well. $\quad\square$

Proof. (of Theorem 16.2)

By Lemma 16.6 and Theorem 16.1. □

Note that the correspondence between D and V is only one-way. It says, roughly speaking, that everything that D does is allowed by V. It does not say that D has to exhibit *all* the possibilities that are allowed by V. For example, extremely fast increases in v that cannot be achieved by accelerations in the allowed ranges, but that keep v within the allowed envelope, are permitted by V, but do not actually occur in D. Also, note that D performs some activities — here, changes to acc and $\dot{v}$ — that are not explicitly represented in V.

Although Theorem 16.2 is very simple, it does demonstrate, at least in a small way, how one can carry out a correctness proof using invariants and simulations, integrating discrete and continuous reasoning, and coping with some uncertainty.

16.5.4 *An Approximate Result*

The lower bound function f is defined essentially as the solution of a differential equation that is extracted from the definition of the trajectories of D. In this case, the differential equation is easy to solve. But what if it were not so easy? In this case, the same methods could still be used, but now the lower bound produced might be a loose bound rather than an exact bound.

For example, suppose that instead of trying to prove a lower bound of f, we only tried to prove a lower bound of h, where h is the function defined in Section 16.3.2.4. Showing that h is a lower bound essentially requires redefining V to use h instead of f. Proving the simulation now rests on the fact, stated in Section 16.3.2.4, that

$$\dot{h}(t) \leq \frac{b - h(t)}{a - t} - \epsilon$$

for all $t \in [0, a)$. Using this fact, it is easy to obtain the analog to part 1 of Lemma 16.4 for h: that in every reachable state of D,

$$\frac{v - h(now)}{a - now} \geq \dot{h}(now) - \dot{v}.$$

This fact follows as in the proof of part 1 of Lemma 16.4 (but using the inequality above at one step instead of an equality as before). Next, we can prove the analog to part 1 of Lemma 16.5 for h: that the ratio $\frac{v - h(now)}{a - now}$

is monotone nondecreasing in w. This is what is needed to complete the analog to the proof of Lemma 16.6.

16.6   Modifications to V and D to Incorporate Periodic Feedback

The discussions and results in Sections 16.4 and 16.5 have dealt with hypothetical systems with continuous control. But recall from the introduction that in the actual implementation in which we are interested, the sampling outputs and control signals are not continuous but periodic, at intervals of d. It turns out that the abstract automata D and V do not quite provide accurate models of the actual implementation. However, they can be modified easily so that they do.

We believe that providing accurate models for the handling of uncertainties is important. It is not sufficient to give a careful analysis of a situation without uncertainty, then argue informally about the variations in behavior that are introduced by uncertainties. Handling uncertainties correctly requires considering them appropriately at all levels of abstraction.

16.6.1   *Modified High Level Specification V_1*

First, we modify V only a tiny bit to get V_1, by changing the lower bound f to the function f_1 defined in Section 16.3.2.3. The upper bound g remains the same as before. (Of course, we could have written the original V with parameters, so that the modifications in this section would just amount to different parameter settings.)

This modification makes the region of allowable values for v bigger by making the lower bound function smaller. The particular way that we make it smaller amount to simply replacing the "goal" of (a, b) in V with the goal of $(a, b - \epsilon d)$ in V_1, for the lower bound function only. Thus, the value of v at time a will be in the range $[b - \epsilon d, b]$, instead of always being exactly b.

It was not obvious to us at first that the high-level effect of the sampling delays is just this simple change of goal point; we discovered this only through detailed analysis of the behavior of the discrete-sampling system. We do not expect to use a general rule for determining the high-level effect of uncertainties; indeed, we expect that this will usually require serious work, perhaps using results of robust control theory. It is important that the high-level effects of uncertainties be described accurately, though the bounds need not be as tight as possible.

16.6.2 Modified Derivative Automaton D_1

Now we modify D to get D_1, again by modifying the lower bound requirement. Here we do this by introducing uncertainty into acc, allowing it to "point to" anywhere between (a, b) (where it points in D) to $(a, b - \epsilon d)$. We still have the same uncertainty in $\dot{v}$ as we do in D. Thus, D_1 expresses two different types of uncertainty. We can think of the uncertainty in $\dot{v}$ as representing propulsion system uncertainty and the uncertainty in acc as encompassing the sampling delays.

The modifications are as follows. The states and start states of D_1 are the same as those of D, except for the following changes: The initial value of acc is any value in the interval $[\frac{b-\epsilon d}{a}, \frac{b}{a}]$, and the initial value of $\dot{v}$ is any value in the interval $[acc - \epsilon, acc]$. The *reset* action now changes slightly, to allow changes in acc as well as $\dot{v}$. These changes keep acc and $\dot{v}$ within the desired ranges.

> *reset*
> > Precondition:
> > > *true*
> > Effect:
> > > $acc :=$ any value in $[\frac{b-\epsilon d - v}{a - now}, \frac{b-v}{a-now}]$
> > > $\dot{v} :=$ any value in $[acc - \epsilon, acc]$

The trajectories of D_1 are all the mappings w from left-closed subintervals I of $[0, a]$ to states of D_1 such that:

(1) $\dot{v}$ is an integrable function in w.

(2) For all $t \in I$, the following conditions hold in state $w(t)$.
   (a) $now = w(0).now + t$.
   (b) If $now \neq a$ then $acc \in [\frac{b-\epsilon d - v}{a - now}, \frac{b-v}{a-now}]$.
   (c) If $now \neq a$ then $\dot{v} \in [acc - \epsilon, acc]$.
   (d) $v = w(0).v + \int_0^t w(x).\dot{v}dx$.

(Again, we could have written the original D with parameters, so that the modifications in this section would amount to different parameter settings.)

16.6.3 Modified Correctness Proof

Our claim now is that the arguments that worked to show that D implements V can be modified slightly (and systematically) to show that D_1 implements V_1. We give the modified result statements.

Lemma 16.7   *Let w be any trajectory of D_1. Then v is a continuous function in w.*

Lemma 16.8   *In every reachable state of D_1, the following are true.*

(1) *If $now \neq a$ then $acc \in [\frac{b-\epsilon d-v}{a-now}, \frac{b-v}{a-now}]$.*

(2) *If $now \neq a$ then $\dot{v} \in [acc - \epsilon, acc]$.*

Lemma 16.9   *In every reachable state of D_1 in which $now \neq a$, the following are true.*

(1) $\frac{v-f_1(now)}{a-now} \geq \dot{f}_1(now) - \dot{v}$.

(2) $\frac{g(now)-v}{a-now} \geq \dot{v} - \dot{g}(now)$.

Proof.   We only prove part 1; part 2 is unchanged from the corresponding proof for D. By definition of f_1, we have that:

$$\dot{f}_1(now) = \frac{b - \epsilon d - f_1(now)}{a - now} - \epsilon.$$

By Lemma 16.8, we have that:

$$\dot{v} \geq acc - \epsilon \geq \frac{b - \epsilon d - v}{a - now} - \epsilon.$$

Therefore,

$$\dot{f}_1(now) - \dot{v} \leq \frac{b - \epsilon d - f_1(now)}{a - now} - \epsilon - \left(\frac{b - \epsilon d - v}{a - now} - \epsilon \right) = \frac{v - f_1(now)}{a - now}.$$

This is as needed.   □

Lemma 16.10   *Let w be any trajectory of D_1 whose now values do not include a, and that starts from a reachable state of D_1. Then:*

(1) *The ratio $\frac{v-f_1(now)}{a-now}$ is monotone nondecreasing in w.*

(2) *The ratio $\frac{g(now)-v}{a-now}$ is monotone nondecreasing in w.*

Now define the relation $fsim_1$ from states of D_1 to states of V_1 as follows. If s_{D_1} is a state of D_1 and s_{V_1} is a state of V_1, then we say that $(s_{D_1}, s_{V_1}) \in fsim_1$ provided that the following hold.

(1) $s_{D_1}.now = s_{V_1}.now$.

(2) $s_{D_1}.v = s_{V_1}.v$.

This definition is essentially the same as that for $fsim$, from D to V.

Lemma 16.11   *$fsim_1$ is a simulation from D_1 to V_1.*

Proof.   Similar to the proof of Lemma 16.6.   □

Theorem 16.3 *If α_{D_1} is a hybrid execution of D_1, then there is a hybrid execution α_{V_1} of V_1 having the same hybrid trace.*

Theorem 16.3 says that the changes in *now* and v that are exhibited by D_1 are allowed by V_1.

Note that the modifications we did to include this uncertainty are quite simple and systematic. A good general strategy for constructing proofs for implementations involving uncertainty is to first carry out the development without the uncertainty, then try to incorporate the uncertainty later, by making simple modifications throughout.

16.7 The Implementation *Impl*

Now we are (finally) ready to describe the actual implementation in which we are interested. This one consists of two components, a *Vehicle* and a *Controller*, interacting by discrete actions. Each component is, formally, an HIOA, and the combination is a composition of HIOAs, interacting via discrete actions only, with the common actions hidden.

16.7.1 *Vehicle*

The *Vehicle* HIOA represents the motion of the vehicle, including its velocity and acceleration. It reports the velocity (accurately, we assume) every d units of time, starting at time d. It is capable of receiving control signals that set an *acc* variable, representing the desired acceleration. However, the actual acceleration can be slightly less than this — within amount ϵ.

The actions are:

Input: Internal:
   accel(c), $c \in \mathsf{R}$ *none*
Output:
   sample(u), $u \in \mathsf{R}$

The variables are the same as those of D_1, with the addition of an internal "deadline variable" *last-sample*. This deadline variable just keeps track of the next (absolute) time at which a *sample* output is scheduled to occur. Also, the initialization of *acc* is more constrained than it is in D_1, reflecting the assumption that the correct acceleration is in effect at the beginning. We can think of the system as if we initialized it with an initial sample output and control signal.

Input: Internal:
   e   *acc* $\in$ R, initially $\frac{b}{a}$
Output: $\dot{v} \in$ R, initially any value in $[\frac{b}{a} - \epsilon, \frac{b}{a}]$
   now $\in [0, a]$, initially 0   *last-sample* $\in$ R$^{\geq 0}$, initially *d*
   v $\in$ R, initially 0

The non-*e* discrete steps are:

accel(c)   *sample(u)*
  Effect: Precondition:
    acc := *c*   *now* = *last-sample*
    $\dot{v}$:= any value in $[acc - \epsilon, acc]$ *u* = *v*
                                  Effect:
                                    last-sample := *now* + *d*

Thus, an *accel* step just sets the *acc* control variable, and resets the actual acceleration $\dot{v}$ accordingly. A *sample* step just announces the current velocity — the only information needed by the controller component. It does so exactly at the time scheduled in *last-sample*. Then it reschedules the sampling time to be exactly *d* in the future.

The trajectories of *Vehicle* are all the mappings *w* from left-closed subintervals *I* of $[0, a]$ to states of *Vehicle* such that:

(1) *acc* and *last-sample* are unchanged in *w*.

(2) $\dot{v}$ is an integrable function in *w*.

(3) For all $t \in I$, the following conditions hold in state *w(t)*.
   (a) *now* = *w(0).now* + *t*.
   (b) *now* $\leq$ *last-sample*.
   (c) $\dot{v} \in [acc - \epsilon, acc]$.
   (c) $v = w(0).v + \int_0^t w(x).\dot{v}dx$.

These trajectories are quite similar to those that are permitted in D_1. The most important difference is that *acc* is now not permitted to change during trajectories; instead, it changes only as a result of discrete inputs (from the controller, presumably). However, $\dot{v}$ can change, as long as it stays within the required bounds. There is also a condition that prevents time from passing beyond the *last-sample* deadline. The following invariants are straightforward to prove.

Lemma 16.12 *In every reachable state of Vehicle, the following are true.*

(1) $\dot{v} \in [acc - \epsilon, acc]$.

(2) *last-sample* $\in [now, now + d]$.

16.7.2 *Controller*

The *Controller* HIOA represents the controller that decides on the desirable acceleration, i.e., the value that should be placed into *Vehicle*'s variable *acc*. It receives reports from the *Vehicle* of its current velocity v, and uses each such report to calculate a desired new acceleration. It sends this, before any further time passage, to the *Vehicle* in an *accel* action.

The external actions of the *Controller* form the "mirror image" of those of the *Vehicle*:

Input: Internal:
    sample(u), $u \in$ R   *none*
    e
Output:
    accel(c), $c \in$ R

The variables are:

Input: Internal:
    none   *now* $\in [0, a]$, initially 0
Output: *sampled-vel* $\in$ R, initially 0
    none   *last-accel* $\in$ R$^{\geq 0} \cup \{\infty\}$, initially ∞

Here, *sampled-vel* is intended to hold the sampled velocity, when the *Controller* receives a report about it. The *last-accel* variable is another deadline variable, intended to keep track of the next scheduled (absolute) time for an *accel* signal. Initially (until the *Controller* receives some velocity report), no signal is scheduled, so *last-accel* $= \infty$.

The non-*e* discrete steps are:

sample(u)   *accel(c)*
    Effect: Precondition:
        sampled-vel := u   *last-accel* = now
        last-accel := now   now $\neq a$

$$c = \frac{b - sampled\text{-}vel}{a - now}$$

                                 Effect:
                                   last-accel := ∞

The *sample* action just records the reported velocity, and schedules an *accel* action to happen before any further real time elapses. (We could alternatively have modelled a system in which there is some bounded delay before the *accel* action occurs.) The *accel* action recalculates the desired velocity, using the same formula as in D — pointing at the desired goal (a, b) — but this time, the calculation is based on the sampled velocity instead of the actual velocity. After the *accel* action, no further *accel* is scheduled, until a new *sample* occurs.

The trajectories of *Controller* are trivial — time just passes up to any time that does not exceed any current deadline. There is no interesting continuous behavior to be modelled. That is, the trajectories are all the mappings w from left-closed subintervals I of $[0, a]$ to states of *Controller* such that:

(1) *sampled-vel* and *last-accel* are unchanged in w.

(2) For all $t \in I$, the following conditions hold in state $w(t)$.
   (a) $now = w(0).now + t$.
   (b) $now \leq last\text{-}accel$.

16.7.3   *Impl*

The complete implementation *Impl* is the composition of the two HIOAs *Vehicle* and *Controller*, identifying the *sample* and *accel* actions, and then hiding those actions (making them internal).

We give some properties of *Impl*. The first lemma gives simple invariants about *last-accel*. It says that *last-accel* is only used to schedule an event immediately, and that when it is being used, the recorded and actual velocities are identical.

Lemma 16.13   *In every reachable state of Impl, the following are true.*

(1) $last\text{-}accel \in \{now, \infty\}$.

(2) *If* $last\text{-}accel = now$ *then* $v = sampled\text{-}vel$.

The next lemma is a key lemma for the simulation proof. It expresses bounds on the *acc* variable, no matter where the reference point is in a sampling interval. The *acc* variable is set accurately initially, and at each sampling time. But in between, the accuracy of the value of *acc* can degrade. Lemma 16.14 gives appropriate guarantees at all times, even within the sampling intervals. Some general statement of this sort is needed for the inductive proof of the simulation of D_1 by *Impl*.

In the statement of Lemma 16.14, the assumption that $last\text{-}accel = \infty$ is used to avoid the case where the implementation automaton is in the middle of processing a new sampling output.

Lemma 16.14   *In every reachable state of Impl, the following are true.*

(1) *If* $now \neq a$ *and* $last\text{-}accel = \infty$ *then* $acc \geq \frac{b - \epsilon(now + d - last\text{-}sample) - v}{a - now}$.

(2) *If* $now \neq a$ *then* $acc \leq \frac{b - v}{a - now}$.

Notice that the lower bound expressed in case 1 varies during each sampling interval. At the beginning of the interval, we have $now + d = last\text{-}sample$, so the bound simplifies to $\frac{b-v}{a-now}$. At the other extreme, at the end of the interval, we have $now = last\text{-}sample$, and the bound simplifies to $\frac{b-\epsilon d-v}{a-now}$. The complete statement fills in guarantees for the intermediate points as well.

Proof.

(1) The lower bound is proved by induction on the length of a hybrid execution, as usual. The lower bound claim is true initially, since initially $acc = \frac{b}{a}$, $now = 0$, $last\text{-}sample = d$, and $v = 0$.

Now consider a discrete step starting from a reachable state. A *sample* step makes $last\text{-}accel = \infty$, which makes the claim vacuously true. On the other hand, an *accel* step explicitly sets acc to $\frac{b-sampled\text{-}vel}{a-now}$, which is equal to $\frac{b-v}{a-now}$ by Lemma 16.13, which suffices to show the inequality. (This uses the fact that $last\text{-}sample \leq now + d$, which follows from Lemma 16.12.)

Finally, consider a $[0, t]$-trajectory w whose first state is reachable. In w, acc is unchanged, and $\dot{v} \geq acc - \epsilon$ everywhere, by Lemma 16.12. Therefore,

$$\frac{w(t).v - w(0).v}{t} \geq acc - \epsilon,$$

that is,

$$w(t).v - w(0).v \geq (acc - \epsilon)t.$$

We know by inductive hypothesis that

$$acc \geq \frac{b - \epsilon(w(0).now + d - last\text{-}sample) - w(0).v}{a - w(0).now}.$$

In other words,

$$w(0).v \geq b - \epsilon(w(0).now + d - last\text{-}sample) - acc(a - w(0).now).$$

Adding, we get:

$$w(t).v \geq b - \epsilon(w(t).now + d - last\text{-}sample) - acc(a - w(t).now).$$

In other words,

$$acc \geq \frac{b - \epsilon(w(t).now + d - last\text{-}sample) - w(t).v}{a - w(t).now}$$

This is what we needed to show.

(2) For the upper bound, the argument is similar. The upper bound claim is true initially, since initially $acc = \frac{b}{a}$, $now = 0$ and $v = 0$.

Now consider a discrete step starting from a reachable state. A *sample* step does not change any of the quantities mentioned in the inequality, and so it preserves the inequality. On the other hand, an *accel* step explicitly sets acc to $\frac{b - sampled\text{-}vel}{a - now}$, which is equal to $\frac{b-v}{a-now}$ by Lemma 16.13, which suffices to show the inequality.

Finally, consider a $[0, t]$-trajectory w whose first state is reachable. In w, acc is unchanged, and $\dot{v} \leq acc$ everywhere, by Lemma 16.12. Therefore,

$$\frac{w(t).v - w(0).v}{t} \leq acc,$$

that is,

$$w(t).v - w(0).v \leq acc \cdot t.$$

We know by inductive hypothesis that

$$acc \leq \frac{b - w(0).v}{a - w(0).now}.$$

In other words,

$$w(0).v \leq b - acc(a - w(0).now).$$

Adding, we get:

$$w(t).v \leq b - acc(a - w(t).now).$$

In other words,

$$acc \leq \frac{b - w(t).v}{a - w(t).now}.$$

This is what we needed to show.

$\square$

16.7.4 *Impl Implements D_1*

We show that *Impl* implements D_1 (see Theorem 16.4 for the formal statement), using a simulation from *Impl* to D_1.

Define the relation $fsim_2$ from states of *Impl* to states of D_1 as follows. If s_{Impl} is a state of *Impl* and s_{D_1} is a state of D_1, then we say that $(s_{Impl}, s_{D_1}) \in fsim_2$ provided that:

(1) $s_{Impl}.now = s_{D_1}.now$.

(2) $s_{Impl}.v = s_{D_1}.v$.

(3) $s_{Impl}.acc = s_{D_1}.acc$.

(4) $s_{Impl}.\dot{v} = s_{D_1}.\dot{v}$.

That is, $fsim_2$ is the identity mapping on all the state components of D_1. Note that all the state components of D_1 are derived from the *Vehicle* state in *Impl*. This is because the abstract system only mentions vehicle behavior, not controller behavior.

Lemma 16.15 *$fsim_2$ is a simulation from Impl to D_1.*

Proof. For the start condition, note that any combination of initial values allowed for all the state components in *Impl* is also allowed in D_1.

Next, consider a discrete step $(s_{Impl}, \pi, s'_{Impl})$ of *Impl*, where s_{Impl} and s_{D_1} are reachable states of *Impl* and D_1, respectively, and $(s_{Impl}, s_{D_1}) \in fsim_2$. There are two cases (again ignoring the trivial e case):

(1) π is a *sample* action.

Then we take the corresponding hybrid execution fragment to be trivial — just the trivial trajectory containing the single state s_{D_1}. It is easy to see that the step and the trivial trajectory have the same hybrid trace. Also, $(s'_{Impl}, s_{D_1}) \in fsim_2$, since this step does not change anything that affects any of the state components of D_1.

(2) $\pi = accel(c)$.

Now we take the corresponding hybrid execution fragment of D_1 to consist of a single *reset* step, $(s_{D_1}, reset, s'_{D_1})$. The state s'_{D_1} is obtained from the state s_{D_1} by modifying the *acc* and $\dot{v}$ components to their values in s'_{Impl}. The two steps have the same hybrid trace. Since π does not modify *now* or v, it should be clear that $(s'_{Impl}, s'_{D_1}) \in fsim_2$. It remains to show that $(s_{D_1}, reset, s'_{D_1})$ is in fact a step of D_1.

The step of *Impl* causes *acc* to be set to $\frac{b - sampled\text{-}vel}{a - now}$, which is equal to $\frac{b-v}{a-now}$ by Lemma 16.13. It also causes $\dot{v}$ to be set to something in the range $[acc - \epsilon, acc]$. These changes are permitted in a *reset* step of D_1.

Finally, we consider a $[0, t]$-trajectory w_{Impl} whose first state is reachable. We allow this to correspond to a trajectory w_{D_1} of D_1, defined by simply projecting the states of *Impl* on the state components of D_1. The correspondence between the trajectories is then immediate. It remains to show that w_{D_1} is in fact a trajectory of D_1. Specifically, we show:

(1) $\dot{v}$ is an integrable function in w_{D_1}.

This follows from the definition of a trajectory of *Vehicle*.

(2) For all $t \in I$, the following conditions hold in state $w(t)$.

   (a) $now = w(0).now + t$.
       This follows from the definition of a trajectory of *Vehicle*.
   (b) If $now \neq a$ then $acc \in [\frac{b-\epsilon d-v}{a-now}, \frac{b-v}{a-now}]$.
       The upper bound follows from Lemma 16.14, part 2. For the
       lower bound, Lemma 16.14, part 1, implies that, throughout
       w_{Impl} (except possibly at the right endpoint, if $now = a$ there),
       we have:

$$acc \geq \frac{b - \epsilon(now + d - last\text{-}sample) - v}{a - now}.$$

   (This uses the fact that $last\text{-}accel = \infty$ throughout a trajectory;
   this is true because if not, then $last\text{-}accel$ must be equal to
   now at the beginning of the trajectory, which would not permit
   time to pass.) Then the fact that $last\text{-}sample \geq now$, stated in
   Lemma 16.12, yields the result.
   (c) If $now \neq a$ then $\dot{v} \in [acc - \epsilon, acc]$.
       This follows from the definition of a trajectory of *Vehicle*.
   (d) $v = w(0).v + \int_0^t w(x).\dot{v}dx$.
       This follows from the definition of a trajectory of *Vehicle*.   □

Now we can give the basic theorem relating *Impl* to D_1:

Theorem 16.4   *If α_{Impl} is a hybrid execution of Impl, then there is a
hybrid execution α_{D_1} of D_1 having the same hybrid trace.*

Proof.   By Lemma 16.15 and Theorem 16.1.   □

Theorem 16.4 implies that the changes in *now* and v that are exhibited
by *Impl* are allowed by D_1. The theorem does not mention the values of
the other variables of D_1, *acc* and $\dot{v}$, but of course those correspond as well.
We could have obtained this conclusion simply by regarding *acc* and $\dot{v}$ as
output variables instead of internal variables.

We can combine the results stated in Theorems 16.4 and 16.3 to obtain
the following result, which relates the implementation *Impl* to the high-level
specification automaton V_1. This is the main result of the chapter.

Theorem 16.5   *If α_{Impl} is a hybrid execution of Impl, then there is a
hybrid execution α_{V_1} of V_1 having the same hybrid trace.*

Theorem 16.5 implies that the changes in *now* and v that are exhibited
by *Impl* are allowed by V_1.

Proof. By Theorem 16.4 and Theorem 16.3. □

16.8 Discussion

We have described a simple vehicle deceleration maneuver as a composition *Impl* of hybrid I/O automata. In this maneuver, deceleration is accomplished using a controller that receives accurate velocity information at equally spaced times, and instantly responds with control signals containing the desired acceleration. However, there is some uncertainty, in that the proposed acceleration might not be exhibited exactly by the vehicle.

We have also given a correctness specification for the range of allowed velocities at various times, as another HIOA V_1. V_1 gives, in a simple closed form, an "envelope" that includes the allowed velocities. The envelope is sufficiently large to encompass the effects of both the acceleration uncertainty and the sampling delays.

We have verified, using extensions of standard computer science techniques (methods for reasoning about discrete systems), that the implementation *Impl* meets the specification V_1. In particular, our proof uses invariants and levels of abstraction. Invariants involve real-world quantities such as the velocity and acceleration, as well as state components of the controller. Our proof interposes an additional level of abstraction between the implementation and the specification, in which the system's behavior is represented using differential equations; uncertainty is included at this level also. Again, the representation is sufficient to encompass the effects of both acceleration uncertainty and sampling delay. Ideas from differential equations and from discrete analysis fit neatly into the appropriate places in the proof.

Our proof that *Impl* satisfies the specification V_1 is broken down into separate pieces, corresponding to different facts to be shown and different types of mathematical tools. It combines continuous and discrete reasoning cleanly, in a single framework. It gives a completely accurate description of the system's guarantees, including correct handling of the uncertainty and the effects of sampling delays.

Note that some complications of continuous mathematics — definability of derivatives, proper handling of infinities, etc. — arise at the intermediate level only, not at the top and bottom level. The top level just gives an envelope demarcated by explicitly-defined continuous functions. The bottom level gives a discrete algorithm. It is only the intermediate level of abstraction that uses the derivative representation, and at which the complications of infinities arise.

Of course, this example is very simplified. It remains to generalize it to cases that include more uncertainty: the sampling times might be known only approximately, or velocity information might be inexact or out-of-date, or the control signal might be sent only after some approximately-known delay. We have considered uncertainty only in the lower bound, but of course there could also be uncertainty in the upper bound. None of these cases appears to introduce any ideas that are different in principle, so we expect that the proofs we have given should extend to these cases. Another extension is that the implementation might be subject to a limit on the achievable acceleration (because of physical limitations or passenger comfort). It should be possible to use our techniques to reason about this situation also.

It should also be possible to continue our example by refining further. A natural extension would be to implement the discrete *Controller* using a more complicated algorithm, for example, a distributed algorithm with its own difficulties of communication and uncertainty. Techniques of discrete reasoning (only) could be used to show the correspondence between the more detailed controller and the more abstract controller of this chapter. Then general composition theorems about HIOAs could be used to show that the combination of the new controller implementation and the given *Vehicle* automaton still guarantee the proper behavior of the vehicle, as expressed by V_1.

Our general strategy can be described as: using levels of abstraction to represent the relationship between a derivative and explicit form of a system representation, and also between a discrete and a continuous form, while incorporating uncertainties accurately throughout. It remains to use the same general strategy to model and verify other maneuvers, in particular, more complex ones. These two splits seem likely to be useful in many other examples.

We could use more levels of abstraction to represent more levels of derivatives. For example, if vehicle position at various times were the important consideration, then vehicle position only might be constrained at the top level, with velocity at the next level, acceleration at another level below that, and jerk at a fourth level, below the acceleration level. The correspondence between each successive pair of levels related by differentiation would use standard methods of reasoning about differential equations (for the continuous parts of the correspondence).

Finally, the sort of reasoning we are doing in this chapter admits assistance by mechanical reasoning tools. We would like to have a combination of a theorem-prover, for carrying out the discrete reasoning, with a tool for manipulating continuous function expressions. The two tools must be integrated so that they can be used together, using a single representation of the system.

Acknowledgments

This work was supported by ARPA contracts N00014-92-J-4033 and F19628-95-C-0118, AFOSR-ONR contract F49620-94-1-0199, AFOSR contract F49620-97-1-0337, NSF grant 9225124-CCR and DOT contract DTRS95G-0001.

We thank Carl Livadas for reading the manuscript and suggesting several improvements.

Chapter 17

Interface Specifications with Conjunctive Timing Constraints

E. Cerny and K. Khardoc

17.1 Introduction

Methods have been developed for the synthesis of interface controllers [Borriello 98] and for the verification of the interface compatibility [Brzozowski 91] of interconnected devices described by timing diagram (TD) specifications. Other works address the issue of efficient algorithms for computing the maximal time separations between events for more complex forms of timing constraints in TDs [MacMillan 92; Burks 93], or for cyclic (process like) TD behavior [Amon 93] defined using the *latest* timing constraints only. However, none of these methods addressed the issue of realizability of such specification in the sense of causality, especially in the presence of conjunctive *linear* constraints. As we shall show, this means that the existing verification methods can become overly pessimistic or even cannot correctly determine the compatibility of interfaces [Brzozowski 91], or they can deal with specifications with the latest constraints only. Also, the synthesis methods [Borriello 98] may not complete the synthesis or may produce devices that do not fully satisfy the specification requirements thus risking eventual incompatibility between independently developed implementations of the interacting devices. Process algebras have emerged [Klusner 93] in which the occurrence times of actions can be related by linear conjunctive constraints. Although such an approach gives exact semantics to the so described system, it again does not guarantee that it is in fact causal and thus realizable using independently developed subsystems, each constructed according to its local specification.

In this chapter, we address the problem of identifying whether an interface specification containing linear conjunctive timing constraints is causal. The definition of a causal behavior yields a well-formedness condition for a specification in terms of the existence of a *causal* partition over the associated constraint graph. The condition is very intuitive, and it guarantees that compatibility of two or more interfaces can be decided exactly and remain valid for any (causal) implementations of the respective interface controllers. The main part of our presentation deals with finite timing diagram specifications containing linear conjunctive constraints, however, we then discuss possible extensions to cyclic behaviors [Amon 93; Khordoc 93; Khordoc 94].

The paper is organized as follows: In Section 2 we define Timing Diagrams and illustrate the problems associated with their verification. We then present the notion of causality in Section 3 and address the verification of interface compatibility in Section 4. In Section 5 we discuss an extension to cyclic behaviors and conclude the presentation in Section 6. The theoretical results are illustrated on a typical example: the causality and compatibility verification of the Motorola MC68360 processor's READ cycle and that of a slave device.

17.2   Timing Diagram Specifications

A timing diagram (TD) defines the behavior on the interface of a device using a set of waveforms, one on each port [Rony 80; Brzozowski 91]. A waveform is a sequence of transitions or **events** between steady state signal values. Events have a **direction** *in* or *out* and are assigned finite occurrence times. Time is a strictly increasing continuous variable (dense time), and an event is said to have occurred when the values of the time variable becomes equal to the occurrence time of the event. The allowed occurrence times of these events relative to the occurrence times of other events (or the origin) are specified implicitly using timing constraints (TC) which indicate allowed separation time intervals between pairs of events. Let $\mathcal{E} = \mathcal{E}_I \bigcup \mathcal{E}_O$ be the set of *in* and *out* events in the TD, $\mathcal{E}_I \bigcap \mathcal{E}_O = \emptyset$; the occurrence time of event $e \in \mathcal{E}$ is denoted as t_e.

Given two events a and b, there can be two **types** of constraints (for a constraint $c : a \to b$, a is called the source and b the sink of c):

Fig. 17.1   Types of constraints: (a) precedence, (b) concurrency

Precedence: $T_{min} \leq t_b - t_a \leq T_{max}$, $T_{max} \geq T_{min} > 0$ (i.e., $t_b - t_a \in [T_{min}, T_{max}]$).

Event a is a predecessor of event b; the graphical appearance of the constraint is in Fig. 17.1(a).

Concurrency: $-T_{min} \leq t_b - t_a \leq T_{max}$, $T_{max} \geq 0, T_{min} \geq 0$ (i.e., $t_b - t_a \in [-T_{min}, T_{max}]$).

Event a can occur concurrently with event b, but their time separation is within $[-T_{min}, T_{max}]$. The graphical appearance of this constraint is in Fig. 17.1(b). Let $C = C_{prec} \bigcup C_{conc}$ be the set of constraints in the TD. $\mathcal{E}$ and C define the directed graph $G(\mathcal{E}, C)$.

When two or more precedence constraints $c_{ij} : e_i \rightarrow e_j$ that have the same sink event e_j, their effect is combined conjunctively: The occurrence times t_j and all t_i, $e_i = \text{source}(c_{ij})$, satisfy **all** the constraints simultaneously. In what follows we consider conjunctive combinations only, since their declarative nature gives rise to non-causality in a specification. The extension to include the *latest* combination is straightforward [Girodias 97], since they are inherently causal, while the *earliest* combination introduces choices in the interpretation of causality. For completeness, these two constraint combinations are defined as follows:

Latest: $max_{i \in predecessors(j)}(T_{ijmin}) \leq t_j \leq$
$$\leq max_{i \in predecessors(j)}(T_{ijmax}), 0 < T_{ijmin} \leq T_{ijmax}.$$
Earliest: $min_{i \in predecessors(j)}(T_{ijmin}) \leq t_j \leq$
$$\leq min_{i \in predecessors(j)}(T_{ijmax}), 0 < T_{ijmin} \leq T_{ijmax}.$$

In the conjunctive system of precedence and concurrency constraints, the largest separation time intervals between any two events can be efficiently computed using an all-pairs-shortest-distance algorithm over a graph CG corresponding to the normalized form of the constraints in the form $t_i - t_j \leq s_{ji}$, where t_i, t_j are connected by an edge from t_j to t_i with the weight s_{ji}. Computing these separations is not very useful, however, unless we first correctly interpret the information provided by the TD.

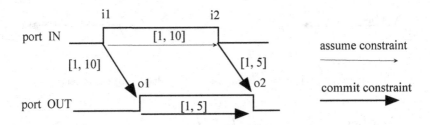

Fig. 17.2   A non-causal specification

Depending on whether an event is generated by the environment or by the device, the constraints have one of two possible **intents** [Khordoc 94]:

— *Assume* constraints (*required timing* [Brzozowski 91]): Such constraints delimit the expected or assumed behavior of the environment - the user of the device. The sink events of precedence constraints are of the *in* direction.

— *Commit* constraints (*produced timing* [Brzozowski 91]): These constraints determine the position of out events. The sink events of precedence constraints are of the *out* direction.

A concurrency constraint between an *in* event and an *out* event must degenerate due to other constraints into strict precedence or is illegal as it would violate the causality conditions (Section 3).

A TD specification can be checked alone for *consistency* [Brzozowski 91] which is a minimal form of realizability — it verifies that the constraint system has a solution and thus an occurrence time can be assigned to every event. Verifying that the specification of one device is compatible with the specification of another device is called *interface satisfiability* [Brzozowski 91] and it is done there by checking that for each pair of events related by an assume constraint c_a, the separation between the same pair of events as implied by the commit constraints is tighter than c_a. The notions of consistency and satisfiability of TDs are insufficient for either constructing correct implementations or for verifying that two or more implementations will interact correctly when built according to their local specifications. We now illustrate these weaknesses.

Consistency: Consider the TD shown in Fig. 17.2. $C = \{i_1 \rightarrow i_2\}_{assume} \bigcup \{i_1 \rightarrow o_1, o_1 \rightarrow o_2, i_2 \rightarrow o_2\}_{commit}$; the constraint system C is consistent and tight. When implementing a device according to this specification, the delay value for event o_1 after the occurrence of event i_1

has to be chosen from within the interval $[1, 10]$. However, this delay value depends on the selected occurrence time of the *in* event i_2 which may occur after o_1. For instance, if we choose $t_{o1} - t_{i1} = 1$ in the implementation, then if i_2 occurs such that $t_{i2} - t_{i1} \in (5, 10]$ (which is within the specified limits) then there is no feasible occurrence time for o_2. The environment would have to track the occurrence time of o_1 and produce i_2 after o_1. Symmetrically, the implementation of the device could decide to do the same, await i_2 and then produce o_1, leading to a deadlock. Clearly, such a specification is non-causal as the decisions made by the device implementation depend on future actions of the environment, and vice versa. A possible solution is that the designer of the environment and the designer of the device analyze the TD and then agree on a joint strategy. Their decision is not part of the specification, however, hence it is impossible to implement each device independently and to verify compatibility of two devices strictly based on the TD specifications. It thus follows that consistency and tightness of C are not sufficient to guarantee a realizable specification, we must also consider *causality*. This situation is similar to the problem of non-realizability of ideal filters (with square frequency response) where the output of the filter would have to start changing before the arrival of a change on its input.

Compatibility: In other works [Brzozowski 91], it has been proposed to verify that the (tightened) assume constraint values of one device include the (tightened) separations of the same actions produced (committed) by the other device. However, the method is exact only if each TD has ports and events of only one direction (i.e., one TD has *in* events, and the other one has *out* events only). Otherwise, it can yield a false negative answer to the compatibility check:

Consider the two TDs in Fig. 17.3. TD1 indicates a simple delay from an *in* event on port p1 to an *out* event on port p2, while TD2 drives p1 depending on the *in* event i_3 on port p2. Both specifications are realizable and devices built according to them can interact without violating the assumptions of their partners. Yet, the previously proposed interface satisfiability procedure [Brzozowski 91] will declare that the two TDs do not satisfy each other: the separation of the commitment between o_3 and o_4 in TD1 is potentially ∞, while TD2 assumes $[4, 10]$. However, when the devices are interconnected, the separation between i_3 and i_4 will fall within the assumed interval, because the separation between events o_1 and o_2 in TD1 is dictated by the behavior of TD2 (i.e., the commit of $[3,3]$ from i_3

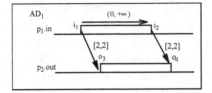 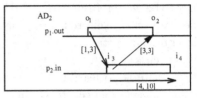

Fig. 17.3   Assumed [4, 10] between i_3 and i_4 in TD2 does not cover [0, +∞) between o_3 and o_4 produced in TD1

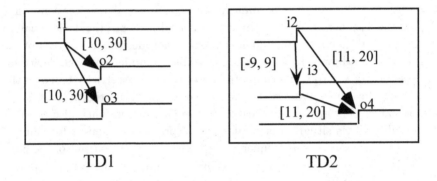

Fig. 17.4   A simple composition of commit constraints does not work here

to o_2). This discrepancy arises because the previously proposed satisfiability procedure [Brzozowski 91] does not take into account the composed behavior of the interconnected system.

A simple attempt to correct the satisfiability procedure can yield **false positive** answers to the compatibility check. For example, we could compose the commit constraints of the two systems and verify that the resulting event separations satisfy the assumptions made by each one of them. This is illustrated in Fig. 17.4: In TD1, the *out* events 2 and 3 can follow the *in* event 1 within [10, 30]. If an implementation is made according to this specification, it should be able to freely choose output delays in the specified intervals, for example, $t_{o2} - t_{i1} = 10$ and $t_{o3} - t_{i1} = 30$. In TD2, the *out* event 4 is to be produced within the interval [11, 20] from both of the *in* events 2 and 3, assuming that these events occurs within 9 units of time from each other. Both constraint systems are consistent and tight. If we now combine the commit constraints of TD1 and TD2 to obtain the total system behavior, and then compute the separation between events 2 and

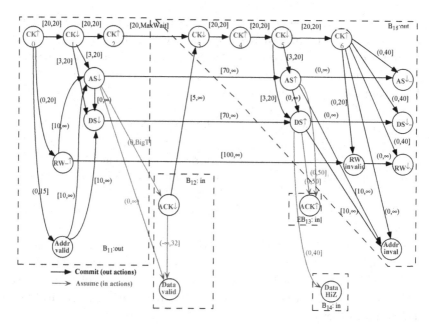

Fig. 17.5 Event graph of the READ cycle of the MC68360 processor (wait states are modeled by a delay interval between CK2 and CK3)

3, we find that the assumption $t_3 - t_2 \in [-9, 9]$ is satisfied. Yet, the implementation of TD1 mentioned above would violate the assumptions made by TD2 (and thus its implementation). This is because the convergent conjunctive commit constraints in TD2 determine the position of events 2 and 3 jointly with those of TD1. That is, the positions of events 2 and 3 in the implementation of TD1 would have to be determined jointly with the occurrence time of the future event o_4 produced by a different component of the system, clearly a non-causal task.

In the following, we propose three conditions that a TD must satisfy to be causal and thus realizable. These conditions are relatively easy to satisfy (e.g., the READ cycle of the MC68360 microprocessor shown in Fig. 17.5), and they lead to an efficient method for verifying the compatibility of TDs.

17.3   Causal Partitions over TD Specifications

As implied by the preceding section, realizability of a TD specification depends not only on the consistency of the TD constraint system, but also on whether the TD describes a causal system. We propose the following intuitive description of a causal TD: The decision that an *out* (*in*) event e should occur at time t_e according to the TD commit (assume) constraints must not depend on the occurrence instants of events that could be performed by the environment (device) at time $t \geq t_e$. We do not eliminate the possibility that the occurrence time of an *out* event depends on future *out* event times (provided that they themselves do not depend on future *in* events) and any past event times. This suggests that, in a causal TD, we should be able to partition the set of events into event blocks $\{B_i\}$ such that, within a block, local event-time computations are possible depending only on past events in preceding blocks. If such a partition exists then the TD has a causal interpretation in the above sense and is considered as realizable.

Let P be a partition over $\mathcal{E}$. For convenience, we also add a block that contains the single event *Origin* which is the source of precedence constraints $(0, \infty)$ to the first event on each port and is involved in no other constraint. **P is a causal partition (CP) if it satisfies the following three conditions:**

Condition 1 [event direction separation]: *In* and *out* events cannot share an event block B_i of P, i.e., $B_i \subseteq \mathcal{E}_I$ or $B_i \subseteq \mathcal{E}_O$.

The blocks delimit events that are controlled locally by either the device (*out* events) or the environment (*in* events). Let $\mathcal{B}_I$ and $\mathcal{B}_O$ be respectively the sets of the *in* and the *out* event blocks.

Let $E_{ij} = \{e_k \in B_i \mid \exists e_l \in B_j \wedge [c(e_k, e_l) \in C \vee c(e_l, e_k) \in C]\}$, i.e., E_{ij} contains all events from B_i related by a constraint to some event in B_j. Furthermore, let s_{kl} be the max. time separation from e_k to e_l (i.e., $t_l - t_k \leq s_{kl}$) computed over the complete constraint graph CG.

Definition 1 [order between two blocks]: $B_i < B_j$ iff $\forall e_k \in E_{ij} \; \forall e_l \in B_j \; s_{lk} < 0$, i.e., $t_k - t_l < 0$, meaning that the events in E_{ij} strictly precede all events in B_j, as determined from the complete constraint graph CG. When $B_i < B_j$ then the events in E_{ij} are called the *triggers* of B_j in B_i.

Condition 2 [partial order over P]: For all pairs of blocks B_i, B_j, if $E_{ij} \neq \emptyset$ then either $B_i < B_j$ or $B_j < B_i$.

Notice that when a partition P satisfies Condition 2 then $\{Origin\} < B_i, B_i \in$ P, and the set of constraints between (the events of) two blocks represents a unique cause-effect relationship through the trigger events and the associated constraints. We call *local constraints* of B_i the set of constraints that either (1) relate pairs of events in B_i or (2) relate events in B_i to the triggers of B_i.

To state the third and last condition, we need to define the execution semantics of the closed system (device . environment) described by a TD and its partition P satisfying Conditions 1 and 2. P can be viewed as describing two abstract machines: the **device** (M_{dev}) and the **environment** (M_{env}), consisting of the sets $\mathcal{B}_O$ and $\mathcal{B}_I$ of P, respectively. The machines communicate through the occurrence of events on the (shared) ports. When we consider the behavior resulting from this cooperation between the two machines, we shall denote the closed system behavior as $M_{dev}.M_{env}$. Either of these machines can be replaced by some other machine, e.g., an implementation I_{dev} or I_{env}. When we wish to describe properties of a closed system of this kind without distinguishing the components, we shall use M to represent the system.

Definition 2 [enabled block]: A block B is enabled when all its triggers have occurred. B becomes enabled at time t if the last trigger(s) occurred at t.

Definition 3 [fixing a block]: An enabled bock B is fixed when the occurrence times of all its events are assigned a value using the occurrence times of B's triggers such that the local constraints of the block are satisfied. If no such assignment exists then the block cannot be fixed.

Definition 4 [execution of M]: An execution of M proceeds as follows:

1. The time variable t is initialized to 0^- and the occurrence time of *Origin* is set to 0. As time advances do:
    While there are un-occurred events do:
    2. Advance time t to the nearest future event occurrence time (t_e). All events assigned to t_e occur.
    3. Fix all the blocks that became enabled at t_e and schedule their events to occur at their projected occurrence times $t > t_e$. If any block cannot be fixed then enter the *error state*.

Finally, we can state the last condition that characterizes a causal partition P over $G(\mathcal{E}, C)$ using the machine M induced by P.

Condition 3 [progress]: No execution of M enters the *error state*.

Next we show how we can effectively verify Condition 3 using the structure of P.

In the following, let pTD = (TD, P) denote a partitioned consistent timing diagram TD with the partition $P = \{B_i, i = 1, \ldots, n\}$. Let *trigger-pairs(B)* denote the set of all the pairs of triggers of block B, and $dist[B](e_i, e_j)$ denote the max. separation of the pair $(e_i, e_j) \in$ *trigger-pairs(B)* of some block B as computed over the union of the local constraints associated with the blocks $B \subseteq P$.

Theorem 1: M can progress if for all blocks $B \in P$ the following condition holds:

$$\forall (e_i, e_j) \in trigger - pairs(B) \ . \ [dist[P](e_i, e_j) < dist[\{B\}](e_i, e_j)]. \ \textbf{(Ex1)}$$

Outline of Proof: We can show that a block B can be fixed for any partial execution up to the fixing of B, provided that the max. separation between all its triggers is determined by the local constraints in blocks $B_j < B$ and is independent from the other constraints, including its local constraints. This can be then translated into the condition that the separation between the triggers as determined by the local constraints of B is strictly greater than that computed over all the constraints of the pTD. ◇

The importance of the theorem is that it gives an **operational method** for verifying Condition 3 of causality of a partition P. Since, regardless which of the causal partitions CP one chooses, all max. separations between pairs of events are determined using the entire constraint graph, the following property of a causal TD holds:

Property 1: A partition P satisfies Conditions 2 and 3 iff the set of solutions to the constraint system (i.e., the assignment of specific occurrence times to all events within the constraints of the TD) is equivalent to the set of possible timed traces of the machine M.

The implication of Property 1 is that a TD is either non-causal in our sense of the word (when no CP exists), or else all its possible interpretations "that make sense", i.e., all causal partitions of the TD are trace equivalent.

Finding a CP of a TD can be achieved by exhaustive enumeration of possible partitions during which impossible combinations are detected early using Conditions 1, 2 and 3 (Theorem 1), before even completing the entire partition. Heuristics based on reconvergence analysis of paths in $G(\mathcal{E}, C)$ can be used to speed up the search.

For example, Fig. 17.5 shows the event graph corresponding to the TD

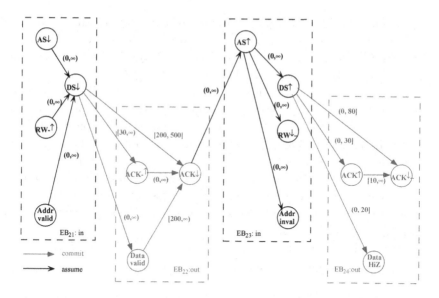

Fig. 17.6   Event graph of the read cycle of a slave device

of the READ cycle of the Motorola MC68360 processor. Blocks of a partition are delimited using dashed lines; e.g., the trigger of block B_{11} is the (implicit) *origin*, event AS↓ is the only trigger of block EB_{12}, events CK↑2 in EB_{11} and ACK↓ are triggers of EB_{15}, etc. Conditions 1 to 3 are satisfied, hence it is a causal partition. Similarly, Fig. 17.6 depicts a read cycle of a slave device that could be connected to the processor in Fig. 17.5. Again, a CP is shown in dashed lines.

The existence of multiple equivalent CPs can be important in the synthesis of interface controllers, because each more refined CP allows smaller implementation granularity with a more distributed control. Multiple CPs also provide the necessary choices for selecting a solution satisfying implementation requirements; however, these considerations are beyond the scope of this paper.

17.4   Compatibility of Realizable Timing Diagrams

Our discussion is limited to the compatibility of two devices, but it can be easily generalized. Consider causal timing diagrams TD_1 and TD_2, with event sets $\mathcal{E}_1$ and $\mathcal{E}_2$ respectively, of two interconnected devices such that

$\mathcal{E}_{I1} \subseteq \mathcal{E}_{O2}$ and $\mathcal{E}_{I2} \subseteq \mathcal{E}_{O1}$ (there are no free *in* events that would not be controlled from the other device). Let CP_1 (CP_2) be a causal partition of TD_1 (TD_2), and $\mathcal{B}_{I1}$ and $\mathcal{B}_{O1}$ ($\mathcal{B}_{I2}$ and $\mathcal{B}_{O2}$) the sets of its *in* and *out* event blocks, respectively. Let $C_{12a} = C_{1a} \bigcup C_{2a}$, the union of the sets of the assume constraints of TD_1 and TD_2. We wish to develop a procedure for verifying whether any implementation based on any CP_1 of TD_1 correctly interacts with any implementation based on any CP_2 of TD_2. Intuitively, a (causal) implementation I_{dev} of M_{dev} is a machine such that when connected to M_{env} it generates the *out* events at time t_{now} as a function of only the occurred *in* and *out* events. The resulting set of time assignments must satisfy the commit constraints of the TD, and any partial execution of $I_{dev}.M_{env}$ can progress. We can define an implementation I_{env} of M_{env} in a symmetrical way.

Definition 5 [CP-based implementation]: A CP-based (causal) I_{dev} satisfies the following two properties:

- *Safety*: I_{dev} fixes occurrence times of events in a block B of CP when its triggers occur and in agreement with the local commit constraints of B.
- *Liveness*: M $= I_{dev}.M_{env}$ satisfies Condition 3.

A CP-based implementation I_{env} of M_{env} can be similarly defined. Unless otherwise stated we assume in the following that all implementations are CP-based.

Definition 6 [compatible implementations]: Let I_{1dev} (I_{2dev}) be an implementation of M_{1dev} (M_{2dev}) of TD_1 (TD_2) based on some CP_1 (CP_2). I_{1dev} and I_{2dev} are compatible if:

(1) (Safety) Any execution of $I_{1dev}.I_{2dev}$ satisfies the constraints in C_{12a}, and
(2) (Liveness) M $= I_{1dev}.I_{2dev}$ satisfies Condition 3.

Definition 7: A set of constraints C_1 *satisfies* a set of constraints C_2 defined over the same events if the set of solutions admitted by C_1 is included in the set of solutions admitted by C_2.

Definition 8 [composed partition machine]: Let P_{12} be the composed partition over $\mathcal{E}_{1O} \bigcup \mathcal{E}_{2O}$ consisting of blocks and their local constraints in $\mathcal{B}_{O1} \bigcup \mathcal{B}_{O2}$, and let C_{12} be the union of these local constraints.

Theorem 2: If TD_1 and TD_2 are causal, the constraint system C_{12} is consistent, and C_{12} satisfies C_{12a} then any CP-based implementation of TD_1 is compatible with any CP-based implementation of TD_2.

The theorem provides operational means for verifying the compatibility of causal interface specifications and thus the compatibility of any of their CP-based implementations. It suffices to verify that the max. separations of events as determined by the composed system of commit constraints C_{12} are contained in the separations required by the assume constraints. In other words, the simple composition as we tried to use in the example related to Fig. 17.4 is correct provided that the participating TD's are causal. This is clearly not the case for TD_2 of Fig. 17.4, since the output block containing (necessarily) the only output event o_4 does not satisfy Theorem 1 — the separation between events i_2 and i_3 using the local commit constraints is $[-9, 9]$, while the separation of its triggers as determined by all the constraints is also $[-9, 9]$. This is not strictly included ($<$) in the former separation, hence the partition is not causal. Since there is no other possible partition that would satisfy the other two conditions, the TD itself is not causal. Consequently, the compatibility check done by composing the commit constraints of the two TDs produced a false positive answer. Note also that when TD_1 and TD_2 are compatible, then $\mathcal{B}_{O1} \bigcup \mathcal{B}_{O2}$ is a CP.

The composition of Figs. 17.5 and 17.6 as shown in Fig. 17.7 satisfies all assume constraints, and since both participating TDs are causal, the compatibility decision is definitive. It is interesting to note that essentially any partition of the MC68360 READ cycle that respects Conditions 1 and 2 satisfies Condition 3 (Theorem 1).

We conclude this section by highlighting an important property of causal specifications that follows from the main results presented above.

Property 2: Let CP $= \mathcal{B}_I \bigcup \mathcal{B}_O$ and CP' $= \mathcal{B}_I' \bigcup \mathcal{B}_O'$ be two causal partitions of a TD. Then $\mathcal{B}_I \bigcup \mathcal{B}_O'$ and $\mathcal{B}_I' \bigcup \mathcal{B}_O$ are also causal partitions of the TD.

This property tells us that the *Env* and *Dev* parts of the TD can be partitioned independently, knowing the complete constraint system. The proof is based on Theorem 2, by composing a mirror image of a TD with itself, while using one partition in the original TD and the other in the mirror TD. In a mirror image, *in* events become *out* events, t*assume* constraints become *commit* constraint, and vice versa.

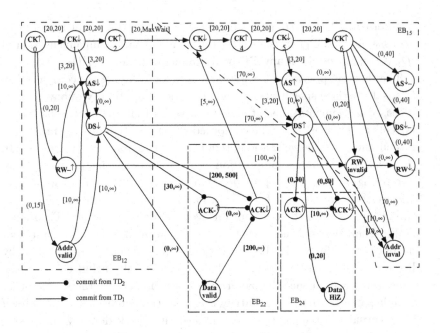

Fig. 17.7   Composition P_{12} resulting from Figures 17.5 and 17.6

17.5   Extension to Cyclic Behaviors

We consider process specifications similar to those of other works [Amon 93; Hulgaard 93], i.e., containing no behavioral choices, however in contrast to those works, the occurrence times of events in our case are determined using a conjunctive system of linear constraints as discussed earlier. Also, to determine causality, we must decide on a partition of the modeled system into components, each being responsible for producing a subset of the system events, as function of the occurrence times of past events and the constraints local to its (eventual) CP blocks. This is a generalization of the notion of input and output events, as the events of a component are its output events, and they are then input events to potentially all components. We wish to determine whether the specification of each component is causal in respect to the specification of the other components. To simplify the presentation and without loss of generality we consider systems consisting of two components, Indigo and Orange; their events thus belong to the sets I and O, respectively.

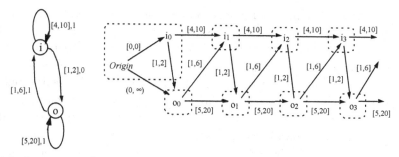

(a) Cyclic process specification.   (b) Unfolded graph till k = 3.

Fig. 17.8   A cyclic process

Definition 9 [conjunctive process graph]: A conjunctive process graph is a directed weighted graph $G(\mathcal{E}, R')$, where $\mathcal{E} = I \bigcup O$ are the nodes of the graph, and $R' \subseteq \mathcal{E} \times \mathcal{E}$ is the set of directed edges, $R' = \{a \xrightarrow{[d,D],\epsilon} b \mid \epsilon \geq 0 \wedge a \in \mathcal{E} \wedge b \in \mathcal{E}\}$, in which $[d, D], d \leq D$, is an interval timing constraint and $\epsilon \in \mathcal{N}$ is the occurrence index offset such that $\forall k.(d \leq t_{b(k+\epsilon)} - t_{a(k)} \leq D)$, where $x(j)$ denotes the j-th occurrence of event x.

As in other works [Amon 93], we can represent each of the iterations (the k-th occurrence of each event in $\mathcal{E}$) explicitly by unfolding the graph, i.e., we construct the infinite digraph $G^\infty(E, R)$ where E is the set of occurrences of events from $\mathcal{E}$, $E = \{e_k \mid e \in \mathcal{E}, k \geq 0\}$, and R is the set of edges obtained by instantiating each directed edge from R' at each occurrence index, i.e.:

$$R = \{a_k \xrightarrow{[d,D]} b_{k+\epsilon} \mid a \xrightarrow{[d,D],\epsilon} b \in R', \ k \geq 0\}. \tag{Ex2}$$

To maintain order in the multiple occurrences of an event, we also include sequencing constraints: $\forall a, \forall k \geq 0.(t_{a(k+1)} > t_{a(k)})$. To define the start-up or initialization of the process behavior we add an *Origin* node, with constraints having $d \geq 0$ to (some) instances of events $e \in \mathcal{E}$ of the unfolded graph. All the above constraints must be satisfied simultaneously. Figure 17.8(a) illustrates a simple cyclic process specification, and Fig. 17.8(b) shows a portion of its unfolding, including the *Origin* event. We could now ask the following questions:

. *Question 1:* Is the process specification consistent, i.e., is there a feasible assignment of occurrence times to all event instances (i.e., satisfying the infinite constraint graph G^∞)?

In the example of Fig. 17.8(b), we can progressively compute the max. separations between events related by the original constraints from Fig. 17.8(b) and see that after a few iterations, the separations do not change anymore, hence they cannot change at any time later. Is it so, however, in general? If consistent, are the separations always converging to a constant value, or can they oscillate or even diverge? Divergence would appear unlikely, since the same constraints keep repeating and we are adding more and more conjunctive constraints, albeit over new event occurrences.

Question 2: Is the process specification causal, i.e., can the occurrence times of O (I) events produced by the Orange (Indigo) component be computed without the knowledge of the occurrence times of future I (O) events? How to find a causal partition?

In the case of Fig. 17.8, a partition satisfying Conditions 1 and 2 can be easily found, and it is shown using dotted lines. There is only one other possible partition which differs from the one shown in Fig. 17.8(b) in that *Origin* and i_0 are in separate blocks, but this is a trivial distinction. We have not yet verified Condition 3, however. In general, we cannot apply Theorem 1 directly, because we do not necessarily know the max. event separations as computed over the infinite constraint graph, but we can use the procedure outlined in the proof of the theorem, i.e., we do not have to compute the separations over the entire G^∞: When checking Condition 3 for block B we need to compute the max. separations over all blocks $B_i < B$. Finding a CP in the general case is an open problem, though.

In our example, $B_0 = (Origin, i_0)$ causes no problem, but these events (with separation $[0, 0]$) are the triggers of block (o_0). The separation between Origin and i_0 using local constraints of (o_0) is $(-2, \infty)$ which is strictly larger than $[0, 0]$. The next trigger events are i_0 and o_0, and the next block to be considered is (i_1). The separation between i_0 and o_0 via the local constraints of (i_1) is $i_0 \xrightarrow{[-2,9]} O_0$, which strictly contains the separation of $[1,2]$ computed over blocks $\{(Origin, i_0), (o_0)\}$. The triggers are now i_1 and o_0, the separation between them is $o_0 \xrightarrow{[2,6]} i_1$ as induced by the current portion of the constraint graph. When the block (o_1) is included, we find, however, that the separation between o_0 and i_1 via the local constraints of (o_1) is $o_0 \xrightarrow{[3,19]} i_1$ which represents a tightening of the lower bound of the interval $[2, 6]$ determined over the past events. This means that to decide the occurrence time of i_1, one would have to consider the occurrence time of o_1 which occurs in the future of i_1 and in a different (and independent) component. Consequently, this partition is not causal. Since no other partition can be constructed due to Conditions 1 and 2, the specification itself is declared non-causal.

We can slightly modify the specification to make it causal, for instance, by changing the constraint $o \xrightarrow{[5,20],1} o$ to $o \xrightarrow{[2,10],1} o$. The verification remains the same until we must consider block (o_1). The separation between o_0 and i_1 via (o_1) becomes $o_0 \xrightarrow{[0,9]} i_1$ which strictly contains $[2, 6]$ computed over the past events. The triggers are now i_1 and o_1, and their tight separation is $i_1 \xrightarrow{[1,2]} o_1$ which is the same as between i_0 and o_0. Since the constraints and the block structure are the same from now on, the computed distances between event instances 0 and 1 repeat themselves, i.e., the partition is causal with $i_k \xrightarrow{[1,2]} o_k$, $i_k \xrightarrow{[4,8]} i_{k+1}$, $o_k \xrightarrow{[2,6]} i_{k+1}$, and $o_k \xrightarrow{[3,8]} o_{k+1}$.

Question 3: Given two events a and b, and an index offset ξ, what is the tightest interval $[\delta, \Delta], \Delta \geq \delta$, such that $\delta \leq t(b_{k+\xi}) - t(a_k) \leq \Delta$ when $k \to \infty$?

To answer this question we could first compute the shortest distances between the trigger events of one iteration to the trigger events of the next iteration, and then within an iteration between the trigger and the destination events of interest. Then all these segments can be combined to find the globally shortest path, etc., until no change in the distances is detected (if such convergence can be achieved in general(?)).

For example, suppose that we wish to compute the max. separation interval from i_k to o_{k+100}: For the max. distance we have, for instance, $t(i_{k+100}) - t(i_k) \leq 100 \times 8$, and $t(o_{k+100}) - t(i_{k+100}) \leq 2$, hence via this path we get $t(o_{k+100}) - t(i_k) \leq 802$. This is the tightest max. separation. The tightest (max. over all paths) min. separation is $(100 \times 4) + 1 = 401$, computed over the path $i_k, i_{k+1}, \ldots, i_{k+100}, o_{k+100}$. Hence $401 \leq t(i_{k+100}) - t(i_k) \leq 802, k \geq 1$.

Finally, if we change the constraint from *Origin* to o_0 to $Origin \xrightarrow{(0,1]} o_0$ then the tight separation of triggers i_0 and o_0 becomes $i_0 \xrightarrow{[1,1]} o_0$. This causes the triggers o_0 and i_1 to become separated by $o_0 \xrightarrow{[3,6]} i_1$ which is tighter than in the original example, and only when we reach the triggers i_1 and o_1 their separation becomes again $[1, 2]$. Thereafter we find again the same periodic behavior as before. The initial segment of the behavior consists of the occurrence indices 0 and 1 here, while in the former case it included only the occurrence index 0.

17.6   Conclusions

We have defined sufficient conditions for a specification based on timing diagrams to be causal and thus realizable, and we developed a method for determining causality of a TD. This leads to a procedure for verifying the interface compatibility of implementation classes of interacting TDs. The classes are based on causal partitions of the TDs. The results are useful for writing TD specifications, verifying interoperability of systems composed of interconnected components, and for implementing interface controllers.

We have also outlined how our method can be generalized to cyclic processes where conjunctive linear constraints relate the occurrence times of events. We are currently researching algorithms for the determination of a causal partition over the constraint graph G^∞ and for computing the max. separation of events in a (causal) graph. A natural extension of the approach is to include the *latest* constraints [Amon 93] in addition to the linear constraints. They are by their nature causal, and efficient methods exist for computing the shortest distances over linear and latest constraint systems [MacMillan 92; Girodias 95]. The inclusion of *earliest* constraints makes the problem of computing event separations NP-complete [MacMillan 92], however, it was shown [Girodias 95; Girodias 97] that CLP (BNR) Prolog and its power of relational arithmetic can be used to solve the constraint satisfaction problem and to perform the necessary exploration and backtracking.

Another application that we explore is the inclusion of causal partitions over linear timing constraint systems in Hierarchical Annotated Action Diagrams [Khordoc 93; Khordoc 94] in which composition rules are used over templates of elementary timed behaviors resembling timing diagrams. The semantics of HAAD are expressed using a real-time process algebra that includes exception and delayed-choice operators and can be extended to express causality. Finally, we envisage using our approach to include linear timing constraints into Message Sequence Charts [CCI 92].

Chapter 18

Experiments on a Fault Tolerant Distributed System

F. Pagani

18.1 Introduction

In this chapter, we report experiments, which have been carried out to formally validate some parts of the fault tolerance mechanisms of the Modulor system. This system was developed at ONERA jointly with the design of a flexible machine architecture. Its goal is to supply the hardware architecture with the ad-hoc software tools.

We have tackled the formal validation of the fault tolerance mechanisms for two main reasons. On one hand, previous versions of the implementation were found erroneous and the formal verification was a good way to check the correctness of the new versions. On the other hand, the selected mechanisms are rather typical in critical embedded systems; as we are involved in the formal validation of this kind of systems, we also aim by this experiment at choosing tools best suited to our purpose.

We have used several model checkers and a theorem prover [Doche 96]. We describe here the results obtained with two tools, Spin [Holzmann 90] and Kronos [Yovine 93], and show how these model checkers can be used in a complementary way. The chapter is structured as follows.

In a first part, we present an overview of the Modulor machine and the verified mechanisms, implemented in Occam.

In the second part, we explain how we used Spin to verify a synchronization algorithm in the nominal cases. In order to build algorithm models very close to the real ones, we have privileged "event based" specification languages. Spin was chosen because its specification language Promela allows to adequately represent communicating processes.

In the third part, we deal with faulty behaviors. We focus on the detection mechanism and explain how nominal models can be modified to take into account the fault presence. The detection mechanism combines real-time aspects and a strategy of message exchange. The communication strategy is validated using Spin whereas we use Kronos to take the real-time features into account.

The use of these two formalisms and tools has led us to make different abstractions of the system: abstraction of the time aspects and highlighting of the communication features in Promela and the complementary view in Kronos. In the last part, we discuss the proposed approach. Moreover, we have chosen to use automatic model checkers rather than interactive theorem provers. We conclude by an analysis of the validity of this last choice.

18.2 The Experiment Context

18.2.1 *The Modulor Project*

The research project named Modulor is directed towards the design and realization of a massively parallel, modular and dynamically reconfigurable computer, as well as the design and realization of the associated software tools. The architecture is a network of processors, and the physical reconfigurability of the hardware links connecting the processors allows us to satisfy two objectives:

- An optimal topology can be chosen for each application or each phase of the application.
- Reconfiguration capabilities can be used to offer the dynamic redundancy needed for fault-tolerant computing (the likelihood of the occurrence of a faulty processor grows with the number of such processors).

Modulor applications
The implemented applications take advantage of this flexibility even if we limited our objectives to explicit and quasi-dynamic reconfiguration. Programmers have to decompose their application into algorithmic phases. Each phase is a graph of communicating processes, written until now in Occam [Pountain 88], and necessitates a specific communication topology.

The model of message-based communicating processes of languages such as CSP [Hoare 85] and Occam handles explicit expression of parallelism in Modulor applications. Moreover it offers parallelism granularity needed for execution on a highly parallel architecture.

Until now, the interest of the approach has been validated by implementing algorithms ranging from numerical algorithms through to tree searching algorithms. The end target is embedded systems. More details about these experiments and their consequences for embedded systems can be found in [David 92] and [Fraboul 93].

Software tools

The development of a reconfigurable application is assisted by a set of tools.

A graphical interface allows the description of the communication graphs of a reconfigurable application. Then an automatic tool makes a partition, the initial graph is divided into loosely interconnected subgraphs according to the number of modules (the communication constraints do not exist inside each module). At last other tools proceed to the mapping of each process (on a processor) and of each communication link (on a network port), and the commands of the networks are computed. An initial validation phase has demonstrated that the architecture and these development steps are valid: if the program is partitioned (it depends of a good choice of the architecture's parameters), then the architecture can run it in spite of the fixed and economical constraints (see [David 92]).

The last step is the generation of a code (Occam), which will be compiled by the standard tools, and which includes:

- The synchronization mechanisms for the phase initialization and completion.
- The fault-tolerance mechanisms.

Our main concern is to validate this additional code.

18.2.2 *Analyzed Mechanisms and Their Properties*

Features of the network of processors

We call "net processors" the processors required by an application. The analyzed mechanisms have been designed for a network of processors having the following features.

All the net processors are connected by oriented links. Considering one link, we call "father processor" the source processor and "son processor" the target one. Each processor has at most four links.

Among the net processors, we distinguish the host processor. It is connected to one of the net processors and is supposed not to break down. It chooses the type of the following phase in accordance with the results of the previous one and synchronizes the beginning and the end of each phase.

Synchronization mechanisms

A round of exchanges of synchronization messages occurs at the phase initialization. The used algorithm allows each processor to receive the phase number to execute, and then to begin the algorithmic phase with the suitable topology.

During the synchronization, the host processor sends the phase number to its son and it begins the execution of the phase. A net processor waits for a phase number from one of its fathers. Then it sends it to all its sons and waits for it from all its potential other fathers; it can send and receive in parallel. Finally, when all the sending and receiving are completed, it begins the execution of the phase.

A second rendezvous system takes place at the phase completion, which is the completion of each process. Then the supervisor physically modifies the communication links for the next phase. At this time, a process of the network must not send messages, it is only waiting in the phase initialization process. All these mechanisms are only written with message exchanges.

Synchronization properties

The synchronization algorithm aims at triggering the computation of the phase and ensuring the consistent use of the exchanged data during the phase. Consistency is reached when a process does not receive synchronization messages while it is waiting for data messages.

So, in the context of our application, we may more precisely express these requirements by:

- P1: each process receives at least one synchronization message before beginning the phase computation;
- P2: each process does not receive any more synchronization messages after entering the phase computation.

This kind of behavioral properties can easily be expressed by using temporal logic.

Fault-tolerance mechanisms

Fault tolerance is achieved thanks to passive redundancy. Detection, isolation and recovery mechanisms have been implemented (fault detection, diagnostic and reconfiguration of the architecture in order to replay the phase). Details of the detection mechanism are given below since it is the main part we have been interested in for the validation.

We assume that *a processor is failed-silent, i.e. the failure of the processor, or of one of the four communication links, will correspond to the total stop of the processor*. Besides, every processor attempting to communicate with a faulty processor is blocked.

At the end of the phase, the topology of the processor net and the specification synchronization are such that if a processor becomes faulty, then its neighbors, and finally the host must become blocked.

In order to detect these deadlocks, the detection mechanism manages timers. Indeed, we also assume the user's code has been already validated and then *we assume given a maximum time for each phase execution*. So exceeding this limit is assimilated to an error, and means that a processor is faulty. The added mechanisms allow to detect the deadlock when timers over-step the given upper bound for the phase.

Finally, the protected code running on each net processor has the following structure. The code is divided in three processes (timer, server and phase) in order to control the state of the whole phase during its execution.

- The phase process is responsible for the execution of the phase. To achieve this execution, it communicates with the processors it is connected with. The phase process can break down at any time during the execution, or it can be blocked while trying to communicate with a processor that has broken down.

  A blocked phase is unlocked by an hardware mechanisms but cannot observe directly when this release occurs. So, the phase process asks the server the current state of the phase after each attempt of remote communication. If the state is not correct, it stops its execution. If it can finish its execution correctly, it signals the correct end to the server.

  The whole behavior of a secured phase is pictured by Figure 18.1. Boxes 3, 5 and 6 must be understood as sub-processes which perform parallel remote communications. The detail of one remote communication is given in Figure 18.2. The transition "!father k of i ok" stands for the

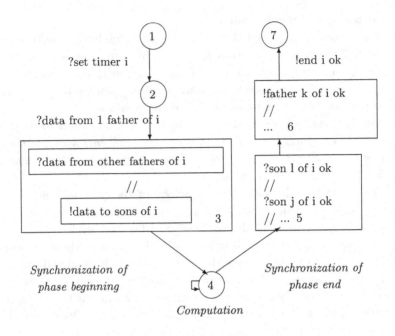

Fig. 18.1   Net process i

successful communication of the processors i and k during the synchronization at the phase end (box 6). "?k block i" models the external event which prevents the success of the communication.

- The server process updates the state of the phase (which becomes in error if a time-out has occurred). The server also gives the state of the phase to the phase process. Finally, it stops the timer when the phase ends correctly (Figure 18.3).
- The timer process initializes a timer at the beginning of the phase. When the execution of the phase does not finish in time (the process has broken down or is blocked), a time-out occurs and the timer process unblocks the phase process if necessary. Otherwise, the server process stops the timer (Figure 18.4).

Detection properties

We focus our experiment on the detection algorithm. We stated at least five requirements which express the correctness of this algorithm:

- P3: there is no wrong alarm, that is to say, when a fault is detected,

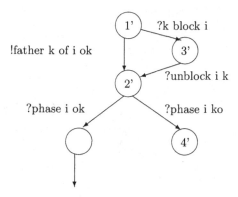

Fig. 18.2 Secured communication between the process i and the process k during the synchronization of phase end

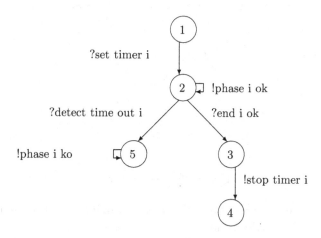

Fig. 18.3 Server associated to process i

one (at least) processor is effectively faulty. This statement may be refined in a local property and a global one:

"Each time a processor is blocked, then one of its sons or one of its father is faulty" and

"Each time the host is blocked then one of the processors is faulty"

- P4: Every failure is detected: "Each time a processor is faulty, the host knows it". This statement may be refined in:

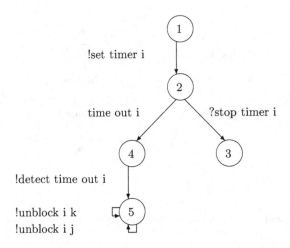

Fig. 18.4   Timer associated to process

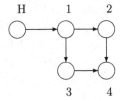

Fig. 18.5   Studied configuration

"Each time a processor is faulty, then one of its sons or one of its father is blocked or faulty" and

"Each time one of the processors is blocked or faulty then the host will be blocked"

- P5: The detection allows to resume communications between non-faulty processors: "All blocked processors will be unblocked or faulty".

18.2.3   *Targeted Experiments*

In all the experiences, we use a simple example of network configuration. We consider the host process (named H and sometimes numbered 0) and four net processes numbered 1, 2, 3, 4 connected as depicted by Figure 18.5.

In some cases, we consider the generalization of this example, that is to say we keep the same number of processors, but we parameterize the specifications by the connections (we describe the behavior of the processes without knowing which connections exist).

We have carried out most of the experiments for the verification with Spin on the same computer: Sparc Station 10 with a memory size of 32Mb and a virtual memory of 75Mb. For the detection verification with Kronos we used another computer: Sparc Station 2 with a memory size of 128Mb and a virtual memory of 280Mb.

18.3   Synchronization Validation with Spin

We now report how we use Spin to validate the synchronization at the beginning of the phase when no fault occurs.

18.3.1   *Promela*

The specification language offered by Spin, called Promela (protocol met-alanguage), allows to define mainly two kinds of objects: processes and communication channels between these processes. Channels are buffers of variable size (channels with size 0 implement synchronous communications). Two primitives are defined for communication: ! and ? which represent respectively the sending and receiving of a message along a channel. The detailed syntax is:

`channel!messagetype(value),channel?messagetype(variable)`

Processes are c-like procedures taking as parameters the channels along which they can send and receive messages. The body of the procedure describes the behavior of the process, using two control structures: `if` and `do` i.e. nondeterministic choice and loop with nondeterministic choice. Other constructions of interest are detailed in the following.

18.3.2   *Specification of the Particular Case*

The specification of the particular case is very simple. The behavior of each processor is described by a process. For example, let p2 be the process running on the processor 2. p2 is connected to two other processes by means of the two channels `in` and `out` (father and son). Its behavior is the following: it just waits for the phase number from its father (`in?numphase(np)`) and then sends it to its son (out!numphase(np)). This is described in Promela as follows:

```
proctype p2(chan in, out)
  { byte np;    /* declaration of variables*/

    in?numphase(np);  /*behavior*/
    out!numphase(np); }
```

Channels are initialized and sized in a kind of main program called init. Processes are also launched by this program:

```
init { chan c01 = [0] of { byte, byte };
  chan c12 = [0] of { byte, byte };

/*c01: name of the channel, [0] size of the channel,
{byte, byte}: size for the message type and for the value*/

  run p0(c01);
  run p1(c01, c12, c13);
  run p2(c12, c23);
  ........}
```

We see here that c12 is the channel connecting p1 and p2.

18.3.3 *Generalization*

For the generalization, we need a structure representing connections between processors. We choose to add connection processes to implement that. Then we can describe behaviors according to the existing connections.

Moreover, we have a great advantage in Promela: it offers parameterization possibilities. So we only have to write two connection processes, one when the connection exists (connectionyes) and one when there is no connection (connectionno). Then we launched these processes as many times as we need. And when connections change, only initializations have to be modified.

We also take advantage of parameterization for process description. We only have to write one procedure that describes the behavior of all the processes (except the host which has its own procedure) and to launch it as many times as the number of processors, with different parameters. So we have the following description:

```
proctype pgen (chan in1, in2, in3, in4, out1, out2, out3,
     c1, c2, c3, c4, co1, co2, co3)
 {

/* at least one reception of the phase number */
if
::c1?connect(5)->in1?numphase(np);received1=true;c1!connect(4)
::c2?connect(5)->in2?numphase(np);received2=true;c2!connect(4)
::c3?connect(5)->in3?numphase(np);received3=true;c3!connect(4)
::c4?connect(5)->in4?numphase(np);received4=true;c4!connect(4)
fi;

/* then other possible receptions and emissions in parallel */
do
::c1?connect(5)->in1?numphase(np);received1=true;c1!connect(4)
.......
::co1?connect(5)->out1!numphase(np);co1!connect(4)
....
od
 }
```

where the connection processes are as follows:

```
proctype connectionyes (chan c1, c2)
/*The process describes the evolution of the link c1-c2*/
{ c1!connect(5); /* The link exists */
 c2!connect(5);
 c1?connect(4); /* The link exists but has no interest*/
 c2?connect(4);
 c1!connect(3); /* The link does no longer exist*/
 c2!connect(3)
}

proctype connectionno (chan c1, c2)
{
  c1!connect(3);
  c2!connect(3)
}
```

Notes:

- The synchronization graph must be acyclic and a net processor has at most four links and at least one father. It is the reason why a generic process foresees at most four inputs links `ini` and three outputs `outi`
- We can see that the `if` is well-suited to express the fact that we do not know from which process the first number will be sent.
- The existence of a connection is represented by the sending of the number 5, while 3 stands for no connection. Once we have received or sent something, we change the state of the connection, by sending a message `connect(4)`, it is exactly how it is done in Modulor.

18.3.4 *Properties*

Spin offers several ways to express properties: assertions, validation labels and temporal properties (depending on the type of properties we want to express).

- Assert (condition): definition of an invariant that has to be satisfied. An invariant is local or global according to where the **assert** is placed (in a procedure or in the main program).
- Labels: some labels can be added in the code. There are three types of labels:
  - **end** labels: identify the correct endings of a process. When the process ends, it must be at a place marked by a **end** label.
  - **progress** labels: detect loops repeating infinitely without making any progress.
  - **accept** labels: express that something cannot happen infinitely often.
- Temporal properties: all the formulae of the linear temporal logic can be expressed in Promela using the primitive **never{body}** that specifies a behavior that can never happen.

For the example of the simple synchronization, the property can be expressed with the primitive **never** by specifying that:
P1: "it is never the case that a process begins the phase without having received the phase number"
P2: "it is never the case that it receives the phase number when it has begun the phase"

For the generalization, we have chosen to express it in a different way, using assertions. So the expression of P1 becomes:

```
assert ((received1 || !b1) && (received2 || !b2) &&
    (received3 || !b3) && (received4 || !b4))
```

The boolean `received` means that the current process has received the phase number from the process i and `!bi` (! is the negation in Promela) means that the current process is not connected to the process i.

18.3.5 *Verification*

RESULTS:

- simple case:

  ```
  P1: OK - 35 states - immediate result
  P2: OK - 35 states - immediate result
  ```

- generalization:

  ```
  P1: no response - 551229 states reached - out of
  memory
  ```

We can notice that Promela is well-suited for this application because it is a system based on communications and Promela was originally meant to describe protocols. Hence we had no problem to specify the synchronization mechanism.

18.4 The Analysis of the Detection Mechanisms

We now consider faulty behaviors and the way they are detected. The detection strategy is split into two parts: locally, a timer allows the local detection of communication errors; then, this detection is propagated through the network as a side effect of the synchronization algorithm at the end of each phase.

We aim at validating this detection mechanism by using:

- Spin to validate how the detection is propagated thanks to the communication strategy at the end of a phase,
- Kronos to validate the local detection with timers.

In both cases, we have to model faults and how they propagate.

18.4.1   *Validation of the Communication Strategy with Spin*

Promela is not meant to express real-time issues. So we abstract the specification of the detection mechanism with respect to time and timer. Hence we will not consider any local timer and consequently no local server. But we use the fact that asynchronous communication can be expressed in Promela to specify the releasing of processes by a server.

The behavior described by this abstract specification does not take into account all the aspects of the real system behavior and it will not allow us to validate every part of the real detection mechanism. But we are going to verify some properties (propagation of an error to the host) and we will see in the next section that Kronos verifies the other aspects (local detection) thanks to real-time features.

18.4.1.1   *Specification*

In the specification, we have one process to describe each processor, one process to describe each processor state (OK or faulty) and one server process. For the processor behavior, at each execution step (i.e. for each communication), we have a non-deterministic choice between three cases: the communication happens normally or the processor breaks down or it is blocked while trying to communicate and will be released by the server.

```
proctype p2(chan in1, out4, in4, out1, statepr, server)
{
  if
  :: in1?data(d)      /*normal behavior*/
  :: statepr!state(0); goto end /*breakdown*/
  :: server?release; goto end /*blocked and so released*/
  fi;
  ...
}
```

When a process breaks down, it sends a message to its state process (which represents the state of the process) and stops. The state process notices the breakdown to the server.

```
proctype stateproc(chan proc, server)
{
  do
  :: proc?state(0) ->
```

```
fault:     server!is_faulty; break
  od
}
```

Then the server sends an asynchronous releasing message to all the other processes (it must be an asynchronous message because if a process is not blocked (i.e. waiting for a releasing message), the server will never succeed in sending it the message).

```
proctype server(chan stateproc1, stateproc2, stateproc3,
  stateproc4,proc0, proc1, proc2, proc3 proc4, in)
{
  if
  :: stateproc1?is_faulty -> proc0!release; proc2!release;
        proc3!release; proc4!release
  :: stateproc2?is_faulty -> proc0!release; proc1!release;
        proc3!release; proc4!release
  :: stateproc3?is_faulty -> proc0!release; proc1!release;
        proc2!release; proc4!release
  :: stateproc4?is_faulty -> proc0!release; proc1!release;
        proc2!release; proc3!release
  :: in?ok
  fi
}
```

When the phase ends correctly (i.e. when the host process receives a message from the process 1 showing it has finished the ending synchronization), then the host process sends a message (ok) to the server (on the channel in).

18.4.1.2 *Properties and Verification*

We have considered the case where only one processor can break down (when we take the breakdown of all the processors into account, no verification can be achieved because the system abort due to a lack of memory). In this case, we have proved that "if a breakdown occurs, the host process knows it" (part of P4).

```
never { stateproc[8]:fault;
    p0[1]:endok}
```

This means that the behavior specified in the {} will never occur, that is to say: it will never be the case that the process 2 breaks down (its state process reaches the label `fault`, we add this label at the line where it receives a message meaning process 2 has broken down) and then process 0 reaches the label `endok` (which characterizes the correct end of the phase).

We have also proved that P5: "if a breakdown occurs, all the stuck processes will be released". We did it by adding `end` labels and verifying that all the processes reach these labels.

RESULTS:

```
P4: OK - 4483 states - almost immediate result
P5: OK - 4483 states - almost immediate result
```

18.4.2   *Validation of the Local Detection with Kronos*

18.4.2.1   *Timed Automata*

A real time system is modeled in Kronos * [Daws 96] by a set of timed automata [Henzinger 94b] running in parallel and synchronizing on transitions of the same label. Each of these automata represents the behavior of one system component and the behavior of the whole system can be obtained by computing the parallel product of these automata.

A timed automaton is basically a labeled transition graph extended with variables called clocks. A clock has a positive real value. It can be set to zero by some transitions and then its value represents the elapsed time since it has been reset. Time progresses only in the nodes of the system whereas transitions between nodes are supposed instantaneous. A clock is local to an automaton in the sense that it can only be reset by transitions belonging to this automaton. However, all the clocks of the system are synchronized, i.e. their values increase at the same rate.

Clock values are used to constrain both transitions and states of the automaton. On one hand, temporal constraints on clocks are the possible guards of the automaton transitions: they give the clock values for which the transitions are enabled. On the other hand, temporal constraints may occur in nodes and give so the limits of the time progress in the corresponding states.

Moreover, each node of an automaton can be labeled by boolean variables that are supposed to be true in that node. They are particularly useful to express properties over states.

---

*http://www-verimag.fr/TEMPORISE/kronos

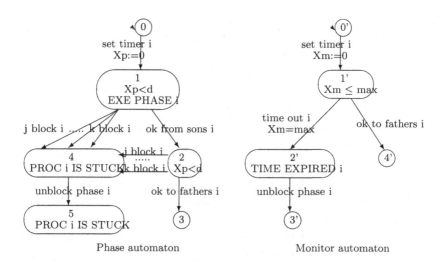

Fig. 18.6   Phase and monitor processes of processor i (partially represented)

Finally, a state of the system is defined by a set of control locations (one for each automaton of the system) and the value of each clock. Since clocks take their values in the positive real number set, the set of states is infinite.

18.4.2.2   *Specification*

The processor behavior is modeled by the following set of automata:

- one for the phase process (left automaton in Figure 18.6),
- one for each link between this processor and its neighbors (very close to the automaton of Figure 18.2),
- one for the monitor (timer+server, right automaton in Figure 18.6)
- one for the processor configuration (Figure 18.7).

The fault of a processor i is modeled by a particular transition *fault i*, respecting the following properties:

- hardware breakdown: The transitions *fault i* must appear on each automaton of the processor.
- irreversible: The transitions *fault i* must lead to a deadlock.
- unpredictable: They must be enabled in every states of each component.

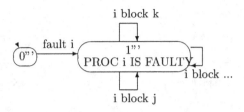

Fig. 18.7   Configuration of processor i

Thus, we chose to add in every automaton and from every node, a undeterministic choice between the nominal behavior of the system and the fault, leading to a new node. For sake of readability, these transitions and the new node are not drawn on the automata of Figure 18.6. Besides, we added an automaton, named "configuration" (see Figure 18.7), that records the current state of the processor and blocks its neighbors when the processor is faulty.

We use two clocks Xp and Xm to specify precisely the role of timers in the detection mechanisms. Xp measures the exact duration of a phase computation in the phase process. In the nominal cases, this duration does not exceed d. This feature is modeled by the temporal constraints occurring in nodes 1 and 2. Xm measures the estimated duration in the monitor process. In the nominal case (node 1'), this duration is equal or less than max. Of course, it is supposed that $d \leq max$.

Moreover, these temporal constraints and the transition guards ensure that the timer on a processor i expires only after a fault of one of i neighbor. The transitions *set timer i* synchronize the value of clocks Xp and Xm at the beginning of the phase computation. Then, the phase and the monitor processes reach simultaneously the control points 1 and 1'. While the phase remains at 1, $Xp = Xm$, $Xp < d$, the guard $Xm = max$ can not be satisfied and then the transition *time out* can not be enabled. Time can go beyond d only after a transition j *block i* has been taken. Thus, a time-out can occur only after a fault.

18.4.2.3   *Properties*

The real-time logic TCTL (Timed Computational Tree Logic) [Alur 90b], a real-time extension of the branching time logic CTL, is used in Kronos to specify properties.

- P3 (wrong alarm, local to processor 1 and global):

$$\forall\sqcup(TIME\_EXPIRED\_1 \rightarrow$$
$$(PROC\_2\_IS\_FAULTY \vee PROC\_3\_IS\_FAULTY))$$
$$\forall\square(TIME\_EXPIRED\_h \rightarrow (\bigvee_{i\in1,2,3,4} PROC\_i\_IS\_FAULTY))$$

- P4 (failure of processor 2 is detected):

$$\forall\square(PROC\_2\_IS\_FAULTY \rightarrow \forall\Diamond(TIME\_EXPIRED\_1))$$

- P5 (stuck processor 2 is unstuck):

$$\forall\square(PROC\_2\_IS\_STUCK \rightarrow \forall\Diamond PROC\_2\_IS\_UNSTUCK)$$

18.4.2.4 Verification

The verification mechanisms offered by KRONOS are based on model-checking and handle the infinite number of states by defining symbolic states. It is very important to note that the verification complexity does not depend on the values given to the temporal bounds, but rather on the relative ordering between clocks. The verifications have been lead with KRONOS 2.2 [Yovine 97].

By modeling each processor of the network of the configuration presented by Figure 18.5 (5 processors including the host one), we managed to built with Kronos a system with 11743 states and 48352 transitions. Nevertheless, the verification of the properties could only be lead on a system composed of 4 processors (3190 states and 14148 transitions).

We can verify P3 but did not succeed for P4 and P5. The P4 and P5 properties are known under the name of inevitability properties. It is very difficult to verify them with Kronos as soon as time progress in nodes is not constrained. Indeed, the guards associated with transitions indicate clocks values for which transitions can be executed and not the time at which they must be executed.

RESULTS

```
P3 (local): true - 2,860s
P3 (global): true - 3,020s
```

Moreover, we tried to verify the P3 properties on a wrong model (6528 states, 31344 transitions), in which the estimated maximal duration of a phase computation is too short. We obtained the following results:

```
P3 (local): false - 30,710s
P3 (global): false - 34,040s
```

This last evaluation shows clearly that the right estimation of the maximal duration of the phase computation is critical for the correctness of this algorithm. It is typically the kind of properties Kronos is interesting for. Nevertheless, we did not manage to verify these properties on the whole system we built from 5 processors because of memory constraints.

18.5   Discussion

We had a practical problem: validate a distributed system quite complex with existing tools as efficiently as possible. We haven take advantage of the system features to propose a pragmatic approach:

- build models of algorithms close to the existing codes by means of an appropriate language: Promela,
- verify all requirements that can be evaluated using the Promela specifications,
- complete the missing verifications (about timing aspect) using a complementary tool, Kronos and the associated specification language,
- use model checkers (Spin and Kronos) to achieve the validation for free with automatic tools.

We thought the experiment would be straightforward. We only have two different kinds of processors, the host and the other ones. Synchronization and fault-tolerance mechanisms are similar for every standard processors. Moreover, the size of the Occam code makes easier the readability and understanding of the mechanisms.

The validation of the synchronization in nominal cases demonstrated the expressiveness of Promela and the adequacy of the choice for our case. We appreciated not only the control structure (selection and use of general guards) to deal with tricky parallel combinations of actions but also the parameterized specification, factorizing the specification effort and the readability.

The validation of the detection shown also that asynchronous communication of Promela is quite adapted to fault modeling. It also confirmed that timed automata were well suited to deal with timing hypothesis.

However, the problem complexity is greater than expected. The likelihood of connection and the induced possible communications are very numerous. Moreover, the occurrences of fault increase the considered cases.

The number of states explored with the tools gives an idea of the problem complexity.[†] Even for a given configuration of the communication network, the combination of the event occurrences is complex enough to demonstrate the need for validation tools.

So, the uses of model checkers were limited. First, model checkers were applied to abstractions of the existing codes in the worse cases. In order to improve our validation results, it is necessary to assess these abstractions.

Then, we only succeeded in dealing with a particular network configuration of at most five processors. The memory consummation was particularly important with the Kronos version used. Since our experiment, new Kronos versions are under developed to overcome such limitations. They integrate several new techniques such as partial order techniques [Pagani 96] [Pagani 97], on-the-fly methods [Bouajjani 97], optimization of the number of clocks [Daws 96] and binary decision diagrams [Bozga 97].

Finally, even if the analyzes of particular configurations are interesting to debug the algorithms, we need to prove the stated properties in any case of configuration of the communication network for N modules of processors. We cannot achieved this result with model checker but we did it using a logical specification in TLA and a theorem prover [Doche 96]. We think that the logical specification allows us to deal better with the notion of "system configuration". This notion is purely state-based and can be expressed easily by temporal logic.

To conclude, one of the most interesting point is the way we have distributed the validation in complementary lemma. The approach raises two questions. On one hand, how general is this decomposition? We believe the decomposition in local proofs and global proofs follows naturally the design approach of Modulor and a wide range of distributed systems in general. The designers often propose well-identified components, with limited interactions to overcome the lack of global clock or to master the system complexity. Each components must guaranty some services so that the whole system behaves correctly.

On the other hand, how can we formally assembly the result to conduct the whole proof? Indeed, we have achieved a similar proof in a rigorous framework using a compositional specification of the detection mechanisms [Seguin 96]. The compositional specification was composed of a set of spec-

---

[†]We did not give precise information on the computation duration because only two cases arose: either the verification succeeded quite immediately or it failed.

ifications (logical theories) combined in a categorical framework. In this study, the specifications was homogeneous and the proof was manual. Now, we would like to tackle properly heterogeneous specifications such as timed automata and Promela text, and combine theorem proving with model checking. One track we follow is the extension of modular specifications [Michel 97], which could encapsulate the heterogeneous specifications and link the proofs through homogeneous interfaces between modules.

Acknowledgments

We would like to thank Marielle Doche for helpful comments and long discussions.

Chapter 19

Specifying Multi-Level Security for an Embedded Real-Time Control System

Jim Alves-Foss, Deborah Frincke and Surekha Ghantasala

Abstract: Multi-level data security is a requirement in many of today's advanced, real-time embedded systems. Current approaches to meeting multi-level security requirements are based on expensive custom or proprietary hardware and software. However, real-time embedded systems are evolving towards open-system architectures and commercial off-the-shelf (COTS) hardware and software. It is therefore important to develop a standard method for evaluating the security aspects of real-time embedded systems, and for handling black-box COTS components in proprietary systems. This chapter presents a brief analysis of multi-level data security in the context of a simplified exemplary real-time, embedded avionics system and discusses mechanisms that can be used to solve the problem of integrating COTS components into a secure system. As is required of high assurance secure systems, a formal model of one such mechanism based on the use of a trusted network interface unit mechanism is provided using the LOTOS formal specification language.

19.1 Introduction

Many modern real-time embedded systems must be designed to handle data at a variety of sensitivity levels, implying that their designers must consider multi-level data security issues. Avionics systems, for example, often include components that manage highly sensitive data as well components that handle less sensitive data. Approaches to managing multi-level secure data in embedded systems are based on expensive custom or proprietary hardware and software. However, real-time embedded system designs are evolving towards open-system architectures and commercial off-the-shelf (COTS) hardware and software. Such designs cannot rely on proprietary solutions. Therefore, it is necessary to develop a standard method for combining COTS components in open architectures. Further, it is important to determine a methodology for evaluating the security aspects of real-time embedded systems. This chapter presents a brief analysis of multi-level data security in the context of a simplified exemplary real-time, embedded avionics system and discusses mechanisms that can be used to solve the problem of integrating COTS components into a secure system. As is required of high assurance secure systems, a formal model of one such mechanism based on the use of a trusted network interface unit mechanism is provided using the LOTOS formal specification language.

Between the 1960s and the 1980s, aircraft such as the F/A-18 were designed as a set of remotely-located processing subsystems under the control of a central mission computer. This design strategy is known as a federated architecture. In such systems, most processing is performed by this central computer. However, in recent years the trend has been towards a more distributed architecture. In these distributed avionics systems, remote subsystems perform preprocessing functions and a central computer is used to perform the final processing and data integration. Distributed architecture are considered advantageous because the central computer no longer needs to communicate as frequently with the subsystems, reducing the aircraft data bus traffic. Further, performing operations on the subsystems will reduce the workload of the central processor and permit increased parallelism, yielding improved overall performance.

As well as using federated architectures, earlier avionics systems were implemented as closed system architectures. These proprietary architecture standards and specifications were not publicly available. However, because the proprietary nature of closed systems effectively locks out competitors and often results in higher costs, in the 1990s aircraft designers have moved towards open system architectures. In an open system architecture, all aspects of the system interfaces are defined and made generally available. Designers can thus independently develop subsystems or modules to be included in the architecture. Ideally, a component can be installed in an open system with only minimal integration. The move to open systems is based both on a desire to increase competition by avionic system manufacturers and by current Department of Defense (DoD) policies. As an example, the next fighter aircraft to be developed is slated to have an open system architecture. The program that is to lead to the development of the new airplane is called the Joint Advanced Strike Technology program. Along with a push for open systems, the DoD is interested in maintaining the security of the integrated system.

There are some drawbacks to using open system architectures. For instance, one advantage of open systems is lower cost due to competition among developers and higher product volumes when the same open architecture is used in more than one system design. However, if a system is to remain open, optimization for an intended application is difficult. In a closed architecture it was possible to optimize a "point solution" for some particular application. Thus, there are some concerns that the open system architecture will result in decreased performance. Further, there may exist a requirements penalty because commercial off-the-shelf (COTS) components may not provide all of the desired properties of the custom components found in closed federated or integrated systems, or may include additional features that are not needed. For instance, they may provide all of the required functions and performance, but may be lacking in non-functional properties such as fault-tolerance, reliability, or security. Fortunately, the increased speed and sophistication of microprocessors has made the performance of non-optimzed open systems acceptable despite the lack of point solutions. COTS components can also be enhanced through the use of additional special-purpose components (e.g., a voting mechanism that provides a level of fault tolerance through redundancy). Thus, it seems likely that the trend towards open systems will continue.

There are several issues that must be resolved when moving from closed systems built from all-proprietary components towards an open system built from COTS components. The security of a system will be affected. For example, the COTS components may not have been developed with the same level of assurance as the locally produced components, and may not have been designed to handle multi-level secure data. Thus, it is necessary to develop a methodology that safely combines trusted components, untrusted components, single-level secure components, and multi-level secure components. As an example of understanding and managing the effects of a transition to distributed open-system architectures, this chapter discusses our analysis of multi-level data security in the context of real-time, embedded computer systems and presents solutions to the problem of integrating off-the-shelf components into a secure system. Even if security is not of concern, the same controls that limit the flow of information in a secure system can be applied to limit the flow of information to restrict possible interference from a faulty unit.

Section 19.2 introduces an exemplary avionics system with a distributed, open-system architecture used to illustrate many of the security concepts discussed later. Section 19.3 provides a brief overview of the Department of Defense "Orange Book" criteria for the evaluation of multi-user general-purpose trusted computer systems and the adaptation of these criteria to multi-level, real-time embedded computer systems. Section 19.4 provides a further discussion of multi-level security in the context of this chapter. A brief overview of the LOTOS specification language as proposed for the assurance and documentation of such systems is presented in Section 19.5. An example of a system configuration and high-level LOTOS specifications for a secure, multi-level, real-time embedded computer system are provided in Sections 19.6 and 19.7.

19.2   An Avionics Real-Time Embedded Computer System

In this section, we discuss our exemplary avionics system, designed as a distributed system that supports a multi-level security policy. A high-level block diagram of the avionics system is shown in Figure 19.1. An expanded view of the integrated processor is shown in Figure 19.2(a), while Figure 19.2(b) depicts one possible implementation of a single signal processor.

The figures show a collection of sensor preprocessors, an integrated core processor, mass memory, and connections to a variety of subsystems such as flight controls. The sensors and subsystems operate and provide data at different sensitivity levels. From a security standpoint, it would be easier to manage this multi-level data if it were possible to assign specific processors and mass memory to specific security levels, so that no information flow between components at differing levels were possible. However, in an avionics system, it is important to maintain a minimal size and weight for the system itself, to reduce the number of unique processor designs, and to provide increased fault tolerance. Therefore, in our design the data processors and signal processors are interchangeable and assigned to tasks dynamically, as

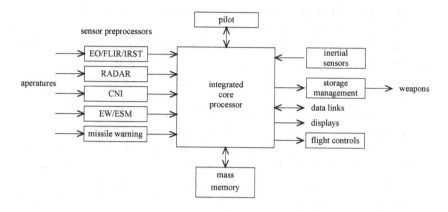

Fig. 19.1   Block diagram of an avionics system

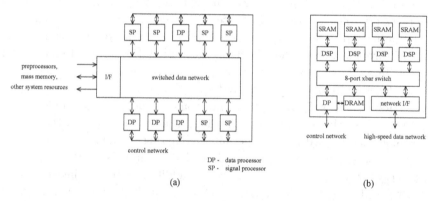

Fig. 19.2   Block diagram of (a) an integrated processor and (b) a signal processor

is the mass memory. Thus, it will be necessary to use a different technique for preventing information flow or contamination.

To illustrate our point, consider the block diagram in Figure 19.1. Assume that one of the data links operates at a lower security level than the RADAR subsystem. Both data link and RADAR subsystem may utilize different data processors or signal processors (see Figure 19.2) at the same time, passing information across the data and control networks at different security levels. They may even use the same data processors or signal processors at different times. In order to maintain security, the data processors and signal processors must be capable of operating at various security levels. This will require that safeguards be built into the hardware and software that prohibit access to secure data by tasks that are not cleared for access to that data. This must be the case whether that data exists in network messages or in processor memory as the result of a previous task. An even more extreme example of the complexity of assuring data security would be when all four of the digital signal processors (DSPs) shown in Figure 19.2(b) operate at different security levels simultaneously.

Proposals for designs of general-purpose secure distributed system architectures vary according to the services offered by the system. In a simple case (e.g., the distributed avionics system shown in Figure 19.1 and Figure 19.2), each processor can support a process or, more generally, several processes operating at the same security level. This situation is described by [Rushby 83], who note that here the burden of assuring security can fall on the network. The network (i.e., the switched data network and the control network in Figure 19.2) can mediate all communication between processors to ensure only those intended to communicate with each other are permitted to do so. Indeed, since users are permitted to communicate only through a few well-defined interfaces the attainment of security for this simple (albeit useful) distributed system is easier than would be the case for a multi-user integrated system.

More complex distributed systems would include multi-level file servers [Rushby 83; Alves-Foss 98] or multi-level processors. Some of these more complex distributed systems permit the sharing of services or processors across the system; processors could be shared through process migration. Such systems require secure processors in addition to trusted interprocessor services. To evaluate the relative security of a multi-level system, one must turn to a standard set of guidelines. In the following section, we outline one such set of guidelines produced by the Department of Defense, and suggest how they should be interpreted for a real-time embedded system environment. The reader should note that the reasoning used in the following section also applies to other criteria such as the Canadian Criteria, the European Criteria and the Common Critieria.

19.3   The TCSEC Guidelines

In 1983 the Department of Defense issued the *Trusted Computer System Evaluation Criteria* (TCSEC) [Dep 83; Dep 85], which defines a criteria for evaluation of trusted computer systems. This document, popularly known as the "Orange Book," defines four divisions of certification. These certifications are labelled from A to D, with Division A as the highest classification and division D is the lowest. Divisions contain one or more subdivisions. Within each division the higher numbered subdivisions consist of additional requirements beyond the requirements of lower numbered subdivisions. Thus, division A1 is the highest defined subdivision, followed by B3, B2 and so on until subdivision D1.

These guidelines were developed for several reasons. First, there were to provide a standard set of security metrics against which a system could be evaluated. Second, the guidelines were intended to make it easier to specify security requirements in procurement documents. Finally, the guidelines were intended to influence vendors to include desirable security features in their products. The intent was to require that products be evaluated against the TCSEC guidelines and assigned a security certification level. To that end, the TCSEC guidelines specify a set of system properties and assurance tasks. These properties cover security concerns ranging from types of security policies to accountability issues. The system properties themselves are specific to a system configuration and are geared for a multi-user general purpose operating system. Network concerns were not included in the original TCSEC.

Within each division of certification (A through D) are a set of requirements. These requirements specify the necessary behavior, design, and operation of the computing system. Each of the requirements is classified into one of four categories: security policy, accountability, assurance, and documentation. In this section we examine the guidelines for each of these categories with respect to a real-time embedded system environment. For a complete discussion of the guidelines for these categories with respect to a real-time embedded system environment [Alves-Foss 97].

19.3.1 *Security Policy*

The first category of the TCSEC evaluation is the security policy, which provides guidelines for the evaluation of discretionary access controls (user-specified controls on who may have read/write access to objects), object reuse, labeling*, import and export of labeled objects, and mandatory

---

* An object's label indicates its classification and a subject's label indicates its clearance. Only subjects having an appropriate clearance may read/write an object having a given classification.

access controls (system-specified controls on who may manipulate objects).

Security Policy guidelines are based on the concept of a *security classification* and the appropriate labeling of subjects and objects. A classification consists of a security level (e.g., top secret, classified) and a security compartment (e.g., NATO, nuclear). The compartment is sometimes referred to as the "need to know" component of the label. Subjects are similarly labeled with a clearance. The security policy specifies a relation between classifications and clearances. For example, let L be a set of security classifications, $L_i \in L$ be the classification of processor i, and $\prec$ be a binary operator on the elements of L such that the transitive closure of $\prec$ on L, written $(L, \prec)$, is a partial ordering (this requires that $\prec$ be antisymmetric, transitive, and non-reflexive.) A security policy for a system can be defined in terms of a particular $(L, \prec)$, such that entities with a security clearance L_i are permitted to view information classified at L_j if and only if $L_j \prec L_i$, where L_i is said to *dominate* L_j. Such a policy is often viewed in terms of a lattice where there exist both a system-high classification that dominates all other classifications and a system-low classification that is dominated by all other classifications.

Security Policy for the Avionics System. In the exemplary Avionics System of Section 19.2, it is possible to revise some of the Security Policy requirements. For example, one of the major assumptions of the TCSEC guidelines is the existence of user-created objects, including files and programs running on behalf of the user. In a real-time embedded system environment, such as the avionics system presented, the core processing element of the system typically consists of a static set of well-defined processes and processing elements. Without such a well-defined set it is not possible to ensure that the required real-time performance constraints of the system will be met. The set of processes currently executing is based on the task(s) requested of the operator (pilot). As these tasks change, so do the current set of executing processes. Thus, we do not have to consider random dynamically constructed objects.

Further, given our sample avionics environment, we do not have to deal with the general concept of *users* in the system. The core processing system has no users, but rather processes information according to a set of well defined functionalities (the pilot's requested tasks). There are no user files, discretionary access controls or dynamically created processes (although processes may be dynamically executed, they are created from a well-defined set of tasks and are not dynamically created in the general sense.) Understanding these specifics of the system allows us to trivially satisfy several of the TCSEC criteria as they relate to providing services to users. For instance, without users it is unnecessary to provide either discretionary access control or user accountability. We must still address the problems of valid interprocess communication and information flow between the pre-established tasks, but need not be concerned with the harder problem.

As mentioned earlier, open system architectures present unique challenges for designers of secure computing systems. Although not intuitively obvious, an open system architecture is a viable alternative in a secure computing environment (especially a distributed environment). Research [Rushby 83; Stoneburner 89] has shown that the use of untrusted, single-level systems, incorporated into a larger multi-level distributed system can still result in a secure system. Specifically for our avionics system, if we allow processors to execute at a single security classification at any point in time, we can define a security policy for the system according to the security classification of the processors. We can state this more formally. Let P be the set of processors in the system and $L_i \in L$ be the classification of processor $P_i \in P$. We can define the *security operator* $S_{i,j} \equiv L_i \preceq L_j$, where $S_{i,j}$ is true, according to the security policy, if and only if processor P_i is permitted to send information to processor P_j.

19.3.2 *Accountability*

The second category of the TCSEC evaluation is accountability, which provides guidelines for the evaluation of identification and authentication mechanisms, auditing, and trusted path access. As the embedded system does not have contact with users, we can avoid the need for authentication and user identification in the system. The real-time system must still maintain an audit trail of accesses to the objects it protects. Read access to the audit data is limited by physical means. The variety of events that must be recorded is reduced for a real-time embedded system because of the lack of dynamically created objects.

19.3.3 *Assurance and Documentation*

The third and fourth categories of the TCSEC evaluation is assurance, and documentation, respectively. Assurance provides guidelines for the evaluation of the system life cycle; including system design, testing, analysis, management, and maintenance. Documentation provides guidelines for the evaluation of the system documentation, both from the user and management perspective as well as from the design and maintenance perspective. These categories are system independent. They provide a mechanism to ensure that reasonable effort was made throughout the system life-cycle to provide correct implementation and operation of the system with respect to the security policy and accountability guidelines. Although the amount of documentation, testing and verification involved may vary among systems, these requirements must be met for every system evaluated. In the next section, the formal LOTOS specification language is presented as a tool that can be used to meet security assurance and documentation requirements as required at the highest levels of assurance defined in the TCSEC (B3 and A1).

19.4   Multi-Level Security

One definition of a secure system requires that it protect the information it stores from unauthorized release or modification. The Multi-level Security Policy (MLS) as described in the TCSEC (for B1 and above) associates security levels with subjects (e.g., program, user) and objects (e.g., data sets, memory), and requires that the contents of objects can only be seen by a subject at its level or lower; that is, information can flow to the same or higher levels but never to lower levels. This mandatory security policy is augmented by a discretionary policy that further restricts information on a need-to-know basis. More abstract and general models of security that avoid the need to consider objects have been formulated [Goguen 82; Goguen 84; Fiertag 77; McCullough 88a; McCullough 88b; McLean 90; McLean 94]. In these models, the information a subject observes is dependent on the actions of subjects at the same level or lower. That is, the actions of higher-level subjects cannot be observed by lower-level subjects.

In a computer system the burden of security falls primarily on the operating system. An operating system that satisfies the MLS policy must enforce access control: it must not permit processes to have access to objects in violation of the security policy. In addition, the operating system itself must not be a channel for the communication of information not in accordance with the security policy. Such unwanted information flow can potentially occur through objects managed by the operating system and shared by more than one subject, or through timed performance of actions on shared resources. The term *covert channel* is often used in referring to such objects. There have been successful attempts to develop systems that implement the MLS policy, mostly for single host/multiple user systems such as mainframes or shared workstations. Regardless of the policy or model used to develop the system, there is the requirement to provide assurance that the implementation satisfies that model. The TCSEC specifies the types of assurance required to meet various levels of security certification. The assurance may consist of informal arguments, test documentation, formal models and descriptions and formal verification.

19.5 LOTOS

LOTOS [Int 89], the Language of Temporal Ordering Specifications, is an executable specification language that was designed by the *International Standards Organization* to specify Open System Interconnection (OSI) protocols and services. However, LOTOS has proven to be appropriate for the specification of many other types of systems as well [Logrippo 90; Logrippo 92].

LOTOS specifications consist of a control component and a data component. The control component describes process behaviors and interactions, while the data component specifies the value expressions and data structures used in the system. The combination of these two components allows for the convenient specification of a system.

LOTOS semantics can be implemented using an interpreter [Guillemot 89]. Specification of complex designs can be implemented during the design cycle. Thus, "fast prototyping" can be accomplished, which allows for the early detection of design errors. Further, LOTOS offers step-by-step execution. At each step, the user can select any of the possible actions to be executed next. In this way, the user can verify that the system behaves as expected.

One of the difficulties facing designers, implementors, and system evaluators is the ambiguous nature of the design and requirement documentation. The LOTOS language permits designers to precisely specify the top-level behavior of a system with respect to individual components and their interactions. The language, and supporting tools, can also be used to specify lower-level behavior (and implementation) of the system, validate the correctness of the implementation, and validate that the system satisfies certain properties. LOTOS fits into the TCSEC criteria and the system life cycle where the requirements insist on formal top-level specification (or even a descriptive top-level specification), and evaluation of the correctness of implementations through prototyping and testing.

19.5.1   *Using LOTOS in the Assurance Cycle*

The TCSEC criteria discuss life-cycle assurance requirements and documentation of the system design and interface. The LOTOS specification language was designed by the International Standards Organization to assist in overcoming the ambiguity of specifications for communication systems. The LOTOS language permits designers to precisely specify the top-level behavior of a system with respect to individual components and their interactions. The language, and supporting tools that have developed, can also be used to specify lower level behavior (and implementation) of the system, validate the correctness of the implementation and validate that the system satisfies certain properties.

Figure 19.3 indicates where we believe LOTOS fits into the TCSEC criteria and the system lifecycle. Next to each of the phases of the system life-cycle we indicate the TCSEC criteria (and reference the appropriate section numbers in the TCSEC) and the LOTOS specifications or tools most likely to be used in those phases.

19.5.2   *LOTOS Specifications*

In general, all LOTOS specifications consist of a collection of process specifications parameterize by gates and values. These specifications can be combined, called and recursively defined. Communication and synchronization between processes occurs through events at the gates. An event occurs at a gate when all processes using that gate are ready to proceed. An event at a gate is denoted by the name of the gate. For example if we have a gate, g, the term g denotes some event at g, g!v denotes that the specific data value, v, is to occur at g while g?x:Type denotes that some value of type Type is to occur at g, and that this value is stored in the local variable x. The symbol [] denotes alternation, or choice of actions and ; denotes sequential ordering. In addition, processes p1 and p2 can

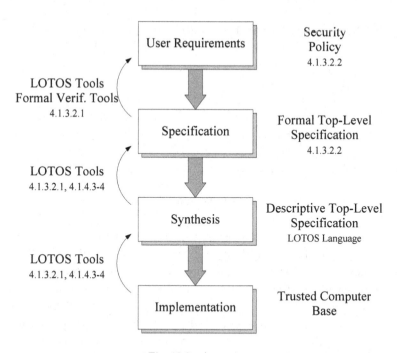

Fig. 19.3 Assurance

proceed in parallel completely synchronized with events at gates g1 and g2 (denoted by p1 |[g1,g2]| p2); completely synchronized with events at all gates (denoted by p1 || p2); or unsynchronized and thus independent (denoted by p1 ||| p2). In addition, actions may be guarded (denoted by [guard expression] -> action) and phases of execution may by sequentially composed (denoted by phase1 >> phase2).

As well as a rich process specification notation, LOTOS has a useful data abstraction specification style. Due to space limitations, we are unable to show the complete data type specifications used in the examples of this chapter. Since we are mostly concerned with events and interactions, this should not be a hindrance to the reader.

19.6   The Formal Security Model

As discussed in the review of the TCSEC guidelines, we are required to have a system security policy. In addition, we also need a formal security

```
PROCESS SeparabilityProcess [dataNetwork, controlNetwork]
          (id : ProcessId, secLabels : SecLabelSet) : noexit :=

  choice label: SecLabel []
    [label ISIN secLabels] ->
        SingleLevelReadProcess [dataNetwork, controlNetwork]
          (id, label)
        |||
        SeparabilityProcess [dataNetwork, controlNetwork]
          (id, REMOVE(label, secLabels))
  ENDPROC
```

Fig. 19.4   Separability process

model for the system that satisfies this policy. In this section we discuss
two security models, separability and restrictiveness, and how they can be
implemented in LOTOS and thus integrated into our system specification.
Since a major requirement of a secure system is the separation of information between security classification, we assume that all messages sent
between processes are appropriately labeled with the correct security classification. Operations that set and extract these labels are assumed to exist
in the system. Details of a system that actually performs these operations
are provided in Section 19.7.

It is important to understand that security models such as these are
at a higher level of abstraction than normal properties. We can model
safety properties such as liveness, fairness and correctness using a temporal
ordering of events as in LOTOS. Security properties require modeling the
set of all possible behaviors [McLean 94]. In effect, normal properties are
applied to a single possible sequence of events in a process; where security
properties are applied to the set of all possible sequences of events. As
such, the following presentations do not specify the security models but
rather provide a framework for the specification of systems that satisfy
these models. A system that is specified based on these frameworks will
satisfy the security model.

19.6.1   *Separability*

Figure 19.4 presents a LOTOS definition of the *separability* security model.
Separability was introduced [McLean 94] to model multi-level secure systems that do not allow information to flow from one security classification

to another. In McLean's presentation of separability, he defines a system with respect to a set of input and output communication channels. A sequence of events on a channel is a *trace* of that channel, and the sequence consisting of events at all channels is a trace of the system. A set of all possible traces for a system, the *trace set*, defines the behavior of the system. We can define an *interleaving* of two traces, t_1 and t_2, by defining for each channel, c_i, whether we use the trace of c_i from t_1 or t_2. If a particular interleaving, f, of two traces, t_1 and t_2 from the trace set, T results in another trace, t of the trace set, then the set is call *closed* under that interleaving. Precisely this is given by:

$$t_1, t_2 \in T \supset t \in T \text{ where } t = f(t1, t2)$$

Assume we have a system with two security levels L_1 and L_2 such that each channel is associated with one of these levels. An interleave function that picks L_1 events from t_1 and L_2 events from t_2 defines the separability security model. In simple terms, if a trace of L_1 events is possible for one trace of the system, then no sequence of L_2 events can make that behavior impossible. Therefore, the behavior of the two levels of the system are completely separate.

Although we do not precisely follow the model of a system as presented by McLean, the specification in Figure 19.4 provides the same restrictions as McLean's separability. In our specification we have provided a separate data and control network to match the avionics example. A modification of these gates to meet system needs does not change the strength of the model. In addition we specify two parameters to the a separability process, a process identifier and a set of security labels. The process identifier is used to uniquely label processes in the system and to specify information flow between processes – this can be used to simulate some of the functionality of McLean's channels. The set of security labels defines all of the security classifications that this system is designed to see. When a specification is designed using this framework it will enforce the restriction that all events of the process be classified with some classification from this set.

In the separability specification we have used a LOTOS specification trick. The intent of the specification is to define a set of processes, specified by **SingleLevelReadProcess**, where each process is parameterized by a different security classification from the set of security labels. The trick is to nondeterministically pick one element of the set (via the **choice** operator) and define the system as a secure process using that element in parallel

```
PROCESS SingleLevelReadProcess [networkIn, networkOut]
     (id: ProcessId, label : SecLabel) : noexit :=
  (
   (* send data messages *)
    choice x: DMessage []
      [label IsLabelOf x] ->
        dataNetwork ! x ;
        exit
  [] (* Receive data messages *)
    dataNetwork ? x: DMessage [label IsLabelOf x];
      exit
  [] (* send control messages *)
    choice x: CMessage []
      [label IsLabelOf x] ->
        controlNetwork ! x ;
        exit
  [] (* Receive control messages *)
    controlNetwork ? x: CMessage [label IsLabelOf x];
      exit
  ) >>
  SingleLevelReadProcess[dataNetwork, controlNetwork] (id,label)
ENDPROC
```

Fig. 19.5   Single-level read process

with the system with the rest of the elements of the set (via the recursive
call using REMOVE in the parameter of the recursion). If there were three
labels in the set, L1, L2, and L3, this is equivalent to any possible ordering
of the three processes:

```
SingleLevelReadProcess[networkIn, networkOut] (id, L1)
|||
SingleLevelReadProcess[networkIn, networkOut] (id, L2)
|||
SingleLevelReadProcess[networkIn, networkOut] (id, L3)
```

Each of these processes behaves as defined in Figure 19.5, which is a
process that can only interact with events at a specified security classification. Any process that is designed to satisfy separability must satisfy these
constraints and be modeled as a single-level reading process.

```
PROCESS RestrictivenessProcess [networkIn, networkOut]
        (id : ProcessId, secLabels : SecLabelSet) : noexit :=

  choice label : SecLabel []
    [label ISIN secLabels] ->
      LatticeProcess[networkIn, networkOut] (id, label)
      |||
      RestrictivenessProcess [networkIn, networkOut]
        (id, REMOVE(label, secLabels))
ENDPROC
```

Fig. 19.6   Restrictiveness process

19.6.2   *Restrictiveness*

The reason we call the process in Figure 19.5 a single-level read process
is that it restricts communication to precisely those messages sent and received with the same security classification. In the notation of Section 19.3,
the security operator $S_{i,j}$ is true only when Li = Lj. However, there are
often cases where we want information to flow up the security hierarchy.
The security model *restrictiveness* can be used to specify this.

The LOTOS specification of the restrictiveness model in Figure 19.6 is
similar to the separability specification. The only major difference here,
is that for each security classification, we execute an instance of a lattice
process. The lattice process is defined such that any message sent will
be sent with the correct security label, but messages received can be of
an security classification dominated by the process's security classification.
This enables any process at a lower security classification to send messages
to a higer process, and for that process to read those messages.

19.7   Specifying Security of Networked Processors

There are several approaches to designing and implementing a secure system. The specific approaches taken by system designers are dependent on
the specifics of the system architecture, the execution environment security
policy, and functional requirements. In this section we review the design of
our exemplary avionics system with respect to security attributes.

As mentioned in the earlier discussion, the avionics system is composed
of a collection of data and signal processors that communicate with each

```
PROCESS LatticeProcess[dataNetwork, controlNetwork]
   (id: ProcessId, label : SecLabel) : noexit :=

 (
  (* send data messages *)
   choice x: DMessage []
   [label IsLabelOf x] ->
      networkOut ! x ;
      exit
 [] (* Receive data messages for this processor *)
   networkIn ? x: DMessage [label Dominates (Label(x))];
      exit
 [] (* send data messages *)
   choice x: DMessage []
   [label IsLabelOf x] ->
      networkOut ! x ;
      exit
 [] (* Receive data messages for this processor *)
   networkIn ? x: DMessage [label Dominates (Label(x))];
      exit
 ) >>
   LatticeProcess [networkIn, networkOut] (id,label)
ENDPROC
```

Fig. 19.7   Lattice process

other over a high speed data bus and a slower speed control bus and also with external system sensors and resources. For such a system to operate in a secure manner, it is essential that the communication between system components does not violate the system security policy. In this section we will provide an outline of a high-level LOTOS specification for one mechanism achieving this goal. For a discussion of other mechanisms see [Ghantasala 97].

19.7.1   *TNIU Mechanism*

One mechanism for achieving secure communications for a system composed of untrusted COTS components is to attach a special processing unit between each data and signal processor and the communication networks. This unit (called the *Trusted Network Interface Unit* (TNIU) [Rushby 83]) labels all messages from a processor with the processor's security classification, and only forwards messages from the network to the processor if they satisfy the security policy. This approach requires each untrusted system component to operate at a single security level.

In the TNIU model, components can communicate with each other over a shared communication network given the following constraints (where M_i is the security classification of a message sent from processor i).

- All messages sent from a component are appropriately labeled with the component id and security level ($M_i = L_i$).
- A component may only read messages specifically sent to it from components at the same security level ($M_i = P_j$, which means that $S_{i,j}$ is true if and only if $L_i = L_j$).
- A component that needs to communicate with many other components at different security levels is considered *multi-level* and must be separately validated to maintain system security.

Using LOTOS, we can specify the correct operation of a system that follows this design. The first thing we need to understand is the constraint-oriented approach to specification. In this approach, system behavior is specified with respect to constraints on allowable interactions through communication gates. The benefit of such an approach is that it permits us to specify normal behavior of the system and additional constraints on that behavior as separate processes, all synchronizing their behavior. This synchronization limits the normal behavior of the system to one that satisfies all of the constraints. In this way we can easily introduce new constraints and modify or remove existing ones without changing the specification of the normal behavior of the system.

A high-level LOTOS specification of the system from Figure 19.2 is depicted in Figure 19.8. Here the system consists of a collection of processors with unique identifiers, a set of initial security classifications for each processor and for each external device, and data and control communication networks.

In this example, assume that the normal behavior of a data processor is specified as a LOTOS process that communicates through data and control gates, and labels messages with its current security level. If we wish to restrict the behavior of this component to one that satisfies additional constraints, we can define the constrained processor as in Figure 19.9. This specification defines a `ConstrainedDataProcessor` as a component that communicates over control and data gates with a processor identification of `id` and a current security level of `level`. This component is divided into

```
PROCESS CompositeSystem [externalinterfaces]
        (IdSet : ValidIdSet,
         InitialSecurityLevels : SecurityMappings,
         ExternalSecurityLevels : SecurityMappings) : noexit :=

HIDE data, control IN

( DataNetwork[data] ||| ControlNetwork[control] )
|[data, control]|
( ExternalDevices[data, control, externalinterfaces]
              (ExternalSecurityLevels)
  |||
  Processors [data, control] (IdSet)
)

ENDPROC

PROCESS Processors [data, control] (IdSet: ValidIdSet)

choice id : ProcessorIdentifier []
    [id IsIn IdSet] ->
      ConstrainedDataProcessor[data, control]
         (id, (LevelOf(id, InitialSecurityLevels))))
      |||
      Processors [data, control] (REMOVE (id, IdSet))

ENDPROC
```

Fig. 19.8   Full system composition

two synchronized subcomponents. The notation |[control, data]| indicates that all communication over the control and data gates must satisfy the specified behavior of both subcomponents. Thus, we can specify the behavior of the labeling data processor in terms of its functional behavior and use the separate SingleLevelSecureProcessor process to enforce the security constraints on the behavior of the labeling data processor.

In the original TNIU design [Rushby 83], a labeling data processor is developed using a normal untrusted processor connected through a TNIU. The purpose of the TNIU is to enforce the security policy by correctly labeling all outgoing messages with the current security level and filtering all incoming messages such that the untrusted processor only receives messages from units at the same security level. Following this model, we can refine the specification of the labeling data processor to consist of two com-

```
PROCESS ConstrainedDataProcessor[control, data]
        (id : ProcessorIdentifier, level : SecurityLevel) : noexit :=

  LabelingDataProcessor[control, data](id, level)
 |[control, data]|
  SingleLevelSecureProcessor[control, data](id, level)

ENDPROC

PROCESS LabelingDataProcessor[control, data]
        (id : ProcessorIdentifier, level : SecurityLevel) : noexit :=

HIDE privatecontrol, privatedata in
  UntrustedDataProcessor[privatecontrol, privatedata](id)
 | [privatecontrol, privatedata] |
  TNIU[privatecontrol, privatedata, control, data](id, level)

ENDPROC
```

Fig. 19.9 Decomposition of constrained data processor as a labeling processor and security constraints and specification of labeling processor

ponents, a data processor and a TNIU (see Figure 19.9). Note that the specification includes the **hide** operator, which keeps the internal communication gates private to the cooperating units. This specification indicates that the untrusted data processor may only communicate with the TNIU.

The specification of the constraints in Figure 19.10 requires that all data and control messages sent by this processor must contain the current security level of the processor. This is based on the separability model discussed in the previous section. All incoming messages (either data or control) must be directly sent to this processor **id** and be labeled with the same security level of this processor. In addition, control messages must be messages destined for single-level processor control. This permits us to specify non-single level processor control messages for overall system management, such as a processor reset and security level change. The overall specification of security here is used to place constraints on the operation of the TNIU.

The TNIU is a device that sends messages between the untrusted processor and the shared network according to the security policy (see Figure 19.11). The TNIU specification is very similar to the single level secure processor specification; it is a simple device that directly implements

```
PROCESS SingleLevelSecureProcess[data, control]
      (id: ProcessId, label : SecLabel) : noexit :=

 ( (* send data messages *)
   choice x: DMessage []
     [(label IsLabelOf x) and (id IsSourceOf x)] ->
       data ! x ;
       exit
 [] (* Receive data messages for this processor *)
   data ? x: DMessage [(id IsDestinationOf x) and (label IsLabelOf x)];
     exit
 [] (* send control message *)
   choice x: CMessage []
     [(label IsLabelOf x) and (id IsSourceOf x)] ->
       control ! x ;
       exit
 [] (* Receive control messages for this processor *)
   control ? x: CMessage
     [(id IsDestinationOf x) and (label IsLabelOf x) and
     (IsSingleLevelControlMessage(x))];
       exit
 ) >>
 SingleLevelSecureProcess[data, control] (id,label)
ENDPROC
```

Fig. 19.10 Specification of security constraints limiting input and output messages to those of the same level as the processor

the security policy. Hence, this specification is a bit redundant when constrained by the single level secure processor specification. We could have removed some of the command checking (such as destination id) to remove the redundancy, but this specification more accurately depicts the behavior of the TNIU. We leave the secure processor constraints in place to enable us to use other models of labeling data processors that may not explicitly repeat all constraints.

19.7.2 *Resettable Processors*

In the sample TNIU-based system we discuss above, each processor is assigned an initial security level. We have provided no explicit mechanism for a processor to execute at a different security level. To enable the ability to reassign a processor to a new security level, we require the processor to remove all traces of information from the previous level (no state informa-

```
process TNIU[privatecontrol, privatedata, control, data]
        (label: SecLabel
         id : ProcessorId) : noexit :=

  (
   (* Receive data messages from this processor and
      pass them on appropriately labeled *)
   privatedata ? x: DMessage;
   data ! (SetId(id, (SetLabel (lavel, x))));
   exit
  [] (* Receive control  messages from this processor and
      pass them on appropriately labeled *)
   privatecontrol ? x: CMessage;
   control ! (SetId(id, (SetLabel (label, x))));
   exit
  [] (* Receive data messages for this processor *)
   data ? x: DMessage [(id IsDestinationOf x) and (label IsLabelOf x)];
      privatedata ! x;
      exit
  [] (* Receive control messages for this processor *)
   control ? x: CMessage
      [(id IsDestinationOf x) and (label IsLabelOf x) and
      (IsSingleLevelControlMessage(x))];
      privatecontrol ! x;
      exit
  ) >>
   TNIU[privatecontrol, privatedata, control, data](label, id)
ENDPROC (* TNIU *)
```

Fig. 19.11   Specification of the TNIU

tion, RAM values, etc). We can then reinitialize the processor and TNIU to operate under the new security compartment. In LOTOS, such a processor can be specified as in Figure 19.9, but implemented as a resettable process. The resettable process would receive a special reset command on the control bus, disable the currently executing process and restart as a newly executing process at the specified level. An example of the specification of such a resettable processor is provided in Figure 19.12. Note that this is identical to the single level secure processor of Figure 19.10, except that the transition from the communication phase to the recusrion step now includes two parameters, a security label and a state. The security label defines the next operating label of the process, while the state defines all past communication known by the process.

Any process specification modeled on this framework should operate

```
PROCESS ResettableSingleLevelProcessor[data, control]
   (id: ProcessId, label : SecLabel, currentState : State) : noexit :=

( (* send data messages *)
   choice x: DMessage []
     [(label IsLabelOf x) and (id IsSourceOf x)] ->
       data ! x ;
       exit (label, Append(Send(x),currentState))
[] (* Receive data messages for this processor *)
   data ? x: DMessage [(id IsDestinationOf x) and (label IsLabelOf x)];
       exit (label, Append(Receive(x),currentState))
[] (* send control message *)
   choice x: CMessage []
     [(label IsLabelOf x) and (id IsSourceOf x)] ->
       control ! x ;
       exit (label, Append(Send(x),currentState))
[] (* Receive control messages for this processor *)
   control ? x: CMessage
     [(id IsDestinationOf x) and (label IsLabelOf x) and
      (IsSingleLevelControlMessage(x))];
       exit (label, Append(Receive(x),currentState))
[] (* Receive Reset Command *)
   (choice newLabel : SecLabel []
      control ! Reset(id,newLabel);
      exit (newLabel, Start)
   )
) >>
ACCEPT nextLabel : SecLabel, nextState: State IN
   ResettableSingleLevelProcessor [networkIn, networkOut]
                        (id,nextLabel,nextState)

ENDPROC
```

Fig. 19.12   Resettable single-level processor

based only on the information in the current state. A processor that is resettable must be able to perform all network interactions as if it started with a clean slate. A TNIU attached to such a device must also intercept the reset command and modify its internal filtering and labeling functions to ensure proper operation.

19.7.3 *A Security Policy Approach*

In the TNIU discussion we have explicitly specified the occurrence of the level event with each communication. A more general approach would permit an arbitrary embedding of the level in a message and provide a set of operations that could determine the level from the message. Such an approach could also go beyond the simple communication between processors at the same security level and instead allow all communication that satisfies the specified security policy. This would be a model based on the restrictiveness policy and the lattice processor of Figure 19.7.

19.8 Conclusion

The DoD Trusted Computer System Evaluation Criteria (TCSEC) [Dep 83] was developed to provide a common yardstick for evaluating system security, as a guide for system developers, and as a procurement standard. However, since then it has become important to consider the security of systems other than the traditional operating systems that influenced the TCSEC's development. Modern real-time systems also may require security. As these systems become more and more integrated and as the amount of data sharing increases, security and validation will become increasingly important.

When compiling a review of TCSEC categories we found that some of the standard TCSEC guidelines were not applicable to a real-time embedded computer system. This discovery led to the review of major TCSEC categories and their applicability to real-time embedded computer systems as presented in this paper. In summary this review points out that certain of the TCSEC guidelines, such as discretionary access control, user authentication, and export labels may be trivially satisfied or not even implemented in a real-time system. Although the claims in the review are generic, we are currently evaluating concrete examples to demonstrate the application of the TCSEC guidelines to specific instances of real-time systems. Given these restrictions, we have provided a model of secure communications for an example of an avionics system. To demonstrate that such a system is obtainable, we have provided an outline of a formal high-level specification for a mechanism that permits the composition of untrusted system components into a MLS system.

Designers of real-time embedded computer systems, such as avionics data acquisition systems, are moving toward open system architectures. This move creates difficulties when trying to manage non-functional system requirements such as fault tolerance, reliability and security. Security is especially a problem for critical real-time systems such as fighter aircraft, where security flaws could endanger the mission or even human life. Inclusion of COTS components in a secure system necessitates the use of mechanisms for maintaining the integrity and enforcing the information flow constraints of the system. We have found that the TNIU approach is an appropriate candidate mechanism for this purpose [Alves-Foss 97; Alves-Foss 98].

In conclusion, we have found that, although the transition to open-system architectures presents challenges, some of them can be overcome through the inclusion of special purpose devices such as TNIU in the system. The behavior of the system will then constitute the composite behavior of the special devices and the untrusted devices, which can be readily specified in a language such as LOTOS. We are continuing to extend this work to other mechanisms and more detail than is presented here. Many challenges remain. In particular, further work still needs to be done on lower-level implementation details and validation of the correctness of the implementations with respect to the high-level specifications.

Chapter 20

An Algebraic Framework for the Feature Interaction Problem

Mohammed Faci and Luigi Logrippo

20.1 Motivation and Background

The problem of augmenting the functionality of a telephone system with new features, without causing unwanted interactions between the features, has received much attention [Bowen 89; Cameron 94; Kimbler 98]. In industrial practice, detection is done not only by analyzing possible conflicts at the design stage, but also by running extensive libraries of test cases against the new system to see that it still behaves properly. Interestingly, the method we propose in this work is similar to the one just described. However, being formal, our method allows precise reasoning, leading to precise criteria for choosing the set of test cases and analyzing the test results. Also, by relating the feature interaction to the well-known conformance testing problem, our approach makes available in this area a wealth of well-established results.

We consider only features that are defined independently and do not "build" on each other, meaning that these features make no assumptions about the behaviors of other features in the system. Also, we consider only single element features [Cameron 94]. In this context, the main idea of our method is that in a system integrating features, the behavior of each feature (which is characterized as the sequences of observable actions generated by the feature) should be the same as its behavior in a system where all features are allowed to execute independently. The fact that this is not always the case is one of the main reasons of interactions in

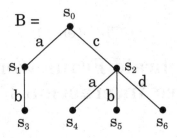

Fig. 20.1   Behavior B represented as a tree

practice. In this framework, feature interactions can be detected at the specification stage by using test cases obtained from a specification which describes the behavior of a 'reference' system where each feature is able to execute independently.

20.2   Basic Concepts and Notation

We use the algebraic specification language LOTOS [Bolognesi 87; Logrippo 92] for feature specification [Faci 97]. LOTOS semantics are based on the concept of labeled transition systems (LTSs). LTSs are a generalization of finite state machines and provide a convenient way for expressing the step-by-step operational semantics of processes. Processes evolve by executing one action at a time, selected from their alphabet set. Formally,

Definition 20.1   Labeled Transition System
A *labeled transition system* (LTS is a 4-tuple $LTS = < S, s_0, L, T >$ where

- S is non-empty set of states;
- s_0 in S is the initial state;
- L is a (finite) set of observable actions; and i is the internal action
- $T = \{-a \rightarrow \subseteq S \times S \mid a \in L'$, where $L' = L \bigcup \{i\}\}$, the transitions, is a L'-indexed family of binary relations on S. So if $s_1 - a \rightarrow s_2$ such that $s_1, s_2 \in S$ then $< s_1, s_2 > \in -a \rightarrow$.

LTSs are usually represented by labeled transition trees, or simply trees, for the obvious pictorial advantage. Figure 20.1 is an example of a behavior B represented by a tree.

In addition to the basic definition, the following notation and definitions are used [Brinksma 87; Leduc 92].

- $L = \{a, b, c, \ldots\}$ is the alphabet of observable *actions* (also called *gates*) and i is the hidden action;

- $B - a \rightarrow B'$ means that after executing the observable action a, the behavior expression B is transformed into another behavior expression B';

- $B - i^k \rightarrow B'$ means that after executing a sequence of k hidden actions, the behavior expression B is transformed into another behavior expression B';

- $B - ab \rightarrow B'$ means that $\exists B''$ such that: $B - a \rightarrow B''$ and $B'' - b \rightarrow B'$;

- $B = a \Rightarrow B'$ means that B is transformed into another behavior expression B' by executing zero or more internal actions, followed by the observable action a, then zero or more internal actions. Formally, $\exists k_0, k_1 \in N$, such that $B - i^{k_0} a i^{k_1} \rightarrow B'$;

- $B = a \Rightarrow$ means that B may accept the action a. Formally, $\exists B'$ such that $B = a \Rightarrow B'$;

- $B \neq a \Rightarrow B'$ means *not* $(B = a \Rightarrow B')$, i.e., B must refuse the action a;

- $B = \sigma \Rightarrow B'$ means that B is transformed into another behavior expression B' by executing a sequence of observable actions. Formally, if $\sigma = a_1 \ldots a_n$ then $\exists k_0, \ldots, k_n \in N$ such that $B - i^{k0} a_1 i^{k1} a_2 \ldots a_n i^{kn} \rightarrow B'$;

- $B = \sigma \Rightarrow$ means that $\exists B'$ such that $B = \sigma \Rightarrow B'$;

- B *after* $\sigma = \{B' \mid B = \sigma \Rightarrow B'\}$, i.e., the set of all behavior expressions reachable from B after executing the sequence σ;

- A *trace* is a sequence of actions; $t \sqsubseteq t'$ expresses the fact that t is a, not necessarily contiguous, subtrace of t'.

- The *trace set* of B is defined as: $Trace(B) = \{\sigma \mid B = \sigma \Rightarrow\}$. Note that $Trace(B) \subseteq L^*$;

- $Refuses(B, \sigma)$ is the *refusal set* of B after executing the sequence σ. Formally, $Refuses(B, \sigma) = \{X \mid \exists B' \in B$ after σ such that $B' \neq a \Rightarrow, \forall a \in X\}$. A set $X \subseteq L$ belongs to $Refuses(B, \sigma)$ iff B may engage in the trace σ and, after doing so, refuse every event of the set X.

Only a subset of LOTOS is used in this chapter, which is described below.

$|[a_1, \ldots, a_n]|$ is the parallel composition operator with synchronization on
   actions $a_1 \ldots a_n$;

$\|$ is the parallel composition operator with synchronization on all actions;

$[]$ is the (exclusive) choice operator between two behavior expressions;

δ is the successful termination action.

20.3 A Method for Analyzing and Detecting Feature Interactions

The steps of the method, shown in Figure 20.2, are as follows [Faci 95]:

❶ Specify each feature independently, within the context of the existing
   system, using the notion of constraints [Faci 91; Faci 97; Vissers 91].

❷ *Integrate* the features into a single specification so that each feature
   is able to perform its function when other features are disabled.
   Consider the resulting behavior as an implementation of the features.

❸ *Compose* the features into a single specification so that they are able to
   synchronize on their common interaction points with the system and
   interleave on the rest of their actions. Consider the results of this
   composition as a specification with respect to the implementation
   obtained in **❷** above.

❹ Derive a set of test cases, using the theory of derivation of tests for
   LOTOS processes, from the specification obtained in **❸** above.

❺ Simulate the system obtained in step **❷** against the test cases obtained
   in step **❹**, and check for deadlocks.

❻ Interpret the results in the following way. A deadlock in **❺** implies that
   the way the features are integrated in the system does not allow for
   their simultaneous activation.

The justification of the method follows.

20.3.1 Specification of Features in the Context of a System (*Step 1*)

Figure 20.3(a) shows the POTS (Plain Old Telephone Service, denoting
a basic featureless telephone system) model defined in [Faci 91] for the
specification of basic call processing. The model is based on the concept of *constraints* which is used to structure the specification [Faci 91;

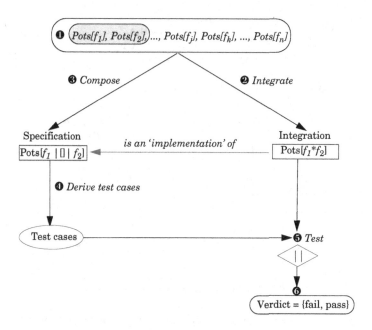

Fig. 20.2   Methodology for detecting feature interactions

Fig. 20.3   Extending the POTS model to support features

Faci 97]. A specification is expressed as a set of *communicating* processes representing three types of constraints: *local constraints*, *end-to-end constraints*, and *global constraints*. Local constraints are used to enforce the appropriate sequences of events at each user's interaction point; they are different according to whether the interaction point connects to a Caller telephone or a Called telephone. End-to-End constraints are related to each connection; they enforce the appropriate sequence of actions between the interaction points for each telephone connection. Finally, global constraints involve action sequencing between connections.

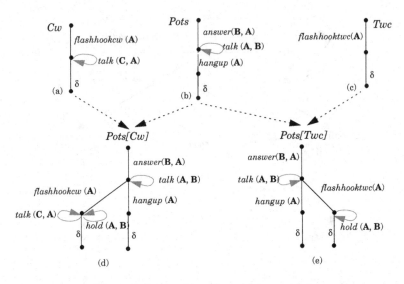

Fig. 20.4   Integrating a feature into a system

This model was generalized to support the specification of features [Faci 94; Faci 95; Faci 97] as shown in Figure 20.3(b). To do this, we first decide on the role of a feature. In general, each feature can be classified as acting on behalf of either the caller process or the called process (or both). Once that decision is made, the integration of the feature behavior into the system is accomplished by integrating the feature, using local constraints, into the process on whose behalf the feature acts. This can be done by specifying the feature as a constraint (operator $|[A]|$, see below), with respect to this process. Of course, a modification of the end-to-end constraints expressed by the controller of POTS is also required. In Figure 20.3(b), C' is obtained by modifying C in order to support the functionality of the new feature. We refer to the resulting specification of integrating f_i into POTS as the behavior of f_i in the context of POTS. Formally,

Definition 20.2   System Context

We say that a feature f_i is specified in the context of a system *Pots*, expressed as Pots$[f_i]$, iff the following condition holds: $\forall t \in Trace(f_i), \exists t' \in Trace(Pots[f_i])$ such that $t \sqsubseteq t'$.

In other words, a feature is said to be specified in the context of a system if every trace of the feature is a sub-trace of some other trace in the resulting system. For example, suppose that we have specified a POTS system which allows a caller **A** to establish a talking session with a called **B**. Figure 20.4(b) shows a portion (obviously very simplified) of the specification. It describes the following sequence, starting from the state where **B** has received a ring signal from **A**. User **B** answers **A**; the two users engage in a talking session; **A** hangs up; and finally the system exits as shown by δ, the LOTOS successful termination.

Suppose now that we wish to integrate *Call Waiting (Cw)* and *Three Way Calling (Twc)* into the system, independently of each other. In the context of POTS, *Cw* allows user **A** to respond to another user **C** while still talking to **B**. Starting from a state where **A** is talking to **B** and **C**'s controller has just sent a *Call Waiting Tone signal* to **A**, **A** may send a *flashhookcw* signal to accomplish two things: (1) to put **B** on hold, and (2) to establish a talking session with **C**, as shown in Figure 20.4(d).

We can also integrate *Twc* into POTS without taking the behavior of *Cw* into consideration. *Twc* is a feature which allows **A** to suspend **B** and establish another talking session with another user (**D** for example) by sending a *flashhooktwc* signal to the controller, and after reaching a talking state with **D**, **A** sends another *flashhooktwc* signal to bring **B** back to the connection, thereby establishing a talking session between **A**, **B**, and **D**. Figure 20.4(e) shows the integration of *Twc* in the context of POTS, but note that only the first action of *Twc* is shown. The LTSs of Figure 20.4 can be represented by the following expressions, using a slightly abused LOTOS syntax, where also the loops have been ignored for simplicity.

(a) $Cw := flashhookcw(A);$ **exit***
(b) $Pots := answer(\mathbf{B}, \mathbf{A}); hangup(\mathbf{A});$ **exit**
(c) $Twc := flashhooktwc(\mathbf{A}); exit$
(d) $Pots[Cw] := answer(\mathbf{B}, \mathbf{A}); (flashhookcw(\mathbf{A});$ **exit** $[]hangup(\mathbf{A});$ **exit**$)$
(e) $Pots[Twc] := answer(\mathbf{B}, \mathbf{A}); (flashhooktwc(\mathbf{A});$ **exit** $[]hangup(\mathbf{A});$ **exit** $)$

It is easy to verify that both *Cw* and *Twc* are specified according to Definition 20.2 by checking their traces.

- $Trace(Cw) = \{<>, < flashhookcw(\mathbf{A}) >,$
  $< flashhookcw(\mathbf{A}); \delta >\} = \{t_1, t_2, t_3\}$

---

*In proper LOTOS, we represent this as: *flashhookcw*!**A**; **exit** where *flashhookcw* is a gate and **A** is a value expression.

- $Trace(Pots[Cw]) =$
  $\{<>, < answer(\mathbf{B}, \mathbf{A}) >,$
  $< answer(\mathbf{B}, \mathbf{A}); flashhookcw(\mathbf{A}) >,$
  $< answer(\mathbf{B}, \mathbf{A}); hangup(\mathbf{A}) >,$
  $< answer(\mathbf{B}, \mathbf{A}); flashhookcw(\mathbf{A}); \delta >,$
  $< answer(\mathbf{B}, \mathbf{A}); hangup(\mathbf{A}); \delta >\}$
  $$= \{t'_1, t'_2, t'_3, t'_4, t'_5, \ t'_6\};$$

Since
$$t_1 \sqsubseteq t'_1 \in Trace(Pots[Cw]), \text{ and}$$
$$t_2 \sqsubseteq t'_3 \in Trace(Pots[Cw]), \text{ and}$$
$$t_3 \sqsubseteq t'_5 \in Trace(Pots[Cw])$$

Then it is the case that $Pots[Cw]$, meaning that Cw is specified in the context POTS. Using similar deductions we can show that the same holds for $Pots[Twc]$, as shown in Figure 20.4(c) and (e).

20.3.2 *Integration versus Composition of Features (Steps 2 and 3)*

Our primary objective, as we have already mentioned, is to answer the following question: is there interaction between features Cw and Twc when they are integrated into an existing system? To answer this question, one must define a reference point against which the answer can be evaluated. Let us first introduce the intuition which motivated the formalism. Our starting point is the notion of simultaneous execution.

For practical purposes, this notion is interpreted in the context of interleaved semantics. Saying that two features can execute simultaneously is equivalent to saying that both features will reach their terminal states and that their actions are allowed to interleave. In many cases, however, when specifiers produce specifications which integrate the functionalities of several features, their primary concern is to include the functionality of each feature, one at time, in the resulting specification. For each feature that is being integrated, the specifier gives no consideration to what effects this will have on other features in the system. The basic idea is explained by way of Figure 20.5. Parts (a) and (b) express the integration of each of the two features in the context of POTS. Parts (c) and (d) express the composition and the integration of both features, respectively.

Note at this point that, while the approach is applicable for n features, for illustration purposes we are using two features only. As mentioned,

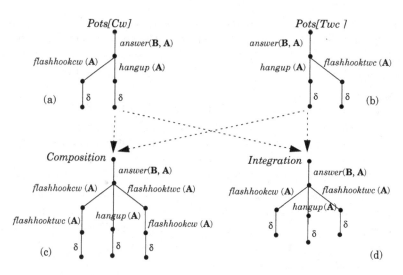

Fig. 20.5   Integration versus composition of features

the composition of features, which reflects the interleaving of the independent actions of Cw and Twc while synchronizing on their common actions with POTS, turns out to be conveniently expressed using the LOTOS composition operator $|[a_{pots}]|$, where a_{pots} are the gates that are common to $Pots[Cw]$ and $Pots[Twc]$. In our example, $answer$ is a common gate between $Pots$, Cw, and Twc. From now on, we will refer to this composition by the following concise notation $(Pots[Cw|[]|Twc])$. Note that this is simply a notation, shorthand for a LOTOS expression, and does not introduce an operator. A question that comes up at this point is: can deadlocks be introduced when doing the composition? This question is worth of further research, and the answer is probably that if such deadlocks come up, this is another symptom of a design problem, which could be a feature interaction. However, we did not encounter such deadlocks in the several features we have specified and composed.

On the other hand, the requirements imposed on the system designer to integrate the two features into the specification, which we will write as $Pots[Cw*Twc]$, are as follows:

- $Trace(Pots[Cw]) \subseteq Trace(Pots[Cw*Twc])$
- $Trace(Pots[Twc]) \subseteq Trace(Pots[Cw*Twc])$

meaning that the functionalities of both features must be preserved in the final integration of Cw and Twc in the context of POTS. However, the integration of Cw and Twc in the context of POTS leaves open the question of whether or not Cw can execute all its traces to completion, even when both features are active at the same time. The same holds for Twc with respect to Cw.

It should be noted that, while composition is formally defined in terms of the LOTOS interleave operator, integration is not. This is because of the fact that integration depends on the way the abstract features are implemented. In other words, composition is a specification-level concept, while integration is an implementation-level concept. The first is formal, the second is not. If the integration is done in such a way that the features cannot exhibit their interleaved behavior, then either the features themselves, or the way they are integrated, should be modified. For example, we shall see below that both features Twc and Cw need a user action to become activated. If, in the integration, both these actions are mapped on the same signal *flashhook*, an interaction arises.

It is possible to see if the traces of the composition are also in the integration by applying to the integration testers obtained from the composition. Thus the following section deals with the problem of testing that the interleaved behavior is realized in the integration.

20.3.3   *Derivation of Test Cases to Detect Interactions; Conformance Testing and the Detection of Feature Interactions (Step 4)*

In this section we briefly review the results reported in [Brinksma 87; Brinksma 88; Brinksma 90] and show how the notion of conformance testing has a direct application in the domain of detecting feature interactions. But first, let us define some concepts which are needed for conformance testing.

Definition 20.3   Deadlocks in Terms of Refusals

Let L be the set of observable events, L^* be the set of traces. Then, for I a labelled transition system, $A \subseteq L, \sigma \in L*$:

- I *Refuses* (σ, A) is defined as: $\exists I'$ such that $(I = \sigma \Rightarrow I'$ **and** $\forall a \in A$ such that $I' \neq a \Rightarrow)$
- I *Deadlocks* (σ) is defined as: I *Refuses*(σ, L)

The first part of the definition says that I may execute the trace σ, and after doing so, refuse every event in the set A. Similarly, the second part of the definition says that I reaches a deadlock if it refuses every observable event, after executing σ.

Conformance allows one to reason about an implementation and a specification using a single formalism. In this context, an implementation is taken to be an abstract representation of a physical realization. *'I is a valid implementation of S'* can be defined as follows [Brinksma 88].

Definition 20.4   Conformance

Let S and I be processes. We say that:

I **conf** S **iff** $\forall \sigma \in Trace(S), \forall A \subseteq L,$
   if I Refuses (σ, A) **then** S Refuses (σ, A).

Informally, I conforms to S if, and only if, testing the implementation I against the traces of the specification S does not lead to deadlocks that would not occur while testing S against those same tests. In other words, testing the implementation does not reveal deadlocks that would not be revealed while testing the specification.

In section 20.3.2 we discussed the relation between composition and integration of features. Using these two notions and the formal definition of conformance, we can now provide our formal definition of the feature interaction problem.

Definition 20.5   Formalization of Feature Interactions: Int

Let $f_1, f_2, \ldots, f_n$ be features,
Let A be the alphabet of POTS and A_i the alphabet of f_i such that:
$\forall i, j : A_i \cap A_j = \emptyset$ and $A \cap A_i \neq \emptyset$, for $1 \leq i \leq n, 1 \leq j \leq n$.
Let S and I be processes, such that:
$S := Pots[f_1|[]|f_2|[]|\ldots|[]|f_n]$ and $I := Pots[f_1 * f_2 * \ldots * f_n]$,

We say that: $int(f_1, f_2, \ldots, f_n)$ **iff** $\neg(I$ **conf** $S)$, meaning that an interaction exists between the n features if, and only if, the *integration* of the features **does not** conform to their *composition*.

Note that in the definition we assume that $A_i \cap A_j = \emptyset$. This is consistent with our intuitive view that features are defined independently, in terms of their interactions only with respect to POTS. However, as already mentioned, it is possible that actions of different features are mapped onto the same element in the integration, and this may cause interactions, which can be detected by our method.

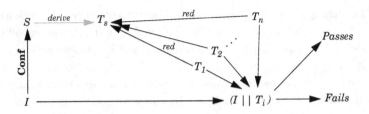

Fig. 20.6 Conformance, canonical tester and testing process

Definition 20.5 is the link that allows us to exploit the *conformance* and *testing* theory of Brinksma et al.

Derivation of Tests

The theory of deriving tests [Brinksma 88] from a LOTOS specification asserts that there exists a *canonical tester* T_s that can discriminate those implementations which conform to the *specification* and those which do not. For an implementation I and a canonical tester T_s, this discrimination is accomplished according to the following *passes* relation.

Definition 20.6   Passes relation
Let I and T be processes, then

$$I \textbf{ passes } T \text{ iff } \forall \sigma \in L^* : \quad \begin{array}{ll} if & (I\|T) \text{ after } \sigma \textbf{ deadlocks} \\ then & T \text{ after } \sigma \textbf{ deadlocks} \end{array}$$

For a specification S, a canonical tester T_s is defined as follows:

- $Trace(T_s) = Trace(S)$, and
- $\forall I : I \textbf{ conf } S$ iff $I \textbf{ passes } T_s$

In addition, each T_s can be expressed as a set of testing processes called the *irreducible reductions* (IR_s) of T_s. Formally,
$IR_s =_{def} \{T | T \textbf{ red } T_s, \forall T' : T' \textbf{ red } T \Rightarrow T' = T\}$, *where*
$B1 \textbf{ red } B2 \text{ iff } B1 \textbf{ conf } B2 \text{ and } Trace(B1) \subseteq Trace(B2).$

Figure 20.6 captures the intuition behind these definitions.

Note that, although we use here a nonconstructive definition of T_s, methods for constructing it are known [Wezeman 90].

The integration of two features in a system is driven by the functionalities of both the features and the existing system. Since it is not possible to define the semantics of a general model for the integration of any two given features, we give an example to show that, depending on the results of the integration, an interaction may or may not occur. In either case, our methodology succeeds in reaching the correct verdict. It is important, however, to keep in mind that the **passes** verdict simply means that more testing is required (noting that for a given specification the set of all testing processes can be infinite), whereas a **fails** verdict means that an interaction is detected.

According to our definition **int** of feature interactions, an interaction exists between Cw and Twc if, and only if, I **does not conform** to S. So, in order to derive the canonical testing process from the composition and execute it against the integration, let us express the trees of Figure 20.5(c) and (d) as LOTOS expressions:

$$S := Pots[Cw|[]|Twc] \quad = \quad answer(\mathbf{B}, \mathbf{A});$$
$$(\quad flashhookcw(\mathbf{A}); flashhooktwc(\mathbf{A});\mathbf{exit}$$
$$[] \quad hangup(\mathbf{A});\mathbf{exit}$$
$$[] \quad flashhooktwc(\mathbf{A}); flashhookcw(\mathbf{A});\mathbf{exit}$$
$$)$$

and

$$I := Pots[Cw*Twc] \quad = \quad answer(\mathbf{B}, \mathbf{A});$$
$$(\quad flashhookcw(\mathbf{A});\mathbf{exit}$$
$$[] \quad hangup(\mathbf{A});\mathbf{exit}$$
$$[] \quad flashhooktwc(\mathbf{A});\mathbf{exit}$$
$$)$$

Following [Brinksma 88], we now express the canonical tester T_s of S in the following way:

$$T_s \quad = \quad T(Pots[Cw|[]|Twc])$$
$$= \quad answer(\mathbf{B}, \mathbf{A});$$
$$(\quad \mathbf{i}; flashhookcw(\mathbf{A}); flashhooktwc(\mathbf{A});\mathbf{exit}$$
$$[] \quad \mathbf{i}; hangup(\mathbf{A});\mathbf{exit}$$
$$[] \quad \mathbf{i}; flashhooktwc(\mathbf{A}); flashhookcw(\mathbf{A}); \mathbf{exit}$$
$$)$$

(where **i** is the internal action). S and T_s are shown in Figure 20.7.

The next step is to express T_s as a set of irreducible test cases, from which a set of useful test cases are selected [Brinksma 91]. Some such test cases are:

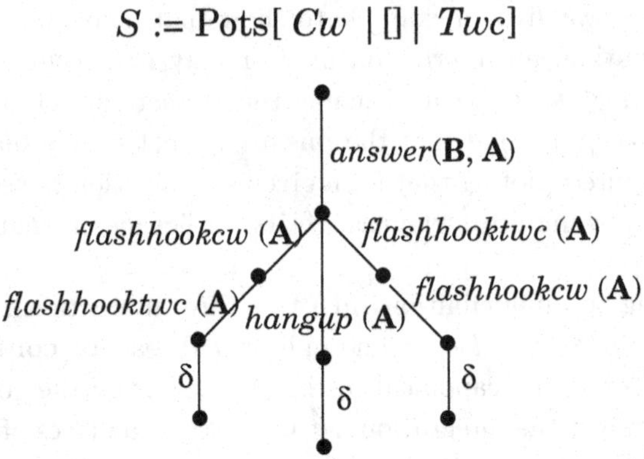

$$S := \text{Pots}[\ Cw\ |\ []\ |\ Twc]$$

(a)

$$T_s = \text{T}(\text{Pots}[\ Cw\ |\ []\ |\ Twc])$$

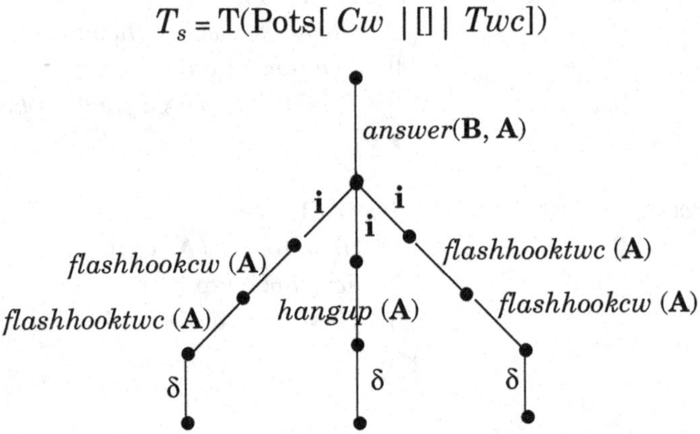

(b)

Fig. 20.7   A specification and its canonical tester

T_1 = $answer(\mathbf{B}, \mathbf{A}); flashhookcw(\mathbf{A}); flashhooktwc(\mathbf{A});$ **exit**

T_2 = $answer(\mathbf{B}, \mathbf{A}); hangup(\mathbf{A});$**exit**

T_3 = $answer(\mathbf{B}, \mathbf{A}); flashhooktwc(\mathbf{A}); flashhookcw(\mathbf{A});$**exit**

T_4 = $answer(\mathbf{B}, \mathbf{A});$

    ($flashhookcw(\mathbf{A}); flashhooktwc(\mathbf{A});$**exit**

     [] $hangup(\mathbf{A});$**exit**

     [] $flashhooktwc(\mathbf{A}); flashhookcw(\mathbf{A});$ **exit**)

)

Although in this very simplified example we have assumed finite behavior trees, in principle the presence of loops is not a problem [Drira 93].

20.3.4 *Executing the System and Analyzing the Results (Steps 5 and 6)*

The final two steps of the method are to execute the specification against a selected subset [Brinksma 91] of the derived test suite in order to check for deadlocks. For our purposes, the set $\{T_1, T_2, T_3\}$ is sufficient to test our integration because every trace of T_4 is a member of another test suite in the selected set. An example of testing the integration with T_1 is shown below. Testing with T_2 and T_3 is similar. The verdicts for the three tests are respectively fail, pass, fail. Since the integration fails at least one of the tests, we conclude that an interaction exists between Cw and Twc. The reason is that once the flashhook is executed, only the feature which participates in its execution is allowed to continue with its behavior, thereby preventing the other one from exhibiting its behavior in the overall system.
Testing with T1:

$$Pots[Cw * Twc] \| T_1 \quad = \quad (\qquad answer(\mathbf{B, A});$$
$$(\qquad flashhookcw(\mathbf{A}); \textbf{exit}$$
$$[] \qquad hangup(\mathbf{A}); \textbf{exit}$$
$$[] \qquad flashhooktwc(\mathbf{A}); \textbf{exit}$$
$$)$$
$$)$$
$$\| answer(\mathbf{B, A}); flashhookcw(\mathbf{A}$$
$$); flashhooktwc(\mathbf{A}); \textbf{exit}$$
$$= answer(\mathbf{B, A}); flashhookcw(\mathbf{A}); \textbf{stop}$$

$\Rightarrow$ test **fails** because it did not reach its **exit**.

20.4 Conclusions and Research Directions

We have proposed a formal algebraic framework for analyzing and detecting certain types of feature interactions in telephone systems at the design level. We used to advantage the characteristics of process algebras: its formal properties allowed us to establish a theoretical framework for the problem; while its executability allowed us to define a testing framework for actually detecting interactions. In [Faci 95], the method is applied on nine examples of feature interactions, mostly very different from the one presented above. Features considered are: Call Waiting, Call Forward on Busy, Call Forward Always, Automatic Recall, Automatic Callback, Originating and Terminating Call Screening, Distinctive Ringing, Calling Number Delivery, Unlisted Numbers.

Of course, many questions remain open. Is the 'conformance' relation the one that best captures the intuition behind detecting feature interaction (it is well-known that this relation has limitations in the area of protocol conformance testing)? Is it possible to better use the concept of 'refusal' for the characterization of features (in our framework, features are characterized by traces and not by refusals)? How can one find appropriate test cases for different types of interactions [Brinksma 91]? How can the method be extended to cover other cases of feature interaction? Our contribution sets the stage for further research on these and other related problems.

Needless to say, the method could be reformulated in terms of other languages using labelled transition models.

Acknowledgment

Funding sources for our work include the Natural Sciences and Engineering Research Council of Canada, the Telecommunications Research Institute of Ontario, Bellcore, Bell-Northern Research, and the National Institute of Standards and Technology. We like to acknowledge the many fruitful discussions that we have had with members of our LOTOS group.

Appendix A

Algebraic Specification

Below is the complete algebraic specification used to generate an implementation of the model checker algorithm.

r_1: $F_e ::= F_e$ or F_t ; $macro(r_1)$: $@_0 := @_1 \cup @_2$;

r_2: $F_e ::= F_t$; $macro(r_2)$: $@_0 := @_1$;

r_3: $F_t ::= F_t$ and F_f; $macro(r_3)$: $@_0 := @_1 \cap @_2$;

r_4: $F_t ::= F_f$; $macro(r_4)$: $@_0 := @_1$;

r_5: $F_f ::=$ not F_e ; $macro(r_5)$: $@_0 := S \setminus @_1$;

r_6: $F_f ::= (\; F_e \;)$; $macro(r_6)$: $@_0 := @_1$;

r_7: $F_f ::=$ p ; $macro(r_7)$: $@_0 := P(p)$;

r_8: $F_f ::=$ true ; $macro(r_8)$: $@_0 := S$;

r_9: $F_f ::=$ false ; $macro(r_9)$: $@_0 := \emptyset$;

r_{10}: $F_f ::=$ ax F_f ;

$macro(r_{10})$: $@_0 := \{ s \in S | successors(s) \subseteq @_1 \}$;

r_{11}: $F_f ::=$ ex F_f ;

$macro(r_{11})$: $@_0 = \{ s \in S | successors(s) \cap @_1 \not\subseteq \emptyset \}$;

r_{12}: $F_f ::=$ a $[\; F_e$ u $F_e \;]$;

$macro(r_{12})$:   let Z, Z' be sets;

               $Z := \emptyset$; $Z' := @_2$;

               while ($Z \neq Z'$) do

                     $Z := Z'$;

                     $Z' := Z' \cup \{ s \in S | s \in @_1 \wedge successors(s) \subseteq Z \}$;

               end while

               $@_0 := Z$;

r_{13}: $F_f ::= \text{e} \ [\ F_e \ \text{u} \ F_e \ ] \ ;$

$macro(r_{13})$:   let Z, Z' be sets;

   $Z := \emptyset \ ; \ Z' := @_2 \ ;$

   while $(\ Z \neq Z' \ )$ do

       $Z := Z' \ ;$

       $Z' := Z' \cup \ \{s \in S | s \in @_1 \wedge successors(s) \cap Z \neq \emptyset\} \ ;$

   end while

   $@_0 := Z \ ;$

Bibliography

J. Adamek & V. Trnkova. Automata and algebras in categories. Kluwer Academic Publishers, 1989.

M. Adelantado, F. Boniol, M. Cubero-Castan, N. Hifdi, B. Lécussan, V. David & R. Porche. *Projet SATURNE: Modèle de Programmation et Modèle d'Exécution pour un Système Temps-Réel d'Aide à la Décision.* Technical report 1/3447.00/DERI, CERT-ONERA Dépt. d'Informatique, Toulouse, January 1993.

M. Adelantado, F. Boniol & S. de Givry. *SATURNE: Étude de cas sur le Copilote Electronique.* Technical report 1/3474.00/DERI, CERT-ONERA Dépt. d'Informatique, Toulouse, February 1994.

R. Alur, C. Courcoubetis & D. Dill. *Model-Checking for Real-Time Systems.* In Proceedings of the 5th IEEE Logic in Computer Science, pages 414–425, 1990.

R. Alur, C. Courcoubetis & D. Dill. *Model-checking for real-time systems.* In Proceedings of the IEEE 5th Symposium of LICS, 1990.

R. Alur & D. L. Dill. *The theory of timed automata.* In Lecture Notes in Computer Science, volume 600, chapter Real-Time: Theory in Practice, pages 45–73. Springer-Verlag, 1990.

R. Alur. *Techniques for automatic verification of real-time systems.* PhD thesis, Stanford University, 1991.

R. Alur, C. Courcoubetis, D. Dill, N. Halbwachs & H. Wong-Toi. *An Implementation of Three Algorithms for Timing Verification Based on Automata Emptiness.* In Proceedings of the Real-Time Systems Symposium, pages 157–166, 1992.

R. Alur & D. Dill. *The Theory of Timed Automata.* In Lecture Notes in Computer Science, volume 600, pages 45–73. Springer-Verlag, 1992.

R. Alur & T. A. Henzinger. *Logics and Models of Real Time: A Survey.* In Lecture Notes in Computer Science, volume 600, pages 74–106. Springer-Verlag, 1992.

R. Alur, C. Courcoubetis, T. A Henzinger & P.-H. Ho. *Hybrid automata: An algorithmic approach to specification and verification of hybrid systems.* In R. L. Grossman, A. Nerode, A. P. Ravn & H. Rischel, editors, Theory of Hybrid Systems, pages 209–229. Springer-Verlag, 1993.

R. Alur, T. A. Henzinger & P.-H. Ho. *Automatic symbolic verification of embedded systems.* In Proceedings of the Real-Time Systems Symposium, pages 2–11, 1993.

R. Alur & D. Dill. *A Theory of Timed Automata.* Theoretical Computer Science, vol. 126, pages 183–235, 1994.

F. Alvarez-Cuevas, F. Oller, M. Bertran & J. Selga. *A Novel Algorithm for Voice Synchronisation in Packet Switching Networks.* IEEE Network Magazine, September 1993.

J. Alves-Foss, D. Frincke & G. Saghi. *Applying the TCSEC guidelines to a real-time enbedded system environment.* In Proceedings of the National Information Systems Security Conference, pages 89–97, October 1997.

J. Alves-Foss. *The architecture of secure systems.* In Proceedings of the Hawaii International Conference on System Sciences, pages 307–316, January 1998.

T. Amon, H. Hulgaard, G. Borriello & S. Burns. *Timing Analysis of Concurrent Systems: An Algorithm for Determining Time Separation of Events.* In Proceedings of ICCD '93, October 1993.

M. Antoniotti & B. Mishra. *Discrete event models + temporal logic = supervisory controller: Automatic synthesis of locomotion controllers.* In Proceedings of IEEE Robotics and Automation, 1995.

M. A. Arbib. *Theories of Abstract Automata.* In Series in Automatic Computation. Prentice Hall, Englewood Cliffs, NJ, 1969.

M. A. Arbib & E. G. Manes. Arrows, structures and functors: The categorical imperative. Academic Press, 1975.

A. Arnold. *MEC: a system for constructing and analyzing transition systems.* In Lecture Notes in Computer Science, volume 407. Springer-Verlag, 1989.

A. Arnold. *Systèmes de transitions finis et sémantique des processus communicants.* MASSON, E. R. I., 1992.

J. C. M. Baeten & J. A. Bergstra. *Real time process algebra.* Formal Aspects of Computing, vol. 3(2), pages 142–188, 1991.

J. C. M. Baeten & J. A. Bergstra. *Real time process algebra.* Formal Aspects of Computing, vol. 3, pages 142–188, 1993.

S. Balemi, G. J. Hoffmann, P. Gyugyi, H. Wong-Toi & G. F. Franklin. *Surpervisory control of a rapid thermal multiprocessor.* IEEE Transactions on Automatic Control, vol. 38(7), pages 1040–1059, 1993.

M. Barbeau, G. Custeau & R. St-Denis. *An algorithm for computing the mask value of the supremal normal sublanguage of a legal language.* IEEE Transactions on Automatic Control, vol. 40(4), pages 699–703, 1995.

M. Barbeau, F. Kabanza & R. St-Denis. *An efficient algorithm for controller synthesis under full observation.* Journal of Algorithms, vol. 25(1), pages 144–161, 1997.

M. Barbeau, F. Kabanza & R. St-Denis. *A method for the synthesis of controllers to handle safety, liveness, and real-time constraints.* IEEE Transactions on Automatic Control, vol. 43(11), pages 1543–1559, 1998.

N. Ben Hadj-Alouane, S. Lafortune & F. Lin. *Variable lookahead supervisory control with state information.* IEEE Transactions on Automatic Control, vol. 39(12), pages 2398–2410, 1994.

N. Ben Hadj-Alouane, S. Lafortune & F. Lin. *Centralized and distributed algorithms for on-line synthesis of maximal control policies under partial observation.* Discrete Event Dynamic Systems: Theory and Applications, vol. 6(4), pages 379–427, 1996.

A. Benveniste & G. Berry. *The Synchronous Approach to Reactive and Real-Time Systems.* In Proceedings of IEEE, Another Look at Real-time Programming, volume 79(9), pages 1270–1282, September 1991.

J. A. Bergstra & J. W. Klop. *Process algebra for syncronous communication.* Information and Control, vol. 60, pages 109–137, 1984.

G. Berry & G. Gonthier. *The Esterel Synchronous Programming Language: Design, Semantics, Implementation.* Science of Computer Programming, vol. 19(2), pages 87–152, 1992.

G. Berry, S. Ramesh & R. K. Shyamasundar. *Communicating Reactive Processes.* In Proceedings of the 20th Annual Symposium on Principles of Programming Languages, 1993.

M. Bertran. *On a Formal Definition and Application of Dimensional Design.* Software — Practice and Experience, vol. 18(11), pages 1029–1045, November 1988.

M. Bertran. *PADD: A Schema Notation Integrating Parallelism and Abstraction.* Report, ETSETB, Universitat Politècnica de Catalunya, Barcelona, 1989. Also in Proceedings of the IEEE Communications Society CAMAD'92, Montebello, Quebec, Canada, September 1992.

M. Bertran & F. Oller. *An Environment for DSP System Development with Extended Abstract Types, and Dimensional Design (PADDE).* In Proceedings of the IEEE International Conference on A. S. Signal Processing (ICASSP'93), pages 449–452, Minneapolis, MN, April 1993.

M. Bertran & F. Alvarez-Cuevas. *A design environment with simulation and formal verification.* In Proceedings of the 5th IEEE Communications Society Conference on Computer Aided Modeling and Design of Communication Links and Networks (CAMAD'94), Princeton, NJ, April 1994.

M. Bertran. *A Transformation of Monitor into Communication Synchronized Parallel Processes: A Systematic Refinement Step in Design.* In Lecture Notes in Computer Science, volume 1213, chapter Proceedings of ARTS'97, pages 199–215. Springer-Verlag, 1997.

M. Bertran, F. Alvarez-Cuevas & A. Duran. *Communication Extended Abstract Types in the Refinement of Parallel Communicating Processes.* In Lecture Notes in Computer Science, volume 1213, chapter Proceedings of ARTS'97, pages 263–279. Springer-Verlag, 1997.

T. Bolognesi & E. Brinksma. *Introduction to the ISO Specification Language LOTOS*. Computer Networks and ISDN Systems, vol. 14, pages 25–59, 1987.

T. Bolognesi, F. Lucidi & S. Trigila. *From Timed Petri Nets to Timed LOTOS*. In Proceedings of the 10th International IFIP Symposium on Protocol Specification, Testing and Verification, pages 377–406. North-Holland, June 1990.

T. Bolognesi & F. Lucidi. *LOTOS-like Process Algebras with Urgent or Timed Interactions*. In Proceedings of FORTE'91: Forma Techniques IV, Sidney, November 1991.

F. Boniol. *Etude d'une sémantique de la réactivité : variations autour du modèle synchrone et application aux systèmes embarqués*. PhD thesis, Ecole Nationale Supérieure de l'Aéronautique et de l'Espace, December 1997.

A. Bonner. *What Was Llull Up To?* In Lecture Notes in Computer Science, volume 1213, chapter Proceedings of ARTS'97, pages 263–279. Springer-Verlag, 1997.

G. Borriello. *A New Interface Specification Methodology and its Application to Transducer Synthesis*. PhD thesis, EECS, University of California at Berkeley, 1998.

A. Bouajjani, S. Tripakis & S. Yovine. *On-the-fly symbolic model-checking for real-time systems*. In IEEE Real-Time System Symposium (RTSS'97), 1997.

F. Boussinot & R. de Simone. *The Esterel language*. In Proceedings of IEEE, Another Look at Real-time programming, volume 79(9), pages 1293–1304, September 1991.

N. Bouteille, P. Brard, G. Colombari, N. Cotaina & D. Richet. Le grafcet. Cepadues Editions, Toulouse, France, 1992.

T. F. Bowen, F. S. Dworak, C. H. Chow, N. Griffeth, G. E. Herman & Y-.J. Lin. *The Feature Interaction Problem in Telecommunications Systems*. In Proceedings of the 7th International Conference on Software Engineering for Telecommunication Switching Systems, pages 59–62, 1989.

M. Bozga, O. Maler, A. Pnueli & S. Yovine. *Some progress in the symbolic verification of timed automata*. Computer Aided Verification, 1997.

B. A. Brandin, W. M. Wonham & B. Benhabib. *Manufacturing cell supervisory control — a modular timed discrete-event system approach*. In Proceedings of the IEEE International Conference on Robotics and Automation, pages 846–851, 1993.

B. A. Brandin. *P(L)C-based supervisory control of discrete event systems*. In Proceedings of the 32nd Allerton Conference, pages 881–889, University of Illinois at Urbana-Champaign, 1994.

B. A. Brandin & M. W. Wonham. *Supervisory control of timed discrete-event systems*. IEEE Transactions on Automatic Control, vol. 39(2), pages 329–343, February 1994.

E. Brinksma, G. Scollo & C. Steenbergen. *LOTOS Specifications, their Implementations and their Tests*. In G. von Bochmann & B. Sarikaya, editors, Protocol Specification, Testing, and Verification, volume VI, pages 349–360.

North-Holland, 1987.

E. Brinksma. *A Theory for the Derivation of Tests.* In S. Aggarwal & K. Sabnani, editors, Protocol Specification, Testing, and Verification, volume VIII, pages 63–74. North-Holland, 1988.

E. Brinksma, R. Alderden, J. Langerak, R. van de Lagemaat & J. Tretmans. *A Formal Approach to Conformance Testing.* In J. de Meer, L. Mackert & W. Effelsberg, editors, Proceedings of the IFIP TC6 2nd International Workshop on Protocol Test Systems, pages 349–363. North-Holland, 1990.

E. Brinksma. *A Framework for Test Selection.* In B. Jonsson, J. Parrow & B. Pehrson, editors, Protocol Specification, Testing, and Verification, volume XI, pages 233–248. North-Holland, 1991.

M. C. Browne & E. M. Clarke. *SML: a High Level Language for the Design and Verification of Finite State Machines.* In Proceedings of the IFIP WG 10.2 International Working Conference from HDL Descriptions to Guaranteed Correct Circuit Designs, pages 269–292, Grenoble, France, September 1986.

R. E. Bryant. *Graph-Based Algorithms for Boolean Function Manipulation.* IEEE Transactions on Computers, vol. 35(8), pages 677–691, 1986.

J. A. Brzozowski, T. Gahlinger & F. Mavaddat. *Consistency and Satisfiability of Waveform Timing Specifications.* Networks, vol. 21, pages 91–107, 1991.

R. J. Buchi. Finite automata, their algebras and grammars. Springer-Verlag, 1989.

P. A. Buhr, M. Fortier & M. H. Coffin. *Monitor classification.* ACM Computing Surveys, vol. 27(1), March 1995.

J. R. Burch, E. M. Clarke, K. L. McMillan, D. L. Dill & L. J. Hwang. *Symbolic Model Checking: 10^{20} states and beyond.* Information and Computation, vol. 98(2), pages 142–170, 1992.

J. R. Burch, E. M. Clarke, D. E. Long, K. L. McMillan & D. Dill. *Symbolic Model Checking for Sequential Circuit Verification.* IEEE Transactions on CAD of ICS, vol. 13(4), pages 401–424, 1994.

T. M. Burks & K. A. Sakallah. *Min-Max Linear Programming and the Timing Analysis of Digital Circuits.* In Proceedings of ICCD'93, pages 152–155, October 1993.

S. Burris & H. P. Sankappanavar. *A Course in Universal Algebra.* In Graduate Texts in Mathematics, volume 78. Springer-Verlag, New York, 1980.

R. Burstall & P. Landin. *Programs and their proofs: an algebraic approach.* Machine Intelligence, vol. 4, pages 17–43, 1969.

E. J. Cameron, N. Griffeth, Y. Lin, M. E. Nilson, W. K. Schnure & H. Velthuijsen. *A Feature Interaction Benchmark for IN and Beyond.* In L. G. Bouma & H. Velthuijsen, editors, Second International Workshop on Feature Interactions in Telecommunications Systems, pages 1–23. IOS Press, 1994. Also in IEEE Communications, volume 31(3), pages 64–69, March 1993.

S. V. Campos & E. M. Clarke. *Real-time symbolic model checking for discrete time models.* In Proceedings of the 1st AMAST International Workshop in Real-time Systems, pages 129–145. World Scientific Publishing Company, 1994.

P. Caspi, N. Halbwachs, P. Pilaud & P. Raymond. *The synchronous dataflow programming language LUSTRE.* In Proceedings of IEEE, Another Look at Real-time Programming, volume 79(9), pages 1305–1319, September 1991.

C. G. Cassandras, S. Lafortune & G. J. Olsder. *Introduction to the modelling, control and optimization of discrete event systems.* In A. Isidori, editor, Trends in Control. A European Perspective, pages 217–291. Springer-Verlag, 1995.

CCITT. *Recommendation Z.120: Message Sequence Charts (MSC)*, 1992.

A. Cerone, A. J. Cowie, G. J. Milne & P. A. Moseley. *Description and Verification of a Time-Sensitive Protocol.* Technical report CIS-96-009, University of South Australia, School of Computer and Information Science, Adelaide, Australia, October 1996. http://www.cis.unisa.edu.au/cgi-bin/techreport?CIS-96-009.

A. Cerone, A. J. Cowie, G. J. Milne & P. A. Moseley. *Modelling a time-dependent protocol using the Circal process algebra.* In Lecture Notes in Computer Science, volume 1201, chapter Hybrid and Real-Time Systems, pages 124–138. Springer-Verlag, 1997.

A. Cerone, A. J. Cowie, G. J. Milne & P. A. Moseley. *Modelling a time-dependent protocol using the Circal process algebra.* In Lecture Notes in Computer Science, volume 1201, chapter Proceedings of the International Workshop on Hybrid and Real-Time Systems, Grenoble, France, March 26-28, 1997, pages 124–138. Springer-Verlag, 1997. Also as Technical Report CIS-96-010, University of South Australia, School of Computer and Information Science, Adelaide, Australia, October 1996. http://www.cis.unisa.edu.au/cgi-bin/techreport?CIS-96-010.

A. Cerone & G. J. Milne. *Modelling a time-dependent protocol using the Circal process algebra.* In Lecture Notes in Computer Science, volume 1349, chapter Algebraic Methodology and Software Technology, pages 108–122. Springer-Verlag, 1997.

A. Cerone & G. J. Milne. *Characterization of Temporal Logic Formulas within Circal.* To appear as Technical Report, University of South Australia, School of Computer and Information Science, Adelaide, Australia, 1999.

A. Cerone. *A temporal logic for simultaneous actions.* Technical report 00-09, University of Queensland, Software Verification Research Centre, March 2000.

G. Champigneux. *Development Environment for Knowledge-Based Systems. Some examples of application: the "Copilote Electronique" project.* In North Atlantic Treaty Organization, AGARD Lecture Series, volume 200, chapter Knowledge-Based Functions in Aerospace Systems. NASA Center for AeroSpace Information, November 1995.

P. Chen. *The entity-relationship model: Toward a unified view of data.* ACM Transactions on Database Systems, vol. 1(1), pages 9–36, March 1976.

I. Christoff. *Testing equivalences and fully abstract models for probabilistic processes.* In Lecture Notes in Computer Science, volume 458, chapter Proceedings of CONCUR'90, pages 126–140. Springer-Verlag, 1990.

E. M. Clarke, E. A. Emerson & A. P. Sistla. *Automatic Verification of Finite-state Concurrent Systems Using Temporal Logic Specifications.* ACM Transactions on Programming Languages and Systems, vol. 8(2), pages 244–263, 1986.

R. Cleveland, S. A. Smolka & A. Zwarico. *Testing preorders for probabilistic processes.* In Lecture Notes in Computer Science, volume 623, chapter Proceedings of ICALP'92, pages 708–719. Springer-Verlag, 1992.

S. Clyde, D. Embley & S. Woodfield. *Tunable formalism in object-oriented systems analysis: meeting the needs of both theoreticians and practitioners.* In Proceedings of OOPSLA'92, pages 452–465, October 1992.

P. Cohn. Universal algebra. Reidel, London, 1981.

T. H. Cormen, C. E. Leiserson & R. T. Rivest. Introduction to algorithms. McGraw-Hill, 1990.

P. Crubillé. *Réalisation de l'outil MEC: spécification fonctionelle et architecture.* PhD thesis, Bordeaux, 1989.

F. Cuartero, D. de Frutos & V. Valero. *A sound and complete proof system for probabilistic processes.* In Proceedings of the 4th AMAST Workshop on Real-Time Systems, 1997.

R. Curtain & A. J. Pritchard. Functional analysis in modern applied mathematics. Academic Press, 1997.

O. J. Dahl, B. Myhrhang & K. Nygaard. Simula 67 common base language. Norsk Regnesentral, Oslo, Norway, 1968.

O. J. Dahl. *Hierarchical program structures.* In Structured Programming. Academic Press, New York, 1972.

V. David, C. Fraboul, J. Y. Rousselot & P. Siron. *Partitioning and mapping communication graphs on a modular reconfigurable parallel architecture.* In Proceedings of CONPAR'92, September 1992.

C. Daws, A. Olivero, S. Tripakis & S. Yovine. *The tool* KRONOS. In Lecture Notes in Computer Science, volume 1066, chapter Workshop on Hybrid Systems and Autonomous Control, DIMACS, New Jersey, October 1996. Springer-Verlag, October 1996.

D. de Champeaux, A. Anderson & E. Feldhousen. *Case study of object-oriented software development.* In Proceedings of OOPSLA'92, pages 377–391, October 1992.

D. de Frutos, G. Leduc, L. Léonard, L. F. Llana-Díaz, C. Miguel, J. Quemada & G. Rabay. *Belgian-spanish proposal for a time extended LOTOS.* ISO/IEC JTC1/SC21/WG1, October 1994.

R. De Nicola & M. C. B. Hennessy. *Testing equivalences for processes.* Theoretical Computer Science, vol. 34, pages 83–133, 1984.

R. De Nicola & F. Vaandrager. *Action versus State based Logics for Trsnsition Systems.* In Lecture Notes in Computer Science, volume 469, pages 407–419. Springer-Verlag, Berlin, 1990.

Department Of Defense Computer Security Center. *Department of Defense Trusted Computer System Evaluation Criteria,* August 1983.

Department Of Defense Computer Security Center. *Department of Defense Trusted Computer System Evaluation Criteria,* December 1985.

D. Dill. *Timing assumptions and verification of finite-state concurrent systems.* In Lecture Notes in Computer Science, volume 407, pages 197–212. Springer-Verlag, 1989.

D. Dill & H. Wong-Toi. *Verification of real-time systems by successive over and under approximation.* In Lecture Notes in Computer Science, volume 939, pages 409–422. Springer-Verlag, 1995.

L. K. Dillon, G. Kutty, L. E. Moser, P. M. Melliar-Smith & Y. S. Ramakrishna. *Graphical Specifications for Concurrent Systems.* In Proceedings of the 14th IEEE International Conference on Software Engineering, pages 214–224, New York, 1992.

L. K. Dillon, G. Kutty, L. E. Moser, P. M. Melliar-Smith & Y. S. Ramakrishna. *A graphical Interval Logic for Specifying Concurrent Systems.* ACM TSEM, vol. 3(2), pages 131–165, April 1994.

M. Doche. Spécification et vérification formelles en vue de la génération de jeux de tests. application au système modulor. Master's thesis, ENSEEIHT, September 1996.

K. Drira, P. Azema & F. Vernadat. *Refusal Graphs for Conformance Tester Generation and Simplification: a Computational Framework.* In A. Danthine, G. Leduc & P. Wolper, editors, Protocol Specification, Testing, and Verification, volume XIII, pages 257–272. Elsevier Science Publishing Company, 1993.

E-LOTOS: ISO/IEC JTC1/SC21/WG7. *Working draft on enhacements to LOTOS,* January 1997.

D. Embley, B. Kurtz & S. Woodfield. Object-oriented systems analysis: A model-driven approach. Prentice Hall, Englewood Cliffs, NJ, 1992.

D. Embley, R. Jackson & S. Woodfield. *OO systems analysis: Is it or isn't it?* IEEE Software, vol. 12(4), pages 19–33, July 1995.

D. Embley. Object database development: Concepts and principles. Addison-Wesley, Reading, MA, 1997.

B. Espiau, K. Kapellos & M. Jourdan. *Formal verification in robotics: Why and how?* In Proceedings of the 7th International Symposium of Robotics Research, Munich, Germany, October 21–24, 1995, pages 201–213. Cambridge Press, October 1995.

M. Faci, L. Logrippo & B. Stepien. *Formal Specifications of Telephone Systems in LOTOS: The Constraint-Oriented Style Approach.* Computer Networks and ISDN Systems, vol. 21, pages 52–67, 1991.

M. Faci & L. Logrippo. *Specifying Features and Analysing their Interactions in a LOTOS Environment.* In L. G. Bouma & H. Velthuijsen, editors, 2nd International Workshop on Feature Interactions in Telecommunications Systems, pages 136–151. IOS Press, 1994.

M. Faci. *Detecting Feature Interactions in Telecommunications Systems Designs.* PhD thesis, University of Ottawa, 1995. http://lotos.site.uottawa.ca.

M. Faci, L. Logrippo & B. Stepien. *Structural Models for Specifying Telephone Systems.* Computer Networks and ISDN Systems, vol. 29, pages 501–528, 1997.

L. M. G. Feijs & H. B. M. Jonkers. Formal specification and design. Cambridge University Press, 1992.

R. J. Fiertag, K. Levitt & L. Robinson. *Proving multilevel security of a system design.* In Proceedings of the Symposium on Operating System Principles, pages 57–95, 1977.

C. Fraboul & P. Siron. *Un environnement de programmation d'applications distribuées et tolérantes aux pannes sur une architecture parallèle reconfigurable.* Aerospace Software Engineering for Advanced Systems Architectures, May 1993.

R. B. France. *Semantically Extended Data Flow Diagrams: A Formal Specification Tool.* IEEE Transactions on Software Engineering, vol. 18(4), pages 329–346, April 1992.

P. Freedman. *Time, Petri Nets, and Robotics.* IEEE Transactions on Robotics and Automation, vol. 7(4), pages 417–433, August 1991.

M. Gardner. *The Ars Magna of Ramon Llull.* In Logic Machines and Diagrams. McGraw-Hill, New York, 1958.

R. Gawlick, R. Segala, J. F. Sogaard-Anderson, N. Lynch & B. Lampson. *Liveness in timed and untimed systems.* Technical report TR-587, MIT Computer Science Laboratory, 1993.

S. Ghantasala. Multi-level data seecurity for an embedded real-time operating system. Master's thesis, University of Idaho, August 1997.

N. Ghezal, S. Matiatos, P. Piovesan, Y. Sorel & M. Sorine. *SYNDEX: un environnement de programmation pour multi-processeur de traitement du signal. Mécanismes de communication.* Technical report 1236, INRIA, June 1990.

A. Giacalone, C. C. Jou & S. A. Smolka. *Algebraic reasoning for probabilistic concurrent systems.* In Proceedings of Working Conference on Programming Concepts and Methods, IFIP TC 2, Sea of Galilee, Israel, 1990.

A. Girault. *Sur la répartition de programmes synchrones.* PhD thesis, Institut National Polytechnique de Grenoble, January 1994.

P. Girodias, E. Cerny & W. J. Older. *Solving Linear, Min and Max Constraint Systems Using CLP Based on Relational Arithmetic.* In Proceedings of the International Conference on Principles and Practice of Constraint Programming (CP'95), Marseille, France, September 1995.

P. Girodias & E. Cerny. *Interface Timing Verification with Delay Correlation Using Constraint Logic Programming.* In Proceedings of the IEEE European Design & Test Conference (ED&TC'97), March 1997.

R. Glabbeek, S. A. Smolka, B. U. Steffen & C. M. N. Tofts. *Reactive, generative and stratified models of probabilistic processes.* In Proceedings of 5th Annual IEEE Symposium on Logic in Computer Science, Philadelphia, 1990.

J. A. Goguen & J. Meseguer. *Security policies and security models.* In Proceedings of the IEEE Symposium on Security and Privacy, pages 11–20, 1982.

J. A. Goguen & J. Meseguer. *Unwinding and inference control.* In Proceedings of the IEEE Symposium on Security and Privacy, pages 75–86, 1984.

M. Gordon. Programming language theory and its implementation. Prentice Hall, 1988.

J. F. Groote. *Transition system specifications with negative premises.* Theoretical Computer Science, vol. 118, pages 263–299, 1993.

R. Guillemot & R. Logrippo. *Derivation of useful execution trees from LOTOS specifications by using an interpreter.* In K. J. Turner, editor, Formal Description Techniques, pages 311–325. North-Holland, 1989.

N. Halbwachs. Synchronous programming of reactive systems. Kluwer Academic Publishers, 1993.

H. Hansson & B. Jonsson. *A calculus for communicating systems with time and probabilities.* In Proceedings of the Real-Time Systems Symposium, Orlando, FL, 1990.

D. Harel. *Statecharts: a Visual Formalism for Complex Systems.* Science of Computer Programming, vol. 8(3), pages 231–275, 1987.

D. J. Hatley & I. A. Pirbhai. Strategies for real time system specification. Dorset House Publishing Company, Inc., New York, 1987.

M. Hennessy & R. Milner. *Algebraic Laws for Nondeterminism and Concurrency.* Journal of ACM, vol. 32, pages 137–162, 1985.

M. Hennessy. Algebraic theory of processes. MIT Press, 1988.

M. Hennessy & T. Regan. *A process algebra for timed systems.* Information and Computation, vol. 177, pages 221–239, 1995.

T. Henzinger, X. Nicollin, J. Sifakis & S. Yovine. *Symbolic model checking for real-time systems.* In Proceedings of the IEEE Symposium on Logic in Computer Science, pages 394–406, 1992.

T. Henzinger, Z. Manna & A. Pnueli. *Temporal Proof Methodologies for Timed Transition Systems.* Information and Computation, vol. 112(2), pages 273–337, 1994.

T. Henzinger, X. Nicollin, J. Sifakis & S. Yovine. *Symbolic model checking for real-time systems.* Information and Computation, pages 193–244, 1994.

J. N. Hillgarth. Ramon Llull and Lullism in XIV Century France. Oxford Press, 1971.

H. Hiraishi. *Design verification of sequential machines based on ε-free regular temporal logic.* In Computer hardware description languages and their applications, pages 249–263. Elsevier Science Publishers, 1990.

C. A. R. Hoare. *Monitors: An Operating System Structuring Concept'.* Communications of ACM, vol. 17(10), pages 549–557, October 1974.

C. A. R. Hoare. Communicating sequential processes. Prentice Hall, 1985.

L. E. Holloway, B. H. Krogh & A. Giua. *A survey of Petri Net methods for controlled discrete event systems.* Discrete Event Dynamic Systems: Theory and Applications, vol. 7(2), pages 151–190, 1997.

G. J. Holzmann. Design and validation of computer protocols. Prentice Hall, Englewood Cliffs, NJ, 1990.

G. J. Holzmann. *Design and Validation of Protocols: A Tutorial.* Computer Networks and ISDN Systems, vol. 25, pages 981–1017, 1993.

H. Hulgaard, S. M. Burns, T. Amon & G. Borriello. *Practical applications of an efficient time separation of events algorithm.* In Proceedings of ICCAD'93, Santa Clara, CA, November 1993.

Institute of Electrical and Electronics Engineers. *ANSI/IEEE 802.3 Standard, ISO/DIS 8802/3*, 1985.

International Organization for Standardization. *LOTOS: A formal description technique based on the temporal ordering of observational behaviour*, international standard, 8807-02-15 edition, 1989.

D. Ionescu. *Designing supervisor for real-time systems.* In T. Rus & C. Rattray, editors, Theories and experiences for real-time system development, pages 103–128. World Scientific Publishing Company, 1994.

K. Jensen. Coloured Petri Nets, Basic Concepts, Analysis Methods and Practical Use, volume 1. Springer-Verlag, Berlin, 1992.

F. Kabanza, M. Barbeau & R. St-Denis. *Planning control rules for reactive agents.* Artificial Intelligence, vol. 95(1), pages 67–113, 1997.

R. Kalman, P. Falb & M. A. Arbib. Mathematical theory of dynamic systems. Academic Press, New York, 1969.

K. M. Kavi. Real-time systems, abstraction, languages and design methodologies. IEEE Computer Society Press, 1992.

Y. Kesten, Z. Manna & A. Pnueli. *Verifying Clocked Transition Systems.* In Lecture Notes in Computer Science, volume 1066, chapter Hybrid Systems III. Springer-Verlag, 1996.

K. Khordoc, M. Dufresne, E. Cerny, P. A. Babkine & A. Silburt. *Integrating Behavior and Timing in Executable Specifications.* In Proceedings of CHDL'93, April 1993.

K. Khordoc & E. Cerny. *Modeling Cell Processing Hardware with Action Diagrams.* In Proceedings of ISCAS'94, June 1994.

K. Kimbler & L. G. Bouma. Feature interactions in telecommunications and software systems, volume V. IOS Press, 1998.

A. S. Klusner. *Models and axioms for a fragment of real time process algebra.* PhD thesis, CWI, Amsterdam, 1993.

J. Knaack. *An Algebraic Approach to Language Translation.* PhD thesis, University of Iowa, Department of Computer Science, Iowa City, IA 52242, December 1994.

J. A. G. M. Koomen. *The TIMELOGIC Temporal Reasoning System in Common Lisp.* Technical report 231, University of Rochester, November 1987.

J. Košecká, H. I. Christensen & R. Bajcsy. *Discrete event modeling of visually guided behaviors.* International Journal on Computer Vision: Special Issue on Qualitative Vision, 1994.

J. Košecká & H. I. Christensen. *Experiments in behavior composition.* In Proceedings of the Conference on Intelligent Robot Control, Pisa, Italy, 1995.

S. Kripke. *Semantical analysis of modal logic I: Normal modal propositional cal-*

culi. Zeitschrift f. Math. Logik und Grundlagen d. Math., September 1963.

R. Kumar & V. K. Garg. Modeling and control of logical discrete event systems. Kluwer Academic Publishers, Boston, MA, 1995.

R. P. Kurshan. Computer-aided verification of coordinating processes: The automata-theoretic approach. Princeton University Press, 1995.

L. Lamport. *The Temporal Logic of Actions.* ACM TPLS, vol. 16(3), pages 872–923, May 1994.

L. Lamport. *TLA in Pictures.* Src Research Report 127, Digital Equipment Corporation, Inc., September 1994.

P. Le Guernic, T. Gauthier, M. Le Borgneand & C. Le Maire. *Programming real time application with SIGNAL.* In Proceedings of IEEE: Another Look at Real-time Programming, volume 79(9), pages 1321–1336, September 1991.

P. Le Parc & L. Marcé. *Synchronous definition of GRAFCET with SIGNAL.* In Proceedings of the IEEE SMC'93 Conference, Le Touquet, France, 1993.

P. Le Parc. *Apports de la méthodologie synchrone pour la définition et l'utilisation du langage GRAFCET.* PhD thesis, Rennes, 1994.

P. Le Parc, Q. Quéguineur & L. Marcé. *Two proof methods for the GRAFCET language.* In Proceedings of the 19th IFAC/IFIP Workshop on Real-Time Programming, Lac de Constance, 1994.

G. Leduc. *A Framework based on the Implementation relations for Implementing LOTOS Specifications.* Computer Networks and ISDN Systems, vol. 25, pages 23–41, 1992.

I. Lee, P. Brémond-Grégoire & R. Gerber. *A Process Algebraic Approach to the Specification and Analysis of Resource-Bound Real-Time Systems.* In Proceedings of the IEEE, pages 158–171, January 1994.

D. R. Lefebvre & G. N. Saridis. *Integrating robotics functions and operator supervision using Petri Nets.* In Proceedings of the IEEE International Conference on Intelligent Robots and Systems, Raleigh, NC, 1992.

Y. Li & W. M. Wonham. *Control of Vector Discrete-Event Systems II — Controller Synthesis.* IEEE Transactions on Automatic Control, vol. 39(3), pages 512–531, 1994.

J. Y. Lin. *Temporal Logic Approach to the Analysis and Synthesis of Discrete Event Systems.* PhD thesis, University of Ottawa, 1993.

B. Liskov & J. Guttag. Abstraction and specification in program development. McGraw-Hill, 1986.

L. Llana-Díaz & D. de Frutos-Escrig. *Denotational semantics for timed testing.* In M. Bertran & T. Rus, editors, Lecture Notes in Computer Science, volume 1231, chapter Transformation-Based Reactive Systems Develoment. 4th International AMAST Workshop on Real-Time and Distributed Software, pages 368–382. Springer-Verlag, 1997.

L. Logrippo, T. Melanchuk & R. J. Du Wors. *The algebraic specification language LOTOS: An industrial experience.* In Proceedings of the ACM SIGSOFT International Workshop on Formal Methods in Software Development, May 1990.

L. Logrippo, M. Faci & M. Haj-Hussein. *An Introduction to LOTOS: Learning by Examples.* Computer Networks and ISDN Systems, vol. 5(23), pages 325–342, 1992.

G. Lowe. *Prioritized and probabilistic models of timed CSP.* Technical report PRG-TR-24-91, Oxford University Computing Laboratory, 1991.

J. Lygeros & D. Godbole. *An interface between continuous and discrete-event controllers for vehicle automation.* Technical report, Intelligent Machines and Robotics Laboratory, University of California at Berkeley, 1994.

N. Lynch, R. Segala, F. Vaandrager & H. B. Weinberg. *Hybrid I/O automata.* In R. Alur, T. Henzinger & E. Sontag, editors, Lecture Notes in Computer Science, volume 1066, chapter Hybrid Systems III: Verification and Control (DIMACS/SYCON Workshop on Verification and Control of Hybrid Systems, New Brunswick, NJ, October 1995, pages 496–510. Springer-Verlag, 1996.

D. M. Lyons. *A process-based approach to task representation.* IEEE Transactions on Robotics and Automation, pages 2142–2150, 1990.

S. Mac Lane. *Categories for the Working Mathematician.* In Graduate Texts in Mathematics. Springer-Verlag, 1971.

K. MacMillan & D. Dill. *Algorithms for Interface Timing Verification.* In Proceedings of ICCD'92, October 1992.

M. Makungu, M. Barbeau & R. St-Denis. *Synthesis of controllers with colored Petri Nets.* In Proceedings of the 32nd Allerton Conference, pages 709–718, University of Illinois at Urbana-Champaign, 1994.

M. Makungu, M. Barbeau & R. St-Denis. *Synthesis of controllers of processes modeled as colored Petri Nets.* Discrete Event Dynamic Systems: Theory and Applications, vol. 9(2), pages 147–169, 1996.

O. Maler, A. Pnueli & J. Sifakis. *On the synthesis of discrete controllers for timed systems.* In E. W. Mayr & C. Puech, editors, Lecture Notes in Computer Science, volume 900, chapter Proceedings of the 12th Annual Symposium on Theoretical Aspects of Computer Science, pages 229–242. Springer-Verlag, Berlin, 1995.

Z. Manna et al. *The Stanford Temporal Prover.* Technical report STAN-CS-TR-94-1518, Department of Computer Science, Stanford University, 1994.

Z. Manna & A. Pnueli. *The anchored version of temporal logic.* In Lecture Notes in Computer Science, volume 354, chapter Linear time, branching time and partial order time in logics and Models of concurrency. Springer-Verlag, 1989.

Z. Manna & A. Pnueli. The temporal logic of reactive and concurrent systems: Specification. Springer-Verlag, New York, 1991.

Z. Manna & A. Pnueli. The temporal logic of reactive and concurrent systems. Springer-Verlag, 1992.

Z. Manna & A. Pnueli. *Models for Reactivity.* Acta Informatica, vol. 30, pages 609–678, 1993.

Z. Manna & A. Pnueli. Temporal verification of reactive and concurrent systems:

Safety. Springer-Verlag, New York, 1995.

D. McCullough. *Foundations of Ulysses: The Theory of Security.* Technical report RADC-TR-87-222, Odyssey Research Associates, Inc., July 1988.

D. McCullough. *Noninterference and the composability of security properties.* In Proceedings of the IEEE Symposium on Security and Privacy, pages 177–187, 1988.

J. McLean. *Security models and information flow.* In Proceedings of the IEEE Symposium on Research in Security and Privacy, pages 180–187, 1990.

J. McLean. *A general theory of composition for trace sets closed under selective interleaving functions.* In Proceedings of the IEEE Symposium on Research in Security and Privacy, pages 79–93, 1994.

K. L. McMillan. Symbolic model checking. Kluwer Academic Publishers, 1993.

G. H. Mealy. *A Mehtod for synthesising sequential circuits.* Bell System Technology Journal, vol. 34, pages 1045–1079, 1971.

P. M. Melliar-Smith. *A graphical representation of interval logic.* In Lecture Notes in Computer Science, volume 335, chapter Proceedings of the International Conference on Concurrence, pages 106–120. Springer-Verlag, Berlin, 1988.

M. D. Mesarovic & Y. Takahara. General systems theory: Mathematical foundations. Academic Press, 1975.

P. Michel & V. Wiels. *A Framework for Modular Formal Specification and Verification.* In Proceedings of FME'97, September 1997.

G. J. Milne. Formal specification and verification of digital systems. McGraw-Hill, 1994.

R. Milner. *Calculi for synchrony and asynchrony.* Theoretical Computer Science, vol. 25(3), pages 267–310, 1983.

R. Milner. *A Complete Inference System for a Class of Regular Behaviours.* Journal of Computer and System Sciences, vol. 28(3), pages 439–466, 1984.

R. Milner. Communication and concurrency. Prentice Hall, London, 1989.

S. Minato, N. Ishiura & S. Yajima. *Shared Binary Decision Diagram with Attributed Edges for Efficient Boolean Function Manipulation.* In Proceedings of the 27th Design Automation Conference, pages 52–57, 1990.

F. Moller. *The Semantics of Circal.* Technical report HDV-3-89, University of Strathclyde, Department of Computer Science, Glasgow, UK, 1989.

E. F. Moore. *Gedanken-experiments on sequential machines.* In Automata Studies, Annals of Mathematics Series, volume 34, pages 192–153. Princeton University Press, Princeton, NJ, 1956.

X. Nicollin & J. Sifakis. *An overview and synthesis on timed process algebras.* In Lecture Notes in Computer Science, volume 575, chapter Computer Aided Design, pages 376–398. Springer-Verlag, 1991.

X. Nicollin, J. Sifakis & S. Yovine. *Compiling real-time specifications into extended automata.* IEEE Transactions on Software Engineering, vol. 18(9), pages 794–804, 1992.

M. Núñez, D. de Frutos & L. Llana-Díaz. *Acceptance trees for probabilistic processes.* In Lecture Notes in Computer Science, volume 962, chapter

Proceedings of CONCUR'95, pages 249–263. Springer-Verlag, 1995.

A. Olivero, J. Sifakis & S. Yovine. *Using abstractions for the verification of linear hybrid systems.* In Proceedings of the 6th Conference on Computer-Aided Verification, California, 1994.

Y. Ortega-Mallén. *En Busca del Tiempo Perdido.* PhD thesis, Departamento de Informática y Automática, Universidad Complutense de Madrid, 1991.

J. S. Ostroff. *Synthesis of controllers for real-time discrete event systems.* In Proceedings of the 27th IEEE Conference on Decision and Control, pages 138–144, December 1989.

J. S. Ostroff. Temporal logic for real-time systems. John Wiley and Sons, New York, 1989.

J. S. Ostroff. *Temporal Logic for Real-Time Systems.* In Advanced Software Development Series. Research Studies Press Limited (distributed by John Wiley and Sons), Taunton, England, 1989.

J. S. Ostroff. *Deciding Properties of Timed Transition Models.* IEEE Transactions on Parallel and Distributed Systems, vol. 1(2), pages 170–183, April 1990.

J. S. Ostroff & M. W. Wonham. *A framework for real-time discrete event control.* IEEE Transactions on Automatic Control, vol. 35, pages 386–397, 1990.

F. Pagani. *Partial orders and verification of real time systems.* In Lecture Notes in Computer Science, volume 1135, chapter Proceedings of the Formal Techniques for Real-Time and Fault-Tolerance (FTRTFT) Conference, Uppsala, Sweden, September 1996. Springer-Verlag, 1996.

F. Pagani. *Ordres Partiels pour la Vérification de Systèmes Temps Réel.* PhD thesis, Ecole Nationale Supérieure de l'Aéronautique et de l'Espace, 1997.

J. Peterson. Petri net theory and the modelling of systems. Prentice Hall, Englewood Cliffs, NJ, 1981.

G. D. Plotkin. *A structural approach to operational semantics.* Technical report DAIMI-FN-19, Computer Science Department, Århus University, Denmark, 1981.

D. Pountain & D. May. *A tutorial introduction to Occam programming.* INMOS Documentation, 1988.

J. Quemada, D. de Frutos & A. Azcorra. *Tic: A Timed Calculus.* Formal Aspects of Computing, vol. 5, pages 224–252, 1993.

P. J. G. Ramadge & W. M. Wonham. *Supervisory control of a class of discrete-event processes.* SIAM Journal on Control and Optimization, vol. 25(1), pages 206–230, 1987.

P. J. G. Ramadge. *Some tractable supervisory control problems for discrete-event systems modeled by Büchi automata.* IEEE Transactions on Automatic Control, vol. 34(1), pages 10–19, 1989.

P. J. G. Ramadge & W. M. Wonham. *The control of discrete event systems.* In Proceedings of the IEEE, volume 77(1), pages 81–98, 1989.

Y. S. Ramakrishna, L. K. Dillon, L. E. Moser, P. M. Melliar-Smith & G. Kutty. *A real-time interval logic and its decision procedure.* In Lecture Notes in Computer Science, volume 761, chapter Proceedings of the 13th Conference on the Foundations of Software Technology and Theoretical Computer Science, pages 173–192. Springer-Verlag, Berlin, 1993.

G. M. Reed & A. W. Roscoe. *A timed model for communicating sequential processes.* In Lecture Notes in Computer Science, volume 226, chapter Proceedings of ICALP'86, pages 214–323. Springer-Verlag, 1986.

P. Rives, R. Pissard-Gibollet & K. Kapellos. *Development of a reactive mobile robot using real time vision.* In Proceedings of the 3rd International Symposium on Experimental Robotics, Kyoto, Japan, 1995.

P. Rony. *Interfacing Fundamentals: Timing Diagram Conventions.* Computer Design, pages 152–153, January 1980.

J. M. Roussel. *Analyse de Grafcets par génération logique de l'automate équivalent.* PhD thesis, Cachan, 1994.

J. Rumbaugh, M. Blaha, W. Premerlani, F. Eddy & W. Lorensen. Object-oriented modelling and design. Prentice Hall, Englewood Cliffs, NJ, 1991.

T. Rus. *Algebraic construction of a compiler.* Technical report 90–01, University of Iowa, Department of Computer Science, Iowa City, IA, 1990.

T. Rus. *Algebraic construction of compilers.* Theoretical Computer Science, vol. 90, pages 271–308, 1991.

T. Rus & T. Halverson. *Algebraic tools for language processing.* Computer Languages, vol. 20(4), pages 213–238, 1994.

T. Rus, T. Halverson, E. Van Wyk & R. Kooima. *An algebraic language processing environment.* In Proceedings of the 6th International Conference on Algebraic Methodology and Software Technology, AMAST'97, December 1997.

T. Rus & S. Pemmaraju. *Using graph coloring in an algebraic compiler.* Acta Informatica, vol. 34(3), pages 191–209, 1997.

T. Rus & E. Van Wyk. *A formal approach to parallelizing compilers.* In Proceedings of the SIAM Conference on Parallel Processing for Scientific Computation, March 1997.

T. Rus & E. Van Wyk. *Integrating temporal logics and model checking algorithms.* In Lecture Notes in Computer Science, volume 1231, chapter Proceedings of the 4th AMAST Workshop on Real-Time Systems. Springer-Verlag, May 1997.

T. Rus & E. Van Wyk. *Model checking tools for parallelizing compilers.* In Proceedings of the 2nd International Workshop on Formal Methods for Parallel Programming: Theory and Applications, April 1997.

J. Rushby & B. Randell. *A distributed secure system.* IEEE Computer, vol. 16(7), pages 55–67, 1983.

T. Sales. *Llull as Computer Scientist or Why Llull Was One of Us.* In Lecture Notes in Computer Science, volume 1213, chapter Proceedings of ARTS'97, pages 263–279. Springer-Verlag, 1997.

J. Sanchez-Allende. *Graphical Designer for LOTOS User Manual.* Department of Telematic Systems Engineering, Technical University of Madrid, October 1994.

S. Schneider. *An operational semantics for timed CSP.* Information and Computation, vol. 116(2), pages 193–213, 1995.

R. Segala. *Modeling and Verification of Randomized Distributed Systems.* PhD thesis, Massachusetts Institute of Technology, 1995.

C. Seguin & W. Wiels. *Using a logical and categorical approach for the validation of fault-tolerant systems.* In Proceedings of Formal Methods Europe (FME'96), March 1996.

K. Seidel. *Probabilistic Communicating Processes.* PhD thesis, Oxford University, 1992.

L. T. Semmens, R. B. France & T. W. G. Docker. *Integrated Structured Analysis and Formal Specifications.* The Computer Journal, vol. 35(6), pages 600–610, 1992.

Y. Shoham & J. Lavignon. *Temporal automata.* Technical report, Stanford University, 1990.

J. F. Sogaard-Anderson, N. Lynch & B. Lampson. *Correctness of communication protocols.* Technical report TR-589, MIT Computer Science Laboratory, 1993.

J. Spivey. Understanding z: A specification language and its formal semantics. Cambridge University Press, Cambridge, UK, 1988.

C. Stirling. *Modal an Temporal Logics for Processes.* In F. Moller & G. Birtwistle, editors, Lecture Notes in Computer Science, volume 1043, chapter Logic for Concurrency — Structure versus Automata, pages 149–237. Springer-Verlag, Berlin, Germany, 1996.

G. R. Stoneburner & D. A. Snow. *The Boeing MLS LAN: Headed towards an INFOSEC security solution.* In Procoddings of the 12th National Computer Security Conference, pages 254–266, October 1989.

J. G. Thistle & W. M. Wonham. *Control of infinite behavior of finite automata.* SIAM Journal on Control and Optimization, vol. 32(4), pages 1075–1097, 1994.

J. G. Thistle & W. M. Wonham. *Supervision of infinite behavior of discrete-event systems.* SIAM Journal on Control and Optimization, vol. 32(4), pages 1098–1113, 1994.

J. G. Thistle. *Supervisory control of discrete event systems.* Mathematical Computer Modelling, vol. 23(11–12), pages 25–53, 1996.

J. K. Turner. Using formal description techniques: An introduction to estelle, lotos and sdl. John Wiley and Sons, 1993.

F. Vazquez. *Automatic File Generator.* In Proceedings of the 2nd Software Engineering Research Forum, Melbourne, FL, pages 141–142, November 1992.

F. Vazquez. Formal design of real time systems. Master's thesis, The George Washington University, Washington, DC, February 1998.

C. A. Vissers, G. Scollo, M. van Sinderen & E. Brinksma. *Specification Styles in Distributed Systems Design and Verification.* Theoretical Computer Science, vol. 89, pages 179–206, 1991.

F. Wang, A. K. Mok & E. A. Emerson. *Symbolic model checking for distributed real-time systems.* In Lecture Notes in Computer Science, volume 670, pages 632–651. Springer-Verlag, 1993.

P. Ward & S. Mellor. Structured development for real-time systems, volume 1. Yourdon Press, Englewood Cliffs, NJ, 1991.

P. Ward & S. Mellor. Structured development for real-time systems, volume 2. Yourdon Press, Englewood Cliffs, NJ, 1991.

P. Ward & S. Mellor. Structured development for real-time systems, volume 3. Yourdon Press, Englewood Cliffs, NJ, 1991.

H. B. Weinberg & N. Lynch. *Verification of automated vehicle protection systems.* In Proceedings of the DIMACS Worshop on Verification and Control of Hybrid Systems, New Brunswick, NJ, 1995.

C. Wezeman. *The CO-OP Method for Compositional Derivation of Conformance Testers.* In E. Brinksma, G. Scollo & C. A. Vissers, editors, Protocol Specification, Testing, and Verification, volume IX, pages 145–158. North-Holland, 1990.

R. W. Witty. *Small scale software engineering.* PhD thesis, Department of Computer Science, Brunel University, Uxbridge, UK, September 1981.

W. M. Wonham & P. J. G. Ramadge. *On the supremal controllable sublanguage of a given language.* SIAM Journal on Control and Optimization, vol. 25(3), pages 637–659, 1987.

W. M. Wonham. *Notes on Control of Discrete-Event Systems.* Report ECE 1636F/1637S, Systems Control Group, University of Toronto, 1994.

M. Woodman. *Yourdon dataflow diagrams: a tool for disciplined requirements analysis.* Information and Software Technology, vol. 30(9), pages 515–533, November 1988.

S. Yamane. *Formal timing verification techniques for distributed system.* In Proceedings of the 5th IEEE CS Workshop on Future Trends of Distributed Computing Systems, pages 454–460, 1995.

S. Yamane. *Verification system for real-time specification based on extended real-time logic.* In Proceedings of the International Workshop on Real-Time Computing Systems and Applications, pages 192–196, 1995.

J. Yang, A. K. Mok & F. Wang. *Symbolic model checking for event-driven real-time systems.* In Proceedings of the Real-Time Systems Symposium, pages 23–32, 1993.

F. Yates. Llull and Bruno. Routledge & Paul Kegan, London, UK, 1982.

W. Yi. *A Calculus of Real Time Systems.* PhD thesis, Department of Computer Science, Chalmers University of Technology, 1991.

W. Yi & K. G. Larsen. *Testing probabilistic and nondeterministic processes.* In Protocol Specification, Testing and Verification, volume XII, pages 47–61. North-Holland, 1992.

E. Yourdon. Modern structured analysis. Yourdon Press, Englewood Cliffs, NJ, 1989.

S. Yovine. *Méthodes et outils pour la vérification symbolique de systèmes temporisès*. PhD thesis, Institut National Polytechnique de Grenoble, 1993.

S. Yovine. *Kronos: A verification tool for real-time systems*. Springer International Journal of Software Tools for Technology Transfer, 1997.

S. Yuen, R. Cleveland, Z. Dayar & S. A. Smolka. *Fully abstract characterization of testing preorders for probabilistic processes*. In Lecture Notes in Computer Science, volume 836, chapter Proceedings of CONCUR'94, pages 497–512. Springer-Verlag, 1994.

Y. Zhang & A. K. Mackworth. *Constraint nets: A unitary model for hybrid concurrent systems*. Technical report, Department of Computer Science, University of British Columbia, Vancouver, BC, Canada, 1994.

Index